DELICT

E. Metzger
Dept. of Law, Taylor Building
University of Aberdeen
Old Aberdeen AB24 3UB
Scotland

GREENS CONCISE SCOTS LAW

DELICT
and
Related Obligations

Third Edition

By
William J. Stewart, L.L.B., L.L.M.
Partner, MacMillans, Solicitors
Formerly Senior Lecturer at the University of Strathclyde

EDINBURGH
W. GREEN
1998

First published 1989
Reprinted 1990, 1992
Second edition 1993
Third edition 1998

Published in 1998 by W. Green & Son Limited
21 Alva Street
Edinburgh EH2 4PS

Typeset by Hewer Text Ltd
Edinburgh

Printed in Great Britain by Redwood Books Ltd
Kennet Way, Trowbridge. Wiltshire

No natural forests were destroyed to make this product;
only farmed timber was used and replanted

A CIP catalogue record of this book is available from the British Library

ISBN 0 414 01239 9

© 1998
W. Green and Son Limited

For Mum and Dad

PREFACE

The publishers reasonably have decided not to print the prefaces to the last two editions but my thanks go, *brevitatis causa*, to those who helped this book off the ground nearly ten years ago. I have kept my promise in the last edition and the book remains at its optimum size. Some older material has been pruned. New material arrives in ever greater quantities: there are more articles in the Journals; there are more journals! One is a dedicated journal of the highest quality – the *Tort Law Review*. There is a series of dedicated law reports now (the *Reparation Law Reports*) and there is the *Reparation Bulletin*, which I have the privilege of editing.

Some extra reading is still necessary for students and *The Digest of Roman Law: Theft, Rapine, Damage and Insult*, trans Kolbert (Penguin) and *Understanding Tort*, Carol Harlow (Fontana) are ideal (and inexpensive) introductions to the subject which is considered in this book from the point of view of contemporary Scots Law. They not only set the scene, they fill the gaps that a black-letter book like this must leave. A more radical contextual discussion can be found in Conaghan, J and Mansell, W *The Wrongs of Tort*, (Pluto, 1993), more expensive but at least in paperback.

The chapter on restitution (new in the 1993 Edition) still charts the traditional heads but retains the Birksian analysis offered in the Second Edition in view of the decision in *Shilliday v. Smith*, particularly that of the Lord President. Teachers may now feel a little more confident in exploring this approach.

Students seeking works of further reference will still find Professor Walker's *Delict* in the library and find it illuminating, especially the general part. Volume 15 of the Stair Encyclopaedia contains a wealth of citation. In this book there are extensive cross-references to my *Casebook on Delict* 2nd. Edition (1997) for those who are too pressed for the time to take their studies further in the Library *every* day. That book also includes either in the text or in the appendix most of the relevant statutes discussed in this book and many that are not. It also has a very full bibliography which should assist busy teachers and be a good resource for the diligent student wanting to improve an essay.

There have been many changes and developments since the last edition in 1993 not least the now usual annual revisions of the law of negligence by the House of Lords by narrow majorities. Chapter 5 has been re-written to take account of this. The head of liability I called 'EuroRep' in the last edition is, as expected, growing.

Legislative developments noted in this edition cover harassment; defamation; damages; conflict of laws and compensation recovery. The main new cases noted cover nuisance; the manual handling regulations; the Animals Act; animals on the road; civil evidence; employer's references; economic loss; indirect property damage; public authority immunity; nervous shock; enticement; professional negligence; occupier's liability; unborn children; and multipliers. There is even a case on one of my old favourites, Lawburrows.

The law is as stated at March 1998.

W. J. Stewart
Dalmarnock

CONTENTS

Preface vii
Table of Cases xi
Alphabetical Table of Statutes xxvii
Chronological Table of Statutes xxxi

1. Introduction 1
2. Delicts with Names I 10
3. Delicts with Names II 33
4. Liability for Unintentional Harm I: An Outline Account.. 47
5. Liability for Unintentional Harm II: Difficult Topics...... 71
6. Statutory Duty and "Eurorep" 113
7. Special Areas of Activity 123
8. Verbal Injuries 158
9. Parties 175
10. Vicarious Liability 190
11. Immunities, Defences, Transfer and Extinction 201
12. Practical Matters 221
13. Principles of Restitution 234

Index 263

TABLE OF CASES

A.B. *v* C.D. (1904) 7 F. 22 .... 8.7
A.K.Z.O. Chemie B.V. *v* Commission of the European Communities,
    1991 T.L.R. 432 .... 3.15
Adam *v* Ward [1917] A.C. 309 .... 8.21
Adams *v* War Office [1995] 3 All E.R. 245 .... 9.4
Adamson *v* Martin, 1916 S.C. 319; 1916 1 S.L.T. 53 .... 11.19
Advocate (Lord) *v* Glasgow Corporation, 1958 S.C. 12 .... 13.6
—— *v* N.B. Rly. (1894) 2 S.L.T. 71 .... 2.13
—— *v* The Scotsman Publications Ltd, 1988 S.L.T. 490; (affd.) *The Times*,
    July 7, 1989. .... 3.6
Airnes *v* Chief Constable, 1998 S.L.T. (Sh.Ct) 15 .... 2.2, 12.7
Alcock *v* Wraith, 1991, T.L.R. 600 .... 10.17
Alcock *et al v* Chief Constable, South Yorkshire [1991] 4 All E.R. 907;
    reported below as Jones *v* Wright [1991] 2 W.L.R. 814; [1991] 3
    All E.R. 88 .... 5.27, 5.28
Aliakmon (The). *See* Leigh & Sillavan Ltd *v* Aliakmon Shipping Co.
    Ltd
Allan *v* Barclay (1864) 2 M. 873 .... 4.41, 4.47, 5.14
—— *v* Gilchrist (1875) 2 R. 587 .... 13.10
Allbut *v* G.M.C. (1889) 23 Q.B.D. 400 .... 8.22
Allen *v* Flood [1898] A.C. 1 .... 3.15
Al-Nakib Investments *v* Longcroft [1900] 3 All E.R. 321 .... 5.7, 5.10
Anderson *v* Forth Valley Health Board, 1997 G.W.D. 39-2016 .... 9.13
—— *v* Lothian Health Board, 1996 Rep. L.R. 88 .... 7.49
Andrea Francovich *v* Italian Republic; Danila Bonifaci & Others *v* Italian
    Republic [1992] I.R.L.R. 84 .... 6.14
Anns *v* Merton London Borough Council [1978] A.C. 728 .... 4.18, 4.19, 5.9, 5.10,
    5.16, 5.18, 5.28, 5.31–5.35, 5.38
Arenson *v* Casson Beckman Rutley & Co. [1977] A.C. 405 .... 5.45
Argyll (Duchess of) *v* Argyll (Duke of) [1967] Ch. 302 .... 3.4
Argyll & Clyde Health Board *v* Strathclyde Regional Council, 1988 S.L.T.
    381 .... 12.8
Armagas Ltd *v* Mundogas Ltd S.A. The Ocean Frost [1986] A.C. 717 .... 10.15
Ashcroft's C.B. *v* Stewart, 1988 S.L.T. 163 .... 11.20
Ashton *v* Turner [1981] Q.B. 137 .... 11.20
Atkinson *v* Newcastle Waterworks Co. (1877) 2 Ex. D. 441 .... 6.1
Att-Gen. *v* Observer Ltd; Att.-Gen. *v* Times Newspapers Ltd [1988] 3 W.L.R.
    776 .... 3.4
—— *v* Nissan [1969] 1 All E.R. 629 .... 10.6
Attia *v* British Gas [1987] 3 All E.R. 455 .... 5.30

B. *v* F., 1987 S.L.T. 6 .... 2.6
B. *v* Harris, 1990 S.L.T. 245 .... 2.3
B.M.T.A. *v* Gray, 1951 S.C. 586; 1951 S.L.T. 247 .... 3.19
B.T. *v* James Thomson & Sons Ltd, 1997 S.L.T. 767 .... 1.8
Baignet *v* McCulloch, 1997 G.W.D. 16-737 .... 8.18
Bain *v* Kings & Co. Ltd, 1973 S.L.T. (Notes) 8 .... 5.26
Baird *v* Hamilton (1826) 4 S. 790 .... 10.1
Baird's Trs. *v* Baird & Co. (1877) 4 R. 1005 .... 13.6
Baker *v* Murdoch, 1979 S.L.T. 145 .... 12.15
Ballantyne *v* SRC, Rep.B. 12-3 .... 7.37
Bank of Scotland *v* 3i plc, 1990 G.W.D. 8-436 .... 13.20
—— *v* ——, 1992 G.W.D. 6-321 .... 5.7
—— *v* Crawford, 1994 S.C.L.R. 913 .... 13.6
—— *v* Grimm-Foxen, 1992 G.W.D. 37-2171 .... 13.24
Banner's Tutor *v* Kennedy's Trs., 1978 S.L.T. (Notes) 83 .... 11.22
Barbour *v* Halliday (1859) 21 D. 453 .... 13.12, 13.27
Barnett *v* Chelsea, etc. Hospital Management Committee [1969] 1 Q.B. 428 .... 4.30
Baron Vernon *v* Metagama, 1928 S.C. (H.L.) 21 .... 4.45
Barr A.G. & Co. Ltd *v* MacGheoghegan, 1931 S.C. (H.L.) 1 .... 2.21
Bartonshill Coal Co *v* Reid (1858) 3 Macq. 266 .... 10.1
Baume & Co. *v* Moore [1958] Ch. 907 .... 3.11
Baxter *v* Pritchard, 1992 G.W.D. 24-1385 .... 10.17
Bell *v* Scottish Special Housing Association, 1987 S.L.T. 320 .... 4.37
Belmont Laundry Co. *v* Aberdeen Steam Laundry (1898) 1 F. 45 .... 3.19
Binnie *v* Rederij Theodoro B.V., 1991 G.W.D. 26-1523 .... 12.4
Black *v* Carmichael, 1992 S.C.C.R. 709 .... 2.22
Blackburn *v* Sinclair, 1984 S.L.T. 368 .... 5.22
Blake *v* Lothian Health Board, 1992 G.W.D. 32-1908 .... 11.34, 11.35
Boal *v* Scottish Catholic Printing Co., 1908 S.C. 667; (1908) 15 S.L.T. 940 .... 8.8
Boardman *v* Sanderson [1964] 1 W.L.R. 1317 .... 5.25
Bogan's Curator Bonis *v* Graham, 1992 G.W.D. 32-1907 .... 11.34, 11.35
Bolam *v* Friern Hospital Management Committee [1957] 1 W.L.R. 582 .... 5.48, 5.49
Bolitho *v* City and Hackney Health Authority [1997] 3 W.L.R. 1151 .... 5.49
Bollinger *v* Costa Brava Wine Co. Ltd [1960] Ch. 262 .... 6.6
Bolton *v* Jameson & Mackay, 1987 S.L.T. 291; (revd.) 1989 S.L.T. 222 .... 5.52
—— *v* Stone [1951] A.C. 850 .... 4.24, 5.43
Bonthrone *v* Secretary of State for Scotland, 1987 S.L.T. 34 .... 2.3, 5.36, 5.38
Borowski *v* Att.-Gen. for Canada (1987) 39 D.L.R. (4th) 371 .... 9.13
Borris *v* Lord Advocate, 1993 G.W.D. 6-435 .... 12.4
Boudier Cass civ. 15th June 1892; D.P. 1892 I. 596, S. 1893, I. 281 .... 13.3
Bourhill *v* Young, 1942 S.C. (H.L.) 78; 1943 S.L.T. 105 .... 4.5, 4.10, 5.25, 5.28
Bowers *v* Strathclyde Regional Council, 1981 S.L.T. 122 .... 12.15
Boy Andrew (The) *v* The St. Rognvald, 1947 S.C. (H.L.) 70 .... 4.35
Boyd & Forrest *v* Glasgow & South-Western Ry, 1912 S.C. (H.L.) 93 .... 3.2
Brasserie du Pecheur S.A. *v* Germany, C-46/93; [1996] 2 W.L.R. 506 .... 6.16
Brice *v* Brown [1984] 1 All E.R. 997 .... 5.27
British Homophone Ltd *v* Kunz [1935] All E.R. 627 .... 3.20
British Motor Trade Association *v* Gray, 1951 S.C. 586 .... 3.19
British Oxygen Co. *v* S.S.E.B., 1959 S.C. (H.L.) 17 .... 13.22
British Telecom *v* Thomson, 1997 Rep. L.R. 23 .... 5.44
Brooks *v* Lind, 1997 Rep. L.R. 83 .... 8.6, 8.24
Brown *v* Lee Constructions, 1977 S.L.T. (Notes) 61 .... 2.11
—— *v* Rolls Royce Ltd, 1960 S.C. (H.L.) 22; 1960 S.L.T. 119 .... 4.28

Brown's Trs. *v* Hay (1898) 25 R. 1112 .... 2.22, 3.3
Bruce *v* Leisk (1892) 19 R. 482 .... 8.18
—— *v* Smith (1898) 1 F. 327 .... 8.28
Bryce Houston Ltd *v* Glass's Fruit Markets Ltd, 1992 S.C.L.R. 1019 .... 13.14
Bryson *v* Somervill (1565) Mor. 1703 .... 9.12
Buron *v* Denman (1848) 2 Ex. 167 .... 10.6
Burrows *v* Rhodes [1899] 1 Q.B. 816 .... 3.2
Burton *v* Moorhead (1881) 8 R. 892 .... 7.24
Byrd *v* Wither, 1991 S.L.T. 206 .... 2.3

C. *v* M., 1923 S.C. 1; 1922 S.L.T. 634 .... 8.10
Cairns *v* Butlins Ltd, 1989 G.W.D. 40-1879 .... 7.5
Cairns *v* Harry Walker Ltd, 1913 2 S.L.T. 379 .... 2.22
Caledonian Ry. Co. *v* Greenock Corporation, 1912 S.C. (H.L.) 56; 1917
  2 S.L.T. 67 .... 2.19, 11.18
Caltex Oil Ltd *v* The Dredge Willemstad (1976–1977) 136 C.L.R. 529 ...... 5.18, 5.19
Cambridge Water Co. Ltd *v* Eastern Counties Leather plc [1994]
  2 A.C. 264 .... 2.19
Cameron *v* Greater Glasgow Health Board, 1993 G.W.D. 6-433 .... 5.51
—— *v* Hamilton Auction Markets Ltd, 1955 S.L.T. (Sh.Ct) 74 .... 1.1
—— *v* Young, 1908 S.C. (H.L.) 7 .... 7.11
Campbell *v* F. & F. Moffat (Transport) Ltd, 1992 S.L.T. 962 .... 4.47
—— *v* Muir, 1908 S.C. 387; (1908) 15 S.L.T. 737 .... 2.20
Candlewood Navigation Corporation Ltd *v* Mitsui OSK Lines [1986] 5
  A.C. 1 .... 5.18
Cantiere San Rocco *v* Clyde Shipbuilding and Engineering Co. Ltd, 1923
  S.C. (H.L.) 105 .... 13.7, 13.26
Caparo Industries plc *v* Dickman [1990] 1 All E.R. 568 .... 5.7
Capital and Counties *v* Mapshire Council; John Munroe *v* London Fire
  Authority; Church of Jesus Christ of Latter-Day Saints *v* West York-
  shire Fire Authority [1997] T.L.R. 141 .... 5.37
Carroll *v* Andrew Barclay and Sons Ltd, 1948 S.C. (H.L.) 100; 1948
  S.L.T. 464 .... 6.7
—— *v* BBC, 1997 S.L.T. (Sh.Ct) 23 .... 8.8
Cassidy *v* Connochie, 1907 S.C. 1112; (1907) 15 S.L.T. 195 .... 8.18
Castellain *v* Preston (1881) 11 Q.B.D. 380 .... 13.18
Castle *v* St. Augustine's Links and Another (1922) 38 T.L.R. 615 .... 4.24
Cavanagh *v* Godfreys of Dundee, 1997 S.L.T. (Sh.Ct) 2 .... 7.39
—— *v* Ulster Weaving Co. Ltd [1960] A.C. 145 .... 4.28
Century Insurance Co. *v* Northern Ireland Road Transport Board [1942]
  A.C. 509 .... 10.14
Chadwick *v* B.R.B. [1967] 1 W.L.R. 912 .... 5.27
Chapman *v* Barber, 1989 S.L.T. 830 .... 8.21
Christie *v* Armstrong, 1996 S.L.T. 948 .... 13.14, 13.15
—— *v* Robertson (1899) 1 F. 1155 .... 8.12
Clark *v* Armstrong (1862) 24 D. 1315 .... 7.24
—— *v* McLean, 1993 S.L.T. 492 .... 11.35
Clayards *v* Dethick (1848) 12 Q.B. 439 .... 11.22
Clayton *v* Woodman & Son (Builders) Ltd [1962] 2 Q.B. 533 .... 5.47
Cohen *v* Shaw, 1992 S.L.T. 1022 .... 9.13
Coleridge *v* Miller, 1997 S.L.T. 487 .... 5.15, 5.44
Comber *v* Greater Glasgow Health Board, 1989 S.L.T. 639 .... 11.35
Comex Houlder Diving Ltd *v* Colne Fishing Co. Ltd, 1987 S.L.T. 443 ...... 11.26
Commercial Bank *v* Biggar; Christie *v* Armstrong, 1996 S.L.T. 948 ...... 13.14
Commission *v* U.K. [1997] All E.R. (EC) 481 .... 7.15

Cooke's Circus Buildings Co. *v* Welding (1894) 21 R. 339 .... 13.11, 13.27
Cope *v* Sharpe [1912] 1 K.B. 496 .... 2.11, 11.16
Coutts Trs. (Sharp) *v* Coutts, 1996 S.C.C.R. 1026 .... 9.16
Craig *v* Glasgow Victoria etc. H.B.H. (O.H.), December 1, 1972
    (unreported) 2.3
Crawford *v* Adams; Crawford *v* Dunlop (1900) 2 F. 987 .... 10.5
Credit Lyonnais *v* George Stevenson & Co. Ltd (1901) 9 S.L.T. 93 .... 13.24
Crindall *v* John Mitchell (Grangemouth) Ltd, 1984 S.L.T. 335; 1987
    S.L.T. 137 .... 9.16
Crofter Hand Woven Harris Tweed Co. *v* Veitch, 1942 S.C. (H.L.) 1 ...... 3.16, 3.19,
                                                                           11.15
Cropper *v* Chief Constable, Dumfries and Galloway Constabulary and
    Secretary of State, 1998 S.L.T. 548 .... 10.18
Crotty *v* McFarlane, unreported Jan. 27, 1891 .... 8.24
Cullen *v* North Lanarkshire Council, 1996 Rep. L.R. 87 .... 7.49
Cumnock & Doon Valley D.C. *v* Dance Energy Associates Ltd, 1992 G.W.D.
    25-1441 .... 2.12
Cunningham & Others *v* Reading Football Club Ltd, 1991 T.L.R. 153 .... 5.43
Cuthbert *v* Linklater, 1935 S.L.T. 94 .... 8.5
Cutler *v* Wandsworth Stadium Ltd (in Liquidation) [1949] 1 All E.R. 544 .... 6.3,
                                                                           6.5, 6.6
D. & F. ESTATES *v* CHURCH COMMISSIONERS [1988] 3 W.L.R. 368 ...... 4.19, 5.7, 5.10,
                                                                           10.17, 11.37
D'Amato *v* Badger [1996] D.L.R. (4th) 129 .... 5.14
Daborn *v* Bath Tramways Motor Co. [1946] 2 All E.R. 333 .... 4.26
Dalgleish *v* Glasgow Corp., 1976 S.C. 32 .... 12.15
Daniell *v* Aviemore Station Hotel Co., 1951 S.L.T. (Notes) 76 .... 11.29
Dash Ltd *v* Philip King Tailoring, 1989 S.L.T. 39 .... 3.12
Davey *v* Harrow Corpn. [1957] 2 All E.R. 305 .... 2.12
Davidson *v* Kerr, 1996 G.W.D. 40-2296 .... 2.12
—— *v* UCS Ltd, 1990 S.L.T. 329 .... 12.14
Davie *v* Newton Merton Board Mills [1959] A.C. 604 .... 7.34
—— *v* Wilson (1854) 16 D. 956 .... 9.11
Davies *v* Mann (1842) 10 M. & W. 546 .... 4.35, 7.33
—— *v* Swan Motor Co. [1949] 2 K.B. 291 .... 11.21, 11.24
Dawson International plc *v* Coats Paton plc, 1988 S.L.T. 854 .... 13.10
De freitas *v* O'Brien [1955] T.L.R. 86 .... 5.49
Dehler *v* Ottawa Civic Hospital (1979) 101 D.L.R. (3d) 686 .... 9.13
Department of the Environment *v* T. Bates Ltd [1990] 3 W.L.R. 457 .... 4.19, 5.10
Devine *v* Colvilles, 1969 S.C. (H.L.) 67 .... 12.4
Devlin *v* Strathclyde Regional Council, 1993 S.L.T. 699 .... 7.8
Diamantis Pateras [1966] 1 Lloyd's Rep. 179 .... 7.14
Dillenkofer *v* Germany, 1996 T.L.R. 564 .... 6.18
Dingwall *v* Alexander, 1981 S.L.T. 313 (affd. on other grounds, 1982 S.C.
    (H.L.) 179) 11.29
Divit *v* B.T., 1997 G.W.D. 1530 .... 7.49
Dobie *v* Lauder's Trs. (1873) 11 M. 749 .... 13.10
Dollar Land *v* CIN Properties Ltd, 1997 S.L.T. 260 .... 13.29
Donaghy *v* N.C.B. 1957 S.L.T. (Notes) 35 .... 4.39
Donald *v* Galloway, 1988 G.W.D. 24-1042 .... 11.35
—— *v* Rutherford, 1984 S.L.T. 70 .... 11.35
Donaldson *v* McNiven [1952] 2 All E.R. 691 .... 9.11
Donlon *v* Colonial Mutual Group (U.K. Holdings) 1997 S.C.L.R. 1088 .... 5.11, 8.23
Donoghue *v* Stevenson, 1932 S.C. (H.L.) 31; 1932 S.L.T. 317 4.5, 4.6, 4.7, 4.10, 4.13,
                         4.18, 4.19, 5.5, 5.10, 5.15, 5.28, 5.38, 5.46, 7.3, 9.11, 13.29

Dorset Yacht Co. *v* Home Office [1970] A.C. 1004 .... 4.15, 4.16, 5.35, 5.40
Doughty *v* Turner Manufacturing Co. [1964] 1 Q.B. 518 .... 4.14
Downie *v* Chief Constable, 1997 S.C.L.R. 603 .... 2.2
Duff *v* Highlands and Islands Fire Board, 1995 S.L.T. 1362 .... 5.37
Dumbreck *v* Addie & Sons (Collieries) Ltd, 1929 S.C. (H.L.) 51; 1929
  S.L.T. 242 .... 7.2
Dunbar *v* Wilson & Dunlop's Trs. (1887) 15 R. 210 .... 13.13
Duncan *v* Dundee, Perth and London Shipping Co. (1878) 5 R. 742 .... 13.16
—— *v* Ross Harper & Murphy, 1993 S.L.T. 105 .... 11.20
Dundas *v* Livingstone (1900) 3 F. 37 .... 8.19
Dunfermline District Council *v* Blyth & Blyth, 1985 S.L.T. 345 .... 11.37
Dunlop *v* McGowans, 1979 S.C. 22; 1979 S.L.T. 34; (affd.) 1980 S.C.
  (H.L.) 73; 1980 S.L.T. 129 .... 11.37
Dunlop Pneumatic Tyre Co. *v* Dunlop Motor Co., 1907 S.C. (H.L.) 15;
  (1907) 15 S.L.T. 362 .... 3.12
Dunnett *v* Nelson, 1926 S.C. 764; 1926 S.L.T. 493 .... 8.17
Duport Steels Ltd *v* Sirs [1980] 1 W.L.R. 142 .... 11.11
Dutton *v* Bognor Regis UDC [1972] 1 Q.B. 373 .... 5.10
Dynamco Ltd *v* Holland and Hannen and Cubitts (Scotland) Ltd, 1971
  S.C. 257 .... 5.15

EIF ENTERPRISE (CALEDONIA) LTD *v* LONDON BRIDGE ENGINEERING LTD
  (1997) T.L.R. 607 .... 11.24
Earl of Fife *v* Samuel Wilson (1864) 3 M 323 .... 13.25
Edgar *v* Lamont, 1914 S.C. 277; 1974 S.L.T. 80 .... 5.46
Edinburgh and District Tramways *v* Courtenay, 1909 S.C. 99 .... 13.22
Edward Wong Finance Co. Ltd *v* Johnson, Stokes & Master [1984] 1
  A.C. 296 .... 5.49
Edwards *v* N.C.B. [1949] 1 K.B. 704 .... 6.8
Elcap *v* Milne's Ex., 1998 G.W.D. 263 .... 13.27
Elliot *v* J. & C. Finney, 1989 S.L.T. 208; (affd.) 1989 S.L.T. 605 .... 11.34, 11.35
—— *v* Joicey, 1935 S.C. (H.L.) 57 .... 9.13
Emeh *v* Kensington, Chelsea and Westminster Area Health Authority [1985]
  Q.B. 1012 .... 9.13
English *v* Wilsons & Clyde Coal Co., 1937 S.C. (H.L.) 46; 1937
  S.L.T. 523 .... 7.34
Esso Petroleum *v* Hall Russell & Co. Ltd, 1988 S.L.T. 874 .... 13.4, 13.18
Evans *v* Slein (1904) 7 F. 65 .... 12.20
Ewing *v* Mar (1851) 14 D. 314 .... 2.2
—— *v* Triplex Safety Glass Co. Ltd [1936] 1 All E.R. 283 .... 7.14, 7.17, 7.21
Exchange Telegraph-Federal Sugar Refining *v* U.S. Sugar Equalisation Board
  268 F. 575 (1920) 13.21
Express Newspapers Ltd *v* McShane [1980] A.C. 672 .... 11.11

F. (IN UTERO) [1998] 2 W.L.R. 1297 .... 9.13
F.C. Finance Ltd *v* Brown & Son, 1969 S.L.T. (Sh.Ct) 41 .... 2.21
Fagan *v* Metropolitan Police Commissioner [1969] 1 Q.B. 439 .... 4.8
Fairlie *v* Carruthers, 1995 S.L.T. (Sh.Ct) 56 .... 7.28, 7.32, 7.33
Farry *v* News Group, 1996 G.W.D. 2-109 .... 8.24
Feely *v* Co-operative Wholesale Society Ltd, 1990 S.L.T. 547 .... 7.4
Fernie *v* Robertson (1871) 9 m. 437 .... 13.13
Ferris-Bank (Anguilla) Ltd *v* Gazar, 1991 T.L.R. 68 .... 8.9
Findlay *v* Blaylock, 1937 S.C. 21; 1936 S.L.T. 596 .... 3.20, 11.15
Fleming *v* Hislop (1886) 13 R. 43 .... 2.12
Forbes *v* Dundee Council, 1997 S.L.T. 1330 .... 5.38, 7.5

Forbes *v* House of Clydesdale Ltd, 1988 S.L.T. 594 .... 11.34
Ford *v* Union Insulation Co. Ltd, 1989 G.W.D. 16-696 .... 11.34, 11.35
Forgie *v* Henderson (1818) 1 Murray 410 .... 12.14
Foskett *v* McClymont, 1998 Rep. L.B. 13 .... 1.1, 7.28, 7.31
Franklin *v* Gramophone Co. Ltd [1948] 1 K.B. 542 .... 7.41
Fraser *v* Greater Glasgow Health Board, 1996 Rep. L.R. 62 .... 7.49
——— *v* Mirza, 1993 S.L.T. 527 .... 8.18
——— *v* Pate, 1923 S.L.T. 457 .... 7.33
Frost *v* Chief Constable [1996] T.L.R. 617 ....: 1.6
——— *v* Chief Constable South Yorkshire [1997] 1 All E.R. 540 .... 5.28
Fry's Metals Ltd *v* Durastic Ltd, 1991 S.L.T. 689 .... 5.43
Fyfe *v* Croudace Ltd, 1986 S.L.T. 528 .... 11.34

G. & A. ESTATES LTD *v* CAVIAPEN TRUSTEES LTD (No. 1), 1993 S.L.T. 1037. 2.19
Garden Cottage Foods Ltd *v* Milk Marketing Board [1984] 1 A.C. 130 .... 3.17, 6.12
Garven *v* White Corries, Fort William Sheriff Court, June 21, 1989,
      unreported 11.19
Gecas *v* Scottish Television plc 1992 G.W.D. 30-1786 .... 8.13
Gemmell *v* Bank of Scotland, Glasgow, Nov. 5 1996 .... 2.22
General Cleaning Contractors *v* Christmas [1953] A.C. 180 .... 7.36
Gibson *v* Smith (1849) 21 Se. Jur. 331 .... 9.7
——— *v* Strathclyde R.C., 1993 S.L.T. 1243 .... 7.5
Gibson & Simpson *v* Pearson, 1992 S.L.T. 894 .... 11.31
Gilchrist *v* D. B. Marshall (Newbridge) Ltd, 1991 S.L.T. 842 .... 4.46
——— *v* Whyte, 1907 S.C. 984 .... 13.10
Gillon *v* Chief Constable, 1996 Rep. L.B. 165 .... 5.43
Girvan *v* Inverness Farmers Dairy (No. 2), 1998 S.L.T. 21 .... 12.15
Glasgow Corporation *v* Inland Revenue, 1959 S.L.T. 230 .... 13.6
Glasper *v* Rodger, 1996 S.L.T. 44 .... 11.37
Glen *v* Roy (1882) 10 R. 329 .... 13.25
Glenrothes Development Corp. *v* Bannerman, 1996 G.W.D. 27-1614 .... 13.24
Gold *v* Haringey Health Authority [1967] 2 W.L.R. 649 .... 2.3, 5.51, 5.55
Goldman *v* Hargrave [1967] 1 A.C. 645 .... 2.18
Gordon *v* Grampian Health Board 1991 S.C.L.R. 213 .... 12.7
Gorris *v* Scott (1874) L.R. 9 Ex. 125 .... 6.7
Gouws *v* Jester Pools Pty. Ltd, 1968 (3) S.A. 563 (T) 13.4, 13.22
Govenor and Company of the Bank of Scotland *v* 3i plc, unreported. O.H.,
      Jan. 18, 1990 .... 13.10
Gow *v* Chief Constable, Strathclyde Police, 1991 G.W.D. 11-662 .... 2.2
Graham *v* Duke of Hamilton (1868) 6 M. 965 .... 2.11
Gramophone Co.'s Application, *Re* [1910] Ch. 423 .... 3.11
Grampian Regional Council *v* Cowan & Linn, 1989 S.L.T. 787 .... 5.7
Grant *v* Australian Knitting Mills Ltd [1935] All E.R. 209 .... 7.13
Gray *v* Dunlop, 1954 S.L.T. (Sh.Ct) 75 .... 1.1, 2.24
——— *v* Kerner, 1996 S.C.L.R. 331 .... 13.14
Greater Nottingham Co-operative Society Ltd *v* Cementation Piling and
      Foundations Ltd [1988] 2 All E.R. 971 .... 5.46
Griffen *v* George MacLellan Holdings, 1992 G.W.D. 30-1787 .... 11.35
Grubb *v* Mackenzie (1834) 13 S. 717 .... 2.22
Gulf Oil Ltd *v* Page [1987] Ch. 327 .... 8.9
Gunstone *v* Scottish Women's Athletic Association, 1987 S.L.T. 611 .... 9.2
Guy *v* Strathkelvin D.C., 1997 S.C.L.R. 405 .... 7.7, 7.11

HAGGARTY *v* GLASGOW CORPORATION, 1963 S.L.T. (Notes) 73; 1964 S.L.T.
      (Notes) 54 and 95 .... 7.11

Haggerty *v* E.E. Caledonia [1997] T.L.R. 69 .... 5.29
Haig & Co. *v* Forth Blending Co., 1954 S.C. 35; 1954 S.L.T. 2 .... 3.8, 3.9, 3.12
Hall *v* Watson (1896) 12 Sh.Ct.Rep 117 .... 2.2
Hallett *v* Nicholson, 1979 S.C. 1 .... 5.35, 5.36, 5.38
Hambrook *v* Stokes Bros. [1925] 1 K.B. 141 .... 5.26
Hamill *v* Lord Advocate, 1994 G.W.D. 33-1960 .... 8.18
Hamilton *v* Fife Health Board, 1993 S.L.T.624.. 9.11, 11.27
—— *v* Wilson, 1994 S.L.T. 431 .... 2.5
Handy *v* Bowman, Dundee Sheriff Court, September 22, 1986 (unreported) 2.4
Harris *v* Abbey National, 1996 G.W.D. 33-1993 .... 2.22
—— *v* Wyre Forest D.C. [1988] 2 W.L.R. 1173; [1989] 2 W.L.R. 790 .... 5.7
Harrison *v* Michelin Tyre Co. [1985] 1 All E.R. 918 .... 10.13
Haseldine *v* C. A. Daw & Son Ltd [1941] 3 All E.R. 156 .... 7.13
Hatherley *v* Smith, 1989 S.L.T. 316 .... 11.29
Hayforth *v* Forrester-Paton, 1927 S.C. 74 .... 8.2
Heath's Garage Ltd *v* Hodges [1916] 2 K.B. 370 .... 7.33
Heaton's Transport (St. Helens) Ltd *v* T.G.W.U. [1972] I.C.R. 308 .... 10.18
Hedley Byrne & Co. Ltd *v* Heller and Partners [1964] A.C. 465 .... 4.18, 5.4, 5.5,
   5.6, 5.7, 5.8, 5.11, 5.12, 5.13, 5.15, 5.16, 5.18, 5.19, 5.20, 5.21, 5.33, 5.39, 9.1
Henderson *v* John Stuart (Farms) Ltd, 1963 S.C. 245; 1963 S.L.T. 22 .... 7.27
—— *v* Chief Constable, Fife Police, 1988 S.L.T. 361 .... 2.6
—— *v* Merrett Syndicates Ltd [1994] 3 W.L.R. 761 .... 5.4, 5.10, 5.46
Highland Dancing Board *v* Alloa Printing Co., 1971 S.L.T. (Sh.Ct) 50 .... 9.7
Hill *v* Chief Constable [1987] 1 All E.R. 1173 .... 5.36
—— *v* Lovett, 1992 S.L.T. 994 .... 7.27
Hillcrest Homecare Services *v* Tartan Home Care Ltd, 1996 G.W.D. 4-215 .... 3.2
Hislop *v* Durham (1842) 4 D. 1168 .... 7.34
Honeywell and Stein Ltd *v* Larkin Bros Ltd [1934] 1 K.B. 191 .... 10.17
Houldsworth *v* City of Glasgow Bank (1880) 7 R. (H.L.) 53 .... 9.6
Hucks *v* Cole [1993] 4 Med. L.R. 393 .... 5.49
Hudson *v* Ridge Manufacturing [1957] 2 Q.B. 348 .... 7.35
Hughes *v* Lord Advocate, 1963 S.C. (H.L.) 31 .... 4.13, 4.16, 4.42, 5.40, 5.41
Hughes' Tutrix *v* G.D.C. 1982 S.L.T. (Sh.Ct) 70 .... 11.19
Hunt *v* Severs [1994] 2 A.C. 350 .... 9.10
Hunter *v* Bradford Property Trust Ltd, 1970 S.L.T. 173 .... 13.17
—— *v* Hanley, 1955 S.C. 200; 1955 S.L.T. 213 .... 5.47, 5.48, 5.51, 5.52, 8.23, 9.1
—— *v* North of Scotland Hydro-Electric Board, 1989 G.W.D. 15-645 .... 11.34
Hunter and 689 Others *v* Canary Wharf Ltd and London Dockland
   Development Corp., [1997] 2 All E.R. 426; 1997 T.L.R. 219 .... 2.14, 11.12

I.C.I. *v* SHATWELL [1965] A.C. 656 .... 6.4, 6.11, 11.19
Inglis *v* L.M.S. Rly, 1941 S.C. 551; 1941 S.L.T. 408 .... 12.5
—— *v* Shotts Iron Co. (1881) 9 R. (H.L.) 78 .... 2.14
Ingram *v* Ritchie, 1989 G.W.D. 27-1217 .... 4.32
International House of Heraldry *v* Grant, 1991 G.W.D. 23-1352 .... 3.12
Invercargill City Council *v* Hamilton [1996] A.C. 624 .... 5.39
Irving *v* Hiddleston, 1998 S.C.L.R. 350 .... 11.32

JACKSON *v* HARRISON (1978) 138 C.L.R. 438 .... 11.20
Jackson *v* McKechnie (1875) 3 R. 130 .... 9.16
Joel *v* Morison (1834) 6 C. & P. 501 .... 10.13
Johnstone *v* City of Glasgow District Council, 1986 S.L.T. 50 .... 12.2, 12.6
—— *v* Traffic Commissioner, 1990 S.L.T. 409 .... 5.36
Jones *v* Lanarkshire Health Authority, 1990 S.L.T. 19 .... 9.13
—— *v* Wright [1991] 2 W.L.R. 814; [1991] 3 All E.R. 88 .... 5.27

Joyce *v* Sengupta 1992 T.L.R. 453 .... 8.1
Junior Books *v* The Veitchi Co., 1982 S.L.T. 492 ..... 1.12, 4.19, 5.8, 5.16, 5.18, 5.19, 5.20, 5.39, 5.44, 9.1
Just *v* British Columbia (1990) 64 D.L.R. (4th) 689 ...... 5.39

K. *v* KENEDY, 1992, 192 S.C.L.R. 386 ...... 12.7
Kay's Tutor *v* Ayrshire and Arran Health Board, 1987 S.L.T. 577 .... 4.32, 5.50, 12.3
Kaye *v* Robertson [1991] F.S.R. 62 ...... 8.9
Kelly *v* Corston [1997] T.L.R. 466 ...... 5.53
—— *v* Kelly, 1997 S.L.T. 896 ...... 9.13
Kelvin Shipping Co. *v* Canadian Pacific Railway Co. 1928 S.C. (H.L.) 21 . 4.45
Kemp & Dougall *v* Darngavil Coal Co. Ltd, 1909 S.C. 1314 ...... 4.3
Kennedy *v* Glenbelle, 1996 S.L.T. 1186 ...... 1.12, 2.16, 2.19, 2.24, 12.8
Kerr *v* Earl of Orkney (1857) 20 D. 298 ...... 2.19
Kidston *v* Annan, 1984 S.C.C.R. 20 ...... 2.22
Killin *v* Weir (1905) 7 F. 526; (1905) 12 S.L.T. 737 ...... 9.3
King *v* Phillips [1953] 1 All E.R. 617 ...... 5.26
—— *v* Strathclyde R.C., Glasgow, Jan. 8, 1991 ...... 7.5
Kirby *v* N.C.B., 1958 S.C. 514; 1959 S.L.T. 7 ...... 10.11, 10.14
Kirkcaldy District Council *v* Household Manufacturing Ltd, 1987 S.L.T. 617 ... 1.1
Kirklands Garage (Kinross) Ltd *v* Clark, 1967 S.L.T. (Sh.Ct) 60 ...... 13.4, 13.22
Koufos *v* Czarnikow (The Heron II) [1969] 1 A.C. 350 ...... 4.40, 4.45
Kozikowska *v* Kozikowski, 1996 S.L.T. 386 ...... 9.10
Kubach *v* Hollands [1937] 3 All E.R. 907 ...... 7.13, 7.18

LAFFERTY *v* ALEX SNOWIE, 1987 G.W.D. 19-743 ...... 4.42
Laing *v* Tayside Health Board, 1996 Rep. L.R. 51 ...... 12.7
Laird Line *v* U.S. Shipping Board, 1924 S.C. (H.L.) 37; 1924 S.L.T. 109..... 11.22
Lambert *v* West Devon [1997] T.L.R. 167 ...... 5.39
Lamond *v* Glasgow Corporation, 1968 S.L.T. 291 ...... 4.24
—— *v* North East Fife District Council (O.H.), 1987 G.W.D. 37-1310 ...... 5.36
Lamont *v* Monklands D.C. 1992 G.W.D. 4-200 ...... 7.5
Lane *v* Holloway [1968] 1 Q.B. 379 ...... 2.3
Lang Brothers *v* Goldwell, 1982 S.L.T. 309 ...... 3.13
Latimer *v* A.E.C. Ltd [1953] A.C. 643 ...... 4.27
Launchbury *v* Morgans [1973] A.C. 127 ...... 10.7
Lawrence Building Co. Ltd *v* Lanark County Council, 1978 S.C. 30 ...... 13.14
Leadbetter *v* NCB, 1952 S.C. 19 ...... 9.13
Leigh *v* Gladstone (1909) 26 T.L.R. 139 ...... 11.16
Leigh and Sillavan Ltd *v* Aliakmon Shipping Co. Ltd [1986] A.C. 785..... 4.19, 5.16, 5.17, 5.18, 9.17
Leitch *v* Leydon, 1931 S.C. (H.L.)..... 12.21
—— *v* Lyal (1903) 11 S.L.T. 394 ...... 8.20
Leon *v* Edinburgh Evening News, 1909 S.C. 1014; 1909 S.L.T. 65 ...... 8.5
Levin *v* Caledonian Produce (Holdings) Ltd, 1975 S.L.T. (Notes) 69 ...... 3.3
Liddle *v* Morton, 1996 S.L.T. 1143 ...... 2.4
Lipkin Gorman *v* Karpnale [1991] 2 W.L.R. 10 ...... 13.24
Lister *v* Romford Ice & Cold Storage Co. Ltd [1957] 1 All E.R. 125 ...... 11.25
Lloyd *v* Grace Smith & Co. [1912] A.C. 716 ...... 9.8
Lockhart *v* Brown (1888) 15 R. 742 ...... 13.3
—— *v* Kevin Oliphant, 1993 S.L.T. 179 ...... 7.50
Longworth *v* Coppas International (U.K.) Ltd, 1985 S.L.T. 111 ...... 7.37
Lonrho Ltd *v* Shell Petroleum Co. Ltd (No. 2) [1982] A.C. 173 ...... 3.16
Lonrho plc *v* Al-Fayed [1991] 3 W.L.R. 188 ...... 3.15, 3.16
Lumley *v* Gye (1853) 2 E. & B. 216 ...... 3.20

Lynch *v* Lynch, 1997 G.W.D. 30-1501 .... 12.7

M. *v* KENNEDY, 1993 S.C.L.R. 69 .... 12.7
M & M Construction Ltd *v* William Reid Engineering Ltd, 1998 S.L.T. 211 ...... 10.17
McAllister *v* ICI plc, 1997 S.L.T. 351 .... 11.29
McArthur *v* Matthew Cleland Public House Proprietors, 1981 S.L.T. (Sh.Ct.)
   76 .... 2.24
MacAusland *v* Dick (1787) Mor. 9246 .... 2.26
McCabe *v* News Group Newspapers Ltd, 1992 S.L.T. 707 .... 8.4
MacColl *v* Hoo, 1983 S.L.T. (Sh.Ct.) 23 .... 2.24
MacDonald *v* Glasgow Western Hospitals Board, 1954 S.C. 453; 1954
   S.L.T. 226 .... 10.10
MacDougall *v* Clydesdale Bank Trustees, 1993 S.C.L.R. 832 .... 5.52
McElroy *v* McAllister, 1949 S.C. 110 .... 12.20
McFarlane *v* Tayside Health Board, 1998 G.W.D. 4-180 .... 9.13
McGhee *v* N.C.B. 1973 S.C. (H.L.) 37; 1973 S.L.T. 14 .... 4.31, 4.32, 12.3
McGlone *v* British Railways Board, 1966 S.C. (H.L.) 1 .... 7.2, 7.8
McGowan *v* Lord Advocate, 1972 S.C. 68 .... 12.7
McGregor *v* AAH Pharmaceuticals, 1995 G.W.D. 32-1656 .... 7.36
McKeen *v* Chief Constable, 1994 S.L.T. 93 .... 2.5
Mackenzie (J.B.) (Edinburgh) Ltd *v* Lord Advocate, 1972 S.C. 231 ..... 13.22
McKillen *v* Barclay Curle & Co. Ltd, 1967 S.L.T. 41 .... 4.46
McKinlay *v* British Steel Corporation, 1987 S.L.T. 522; (affd.) 1988 S.L.T. 810. 4.25
McLachlan *v* Bell (1895) 23 R. 126 .... 9.1
McLaren *v* Procurator Fiscal for Lothian and Borders, 1991 G.W.D.
   24-1407 .... 2.6, 10.18
McLean *v* Remploy Ltd, 1994 S.L.T. 687 .... 7.35, 10.13
McLeod *v* Hellyer Bros. Ltd [1987] 1 W.L.R. 728; [1987] I.R.L.R. 232 ...... 10.10
Macleod *v* MacAskill, 1920 S.C. 72; 1919 S.L.T. 256 .... 2.8
McLoughlin *v* O'Brian [1983] A.C. 410 .... 5.9, 5.26, 5.27, 5.28
McMeechan *v* Secretary of State for Employment [1997] I.R.L.R. 353 .... 10.10
McMillan *v* Ministry of Defence, 1991 S.L.T. 150; 1990 G.W.D. 5-271 ...... 7.7
McMullan *v* Lochgelly Iron and Coal Co., 1933 S.C. (H.L.) 64; 1934
   S.L.T. 114 .... 6.5
McMurdo *v* Ferguson, 1993 S.L.T. 193 .... 8.9
McNab *v* Guild, 1989 S.C.C.R. 138 .... 2.11
McNaughton Paper Group Ltd *v* Hicks Anderson *v* Co. [1991] 1 All
   E.R. 134 .... 5.7
MacPhee *v* Macfarlane's Exr., 1933 S.C. 163; 1933 S.L.T. 148 ...... 2.7, 11.7
McQueen *v* Glasgow Garden Festival, 1994 G.W.D. 9-557 .... 12.4
MacRostie *v* Ironside (1849) 12 D. 74 .... 8.6
McTighe *v* East & Midlothian NHS Trust (1998) Rep. L.R. 21 .... 7.46
McWilliams *v* Lord Advocate, 1992 S.L.T. 1045 .... 9.11
—— *v* Sir William Arrol & Co. Ltd, 1962 S.C. (H.L.) 70; 1962
   S.L.T. 121 .... 7.40
Mackle *v* Mackle, 1984 S.L.T. 276 .... 13.14
Maloco *v* Littlewoods Organisation, 1986 S.L.T. 272; (affd.) 1987
   S.L.T. 425 .... 4.37, 4.42, 5.41, 5.42
Manners *v* Whitehead (8998) 1 F. 171 .... 5.54
Marc Rich & Co. A.G. and Others *v* Bishop Rock Marine Co. Ltd and
   Others (The Nicholas H) [1995] 3 All E.R. 307 .... 5.12, 5.38, 5.44
Margarine Union GmbH *v* Cambay Prince S.S. Co. [1969] 12 Q.B. 219 ...... 5.16
Marshall *v* William Sharp, 1991 S.L.T. 114 .... 10.17
Martin *v* Bell Ingram, 1986 S.L.T. 575 .... 5.13
Mason *v* Orr (1901) 4 F. 220 .... 2.2

May v Teague Homes, 1996 G.W.D. 23-1344 .... 8.21
Mellor v Wm Beardmore & Co., 1927 S.C. 597 .... 13.3
Melrose v Davidson and Robertson, 1993 S.L.T. 611 .... 5.13
Melville v Cummings, 1912 S.C. 1185; 1912 S.L.T. 130 .... 9.8
Mercedes-Benz Finance Ltd v Clydesdale Bank plc, 1996 S.C.C.R. 1005.... 13.8, 13.14
Mercury Communications Ltd v Scott-Garner and P.O. Engineering Union
   [1984] Ch. 37 .... 11.11
Merkur Island Shipping Corporation v Laughton [1983] A.C. 570 .... 3.21, 11.12
Merivale v Carson (1887) 20 Q.B.D. 275 .... 8.24
Mersey Docks & Harbour Board v Coggins & Griffiths Ltd [1947] A.C. 1 .... 10.16
Metall und Rostoff A.G. v Donaldson Lufkin and Jenrette Inc. [1990] 1
   Q.B. 391 .... 3.16
Middleton v Douglass, 1991 S.L.T. 726 .... 1.1
Midland Bank plc v Cameron, Thom, Peterkin & Duncans, 1988 S.L.T. 611 .... 5.52
Millar v Fife Regional Council, 1990 S.L.T. 651; 1989 G.W.D., 40-1880 ..... 7.7
Miller v City of Glasgow District Council, 1989 G.W.D. 29-1347 .... 7.6
—— v ——, 1989 S.L.T. 44 .... 1.1
Miller v SSEB, 1958 S.L.T. 229 .... 12.16
Milne v Tudhope, 1981 S.L.T. (Notes) 42 .... 2.22
Mitchell v Inverclyde D.C., 1997 G.W.D. 31-1593 .... 7.46, 7.47, 7.49
Mogul S.S. Co. Ltd v McGregor, Gow & Co. [1892] A.C. 25 .... 3.15
Monson v Tussauds [1894] 1 Q.B. 671 .... 8.2
Monteith v Cape Insulations, 1997 G.W.D. 1431 .... 11.29
Montreal Tramways v Leveille [1933] 4 D.L.R. 337 .... 9.13
Moorcraft v W. Alexander & Sons, 1946 S.C. 466 .... 9.13
More v Boyle, 1967 S.L.T. (Sh.Ct) 38 .... 2.20
Morgan v Morgan's Judicial Factor, 1922 S.C. 247 .... 13.3
Morgan Crucible plc v Hill Samuel [1991] 1 All E.R. 148 .... 5.7
Morgan Guaranty Trust Co. of New York v Lothian R.C., 1995 S.L.T.
   229 .... 13.1, 13.6, 13.29
Morley v Most Noble Ian Campbell 1997 G.W.D. 8-844 .... 7.5
Morris v West Hartlepool Steam Navigation Co. Ltd [1956] A.C. 552 .... 4.23
Morrison v Kelly, 1970 S.C. 65 .... 12.7
—— v Ritchie (1902) 4 F. 645; (1902) 9 S.L.T. 476 .... 8.9
Morrow v Neil, 1975 S.L.T. (Sh.Ct) 65 .... 2.4
Mortgage Corporation, The v Mitchells Roberton, 1997 S.L.T. 1305 .... 13.7
Morton v Wm Dixon, 1909 S.C. 807; 1909 1 S.L.T. 346 .... 4.28
Moss v Howdle, 1997 S.L.T. 782; 1997 S.C.C.R. 215 .... 2.11, 11.16
—— v Penman, 1994 S.L.T. 19 .... 13.15
Moyes v Lothian Health Board, 1990 S.L.T. 444 .... 2.3, 5.48, 5.51
Muir v Cumbernauld and Kilsyth District Council, 1993 S.L.T. 287 ..... 12.3
—— v Glasgow Corporation, 1943 S.C. (H.L.) 3; 1944 S.L.T. 60 ...... 4.20, 4.21, 9.6
Muir's Tr. v Braidwood, 1958 S.C. 169; 1958 S.L.T. 149 .... 9.16
Mulcahy v MOD [1996] 2 W.L.R. 474 .... 9.4
Mull Shellfish Ltd v Golden Sea Produce Ltd, 192 S.L.T. 703 .... 5.16
Murphy v Brentwood District Council [1990] 3 W.L.R. 414 .... 5.10, 5.33, 5.38, 5.39, 5.44, 7.14
—— v —— [1991] 1 A.C. 398 .... 4.19
Murray v Fraser, 1916 S.C. 623; 1916 1 S.L.T. 300 .... 2.8
—— v Harringay Arena Ltd [1951] 2 K.B. 529 .... 11.19
Mustard v Paterson, 1923 S.C. 142; 1923 S.L.T. 21 .... 2.28

N.V. Devos Gebroeder v Sunderland Sportswear Ltd., 1990 S.L.T. 473   13.14
Nacap Ltd v Moffat Plant Ltd, 1987 S.L.T. 221 .... 5.16, 9.1, 9.17
Naftalin v LMS Ry, 1933 S.C. 259 .... 12.20

National Bank of Greece *v* Pinios Shipping Co. (No. 1) (The Maria) [1989] 1
  All E.R. 213 .... 5.46
Nea Tyhi (The) [1982] 1 Lloyd's Rep. 606 .... 5.16
Nelson Holdings Ltd *v* British Gas [1977] T.L.R. 122 .... 5.37
Nethermere (St Neots) Ltd *v* Taverna [1984] I.C.R. 612 .... 10.10
Newton *v* Edgerley [1959] 1 W.L.R. 1031 .... 9.11
——— *v* Newton, 1925 S.C. 715 .... 13.14, 13.26
Nicolls *v* City of Glasgow, unreported, Glasgow Sh.Ct, Dec. 23, 1996 .... 7.49
Nimmo *v* Alexander Cowan & Sons Ltd, 1967 S.L.T. 277 .... 7.50
Norsk Pacific Steamship Co. Ltd *v* Canadian National Ry, Supreme Court of
  Canada, April 30, 1992 (unreported) 5.19
North Scottish Helicopters *v* United Technologies, 1988 S.L.T. 77, 778 .... 9.1

O'BRIENS *v* WATTS, 1987 S.L.T. 101 .... 3.11
O'Brien's C.B. *v* British Steel, 1991 S.L.T. 477 .... 12.13
O'Donnell *v* Murdoch McKenzie & Co., 1967 S.C. (H.L.) 63 .... 12.6
O'Kelly *v* Trusthouse Forte plc [1984] Q.B. 90 .... 10.10
O'Neil *v* Coyle, 1995 G.W.D. 21-1185 .... 7.30
Oll Ltd *v* Secretary of State for the Home Dept, unreported Q.B., June 16,
  1997 .... 5.37
Oropesa (The) [1943] P. 32 .... 4.34
Overseas Tankship (U.K.) Ltd *v* Morts Dock & Engineering Co. Ltd [1961]
  A.C. 388 (The "Wagon Mound" No. 1) 4.44, 4.46
——— *v* Miller S.S. Co. [1967] 1 A.C. 617 (The "Wagon Mound" No. 2) 4.22

P's C.B. *v* CICB, 1996 G.W.D. 39-2243 .... 9.14
Pacific Associates Inc. *v* Baxter [1989] 2 All E.R. 159 .... 5.46
Page *v* Smith [1996] 1. A.C. 155 .... 5.28
Paris *v* Stepney B.C. [1951] A.C. 367 .... 4.25
Park *v* Tractor Shovels Ltd, 1980 S.L.T. 94 .... 10.16
Parker Knoll *v* Knoll International [1962] R.P.C. 265 .... 3.11
Parry *v* Cleaver [1970] A.C. 1 .... 12.14
Peebles *v* MacPhail, 1990 S.L.T. 245 .... 2.3
Pepper *v* Hart [1992] 3 W.L.R. 1032 .... 11.27
Percy *v* Glasgow Corporation, 1922 S.C. (H.L.) 144; 1922 S.L.T. 352 .... 10.7
Petch *v* Customs and Excise Commissioners [1933] I.C.R. 789 .... 7.37
Phelps *v* Hillingdon L.B.C. [1997] T.L.R. 502 .... 5.39
Phestos Shipping Co. Ltd *v* Kurmiawan, 1983 S.L.T. 388 .... 2.11
Philips *v* William Whiteley Ltd [1938] 1 All E.R. 566 .... 5.55
Phillips *v* Grampian Health Board, 1988 S.L.T. 628; (revd) 1989 S.L.T. 538 .... 11.29
Pitts *v* Hunt [1991] 1 Q.B. 24 .... 11.20
Plato Films *v* Speidel [1961] A.C. 1090 .... 8.10
Polemis and Furness, Withy & Co. Ltd, *Re* [1921] 3 K.B. 560   4.43, 4.44, 4.46, 4.47
Poliskie *v* Lane, 1981 S.L.T. 282 .... 7.4
Porteous *v* Rutherford, 1980 S.L.T. (Sh.Ct) 129 .... 2.4
Porteous (George) (Arts) Ltd *v* Dollar Rae, 1979 S.L.T. (Sh.Ct) 51 .... 11.37
Porter *v* Dickie, 1983 S.L.T. 234 .... 11.29
Post Office *v* Morton, 1992 G.W.D. 26-1492 .... 3.2
Prentice *v* Chalmers, 1985 S.L.T. 168 .... 11.29
Pritchard *v* Tayside Health Board, 1989 G.W.D. 15-643 .... 11.35
Progress and Properties *v* Craft (1976) 135 C.L.R. 651 .... 11.20
Prophit *v* BBC, 1997 S.L.T. 745 .... 8.2
Pullar *v* Window Clean, 1956 S.L.T. 18 .... 5.38, 6.1, 6.3

R. *v* H.M. TREASURY, EX P. BRITISH TELECOMMUNICATIONS PLC [1996] 3 W.L.R. 203 .... 6.18
R. *v* Ministry of Agriculture and Fisheries, ex p. Hedley Lomas (Ireland) Ltd [1996] T.L.R. 353 .... 6.18
R. *v* Secretary of State for Transport, ex parte Factortame Ltd [1990] 2 A.C. 85, H.L.; [1991] 1 A.C. 603, ECJ C-48/93 .... 6.16
R.H.M. Bakeries (Scotland) Ltd *v* Strathclyde Regional Council, 1985 S.L.T. 214 .... 1.12, 2.15, 2.18, 2.19, 2.24, 12.8
Rae *v* Chief Constable, 1998 G.W.D. 406 .... 12.7
Rae *v* Hay (1832) 10 S. 303 .... 2.26
Ramsay *v* MacLay (1890) 18 R. 130 .... 8.2
Rankin *v* Wither (1886) 13 R. 903 .... 13.14
Ravenscroft *v* Rederiaktiebolaget Transatlantic [1991] 3 All E.R. 73 .... 5.19
Reading *v* Att.-Gen. [1951] A.C. 507 .... 13.21
Reavis *v* Clan Line Steamers, 1925 S.C. 725 S.L.T. 538 .... 5.14
Reid *v* Mitchell (1885) 12 R. 1129 .... 2.2
Renfrew Golf Club *v* Ravenstone Securities, 1984 S.L.T. 170 .... 11.37
Riches *v* Secretary of Sate for Social Security, 1994 S.L.T. 730 .... 13.17
Riverstone Meat Co. Ltd *v* Lancashire Shipping Co. Ltd [1961] A.C. 807 .... 10.17
Robbie *v* Graham & Sibbald, 1989 S.L.T. 870 .... 5.13
Roberts *v* Ramsbottom [1980] 1 All E.R. 7 .... 9.15
Robertson *v* Fleming (1861) 5.52
—— *v* Forth Road Bridge Joint Board, 1996 S.L.T. 263 .... 5.27, 5.28
—— *v* Landell (1843) 6 D. 170 .... 13.22
—— *v* Tennent Caledonian Brewers, 1994 G.W.D. 11-679 .... 12.2
—— *v* Turnbull, 1982 S.L.T. 96 .... 5.22
Rochester Poster Services Ltd *v* A.G. Barr plc, 1994 S.L.T. (Sh.Ct) 3 .... 13.25
Roe *v* Minster of Health [1954] 2 Q.B. 66 .... 4.17
Rondel *v* Worsley [1969] 1 A.C. 191 .... 5.53
Rookes *v* Barnard [1964] A.C. 1129 .... 3.22
Rose *v* Colvilles, 1950 S.L.T. (Notes) 72 .... 7.39, 7.41
—— *v* Plenty [1976] 1 All E.R. 97 .... 10.13
Ross *v* Associated Portland Cement Manufacturers [1964] 2 All E.R. 452 .... 12.6
—— *v* Bryce, 1972 S.L.T. (Sh.Ct) 76 .... 2.3, 11.17
—— *v* H.M. Advocate, 1991 S.L.T. 564 .... 9.15
—— *v* McCallum's Trs, 1922 S.C. 322; 1922 S.L.T. 254 .... 7.7
—— *v* Secretary of State, 1990 S.L.T. 13 .... 5.36
Rosses *v* Sir Bhagral Sinjie (1891) 19 R. 31 .... 12.20
Rossleigh Ltd *v* Leader Cars Ltd, 1987 S.L.T. 355 .... 3.20
Rothfield *v* N.B. Ry, 1920 S.C. 805; 1920 2 S.L.T. 269 .... 3.14
Rouse *v* Squires [1973] Q.B. 889 .... 4.36, 4.38
Rowling *v* Takaro Properties Ltd [1988] 2 W.L.R. 418 .... 4.19, 5.7, 5.33, 12.10
Roxburgh *v* Seven Seas Engineering Ltd, 1980 S.L.T. (Notes) 49 .... 3.3
Royal Bank of Scotland *v* Watt, 1991 S.L.T. 138 .... 13.23
Runciman *v* Borders Regional Council, 1988 S.L.T. 135 .... 4.41
Russell *v* Dickson, 1998 S.L.T. 96 .... 11.7
Russell *v* Motherwell Bridge Fabricators Ltd, 1992 G.W.D. 14-827 .... 7.36
Rylands *v* Fletcher (1868) L.R. 3 H.L. 330 .... 2.18

S.M.T. SALES & SERVICES CO. LTD *v* MOTOR AND GENERAL FINANCE CO. LTD., 1954 S.L.T. (Sh.Ct) 107 .... 13.13
Sabri-Tabrizi *v* Lothian Health Board, unreported, O.H., Dec. 17, 1997 ...... 9.13
Saif Ali *v* Sydney Mitchell & Co. [1978] 3 All E.R. 1033 .... 5.53
Sanderson *v* Lees (1859) 22 D. 24 .... 9.17
Sanderson *v* Paisley Burgh Commissioners (1899) 7 S.L.T. 255 .... 10.17

Schiffahrt & Kohlen GmbH *v* Chelsea Maritime Ltd [1982] Q.B. 481 .... 5.16
Scobie *v* Steele & Wilson, 1963 S.L.T. (Notes) 45 .... 10.7
Scott *v* London & St Katherine's Docks (1865) 3 H. & C. 596 .... 12.4
Scott Lithgow Ltd *v* G.E.C. Electrical Projects Ltd, 1992 S.L.T. 244 .... 1.1
Scott's Trs *v* Moss (1889) 17 R. 32 .... 5.40
Scottish Milk Marketing Board *v* Dryburgh Ltd, 1985 S.L.T. 253 .... 3.12
Scottish Old People's Welfare Council, 1987 S.L.T. 179 .... 9.17
Secretary of State for Defence *v* Mary Johnstone, unreported, Elgin Sheriff
    Court, July 18, 1996 .... 13.25
Secretary of State for Scotland *v* Scottish Prison Officers Association, 1991
    S.L.T. 658 .... 11.13
Shanks *v* B.B.C., 1991 G.W.D. 27-1641 .... 8.4
Sharp *v* Thomson, 1995 S.L.T. 837 .... 13.8
Shaw *v* Morgan (1888) 15 R. 865 .... 8.21
Shell U.K. Ltd *v* McGillivray, 1991 S.L.T. 667 .... 2.11, 3.15
Shields *v* Dalziel (1897) 24 R. 849 .... 11.19
Shilliday *v* Smith, 1998 S.C.L.R. 502 .... 13.19, 13.26
Short *v* J. & W. Henderson, 1946 S.C. (H.L.) 24; 1946 S.L.T. 230 .... 10.10
Sidaway *v* Governors of the Bethlem Royal Hospital [1985] A.C. 871   2.3, 5.49, 5.51
Sime *v* Sutcliffe Catering (Scotland) Ltd, 1990 S.L.T. 687 .... 10.17
Simpson *v* I.C.I., 1983 S.L.T. 601 .... 5.23
Simpson & Co. *v* Thomson (1877) 5 R. (H.L.) 40 .... 5.4, 5.14, 5.16, 5.27
Sinclair *v* MacDougall Estates Ltd, 1992 G.W.D. 17-1002 .... 11.37
Sloan *v* Triplett, 1985 S.L.T. 294 .... 11.20
Smith *v* Comrie's Exrx, 1944 S.C. 499; 1945 S.L.T. 108 .... 11.29
—— *v* Crossley Bros Ltd (1951) 95 Sol.Jo. 655 .... 7.35
—— *v* Eric S. Bush and Harris *v* Wyre Forrest D.C. [1989] 2 W.L.R. 790 .. 5.13
—— *v* Jenkins (1970) 119 C.L.R. 397 .... 11.20
—— *v* Leech Brain *v* Co. [1962] 2 Q.B. 405 .... 4.46
—— *v* Littlewoods Organisation. *See* Maloco *v* Littlewoods Organisation.
—— *v* Saville, Outer House, May 12, 1989 .... 13.16
Snare *v* The Earl of Fife's Trs (1850) 13 D. 286 .... 2.21
Solicitors of Edinburgh *v* Robertson (1781) Mor. 13935 .... 9.6, 9.7
Somerville *v* Hamilton (1541) Mor. 8905 .... 9.12
Southern Bowling Club *v* Ross (1902) 4 F. 405 .... 2.11
Spartan Steel & Alloys Ltd *v* Martin & Co. (Contractors) Ltd [1973] Q.B. 27.... 5.15
Spring *v* Guardian Assurance Co., 1992 T.L.R. 628 .... 5.11, 8.23
—— *v* —— [1995] 2 A.C. 296 .... 5.11
Square Grip Reinforcement Co. *v* Macdonald, 1966 S.L.T. 232; 1968
    S.L.T. 65 .... 11.11
Squires *v* Perth and Kinross District Council, 1986 S.L.T. 30 .... 4.37, 5.41
Steele *v* Scottish Daily Record, 1970 S.L.T. 53 .... 8.26
Stephen *v* Thurso Police Commrs (1876) 3 R. 535 .... 10.17
Stevenson *v* Glasgow Corporation, 1908 S.C. 1034 .... 7.8
—— *v* Wilson, 1907 S.C. 445 .... 13.8
Stewart *v* Thain, 1981 S.L.T. (Notes) 2 .... 2.3
Stillie *v* Wilson, 1988 S.C.L.R. 108; (revd) 1989 G.W.D. 19-781 .... 7.29
Stirling *v* Earl of Lauderdale (1733) Mor. 2930 .... 13.6
Stovin *v* Wise [1996] A.C. 923 .... 5.34, 5.38, 7.5
Stratford *v* Lindley [1964] 3 All E.R. 102 .... 3.20, 3.23
Strathclyde R.C. *v* W.A. Fairhurst, 1997 S.L.T. 658 .... 11.37
Strathford East Kilbride Ltd *v* HLM Design Ltd, 1997 Rep.L.R. 112; 1997
    S.C.L.R. 877 .... 5.10, 5.19, 5.39, 5.52
Style Financial Services Ltd *v* Bank of Scotland, 1997 G.W.D. 255 .... 13.8, 13.14
Summers *v* Frost [1955] A.C. 740 .... 6.8, 7.38

Sutherland Shire Council *v* Heyman (1985) 157 C.L.R. 424 .... 5.38
Swan *v* Minto & Son, unreported, Lanark Sheriff Court, May 19, 1997 ..... 7.33
Symington *v* Campbell (1894) 21 R. 434 .... 9.17

TAHIR *v* GOSAL, Glasgow Sheriff Court, May 16, 1974 .... 2.4
Tai Hing Cotton Mill Ltd *v* Lui Chong Hing Bank [1986] A.C. 80 .... 5.46
Tate & Lyle Foods *v* Greater London Council [1983] 2 A.C. 509 .... 5.10
Taylor *v* City of Glasgow, 1997 Rep.L.R. 17; 1996 Rep.L.R. 69 .... 10.15
—— *v* Glasgow Corporation 1922 S.C. (H.L.) 1; 1921 S.L.T. 254 .... 7.7
—— *v* Wilson's Trs, 1975 S.C. 147 .... 13.17
Telfer *v* Glasgow Corporation, 1974 S.L.T. (Notes) 51 .... 7.4, 7.7
Thin & Sinclair *v* Arrol (1896) 24 R. 198 .... 3.2
Thomas *v* N.U.M. (South Wales Area) [1985] 2 W.L.R. 1081 .... 11.12
Thomson *v* British Steel Corporation 1977 S.L.T. 26 .... 10.11
—— *v* Devon (1899) 15 Sh.Ct Rep. 209 .... 2.3
Thomson (D.C.) *v* Deakin [1952] 2 All E.R. 361 .... 3.20
Thurogood *v* Van den Berghs and Jurgens Ltd [1951] 2 K.B. 537 .... 4.46
Titchener *v* British Railways Board, 1984 S.L.T. 192 .... 7.8, 7.10
Tolstoy *v* U.K., unreported, ECHR, July 13, 1995 .... 8.10
Topp *v* London Country Bus Ltd, 1991 T.L.R. 552 .... 5.43
Torquay Hotel Co. Ltd *v* Cousins [1969] 1 All E.R. 522 .... 3.21
Transocean Maritime Agencies S.A. Monegasque *v* Petit, 1997 S.C.L.R. 534 .... 13.7
Trapp *v* Mackie, 1979 S.C. (H.L.) 38; 1979 S.L.T. 126 .... 8.16
Treadwell's Drifters Inc. *v* RCL Ltd, 1996 S.L.T. 1048 .... 3.7, 3.10
Tuttle & Buck (1909) 119 N.W. 946 .... 3.15

UNITED WHOLESALE GROCERS LTD. *v* SHER, 1993 S.L.T. 284 .... 10.10
United States *v* Carroll Towing Co. (1947) 159 F. (2d) 169 .... 4.23
United Technologies Corp. Inc. *v* North Scottish Helicopters Ltd, 1988
    S.L.T. 77 .... 5.16
—— *v* —— (No. 2) 1988 S.L.T. 778 .... 5.16
Uxbridge Permanent Building Society *v* Pickard [1939] 2 K.B. 248 .... 10.15

VAN GEND EN LOOS *v* NEDERLANDSE TARIEF COMMISSIE [1963] C.M.L.R. 105 ... 6.13
Varney (Scotland) Ltd *v* Burgh of Lanark, 1976 S.L.T. 46 .... 13.14
Vize *v* Scott Lithgow Ltd, 1991 G.W.D. 9-549 .... 12.3
Vulcan *v* Berlin (1882) 9 R. 1057 .... 13.16

WADDELL *v* BBC, 1973 S.L.T. 246 .... 8.9
Walker *v* Eastern Scottish Omnibuses, 1990 G.W.D. 3-140 .... 7.6
—— *v* Henry Ost & Co. Ltd [1970] 1 W.L.R. 917 .... 3.13
—— *v* Milne (1823) 2 S. 379 .... 13.9
—— *v* Northumberland C.C. [1995] 1 All E.R. 737 .... 7.37
Walker (John) & Sons Ltd *v* Douglas Laing & Co., 1993 S.L.T. 156 .... 3.12
Wallace *v* City of Glasgow District Council, 1985 S.L.T. 23 .... 7.6
Walsh *v* Secretary of State for Scotland, 1990 G.W.D. 7-385 .... 2.6
Ward *v* Chief Constable, 1991 S.L.T. 292 .... 5.36
Wardlaw *v* Bonnington Castings, 1956 S.C. (H.L.) 26; 1956 S.L.T. 135 .... 6.9
Warnink B.V. *v* Townend & Son Ltd [1979] A.C. 731 .... 3.10
Watt *v* Jamieson, 1954 S.C. 56; 1954 S.L.T. 56 .... 2.14, 2.16
Waugh *v* James K. Allan Ltd, 1964 S.C. (H.L.) 102; 1964 S.L.T. 269 .... 9.15
Waverley Housing Management *v* BBC, 1993 G.W.D. 17-1117 .... 9.6
Webster *v* Lord Advocate, 1984 S.L.T. 13; varied at 1985 S.L.T. 361 .... 2.12
Weir *v* J. M. Hodge & Son, 1990 S.L.T. 266 .... 5.22
Weir *v* Wyper, 1992 S.L.T. 579 .... 11.20

West *v* Secretary of State for Scotland, 1992 S.L.T. 636 .... 12.10
Wheeler *v* New Merton Board Mills Ltd [1933] 2 K.B. 669 .... 6.11, 7.40
White *v* Jones [1995] 2 A.C. 207 .... 5.4, 5.21, 5.52
—— *v* McIntyre (1841) 3D.334.. 13.3
Whitefield *v* Barton, 1987 S.C.L.R. 259 .... 4.24
Wilkinson *v* Downton [1897] 2 Q.B. 57 .... 3.2
William Grant & Son *v* Glen Catrine Bonded Warehouse, 1995 S.L.T. 936 .... 9.1
Williams *v* Hemphill, 1966 S.C. (H.L.) 31 .... 10.12, 10.13
Willis *v* Brooks [1947] 1 All E.R. 191 .... 9.9
Willis Faber Enthoven (Pty) Ltd *v* Receiver of Revenue, 1992 (4) S.A.
    202 (A) 13.6
Wilsher *v* Essex Area Health Authority [1988] 2 W.L.R. 557 .... 4.32, 5.50
Wilson *v* Housing Corporation [1996] T.L.R. 733 .... 3.20
—— *v* McCaffrey, 1989 G.W.D. 1-37 .... 5.36
—— *v* Price, 1989 S.L.T. 484 .... 11.20
—— *v* Shepherd, 1913 S.C. 300 .... 2.21
Wilsons *v* McKnight (1830) 8 S. 398 .... 2.22
Winnik *v* Dick, 1984 S.L.T. 185 .... 1.8, 11.20
Winter *v* News Scotland Ltd, 1991 S.L.T. 828 .... 8.9
Wood *v* Fullerton (1710) Mor. 13960 .... 10.1
—— *v* Wood 1935 S.L.T. 431 .... 9.11
Wolfson *v* Forrester, 1910 S.C. 675; 1910 1 S.L.T. 318 .... 10.17
Wooldridge *v* Summer [1962] 2 All E.R. 978 .... 11.19
Woolwich Equitable Building Society *v* Inland Revenue [1991] 4 All E.R. 577... 13.17
Woolwich *v* Inland Revenue [1992] 3 W.L.R. 366 .... 12.10
Wright *v* Outram (1889) 16 R. 1004 .... 8.16

X. *v* Bedfordshire C.C. [1995] 3 All E.R. 353 .... 5.34, 5.38, 6.3

Yorkshire Dale S.S. Co. *v* MOWT [1942] A.C. 691 .... 4.31
Youle *v* Cochrane (1868) 6 M. 427 .... 13.6
Young *v* Cockburn (1674) Mor. 11,624 .... 13.25
Youssoupoff *v* M.G.M. (1934) 50 T.L.R. 581 .... 8.2
Yuen Kun Yeu *v* Att.-Gen. Hong Kong [1988] 1 A.C. 175 .... 4.19, 5.7, 5.33

Zemhunt Holdings *v* Control Securities plc, 1991 S.L.T. 653 .... 13.7

ALPHABETICAL TABLE OF STATUTES

Administration of Justice Act 1982 .... 5.22, 9.10–11, 11.27, 11.29–30, 12.14
Age of Legal Capacity (Scotland) Act 1991 .... 9.12, 11.34, 11.37
Animals Act 1971 .... 7.33
Animals (Scotland) Act 1987 .... 1.5, 6.2, 6.11, 7.21, 7.23, 7.28, 7.33
Bankruptcy (Scotland) Act 1985 .... 9.16
Betting Gaming and Lotteries Act 1934 .... 6.3
Bills of Lading Act 1855 .... 5.16
Carriage of Goods by Sea Act 1971 .... 2.26, 10.17
Carriage of Goods by Sea Act 1992 .... 5.16
Carriers Act 1830 .... 2.26
Children (Scotland) Act 1995 .... 9.12
Civil Aviation Act 1982 .... 2.11
Civil Evidence (Scotland) Act 1988 .... 12.7
Civil Jurisdiction and Judgements Act 1982 .... 12.19
Coal Mines Act 1911 .... 6.5
Congenital Disabilities (Civil Liability) Act 1976 .... 9.13
Consumer Protection Act 1987 .... 6.2, 7.12, 7.15, 11.9, 11.33
Copyright Act 1911 .... 3.3
Criminal Justice (Scotland) Act 1980 .... 1.3
Criminal Procedure (Scotland) Act 1995 .... 2.7
Crown Proceedings Act 1947 .... 9.4, 10.18
Crown Proceedings (Armed Forces) Act 1987 .... 9.4, 10.18
Crown Suits (Scotland) Act 1857 .... 9.5
Damages (Scotland) Act 1976 .... 1.3, 5.2, 9.11, 11.27, 11.30, 12.13, 12.15
Damages (Scotland) Act 1993 .... 11.27, 11.28, 11.29, 12.13, 12.15
Damages (Scotland) Act 1996 .... 12.14
Dangerous Wild Animals Act 1976 .... 7.30, 7.31, 7.33
Defamation Act 1952 .... 8.10, 8.13, 8.22
Defamation Act 1996 .... 8.2, 8.15, 8.16, 8.25
Diplomatic Privileges Act 1964 .... 11.6
Dogs Act 1906 .... 7.26
Education Act 1986 .... 2.3
Education Act 1993 .... 2.3
Employers' Liability Act 1880 .... 7.34
Employers' Liability (Compulsory Insurance) Act 1969 .... 11.23
Employers' Liability (Defective Equipment) Act 1969 .... 7.34
Employment Act 1980 .... 11.8, 11.13
Employment Act 1988 .... 11.8
Employment Act 1990 .... 11.8
Factories Act 1937 .... 6.7

Factories Act 1961 .... 7.9, 7.38, 7.45, 7.46, 10.17
Guards Dogs Act 1975 .... 6.2, 7.26, 7.33
Health and Safety at Work etc Act 1974 .... 1.5, 6.2, 7.38, 7.42, 7.50
Hotel Proprietors Act 1956 .... 2.27
Housing (Scotland) Act 1987 .... 7.11
Industrial Relations Act 1971 .... 11.8
Interest on Damages (Scotland) Act 1971 .... 12.13, 12.15
International Organisations Act 1968 .... 11.6
International Organisations Act 1981 .... 11.6
Law Reform (Contributory Negligence) Act 1945 .... 11.21
Law Reform (Husband and Wife) Act 1962 .... 9.10
Law Reform (Husband and Wife) (Scotland) Act 1984 .... 2.5, 9.10
Law Reform (Misc. Prov.) Act 1971 .... 11.29
Law Reform (Misc. Prov.) (Scotland) Act 1940 .... 4.38, 11.24–25
Law Reform (Misc. Prov.) (Scotland) Act 1968 .... 12.7
Law Reform (Misc. Prov.) (Scotland) Act 1980 .... 11.33–40
Law Reform (Misc. Prov.) (Scotland) Act 1985 .... 5.54, 11.33–40
Law Reform (Misc. Prov.) (Scotland) Act 1990 .... 5.13
Law Reform (Personal Injuries) Act 1948 .... 10.11
Lawburrows Act 1429 .... 2.4
Lawburrows Act 1581 .... 2.4
Married Women's Property (Scotland) Act 1881 .... 9.10
Married Women's Property (Scotland) Act 1920 .... 9.10
Medicines Act 1968 .... 6.2
Mental Health (Scotland) Act 1984 .... 2.6
Merchandising Marks Act 1887 .... 6.6
Merchant Shipping Act 1995 .... 2.6, 2.26
Occupiers Liability Act 1984 .... 7.2
Occupiers Liability (Scotland) Act 1960 .... 1.5, 6.2, 6.11, 7.2–11, 9.4, 11.19
Parliamentary Papers Act 1840 .... 8.15
Partnership Act 1980 .... 9.8
Police (Scotland) Act 1967 .... 10.18
Policyholders Protection Act 1975 .... 11.23
Prescription and Limitation (Scotland) Act 1973 .... 11.26, 11.33–40
Prescription and Limitation (Scotland) Act 1984 .... 11.33–40
Protection from Harrassment Act 1997 .... 2.9, 12.10
Rehabilitation of Offenders Act 1974 .... 8.13
Rent (Scotland) Act 1984 .... 2.10
Representation of the People Act 1983 .... 8.18
Road Traffic Act 1972 .... 11.23
Sale of Goods Act 1893 .... 2.21
Sale of Goods Act 1979 .... 5.16
Social Security Act 1989 .... 12.14
Social Security (Recovery of Benefits) Act 12.14
State Immunity Act 1978 .... 11.6
Summary Jurisdiction (Scotland) Act 1908 .... 2.7
Third Parties (Rights Against Insurers) Act 1930 .... 11.23
Trade Disputes Act 1906 .... 3.22, 11.8
Trade Disputes Act 1965 .... 3.22, 11.8
Trade Marks Act 1938 .... 3.11
Trade Union Act 1984 .... 11.13
Trade Union and Labour Relations Act 1974 .... 11.8
Trade Union and Labour Relations (Conslidation) Act 1992 ...... 9.9, 10.18, 11.8–13
Trade Union Reform and Employment Rights Act 1993 .... 11.8, 11.13
Trespass (Scotland) Act 1865 .... 2.11

Unfair Contract Terms Act 1977 .... 5.13, 7.9
Visiting Forces Act 1952 .... 11.6
Winter Herding Act 1686 .... 7.26
Workmen's Compensation Act 1887 .... 7.34

CHRONOLOGICAL TABLE OF STATUTES

(Acts within a year are sorted by Chapter)

1429	Lawburrows Act	2.4
1581	Lawburrows Act	2.4
1686	Winter Herding Act	7.26
1830	Carriers Act	2.26
1840	Parliamentary Papers Act	8.15
1855	Bills of Lading Act	5.16
1857	Crown Suits (Scotland) Act	9.5
1865	Trespass (Scotland) Act	2.6, 2.11
1880	Employer's Liability Act	7.34
1881	Married Women's Property (Scotland) Act	9.10
1887	Workmen's Compensation Act	7.34
	Merchandising Marks Act	6.6
1890	Partnership Act	9.8
1893	Sales of Goods Act	2.21
1906	Dogs Act	7.26
	Trade Disputes Act	3.22, 11.8
1908	Summary Jurisdiction (Scotland) Act	2.7
1911	Coal Mines Act	6.5
	Copyright Act	3.3
1920	Married Women's Property (Scotland) Act	9.10
1930	Third Parties (Rights Against Insurers) Act	11.23
1934	Betting Gaming and Lotteries Act	6.3
1937	Factories Act	6.7
1938	Trade Marks Act	3.11
1940	Law Reform (Misc. Prov.) (Scotland) Act	11.24–25
1945	Law Reform (Contributory Negligence) Act	11.21
1947	Crown Proceedings Act	9.4, 10.18
1948	Law Reform (Personal Injuries) Act	10.1
1952	Defamation Act	8.10, 8.13, 8.22
	Visiting Forces Act	11.6
1956	Hotel Proprietors Act	2.27
1960	Occupiers' Liability (Scotland) Act	1.5, 6.2, 6.11, 7.2–11, 9.4, 11.19
1961	Factories Act	7.45, 7.46, 10.17
1962	Law Reform (Husband and Wife) Act	9.10
1964	Diplomatic Privileges Act	11.6
1965	Trade Disputes Act	3.22, 11.8
1967	Police (Scotland) Act	10.18
1968	International Organisations Act	11.6
	Medicines Act	6.2
	Law Reform (Misc. Prov.) (Scotland) Act	12.7

1969	Employers' Liability (Defective Equipment) Act	7.34
	Employers' Liability (Compulsory Insurance) Act	11.23
1971	Carriage of Goods by Sea Act	2.26, 10.17
1971	Animals Act	7.33
	Interest on Damages (Scotland) Act	12.13, 12.15
1971	Law Reform (Misc. Prov.) Act	11.29
	Industrial Relations Act	11.8
1972	Road Traffic Act	11.23
1973	Prescription and Limitation (Scotland) Act	11.26, 11.33–40
1974	Health and Safety at Work etc. Act	1.5, 6.2, 7.38, 7.42, 7.50
	Trade Union and Labour Relations Act	11.8
	Rehabilitation of Offenders Act	8.13
1975	Guard Dogs Act	6.2, 7.33, 7.26
	Policyholders Protection Act	11.23
1976	Damages (Scotland) Act	1.3, 5.22, 9.11, 11.27, 11.28, 11.30, 12.13, 12.15
	Congenital Disabilities (Civil Liability) Act	9.13
	Dangerous Wild Animals Act	7.30, 7.31, 7.33
1977	Unfair Contract Terms Act	5.13, 7.9
1978	State Immunity Act	11.6
1979	Sale of Goods Act	5.16
1980	Employment Act	11.8, 11.13
	Law Reform (Misc. Prov.) (Scotland) Act	11.33–40
	Criminal Justice (Scotland) Act	1.3
1981	International Organisations Act	11.6
1982	Civil Aviation Act	2.11
	Civil Jurisdiction and Judgements Act	12.19
	Administration of Justice Act	5.22, 9.3, 9.10-11, 11.27, 11.29, 11.30, 12.14
1983	Representation of the People Act	8.18
1984	Occupiers Liability Act	7.2
	Law Reform (Husband and Wife) (Scotland) Act	2.5, 9.10
	Mental Health (Scotland) Act	2.6
	Prescription and Limitation (Scotland) Act	11.33–40
	Trade Union Act	11.13
	Rent (Scotland) Act	2.10
1985	Bankruptcy (Scotland) Act	9.16
	Law Reform (Misc. Prov.) (Scotland) Act	5.54, 11.33–40
1986	Education Act	2.3
1987	Animals (Scotland) Act	1.5, 6.2, 6.11, 7.21, 7.23, 7.28, 7.33
	Crown Proceedings (Armed Forces) Act	9.4, 10.18
	Housing (Scotland) Act	7.11
	Consumer Protection Act	6.2, 7.12, 7.15, 11.9, 11.33
1988	Employment Act	11.8
	Civil Evidence (Scotland) Act	12.7
1989	Social Security Act	12.14
1990	Employment Act	11.8
	Law Reform (Miscellaneous Provisions) (Scotland) Act	5.13
1991	Age of Legal Capacity (Scotland) Act	9.12, 11.34, 11.37
1992	Carriage of Goods by Sea Act	5.16
	Trade Union and Labour Relations (Consolidation) Act	9.9, 10.18, 11.8–13
1993	Damages (Scotland) Act	11.27, 11.28, 11.29, 12.13, 12.15
	Education Act	2.3
	Trade Union Reform and Employment Rights Act	11.8, 11.13
1995	Children (Scotland) Act	9.12
	Criminal Procedure (Scotland) Act	2.7
	Merchant Shipping Act	2.6, 2.26

1996   Defamation Act 8.2, 8.15, 8.16, 8.25
1997   Protection from Harassment Act 2.9, 12.10
       Social Security (Recovery of Benefits) Act 12.14

CHAPTER 1

INTRODUCTION

THE SUBJECT

A cow falls through the ceiling of your shop, some unidentified person 1.1 pours a pot of urine over your head, you fall through the floor of a building or you are butted by a bull over a wall on to stinging nettles having tried to ward it off by tapping it on the nose. It is with stories like these that the law of delict deals and indeed has had to deal in the past.[1] But first it is only fair to explain what is meant by the strange name of the subject.[2]

For the moment, the reader may conveniently consider delict to be the area of law which makes certain legally disapproved conduct by a defender actionable (usually for damages or by interdict) in the civil courts by a pursuer who often, but not always, will have suffered some loss as a result of the conduct. It applies to much of the same area of the law as the English "tort". The same subject-matter is often considered in Scotland under the heading "reparation" but that term more accurately describes a response to a breach of a legal obligation: one commits a delict; one must make reparation.[3]

Calling the subject "delict" is consistent with a division of obligations according to the events which trigger various responses, *i.e.* contract, delict and unjust enrichment at the expense of another.[4] The

---

[1] See *Cameron v. Hamilton's Auction Marts Ltd*, 1955 S.L.T. (Sh.Ct.) 74; *Gray v. Dunlop*, 1954 S.L.T. (Sh.Ct.) 75; and *Foskett v. McClymont*, 1998 Rep.L.R.13.

[2] " '*Delinquo*', supine *delictum* means 'to be lacking' or 'fail'. It was already used in classical Latin to mean 'fail in one's duty, offend' ": Birks, "The Concept of a Civil Wrong" in *Philosophical Foundations of Tort Law* (Owen ed., Oxford, 1995), p. 39, n. 28.

[3] Reparation is no longer thought to refer to breach of contract: *Miller v. Glasgow D.C.*, 1989 S.L.T. 44; *Middleton v. Douglass*, 1991 S.L.T. 726. The practitioner publications are called the "*Reparation Law Reports*" and the "*Reparation Bulletin*".

[4] For a full discussion of the problems of terminology see Walker, *Delict*, pp. 3–8; Birks, "Six questions in search of a subject", 1985 J.R. 227; Stewart, "Smith's question-mark", 1990 J.R. 71; and see the following cases decided after that article was written: *Kirkcaldy D. C. v. Household Manufacturing Ltd*, 1987 S.L.T. 617; *Scott Lithgow Ltd v. GEC Electrical Projects Ltd*, 1992 S.L.T. 244.

word "delict" formerly had the same "bad" connotation as has "delinquent" and classically dealt with matters which were essentially crimes and generally required *mens rea*.

The term "quasi-delict" is used by the legal community in at least two ways: to describe cases involving actionable conduct not quite so morally wrong as delicts proper, such as, for example, negligence; and, more particularly, to describe those obligations imposed in Scots law which are derived from certain Roman actions [2.23–2.28].

Difference from other subjects

1.2 The traditional explanation is that the commission of a delict is a breach of an obligation created by the law between the wrongdoer and the victim, as opposed to contract where any liability to perform or to pay damages depends upon the consent of the parties or the will of a party (in the case of the unilateral gratuitous obligation).[5] Unjust enrichment,[6] with which delict is frequently associated, has more in common with delict than contract, the obligation being quite clearly imposed by the law: it differs from delictual duties only in that in unjust enrichment cases the duty to pay or to do something arises without the necessity of any wrong being done by the defender. It is only right to say that there is considerable academic discussion concerning the interrelation of the various categories of the law of obligations.[7]

HISTORY

1.3 Scots law has been influenced by Roman law over the centuries and further reading should, in the first instance, be directed towards some comprehension of that (now quite distant) relationship.[8] There are also parallels. The Roman law began by treating delict and crime as much the same thing. The most significant delicts for the Romans were

---

[5] See Woolman, *Introduction to the Scots Law of Contract* (2nd ed., W. Green, 1987), pp. 11–12.

[6] Until recently misleadingly dealt with under the heading of quasi-contract, this is the body of law which deals with the restitution of gains unjustly made by a defender at the expense of the pursuer, rather than reinstating the pursuer to the position he was in before a wrong was done to him or her, as in delict. A general principle of restitution is recognised in Scotland but the cases are collected under certain categories such as, for example, recompense or repetition. See Chap. 13.

[7] Atiyah, *Rise and Fall* (Oxford, 1979), Chap. 20 and Birks, *Introduction to the Law of Restitution* (Oxford, 1989).

[8] See generally, Evans-Jones, *The Civilian Tradition in Scots Law* (Stair Society, 1995); Zimmerman, *The Law of Obligations: Roman Foundations of the Civilian Tradition* (Oxford, 1996).

things like assault or theft. In the absence of a state apparatus, such as a police force, to investigate and deal with such matters, the Roman law attempted to control the self-help to which Romans might resort. Roman law arranged for people to be able to buy off vengeance. For example, the first piece of Roman legislation, the Twelve Tables, promulgated about 450 B.C., provided that the killing of an armed thief resulted in no penalty. The law later tried to intercede so that a thief caught red-handed could not have vengeance visited upon him except as permitted by the court. At first the court permitted restricted reprisals but eventually a monetary penalty was substituted. The penalty was not, however, an amount intended to compensate, as is now the general rule; instead, sometimes two, three or four times the value of the object stolen had to be paid.

Scots law developed a similar way. In the modern Scots law theft and assault remain delicts as much as they are crimes. Beginning about the fourteenth century, when a person had killed another as a result of a criminal act, he might be called upon to pay a reasonable sum to the deceased's kin. This remedy became known as assythment and was only formally abolished by the Damages (Scotland) Act 1976.[9] This is only one example of a more native non-Roman source. In principle, Scots law parted from crime when Stair, under reference to Romans, xii, 19,[10] was quite clear that the breach of delictual obligations should be visited by an obligation to make reparation and should not be concerned with revenge. Interestingly though, since the Criminal Justice (Scotland) Act 1980, Part IV, a criminal court can in certain circumstances make an order called a compensation order. Such an order makes an offender pay a sum compensating the victim of the crime, as well as any fine or sentence of imprisonment that may be imposed. Compensation orders cannot be made in motor collision cases. The offender who does not pay the order—which can be paid by instalments—can be imprisoned for a specified period.

There are traces running through Scots law of two Roman law 1.4 remedies which have certainly influenced the systems in the civilian family: the *actio injuriarum* and the *actio legis Aquiliae*.[11] The first gave an action for insult and the second allowed for damages in respect of loss wrongfully caused (*damnum injuria datum*). *Injuria* in the *actio injuriarum* meant affront or insult but meant contrary to law in the context of the *lex Aquilia*.[12] The *lex Aquilia* was an ancient Roman

---

[9] See *Casebook*, Appendix, Ext. 11, and see Sutherland, "The Resuscitation of Assythment?" 1992 J.R. 242.

[10] I, ix, 2 (*Casebook*, Ext. 11. 2.1.3).

[11] Until relatively recently the modern significance of these antecedents in Scots law were not clearly understood by many: see Stein (1955); T.B. Smith (1972) (1984) (Casebook, Ext. 14).

[12] D.9.2.5.1 (Ulpian).

statute which provided for liability for certain damage to certain property caused in certain ways.[13] Its practical significance is that it is this statute and its interpretation which attracted the attention of the great Roman Jurists, featured in the *Digest* and was rediscovered in post-medieval Europe. Eventually *injuria* meaning "contrary to law" was expanded to mean blameworthiness or *culpa*.[14]

Scots law did not follow the classical Roman law but the thinking, concepts and terminology of Roman law have been extensively appropriated. By the time of Erskine it was possible to state the law quite broadly: "every one who has the exercise of reason, and so can distinguish between right and wrong, is naturally obliged to make up the damage befalling his neighbour from a wrong committed by himself. Wherefore every fraudulent contrivance, or unwarrantable act by which another suffers damage, or runs the hazard of it, subjects the delinquent to reparation."[15] This comes close to the position reached in the French and German Civil Codes—a general principle of reparation not requiring nominate heads.[16]

1.5   Industrialisation brought about more opportunity for loss to be caused in the form of physical injury whether in the factory, the mill, the mine or by the railway or the motor car. Mass production separated the maker from the product and in many cases resulted in no individual being solely responsible for the finished product. In these situations the wrongfulness which triggered liability in theft or assault or in insult was not quite so apparent. Thus began the rapid development of the law of negligence. The concept of fault (*culpa*) recognised in Scots law was a fertile theoretical compost in which liability for lack of care could grow.

This rapid change of social factors could not always be accommodated by the common law, which requires a litigation between real parties to declare the law, and often Parliament has been compelled to intervene to provide remedies for appropriate causes, or to remedy perceived deficiencies in the common law as it develops. It shall be seen that many areas are no longer covered by the common law but by statute—for example, the Health and Safety at Work etc. Act 1974, the Occupiers' Liability (Scotland) Act 1960 and the Animals (Scotland) Act 1987 (see Chapter 7 below).

---

[13] See generally Kolbert (1989).
[14] MacCormack, "Aquilian Culpa" in *Daube Noster* (Watson ed., 1974).
[15] Erskine, *Inst*. III, 1, 13 (Casebook, Ext. 12).
[16] Although it should be noted that there are different strands in the civilian tradition: see Zimmerman. Stair has a rights-focused general principle which is similar to the German Code and Erskine's is closer to the French.

FUNCTION

Function changes with time. As indicated above, initially delict had a quasi-criminal function of penalising wrongdoers. To some extent it still has that function: if you strike me or insult me I will get damages from you. This is sometimes described as a hortatory/deterrent function: as well as punishing, the possibility of delictual liability deters people by creating a fear of punishment, encouraging people to organise their behaviour accordingly.[17] But this criminal/hortatory/ deterrent function only operates to a certain extent: if you are unemployed and in receipt of state benefit then you pay no damages and so you may not be so concerned to plan your conduct within the law. If you carelessly run me down in your company car, your employer's insurers pay the damages and it is your employer who loses his "no claims" bonus. The criminal law now fulfils this function: you drive carelessly—you are fined—you may lose your driving licence. 1.6

The next major function (and that which concerns the practitioner) is compensation. Instead of concentrating on penalising the wrongdoer we compensate the victim. If compensation is based on fault [1.12] then not every injured person is compensated and so it might be said that delict is a poor compensation scheme. If a regime of strict liability [1.12] is applied more people are compensated. Because a quite significant amount of compensation is achieved through the delict system, those who wish to extend compensation often urge a strict liability regime. Strict liability is also likely to cover the cost of compensating.[18] 1.7

Aside from penalising some wrongdoers quite effectively (for example, defamation actions between persons with money), delict redistributes the cost of certain accidents within the community—a function most clearly seen in the rule that an employer is vicariously liable for his or her employees (see Chapter 10). 1.8

The practice of insuring against certain risks, although it has had a considerable influence on the law, is nonetheless legally irrelevant.[19] It therefore does not matter that a pursuer may already have recovered from his insurers. For example, if a contractor wrongly cuts a power

---

[17] This rather unfashionable view is still, it is submitted, valid: see the recent support from Henry L.J. in *Frost v. Chief Constable* [1996] T.L.R. 617.

[18] See the references in Chap. 7, "Product Liability"; Atiyah, *Accidents, Compensation and the Law* (4th ed., P. Cane, Weidenfeld). The consultation paper "Compensation for Road Accidents" from the Lord Chancellor's Department (May, 1991) is still under consideration.

[19] See, *e.g. Winnik v. Dick*, 1981 S.L.T. (Sh.Ct.) 23. But insurance can be a factor in other enquiries such as fairness: see Lord Rodger in the Outer House in *B.T. v. James Thomson & Sons Ltd*, 1997 S.L.T. 767 at 774D.

cable which deprives millions of people of power and causes millions of pounds of financial loss, it would be expensive to insure against such a contingency, whereas if individuals are aware that a power cut is a risk they themselves must carry, they will take steps to minimise the loss they might suffer, for example by buying a petrol-powered generator. Alternatively, people who would suffer from a power cut could arrange insurance themselves.[20]

1.9 Finally, the modern welfare state interacts with the law of delict. People who are the victims of crime may recover compensation from the Criminal Injuries Compensation Scheme[21] and workers injured at work may receive industrial injury benefit. Rules have been worked out to balance the desire not to overcompensate a victim and the law's reluctance to let a wrongdoer off the hook because the person who has title to sue may already have been compensated [12.15].

DIFFERENCES BETWEEN SCOTS AND ENGLISH LAW

1.10 The English law of torts itself grew out of English criminal law. After that its development was closely linked to the forms of action. Basically, unless a person could fit his or her claim into one of the forms of action there was no remedy. Accordingly, English law is most appropriately seen as being a series of separate torts and not as a number of frequently occurring instances of a general principle of delictual or tortious liability. On the other hand, with the passage of time, the expansion of each of the torts resulted in there being fewer gaps between the torts, and indeed the extension of existing torts or the creation of new torts seems to have been based on principles similar to those informing Scots law, such as liability based on fault.[22] It is fair to say that there are still differences between the two systems—outwith careless conduct, considerable differences. The English law is still affected by precedents which say that a man acts at his peril, or that there is no liability for a pure omission. The English law of defamation makes a technical distinction between libel and slander, which Scots law does not. English law makes a technical distinction between public and private nuisance which again does not seem to have been adopted in Scotland. The English courts can award exemplary or penal damages and the rules on prescription and limitation are different. The rules on remoteness of damage may be different. The English law in relation to property

---

[20] For an excellent examination of this issue, see Davies, "The End of the Affair: Duty of Care and Liability Insurance" (1989) 9 L.S. 67.

[21] Fully explained in Pollock, "Criminal Injuries Compensation: the Tariff" (1996) 41 J.L.S.S 93.

[22] Salmond and Heuston, *The Law of Torts* (20th ed., Sweet & Maxwell, 1992), Chap. 1

interests is quite different both in concept and result.[23] The law of trespass is much more significant in England than in Scotland. However, in the most frequently litigated area, that of negligence, it cannot be said that the law is not now the same in both jurisdictions.[24]

GENERAL PRINCIPLES OF DELICTUAL LIABILITY

At the highest level of generality there is the precept that one person 1.11 should not harm another. Below that is the principle that one should not cause loss wrongfully. "Wrongfully" refers to fault or conduct in breach of a duty of care, or conduct causing reasonably foreseeable harm of the kind which in fact results. However, there are cases where loss is caused but no action is possible—for example, some of the secondary pure economic loss cases [5.14–5.19]. These may be explained on the basis that "wrongfully" can be dependent upon a duty of care which can only be said to exist in certain limited circumstances or, more convincingly, that sometimes as a matter of public policy, discernible from precedent, the courts will not allow recovery.

Nonetheless, given Stair's broad statement of the basis of liability,[25] the nineteenth-century emphasis on *culpa*[26] and the frequent express reliance upon principle in negligence cases,[27] it can be said that the outcome of cases not directly covered by authority can be predicted with some degree of certainty on the strength of these principles.

So far as the idea of *culpa* or fault is concerned, the present writer's 1.12 view is that it can be said that, so far as the common law is concerned, in most cases there is no liability without fault, but that proof of fault is not a guarantee of success. What is not settled in the literature is what *culpa* actually means[28]; neither is it agreed to which factual circumstances *culpa* is relevant. Nuisance [2.12–2.17] is an excellent example. At one time it was thought not to involve fault, but now it does. One recent nuisance case has provided an opportunity for a restatement of the civilian approach. In *Kennedy v. Glenbelle*[29] Lord President Hope said:

> "Culpa which gives rise to a liability in delict may take various forms. In *Stair Memorial Encyclopaedia*, vol 14, "Nuisance" para 2087 it is stated that the usual categories of culpa or fault are

---

[23] See Torts (Interference with Goods) Act 1977.

[24] See Chaps 4 and 5, but especially Rodger, "Lord MacMillan's Speech in *Donoghue v. Stevenson*" (1992) 108 L.Q.R. 236.

[25] I, ix, 6 (*Casebook*, Ext. 11).

[26] *e.g. per* Lord Fraser in *R H M Bakeries v. Strathclyde R.C.*, 1985 S.L.T. 214 at 217.

[27] *e.g. per* Lord Roskill in *Junior Books v. Veitchi*, 1982 S.C. (H.L.) 244.

[28] See the articles in the further reading section.

[29] 1996 S.L.T. 1186 at 1188.

malice, intent, recklessness and negligence. To that list there may be added conduct causing a special risk of abnormal damage where it may be said that it is not necessary to prove a specific fault as fault is necessarily implied in the result".

Although it may be said to be a unifying feature, *culpa* really does not help to solve problems (as can be seen from the range of conduct which it can be said to encompass, listed in the foregoing quotation). In this respect Professor MacCormack has made some very good points: "statements which assert that the law of reparation is founded upon a principle of culpa derived from the Roman law are of a fairly late date"; "The judges have simply taken the word culpa and used it in the construction of arguments which consider the incidence of fault or negligence"; and finally, "the sporadic reliance on texts from the Digest or the Institutes which use the term culpa does not prove that Scots law extracted from the Roman sources and applied a principle of culpa".[30] In modern times, when the law of delict will act against conduct which is in no sense morally blameworthy, fault becomes as technical a device as the duty of care. To use the Latin term *culpa* does not help solve practical problems. Instead it is perhaps more useful and more realistic to see the law of delict for what it really is—a large amount of precedent on top of some solid principle, a body of norms which are not always consistent. Taking that view there are areas where the law is reasonably clear because of precedent, or institutional authority. In other areas the law is less clear but there are themes—if not precepts or principles—which run through much of the authority which can assist a court, practitioner or student in determining the law. It is all a matter of emphasis: there is no danger in saying that the law of delict is based upon certain principles, so long as one is aware of all of the exceptions and anomalies. The law of delict is largely in the cases (and statutes)—the first task for the student is to know them.

> "Hence we shall insist no further, but come to the obligations by delinquence, which are civilly cognoscible by our custom, according to their known names and titles in our law; which though they do rather signify the acts or actions whereby such obligations are incurred or prosecute, than the obligations themselves, yet will they be sufficient to hold out both."[31]

Following this practical and sensible approach, in the next two chapters we look at a large number of delicts which have recognised names and association cases based on principle.

---

[30] MacCormack, "Culpa in the Scots Law of Reparation", 1974 J.R. 13 at 14, 18, 27.
[31] Stair, I, ix, 5. See this in context, *Casebook*, Ext. 11.

Further reading

Black, R., "An Historical Survey of Delictual Liability in Scotland for Personal Injuries and Death", 1975 C.I.L.J.S.A. 46, 189, 316; 1976 9 C.I.L.J.S.A. 57.

Cane, P., "Does No-Fault Have a Future", 1994 J.P.I.L. 302.

Davies, M., "The End of the Affair: Duty of Care and Liability Insurance", 1989 L.S. 67.

Elliot, W.A., "Reparation and the English Tort of Negligence" (1952) 64 J.R. 1.

Elliot, W.A., "What is culpa?" (1954) 66 J.R. 6.

Gow, J.J., "Is culpa ammoral?" (1953) 65 J.R. 17.

Hadden, J., "Contract Tort and Crime: the Forms of Legal Thought" (1971) 87 L.Q.R. 240.

Kamba, W.J., "Concept of Duty of Care and Aquilian Liability in Roman Dutch Law", 1975 J.R. 252.

McBryde, W.W., "The Advantages of Fault", 1975 J.R. 32.

MacCormack, G., "Aquilian Culpa" in *Daube Noster* (Watson ed., 1974).

MacCormack, G., "Culpa in the Scots Law of Reparation", 1974 J.R. 13.

Mackay, Robert E., "The Resuscitation of Assythment?" 1992 J.R. 242.

McKenzie, D.W., and Evans-Jones, R., "The Development of Remedies for Personal Injuries and Death" in *The Civilian Tradition in Scots Law* (Evans-Jones ed., Stair Society, supplementary volume 2 (1995)).

McLaren, J.P.S., "Nuisance law and the Industrial Revolution" (1983) 3 O.J.L.S. 155.

McManus, F., "Culpa and the Law of Nuisance", 1995 J.R. (note) 462.

McManus, F., "Culpa and the Law of Nuisance", 1997 J.R. 259.

Markesinis, B.S., "The not so Dissimilar Tort and Delict" (1977) L.Q.R. 78.

Pollock, A.S., "Criminal Injuries Compensation: The Tariff" (1996) 41 J.L.S.S. 93.

Smith, T.B., "Damn *Injuria* Again", 1984 S.L.T. (News) 85.

Thomson, J., "Who Could Sue on The Lex Aquilia?" (1975) 91 L.Q.R. 207.

Walker, D.M., "The Development of Reparation" (1952) 64 J.R. 101.

Walker, D.M., "Strict Liability in Scotland" (1954) 66 J.R. 231.

CHAPTER 2

DELICTS WITH NAMES I

INTRODUCTION

2.1 Usually called the "nominate" delicts, these are often the clearest cases of delictual liability. Assault is a good example. Others are clear in theory but raise difficult questions of application—for example, passing off. Some are not particularly relevant today whereas others are an important background to commercial practice. Some protect one particular interest (*e.g.* assault protects the individual's interest in his personal integrity) but others, such as fraud, protect a number of interests (such as personal integrity or economic well-being). Many of the most important protect interests in property. The division into two chapters is simply for convenience. This chapter deals with delicts most frequently used to protect interests in the person or property and concludes with a treatment of the obligations which are based on or derived from certain Roman quasi-delicts. Chapter 3 covers what are sometimes described as economic delicts. Some delicts known by specific names but which developed in part from the *actio injuriarum* are dealt with in Chapter 8: Verbal Injuries.

It will be seen that the state of mind of the defender varies quite considerably. Sometimes we look for an intentional act, sometimes for a malicious act and often the act implies whatever mental element is required. Sometimes reasonable care has to be taken to avoid some result but sometimes there is liability simply because the result occurs. The nominate delicts are brought up to date in this and the next chapter and relevant analogous obligations discussed.

INTERESTS IN PERSONALITY

Assault

2.2 Assault is an overt act intended to insult or harm another done without justification or excuse. In one example, police officers went to a bedsit and made enquiries of a man. One of the officers was rather intimidating; the pursuer swiftly went into the corridor of the flat, where he was punched and truncheoned. This police action was held to be unjustifiable.[1] The *actio injuriarum* root of Scots law infuses the delict of assault as much as any development of the *lex Aquilia*. Accordingly, assault as a delict includes notional assaults, such as threats of harm, if sufficiently immediate.[2] Assault includes conduct which might also be criminal. However, the issue of *mens rea* (guilty mind) in the criminal law does not feature to any significant extent in the civil law. Where four farm labourers were building a straw stack and three of them began frolicking, when one of the frolicking workers hit the labourer who had continued to work, this was held to be an assault. Lord Young treated it as a case of assault: "technically he assaulted him, although he did it playfully and without any bad intention, for if a man playfully attacks another to make him engage in sport, I am of the opinion that that is an assault, and if harm results that is an actionable wrong."[3] An accident is not actionable as assault.[4]

Even a good motive does not justify an assault; thus medical 2.3 treatment without a patient's consent is an assault and actionable.[5] However, in an English case[6] the court refused to impose a rule that a patient's consent has to be fully informed, a rule which does apply in some of the United States of America. The rationale of the informed consent doctrine is that if to touch is prima facie actionable as assault, then if the patient's consent has been obtained on the basis of misinformation or a withholding of available information, the consent given is vitiated and the treatment given thereafter becomes actionable even if the treatment that follows is carried out without fault or negligence. While this reasoning appears quite sound, it was rejected by a majority in the House

---

[1] *Downie v. Chief Constable*, 1997 S.C.L.R. 603. See also *Gow v. Chief Constable, Strathclyde Police*, 1991 G.W.D. 11–662; *Airnes v. Chief Constable*, 1998 S.L.T. (Sh.Ct.) 15. Cases against the police are very likely to meet the defence of justification: *Mason v. Orr* (1901) 4F. 220. If force is *ex facie* justified it will still be actionable if manifestly in excess of the requirements of the case.

[2] See the charge to the jury of Lord President Boyle in *Ewing v. Mar* (1851) 14 D. 314.

[3] *Reid v. Mitchell* (1885) 12 R. 1129.

[4] *Hall v. Watson* (1896) 12 Sh. Ct. Rep. 117; although a negligence action might attack some "accidents".

[5] *Thomson v. Devon* (1899) 15 Sh. Ct. Rep. 209.

[6] *Sidaway v. Board of Governors of the Bethlem Royal Hospital* [1985] A.C. 871, HL; and see also *Gold v. Haringey Health Authority* [1987] 3 W.L.R. 649. For Scotland see the case *Bonthrone v. Secretary of State for Scotland*, 1987 S.L.T. 34 (*Casebook*, Ext. 56); *Craig v. Glasgow Victoria and Leverndale HBH*, O.H., Dec. 1, 1972; *Moyes v. Lothian Health Board*, 1990 S.L.T. 444.

of Lords on the basis that the whole matter fell to be dealt with on principles of negligence, asking the question: Would a reasonable doctor have given more information than that upon which the consent was based? There is support for the *Sidaway* approach in Scotland.[7]

An assault can be justified by, for example, judicial authority and self-defence. Scots law allows a defence to a claim of assault (both criminal and civil) in the case of certain instances of the beating of children. The defence applies in criminal cases and probably in the same way to civil cases. However, the defence is limited to reasonable chastisement—it is supposed to be a disciplinary matter. The defence is available to parents of children and to others having a position of authority and responsibility over the child, such as teachers[8] and probably cohabitants.[9] What is or is not considered reasonable is a matter for the court and clearly there is likely to be uncertainty as a result.[10] In the case of teachers the defence was limited by the Education Act 1986 in the public sector and removed completely for all schools by the Education Act 1993. It is not corporal punishment, however, to strike a child out of the way of immediate danger of harm or to prevent immediate danger to property of a person, as by rugby tackling a child about to throw a brick through the windscreen of someone's car.

After an exhaustive consultation and consideration of the works of psychologists and after surveying a sample of the populace,[11] the Scottish Law Commission recommended restriction of the parent's defence. Clause 4 of the draft Family Law (Scotland) Bill provided, *inter alia*:

> "(1) In any proceedings (whether criminal or civil) against a person for striking a child, it shall not be a defence for the person to establish that he or she struck the child in the purported exercise of any parental right if he or she struck the child—
>
> > (a) with a stick, belt or other object of whatever description; or

---

[7] The Outer House decision in *Moyes v. Lothian Health Board*, 1990 S.L.T. 444 is support for the *Sidaway* case: indeed it is argued that Scots law had already come down against the need in all cases for informed consent.

[8] *Stewart v. Thain*, 1981 S.L.T. (Notes) 2.

[9] *Byrd v. Wither*, 1991 S.L.T. 206.

[10] *B. v. Harris*, 1990 S.L.T. 245; *Peebles v. MacPhail*, 1990 S.L.T. 245.

[11] Nearly one in five people over 65 were in favour of the hitting with the stick option for the child of 15 years; the Free Presbyterian Church drew attention to Proverbs 13, 24.

(b) in such a way as to cause, or to risk causing—
    (i) injury; or
    (ii) pain or discomfort lasting more than a very short time."[12]

Provocation is not a defence but will serve to mitigate (reduce) the damages.[13]

Contravention of lawburrows

A person who has been required to find caution (a sum of money or 2.4 an insurance bond for a sum of money) not to harm another or his family (called "lawburrows") may, if he contravenes the non-molestation order, be sued in an action of contravention of lawburrows for forfeiture of the caution.[14] This procedure, it may be said, is not often used, but that may simply be because few are aware of it. It is today still used in disputes between neighbours.

In *Liddle v. Morton*[15] the defender admitted breaking the pursuers' windows. He threatened violence and shook his fist. He left a gate off its hinge so that it would fall. It did—but on the postman. A log was thrown through the pursuers' front window. The sheriff granted lawburrows. On appeal to the High Court of Justiciary, counsel for the appellant accepted, as did the Court, that the test for granting lawburrows was that set out by Sheriff Macphail in *Morrow v. Neil*[16]: "The pursuer must establish that he has reasonable cause to apprehend that the defender will harm the person or property of the pursuer or his family, tenants or servants." The "reasonableness" aspect of this may require to be reviewed if challenged—such subtlety was not a feature of fifteenth-century Scottish jurisprudence.[17]

Relatively recently it has been unsuccessfully used in two tenement

---

[12] Johnson's biographer, the advocate Boswell, appeared to argue a schoolmaster's case (Hastie) in the House of Lords after "a couple of bumpers of white wine". In the course of his address, Boswell said: "I speak with warmth for this schoolmaster, for I am sensible that if I had not been very severely beat by my master, I should not have been able to make even the weak defence which I now make for this schoolmaster." Lord Mansefield, he says, smiled. Others of the Lords, in the chamber, called out "Bravo": Wimsatt and Pottle, *Boswell for the Defence* (1960, Heinemann), p. 120.

[13] *Stewart v. Thain*, 1981 S.L.T. (Notes) 2 (chastisement); *Ross v. Bryce*, 1972 S.L.T. (Sh.Ct.) 76 (*Casebook*, Ext. 17); see *contra* in England, *Lane v. Holloway* [1968] 1 Q.B. 379 (provocation).

[14] Lawburrows Acts 1429 and 1581. See generally Walker, *Legal History*, Vol. II, pp. 615–616.

[15] 1996 S.L.T. 1143.

[16] 1975 S.L.T. (Sh.Ct.) 65 at 67.

[17] See *Porteous v. Rutherford*, 1980 S.L.T. (Sh.Ct.) 129; and *Tahir v. Gosal*, Glasgow Sheriff Court, May 16, 1974.

disputes.[18] In 1986 an unsuccessful attempt was made to have a chief constable find caution for the alleged behaviour of his officers: it was held that lawburrows would only be granted in respect of the personal behaviour of the defender and not on the basis of his vicarious responsibility[19] (see Chapter 10). That named delicts can cover more than one interest is demonstrated in that lawburrows was designed to protect against intrusion on property [2.11] as well as injury to the person.

Enticement

2.5   A right of action exists where a person, even a relative, entices a member of someone's family away from him or her, without justification. There is now, however, no delictual liability in the most common instance of enticement—where a person has induced someone's spouse to leave, or remain apart from, the other spouse.[20] This delict might provide a remedy in cases where children are "attracted" to a religious cult. Contrary to that view is the case of *McKeen v. Chief Constable*,[21] where a man was claiming a sum for the intervention of the police in taking away his child during a custody dispute with his wife. A particular statement of Professor Walker's was relied upon: "A claim may even lie against a parent not entitled to custody who seeks to entice a child out of the custody of the parent lawfully entitled thereto."[22] Lord Morton thought that if such a right existed it was strange that it had not come before the court.[23] He hazarded the opinion that there might be social reasons why recognition of such a right might be inappropriate. It is submitted that the authorities on enticement generally support Professor Walker's view. Contempt of court and criminal sanctions (*plagium*) might explain why such cases are rare.[24] Many custody disputes involve the social work department and they take a dim view of enticing conduct or conduct inverting possession; if they are involved would-be enticers are nervous and wary of the social workers. The fact that legislation was needed to exempt the enticement of a spouse might support the view that it was needed.

---

[18] *Morrow v. Neil*, 1975 S.L.T. (Sh.Ct.) 65; *Porteous v. Rutherford*, 1980 S.L.T. (Sh.Ct.) 129.
[19] *Handy v. Bowman*, Dundee Sheriff Court, Sept. 22, 1986; see Stewart (1988).
[20] Law Reform (Husband and Wife) (Scotland) Act 1984, s. 2(2) (*Casebook*, Appendix, Ext. 14).
[21] 1994 S.L.T. 93.
[22] *Delict*, p. 713.
[23] 1994 S.L.T. at 96A.
[24] See, e.g. *Hamilton v. Wilson*, 1994 S.L.T. 431.

Physical detention

Generally, the simple act of preventing a person moving around 2.6
freely is actionable and sounds in damages for the affront caused.
Perhaps the most practical modern significance of this particular delict
relates to store detectives detaining persons suspected of shoplifting.
Wrongful detention is enough to constitute the delict. There is no need
to establish defamation of character.

The following case[25] is a good illustration of how the law applies.
Indeed it might be seen as advancing the law: the reasoning is directed
at the individual's interest in personal integrity. Some workers
barricaded themselves in their employer's laboratory. Action was
taken by the police under the Trespass (Scotland) Act 1865. They
arrested the workers, who sued for damages on four counts: (1) the
arrest and detention were unjustified; (2) if detention was justified
there was no need to detain in cells; (3) if detention in cells was
necessary then the removal of one worker's brassiere was unjustified;
(4) there was no justification for handcuffing one of the individuals.

It was held that in terms of the 1865 Act the police had been given a
discretion to arrest or detain and that they had exercised it reasonably.
Moreover, it was also reasonable in the circumstances to keep the
admittedly intelligent and articulate employees in cells. However, the
claim in respect of the request to remove the brassiere succeeded.
Although there had been no previous case where a request to remove
clothing had been held to be actionable, Lord Jauncey, then in the
Outer House, said that such a request, "must amount to an infringement of liberty . . . I see no reason why the law should not protect the
individual from this infringement, just as it does from other infringe-
ments." It was conceded that it was wrongful in the circumstances to
handcuff one of the workers. The case illustrates how this delict, like
many others, is based upon the protection of the legitimate interests of
the citizen.

In many cases it may be permissible to detain a person either at
common law or under a statute, for example, where someone wants to
leave in breach of contract; or a child may be detained so far as
reasonable and necessary in his interests. The master of a ship may
detain people for the preservation of good order or the safety of
persons, property or the vessel itself, and a mentally ill person may be
detained if a danger to himself.[26] To keep a person in prison longer
than necessary is a form of wrongful detention.[27] The opinion has

---

[25] *Henderson v. Chief Constable, Fife Police*, 1988 S.L.T. 361 (*Casebook*, Ext. 18).
[26] Merchant Shipping Act 1995, s.105 and the Mental Health (Scotland) Act 1984, ss.
17 and 24. For a full discussion of issues of principle see *B. v. F.*, 1987 S.L.T. 681.
[27] *Walsh v. Secretary of State* for *Scotland*, 1990 G.W.D. 7–385.

been expressed that detention based on identification of a person's photograph as resembling a perpetrator, together with another accusation, was not unlawful.[28]

Wrongful imprisonment

2.7   To be actionable the imprisonment has to be shown to have been legally unjustifiable in the first place. Superior court judges are immune [11.7]. Magistrates may be liable for a grossly *ultra vires* sentence, without proof of malice or lack of probable cause but not for an honest error in statutory interpretation. In *MacPhee v. Macfarlane's Executor*,[29] Lord President Clyde thought it clear that there could be no liability for an honest error in statutory interpretation. In that particular case, if there had been an error in interpretation of the Summary Jurisdiction (Scotland) Act 1908, it would have been one which magistrates all over the country would have been applying since 1908 and so would not be actionable as grossly *ultra vires*. Generally, in terms of section 170 of the Criminal Procedure (Scotland) Act 1995, the wrongfully imprisoned pursuer must aver and prove both malice and lack of probable cause and the action must be commenced within two months of the act complained of.

Seduction

2.8   Seduction is a delict perhaps not litigated nearly as often as it is committed. Professor Walker defines it as "obtaining sexual relations with a virgin by fraud, circumvention, guile, misrepresentations or other persuasive practices and deflowering her."[30]

The difference between seduction and fornication (or adultery in particular) is that in the latter there is genuine and full consent. In rape, which is itself actionable, consent is never given at all. In seduction there is consent but it is vitiated by the trickery or wiles involved. An example is *Murray v. Fraser*:[31]

> The pursuer was a headmaster's daughter and alleged that sexual intercourse took place on two occasions, once in a bicycle shed and another time in a wood. She became pregnant. The defender was a tenant farmer about 30 years of age. He was a friend of the family. He said he regarded the girl as a child and the girl said he treated her as such. She was ignorant of sexual matters and believed his assurance that she would come to no harm.

---

[28] *McLaren v. Procurator Fiscal for Lothian and Borders*, 1991 G.W.D. 24–1407.
[29] 1933 S.C. 163.
[30] Walker, p. 698.
[31] 1916 S.C. 623.

Lord Dundas pointed out that the popular meaning of seduction is different from its legal meaning. In general speech full consent is implied. What he considered important was the defender's relationship with the family and the girl's amazing ignorance of matters sexual. Other examples of wiles are promises to marry not later implemented, courtship with apparent intention to marry and taking advantage of the woman's dependency, as when she is in the man's employment.[32]

Harassment

Under the Protection from Harassment Act 1997, every individual 2.9 in Scotland has a right to be free from harassment and, accordingly, a person must not pursue a course of conduct which amounts to harassment of another and—(a) is intended to amount to harassment of that person; or (b) occurs in circumstances where it would appear to a reasonable person that it would amount to harassment of that person.[33] Conduct includes speech.[34] Harassment of a person includes causing the person alarm or distress.[35] A course of conduct must involve conduct on at least two occasions.[36] It is not otherwise defined and the matter will be for the courts.

A potential pursuer who complains that they are being followed by tall, dark, handsome men with size 11 feet may well find that their case vanishes as a result of the Secretary of State certifying that the conduct related to national security, the economic well-being of the United Kingdom or the prevention or detection of serious crime.[37] Alternatively, it is a defence to show that the conduct complained of was pursued for the purpose of preventing or detecting crime.[38] The other defences are legal authority[39] and that the conduct was reasonable.[40]

HERITABLE PROPERTY

Ejection and intrusion

Ejection is where someone enters on to lands and removes another 2.10 or stays on when his right to stay there has expired. Intrusion is sneaking on to the subjects when the possessor holds *animo* (by will) rather than *corpore* (in person):

---

[32] *Macleod v. MacAskill*, 1920 S.C. 72.
[33] s.8 (1).
[34] s.8 (3).
[35] s.8 (3).
[36] s.8 (3).
[37] s.12 (1). The certificate is conclusive. A certificate which purports to be of such type is presumed to be so unless the contrary is proved: s.12 (3).
[38] s. 8 (4) (b).
[39] s. 8 (4) (a).
[40] s. 8 (4) (c).

"they differ in this; that intrusion is the entering in possession, being for the time void, without consent of the parties interested, or order of law . . . but ejection . . . is not only the unwarrantable entering in lands, but the casting out violently of the then possessor."[41]

The remedies are: (a) summary ejection[42]; (b) violent profits, being the greatest profit the pursuer could have made if in possession[43]; and (c) actual compensatory damages. Caution for violent profits may be made a condition of proceedings. It was delicts such as these that lawburrows [2.4] was introduced to prevent.

Trespass

2.11   Trespass, in Scotland, is a temporary intrusion without permission or justification, such as entering upon someone else's property. The Trespass (Scotland) Act 1865, as amended, criminalises certain trespasses, being "an Act to provide for the better Prevention of Trespass in Scotland." The Act is important in making conduct "wrongful" but it has not been decided whether it can be founded on in a breach of statutory duty case. (See 2.6 and further below in this paragraph.)

> "3. Every person who lodges in any premises, or occupies or encamps on any land, being private property, without the consent and permission of the owner or legal occupier of such premises or land, and every person who encamps or lights a fire on or near any private road or enclosed or cultivated land, or in or near any plantation, without the consent and permission of the owner or legal occupier of such road, land, or plantation, or on or near any . . . highway, shall be guilty of an offence."

Premises for these purposes includes any home, barn, stable, shed, loft, granary, outhouse, garden, stockyard, court, close or enclosed space. Because land is owned *a caelo usque ad centrum* (from the heavens to the centre of the earth) the law is concerned as much with the pursuer's airspace and the ground under his property as with the surface. The matter was considered in *Brown v. Lee Constructions Ltd*[44]:

> A homeowner petitioned for interdict against builders to restrain the respondents' crane sweeping over the petitioner's property. The builders argued that there was a difference between a permanent overhang and a transient one. The interdict was granted.

---

[41] Stair, I, ix, 25.
[42] Subject to, *inter alia*, the Rent (Scotland) Act 1984.
[43] This is arguably an instance of restitution for wrongs: see 13.21.
[44] 1977 S.L.T. (Notes) 61.

The court mentioned that there was some risk of personal injury but quite properly did not treat that as important, for trespass essentially protects the pursuer's interest in his land. Special statutory provision is made to allow aircraft to fly over land without being sued for trespass.[45] Damages are not recoverable for trespass where no damage is done to the property, especially if the trespassing is innocent.[46] Interdict is possible if repetition is feared and self-help is allowed so long as reasonable in the circumstances.

The red-faced farmer of the comic books may shout you off his land or lock his gate against you but should not discharge his shotgun in your direction. Necessity and justification, as by having a legal warrant, are defences: a fireman can crash through your gate and axe your door—providing, of course, there is a fire![47]

An example of the reluctance (or inability) of Scots lawyers to analyse wrongful interference with property can be found in *Shell U.K. Ltd v. McGillivray*.[48] In this case, trespass was pled as the basis of an action for interdict (an interdict, incidentally, which in preventing continued occupation had the positive result of requiring the respondents to leave on transport becoming available). The action was against workmen of contractors of the petitioners who were "occupying" oil installations where they worked. It was argued for the respondents that as the property was moveable the law of trespass did not apply. Lord Cameron of Lochbroom applied dicta in a case dealing with non-heritable property.[49] He said: "In my opinion, the use of the word trespass has no particular significance in these petitions other than indicating that the actings of the respondents are averred to be wrongful acts of occupation of parts of property of which the petitioners have the exclusive right of occupation." He then proceeded on the basis that such occupation was a delict.[50]

Nuisance

What is a nuisance?

A nuisance is a continuing harm and not an isolated incident. A 2.12 trivial matter will not be actionable. The nuisance must not be a

---

[45] Civil Aviation Act 1982, s. 76. The section also protects against nuisance.

[46] *Graham v. Duke of Hamilton* (1868) 6 M. 965.

[47] *Cope v. Sharpe* [1912] 1 K.B. 496 (necessity); *Southern Bowling Club Ltd v. Ross* (1902) 4 F. 405 (justification). Necessity called "duress of circumstances" has recently been reinvigorated in the criminal law. Taking into account the close relationship of crime and intentional delicts these cases may be helpful in future delictual cases. See *McNab v. Guild*, 1989 S.C.C.R. 138 and *Moss v. Howdle*, 1997 S.L.T. 782.

[48] 1991 S.L.T. 667.

[49] *Phestos Shipping Co. Ltd v. Kurmiawan*, 1983 S.L.T. 388.

[50] 1991 S.L.T. 667 at 669.

matter of nature and must therefore be as a result of the defender's acts or omissions.[51]

Webster v. Lord Advocate[52] is an interesting discussion of what constitutes a nuisance.

> The pursuer moved into her flat in 1977. She sought interdict because of the noise involved in the construction nearby of the grandstand for the Edinburgh Tattoo. The tattoo had been going on for some time before the complainer moved in. Both sides accepted that the simple fact that the conduct had been going on before the complainer arrived was not a defence.[53]

The court had to balance the various circumstances and interests: "I was left in no doubt that the Tattoo is a spectacle appreciated by the public and a valuable publicity and commercial asset to the city."[54] But the court was clear that it was not generally the case that the greater good would allow a nuisance—in this case the noise involved in erecting the grandstand rather than the Tattoo itself—to continue. It rejected the contention that Miss Webster could reduce the effect of the noise by closing her windows or having double glazing: "one of the nice things about summer is that you are able to open your windows." Interdict was granted.

The essence of the delict is that the defender's conduct is, in the circumstances, more than the pursuer should reasonably have to tolerate, *i.e.* that the conduct is *plus quam tolerabile*. In a recent case it was held that a "rave"—an all-night dance party with very loud music—held in an isolated location did not exceed what was *plus quam tolerabile*, being a one-off event.[55] A next-door neighbour failed when all that could be shown was noise arising from normal domestic use such as would not seriously disturb nor substantially inconvenience an average reasonable person in the locality.[56]

2.13 The court in *Webster* reiterated the long-established point that it is not a good defence to plead that the pursuer came to the nuisance. Thus long practice of a nuisance does not give a potential defender a right to continue it when one acquires a new neighbour. On the other hand, the different point should be noted that if someone has put up with a nuisance for the 20 years of the long negative prescription then,

---

[51] *Davey v. Harrow Corp.* [1957] 2 All E.R. 305.
[52] 1984 S.L.T. 13, and on appeal at 1985 S.L.T. 361.
[53] And see *Fleming v. Hislop* (1886) 13 R. 43: "It is clear that whether the man went to the nuisance or the nuisance came to the man the rights are the same."
[54] 1984 S.L.T. 13, *per* Lord Stott at 14.
[55] *Cumnock & Doon Valley District Council v. Dance Energy Associates Ltd*, 1992 G.W.D. 25–1441.
[56] *Davidson v. Kerr*, 1996 G.W.D. 40–2296.

so long as the behaviour has not changed, the potential pursuer has no right to interdict or damages. But it would be open to some other person in the same neighbourhood to complain.

A possible defence is statutory authority, *i.e.* the "nuisance" is really obedience to some Act of Parliament or subordinate legislation. A distinction has to be made between cases where a statute actually permits some conduct to be done even though it is a nuisance, and statutes which require certain matters to be carried out but which need not be carried out in such a way as to cause a nuisance.[57] Statutory authority will not be a defence if the act carried out could have been executed without causing a nuisance.

The Scots law is reflected in the maxim *sic utere tuo ut alienum non laedas* (use your own property in a way that you do not do harm to others). As Lord President Cooper said: **2.14**

> "If any person so uses his property as to occasion serious disturbance or substantial inconvenience to his neighbour or material damage to his neighbour's property, it is in the general case irrelevant as a defence for the defender to plead merely that he was making a normal and familiar use of his own property."[58]

Nuisance is a delict which arises from the interests involved in the ownership or occupation of property. It probably also protects the interests of the individual even temporarily in the neighbourhood of the property in his or her life and health.[59]

It is largely a matter of fact and degree depending upon the circumstances of the case whether or not a nuisance has been or is being committed: "Things which are forbidden in a crowded urban community may be permitted in the country. What is prohibited in enclosed land may be tolerated in the open."[60] Interdict will be granted to prevent a nuisance being continued or repeated and damages will be granted in respect of loss caused by it. The main point is that it is conduct *plus quam tolerabile* which constitutes this special kind of fault—independent of negligence.

The basis of liability

Until recently the view was often expressed that nuisance was an example of strict liability, in that it was not open to a defender to show **2.15**

---

[57] *Lord Advocate v. N.B. Ry* (1894) 2 S.L.T. 71.

[58] *Watt v. Jamieson*, 1954 S.C. 56 at 58.

[59] Lord Hope in an English appeal agreed with his brethren that a licensee was not protected by the law of nuisance: *Hunter and 689 Others v. Canary Wharf Ltd and London Dockland Development Corp.*, 1997 T.L.R. 219.

[60] *Inglis v. Shotts Iron Co.* (1881) 8 R. 1006 at 1021, *per* Lord Shand.

that he had taken all reasonable care to prevent the nuisance, *i.e.* that he was not at fault. The position has now been resolved by the House of Lords' decision in *R H M Bakeries v. Strathclyde Regional Council*.[61]

> A bakery was flooded as the result of the collapse of a sewer. The pursuers sued for damages but did not allege that the flood was the defenders' fault, just that they had committed a nuisance. The House held that this was not sufficient—it was essential to allege some degree of fault.

However, in nuisance cases it will often be very simple to infer [12.2–12.8] fault from the happening of the incident and the onus will be upon the defender to show that the nuisance was not his fault.[62] This, it must be said, is not the same as saying that negligence will be inferred.

2.16 The law was subject to further review in *Kennedy v. Glenbelle and Charles Scott*.[63] Building work was done on the pursuers' premises by the first-named defenders on advice from the second-named defenders (who had been engaged by the first defenders). It caused damage to the pursuers' subjects. The Lord President said that negligence is not required for nuisance although *culpa* is. For a damages action, other conduct may infer the necessary responsibility. When taken with conduct *plus quam tolerabile*, that can be nuisance.[64]

2.17 Finally, a distinction can be made between cases where interdict is sought, on the one hand, and cases where damages are sought, on the other. In the case of interdict the court will generally look at the matter from the point of view of the complainer, concentrating less on the issue of fault and more on the issue of whether the defender is going to continue to do the act complained of.[65]

Non-natural use of land and the escape of dangerous things from land

2.18 Since the decision of the House of Lords in *R H M Bakeries v. Strathclyde Regional Council*, it is now possible to deal with this formerly awkward category of cases very briefly. As a general rule, liability for nuisance is based on *culpa*. If someone does something with his land which is out of the ordinary he cannot be held liable just

---

[61] 1985 S.L.T. 214.
[62] *ibid.* at 219.
[63] 1996 S.L.T. 1186.
[64] See the more general quotation in relation to *culpa* at 1.12 above.
[65] 1985 S.L.T. at 218; *Watt v. Jamieson* is accordingly still good authority on the question of interdict.

because something goes wrong: unlike the law in England there is no rule that a man acts at his peril.[66] However, where, for example, someone brings something inherently dangerous like dynamite on to his or her land and damage results from its escape (*e.g.* by explosion), the action is based on his or her fault in so bringing it on and his or her fault in not preventing it from exploding, or his or her fault in not taking steps to prevent parties who would foreseeably interfere with it from doing so, and such fault will be easily inferred—indeed the defender will have to explain why it is not his or her fault.

When the House of Lords was restating the law of nuisance in *R H M Bakeries* it distinguished an earlier House of Lords case in a Scots appeal: *Caledonian Ry v. Greenock Corporation*.[67] Greenock Corporation altered the channel of a burn to make a paddling pool. Rainfall which was exceptional for Greenock, but not for Scotland, caused it to flood and damage occurred to the railway company's property. The corporation were held liable. Lord Fraser acknowledged that the House of Lords, in making that decision, may have applied strict liability rather than liability based upon *culpa*; because the decision was not strictly in point, the House did not require to overrule the case. In *Kennedy v. Glenbelle Ltd and Charles Scott*[68] it was accepted this may be an anomalous category of case. It seems to have been accepted in principle in *G. & A. Estates Ltd v. Caviapen Trustees Ltd (No. 1)*.[69] Accordingly, it remains the case that while liability for non-natural use of land or the escape of dangerous things is now based on *culpa*, liability may remain strict where damage is caused by the alteration of the natural direction of a stream, at least until a case in point comes before the House of Lords.

2.19

---

[66] *Rylands v. Fletcher* (1868) L.R. 3 H.L. 330 applied that principle to establish a strict liability for the escape of dangerous things where there was a non-natural use of land. Even in England there is a trend to restrict the application of this type of liability to cases where the whole danger is man-made and in other cases to impose liability based on fault: *Goldman v. Hargrave* [1967] 1 A.C. 645. The House of Lords in *Cambridge Water Co. Ltd v. Eastern Counties Leather plc* [1994] 2 A.C. 264 held that the case should be restricted to isolated escapes from land and not extended to be a rule of strict liability for ultra-hazardous operations on land. It was also said that even under this head there had to be foreseeability of damage of the type which occurred. The exercise of due care is not, however, a defence. See Fleming, J.G., "The Fall of the Crippled Giant" (1995) 3 Tort L. Rev. 56.

[67] 1917 S.C. (H.L.) 56; cases which the court reconsidered and explained as being truly based upon *culpa* included what could be called a "Scottish *Rylands*": *Kerr v. Earl of Orkney* (1857) 20 D. 298, where the language of strict liability was used, especially at 302.

[68] discussed above.

[69] 1993 S.L.T. 1037.

Use of land in aemulationem vicini

2.20   This is a recognised but difficult area of liability.[70] Under this head
there is liability for harm caused by a legitimate and non-continuing
use of land which is carried out with malice and spitefully to harm a
neighbour. It is clearly associated with nuisance but differs in that one
incident is sufficient and that the defender's mental state must be
demonstrated.[71] An example is *Campbell v. Muir*[72]:

> The defender was exercising his entitlement to fish from a boat in
> a river. He did so in such a way as to prevent anglers on the
> opposing bank from being able to cast. It was held that to do this
> spitefully was actionable and amenable to interdict.

MOVEABLE PROPERTY

Spuilzie and wrongful interference with moveables

2.21   Spuilzie (pronounced, approximately, "spoolly") both describes: (a)
the act of interfering with property, namely, spoliation; and (b) a
remedy known to the law of Scotland in respect of such actings. It is
a delict said by some to be obsolete but which may yet be found to
be useful.[73] It long ago ceased to be important in relation to heritage.
It is committed by a person who takes away moveables without the
consent of the possessor or without order of law. It is not even
necessary for the pursuer to establish ownership of the property so
long as there is a right of possession or custody.[74]

The primary obligation is to restore the goods to the pursuer but
there is also a liability to violent profits. These are the profits which
could have been made with the goods value originally by the pursuer's
own oath.

Although there is an urge to interpret this remedy as combination of
restitution and damages for delict, this may be misleading. It is the
element of violent profits which is of interest. This is not necessarily a
matter of delictual damages. Indeed the exciting thing about such a
claim is that it means that the pursuer does not have to show the loss

---

[70] Johnston, "Owners and Neighbours: from Rome to Scotland" in *The Civil Law
Tradition in Scotland* (Evans-Jones ed., 1995), Stair Society Supplementary Volume
2, p. 176.

[71] See Hume, *Lectures*, III, 208.

[72] 1908 S.C. 387. Another is *More v. Boyle*, 1967 S.L.T. (Sh.Ct.) 38 (*Casebook*, Ext.
27).

[73] Its relevance can be seen from the full treatment it has obtained from Dr Carey
Miller in *Corporeal Moveables in Scots Law* (W. Green/SULI, 1991).

[74] Stair, I, ix, 16.

which would be required if the case were based on loss wrongfully caused. The better rationalisation might be that this award is essentially restitutionary and is an example of restitution for wrongs.[75] The recognition of loss of use as a head of claim in ordinary delictual actions makes it unlikely that spuilzie arguments will be heard often.

An example of the sort of modern context into which spuilzie may be thrust is *F.C. Finance Ltd v. Brown & Son*[76]:

> The pursuers entered into a hire-purchase agreement with West of Scotland Refractories Ltd. The car in question, a Daimler, was sold by the defender on the instructions of the hire-purchaser to Deanside Motors Ltd, the vehicle eventually ending up in the hands of one McMaster, a private purchaser under the 1964 Act, from whom, accordingly, it was impossible for the pursuers to seek the normal remedy of restitution and damages. The action was by the pursuers as owners against the defenders for the price which the defenders received, namely £825. The defenders, it was later established, had sold as agents for the hire-purchasers and applied the cheque to an account which the hire-purchasers owed to the garage. Indeed the hire-purchasers continued to pay the instalments. It was only when they went into liquidation that the issue became live.

The sheriff substitute proceeded by way of spuilzie, but found that a case of spuilzie was not made out. They failed, in the learned sheriff substitute's view, because the defenders had not committed an offence against possession. At the time when the sale took place the owners had not terminated the agreement. Had he been able to find for the pursuers he would have awarded the sum sued for and made no allowance for the sums that had been paid to the pursuers by the hire-purchasers.

The case was appealed to the sheriff who instead found for the pursuers and awarded damages as claimed. His decision is not based upon spuilzie but upon a different line of reasoning. It is not entirely clear precisely how he reached his conclusion but it seems to proceed on the basis of fault in a situation where there would be a duty of care based upon the custody of the goods of another. It should be emphasised that no mention was made of *culpa* or of a duty of care. However, the focus of the decision was clearly on the agent's knowledge of the ownership and his failure to apply the proceeds for the benefit of the owner. *Obiter*, it was said that the ground of decision might be spuilzie in a modern form.

This decision prompted highly critical comment.[77] The main defect

---

[75] See below 13.2.
[76] 1969 S.L.T. (Sh.Ct.) 41.
[77] Rodger, "Spuilzie in the Modern World", 1970 S.L.T. (News) 33.

relates to the measure of damages: "In concrete terms: under the H.P. agreement, the finance company were entitled to £1,932 1s 11d; at the time of the action they had already received all but £617 10s 4d. Nonetheless they were awarded damages of £825, thus ensuring a windfall to them of £207 9s 8d." Adding to this a penetrating *reductio ad absurdum*, Rodger points out that if 95 per cent of the payments had been made the owner would in effect be paid almost twice the value. He argues instead that the sum awarded should have been their loss of £617 10s 4d.

On the other hand, there is something else lost in the cases like *Brown* other than the right to the payments—that is, the residual right to the property. Neither is this a freak case nor an accident. Apart from the primary economic purpose of obtaining the price with interest, the hire-purchase contract has as an important feature the retention of ownership in the goods with the lessor–seller.

Spuilzie is similar to the English tort of conversion which in that jurisdiction is but one form of wrongful interference with goods.[78]

If we look now at the wider notion of wrongful interference it can be said that spuilzie is a species of this wider delictual concept (which is likely to have both proprietary and restitutionary aspects). There are sufficient markers in the Scots authorities for this wider notion. In *Snare v. The Earl of Fife's Trustees*,[79]

> Snare, a bookseller in Reading, bought a picture which he discovered to be Charles I, by Velasquez. He exhibited it and produced pamphlets showing it to have been in the possession of the Earl of Fife. The result of this information was that the Earl of Fife's trustees petitioned the sheriff that the picture had been stolen or surreptitiously abstracted from their possession and craved (i) restitution or (ii) warrant to the clerk of court to take possession and retain until caution found. Warrant was granted, the painting seized and retained, and eventually returned. Snare claimed for damages for loss of exhibition. The court allowed the case to go to trial on the basis of the wrongful detention—they "obtained and acted upon an illegal warrant". Neither did they require to aver malice and lack of probable cause.

Even more interesting are the bottle cases. An interdict was granted in *Wilson v. Shepherd*,[80] where one trader allowed people to fill another's bottles with paraffin. While there is an element of the law of property about this the interdict was granted on the basis of a wrong to property and therefore was essentially a delict for which

---

[78] See Salmond & Heuston, *Law of Torts* (20th ed., Sweet & Maxwell, 1992), Chap. 6.
[79] (1850) 13 D. 286.
[80] 1913 S.C. 300.

damages could be sought. In a later case, *Leitch v. Leydon*,[81] a grocer filled bottles belonging to another with aerated water. It had already been intimated to him that the owners retained ownership. It would have taken a careful glance to check the origin of a bottle. It was held there was no duty to inspect bottles. For Viscount Dunedin there was no *culpa*. Interdict was refused. Although *Wilson* was cited in argument, the respondents were not called upon and the case was not mentioned in the speeches. There was no mention of the provisions of the Sale of Goods Act 1893 that allowed a non-owner to pass title if a buyer was in possession of the goods although the notice on the bottle might well deprive the "consumer" of the right to rely upon it. So far as it goes the case is correct but the real issue is whether, if it were clear *ex facie* that a bottle was one of a specific type which was always sold under a retention if there was no specific intimation that the owners expressly prohibited re-filling, interdict or damages should be granted.

In modern life it seems strange that we can do what we like with a bottle that says "Property of X—do not refill, return or destroy" but cannot do as we please with a video cassette or computer disk which contains its restriction only in particles of ferrous oxide. The analysis used by the software "vendors" is that the "buyer" pays for a licence.

A practical analysis until the law is restructured is that there is 2.22 liability as follows:

1. Property destroyed

The *lex Aquilia* principle applies—loss wrongfully caused. In this case (for a long time) deliberate destruction has fallen clearly within the idea of wrongfulness. This does not depend in any way upon the law of negligence. Examples include the destruction of a horse[82] and the destruction of stakenets.[83] Spuilzie is not appropriate in destruction *simpliciter* for there is no taking.

2. Property of another taken

It is the kind of activity which would have been struck at by spuilzie and in modern times attracts an award of damages albeit damage need not be proved in the sense of loss but rather by proving that the property was taken and evidence given as to its value.

3. Property of another used without permission

In addition to the bottle cases discussed there is *Brown's Trustees v. Hay*.[84] Hay was an employee of a firm of solicitors who, while

---

[81] 1931 S.C. (H.L.) 1. This case ran along with, and was reported with, *A.G. Barr & Co. Ltd v. MacGheoghegan* and was decided in exactly the same way.

[82] *Wilsons v. McKnight* (1830) 8 S. 398.

[83] *Grubb v. Mackenzie* (1834) 13 S. 717.

[84] (1898) 25 R. 1112.

involved with an estate, discovered papers which he thought impli-
cated the estate in false returns to the revenue. He was held liable in
damages for the ultroneous use of the property even although there
was no actual loss and no taking. A defender who took possession of a
car in a sale from a trustee of a garage proprietor which had not been
included in the sale was held liable in damages to the owner of the
car.[85] That case may come within this category because the taking was
permitted. In *Cairns v. Harry Walker Ltd*[86] the owners of a ship were
fined for an excise offence. The cause was the conduct of the steward
in conjunction with the defenders. They were held to be liable for the
wrongful and illegal use of the ship.

4. *Property detained*

In addition to *Snare*, cited above, a person who stopped a coach
taking people to a funeral was held liable in damages.[87]

Another approach

As the issue in these cases is intentional violation of interests in
moveables, the general theme that all crimes are delicts might help in
this sphere. The Scots indigenous criminal law has developed carefully
over the years while the civil counterpart has been obscured by negligence
and duties of care. Thus it is submitted that in cases where the facts fit
Milne v. Tudhope[88] or *Kidston v. Annan*[89] or *Black v. Carmichael*,[90] civil
liability based on wrongfulness ought to succeed without difficulty.
Looking at cases that way means that they can become rather simple,
as in *Gemmell v. Bank of Scotland*,[91] where the bank repossessed and the
pursuers' goods were missing. The learned sheriff thought it did not
matter that the case was one of spuilzie or restitution—there would be
damages including damages for loss of use.[92]

THE ROMAN QUASI-DELICTS

General

2.23   This is a special category of obligations which certainly arise *ex lege*
and are therefore appropriately treated in the law of delict. Unfortunately they have little in common in either Roman or Scots law.

---

[85] *Mackintosh v. Galbraith & Arthur* (1900) 3F. 66.
[86] 1913 2 S.L.T. 379
[87] *Crawford v. Mill* (1830) 5 Mur. 215.
[88] 1981 S.L.T. (Notes) 42.
[89] 1984 S.C.C.R. 20.
[90] 1992 S.C.C.R. 709.
[91] Glasgow, Nov. 5, 1996.
[92] Compare with *Harris v. Abbey National*, 1996 G.W.D. 33–1993 in which the
pursuer was also successful.

However, when it is remembered that the term delict originally had a morally blameworthy connotation, this may help explain why they were put together, in that in these cases the defender has not been especially bad. With perhaps the difficult exception of the *judex qui litem suam fecerit* (the judge who makes a cause his own) they involve liability being established without proof of fault on the part of the defender and have suggestions of vicarious liability (see Chapter 10). Their reception into Scots law is not, as shall be seen, without difficulty. The interests protected are sometimes integrity of the person but extend also to property. As there are no Scots cases directly in point on the strict liability of the *judex* and as most judges would be immune anyway, that head of liability is not dealt with in this book.[93]

The *actio de effusis vel dejectis* and the *actio de positis vel suspensis*

Roman law imposed a penalty on the occupier of premises (i) from 2.24 which something was poured or thrown out, striking the victim (the *actio de effusis vel dejectis*), and (ii) where something was placed or suspended from a building which fell causing loss, injury or damage (the *actio de positis vel suspensis*). The remedy has been recognised as part of Scots law but not clearly so.[94]

The difficulties concerning reception of these obligations can be seen in two sheriff court cases. In *Gray v. Dunlop*[95]:

> the pursuer's pupil son was walking along a street about 5 p.m. when some, understandably unidentified, person emptied a pot of urine upon him. An action was raised against the occupier of the premises which were a model lodging house (a sort of hostel for down-and-outs). No fault could be proved against the occupier and so it was important for the pursuer that strict liability should be established. The sheriff refused to accept that there could be liability without fault and refused the claim.

Notwithstanding that decision, Professor Walker and Professor Stein incline to the view that the *actio de effusis vel dejectis* is part of the law of Scotland.[96]

The *actio de positis vel suspensis* was considered in *MacColl v. Hoo*[97]:

---

[93] See Walker, pp. 285–286.
[94] Bankton, I, iv, 32; Kames, I, i, 1; Hume, *Lectures*, iii, 186; and see Stein (1955) 4 I.C.L.Q. 356 (*Casebook*, Ext. 14); and Walker, pp. 284 *et seq.*
[95] 1954 S.L.T. (Sh.Ct.) 75.
[96] Stein and Walker, n. 58 above.
[97] 1983 S.L.T. (Sh.Ct.) 23 (*Casebook*, Ext. 24).

Miss MacColl discovered that her motor car had been dented by a tile which had fallen from premises occupied by Mr Hoo. She sued relying on the *actio*. The sheriff at first instance allowed the claim, accepting that it was part of the law of Scotland, and did not require proof of fault. On appeal the sheriff principal rejected the claim, taking the view that there can be no liability without fault.

The question thus remains for decision by a higher court. On analogy with *R H M Bakeries* [2.15] and *Kennedy v. Glenbelle* [1.12] it might be considered that these are cases where there is an overwhelming inference of fault from the facts, putting an onus of proof on the occupier which will usually be difficult to shift. Alternatively, the courts might choose to accept that liability is indeed strict.

In *McArthur v. Matthew Cleland Public House Proprietors*,[98] which was before the sheriff, but perhaps not before the sheriff principal referred to in *MacColl*, another lady was unsuccessful in claiming for damages for injury caused by a slate falling from the roof of the defenders' public house. The sheriff had allowed the case to proceed on the basis of the possibility of *res ipsa loquitur* being established. The sheriff correctly rejected *res ipsa loquitur* because the fall of a slate could be explained other than by the defenders' negligence. However, it may well be that if there had been more facts alleged in the pleadings sufficient to infer fault, the case would have proceeded—averments that the roof was generally in a poor state of repair prior to the accident, or (in the sheriff principal's view) that the building was newly built.[99]

The praetorian edict *nautae caupones stabularii*

2.25   The praetor was a Roman magistrate elected annually. When he demitted office his edicts were handed down to the next praetor and eventually this grew into a body of law equivalent to legislation—most praetors being content to leave the previous edicts alone. This particular edict related to the liability of sailors (*nautae*), innkeepers (*caupones*) and stable keepers (*stabularii*). These particular trades are said to have been singled out because of the propensity of people involved in them to be in league with pirates or highwaymen. The hotel keeper or carrier could arrange to have the guest's baggage or the consigned goods stolen for a share in the booty. The carrier or innkeeper would then be able to plead that it was not his fault. To remedy this, the edict imposed strict liability for the simple happening

---

[98] 1981 S.L.T. (Sh.Ct.) 76.
[99] *ibid*. at 77. In *MacColl* the home was completed in July 1979 and the slate fell in December of that year.

unless there had been a *damnum fatale* [11.18]. In its modern form in
Scots law, it applies to carriers of goods (not carriers of passengers),
hotel keepers and stable keepers.

While the law of contract will often be applicable in many such
cases, since we are concerned with liability in delict it is not essential
that a contract exists: for example, in a case where a purported
contract for accommodation is void, if goods are stolen from the
hotel there is still liability under the edict. The liability of both the
carrier and hotel proprietor has been adjusted by statute.

Carriers

Nautae, or carriers by sea, are strictly liable unless they can show the   2.26
damage to goods was caused by *damnum fatale* or act of the Queen's
enemies. It is therefore to no avail to show that all reasonable
precautions were taken.[1] The law is, however, affected by, *inter
alia*, the Carriage of Goods by Sea Act 1971 and the Merchant
Shipping Act 1995, and is not dealt with in this book.[1a]

The common carrier of goods (but not of people) by land is, by
analogy, held strictly liable for the goods carried. It is no defence to
show that the goods were stolen.[2] Only the defences of *damnum fatale*
and act of the Queen's enemies are available.

The Carriers Act 1830 affects the edictal liability. It prevents the
carrier excluding liability by advertisement or notice. It does allow
special contracts to be made so long as reasonable care is taken to
bring the terms to the attention of the consignor. It also excludes the
carrier's liability for certain specified goods[3] unless their nature and
value, if over £10, was declared when deposited.

Hotel proprietors

The Hotel Proprietors Act 1956 now regulates the inn keeper's   2.27
liability: "An hotel within the meaning of this Act shall, and any other
establishment shall not, be deemed to be an inn." Hotel "means an
establishment held out by the proprietor as offering food, drink and, if
so required, sleeping accommodation, without special contract, to any
traveller presenting himself who appears able and willing to pay a
reasonable sum for the services and facilities provided and who is in a
fit state to be received."[4]

On such a proprietor there falls strict liability subject to the defences
of *damnum fatale* and act of the Queen's enemies. But the Act offers

---

[1] *Rae v. Hay* (1832) 10 S. 303.
[1a] See Gloag and Henderson, *The Law of Scotland* (10th ed., 1995) Chaps 26 and 27.
[2] *MacAusland v. Dick* (1787) Mor. 9246.
[3] For example, jewellery, watches and lace.
[4] s. 1. And see *Casebook*, Ext. 31 for more of the text of the Act.

additional protections to the hotel proprietor: sleeping accommodation has to have been booked at the time of the loss; and the loss must have occurred between the midnight before arrival and the midnight after departure. There is no special strict liability in respect of motor vehicles in hotel car parks.

The proprietor can limit his liability to £50 for any one article and £100 in aggregate if he has conspicuously displayed a notice in terms of the Schedule to the Act.[5] But the restriction does not apply: where fault or vicarious liability is actually established; where the property was deposited for safe custody; or if the goods were offered for deposit and not accepted.

Stable keepers

2.28 Stable keepers have not received the benefit of any special legislation and are strictly liable for any damage to the beast subject to the defences of *damnum fatale* and act of the Queen's enemies.[6]

Further reading

Gordon, W.M., "Householders' Liabilities" (1982) 27 J.L.S.S. 253.
Mackenzie Stuart, "Liability of Common Carriers" (1926) 38 J.R. 205.
MacKintosh, J., "The Edict *nautae caupones stabularii*" (1891) 3 J.R. 306.
McLaren, J.P.S., "Nuisance Law and the Industrial Revolution" (1983) 3 O.J.L.S. 155.
McManus, F., "Bye-bye *Rylands*—Again!" 1995 J.R. (note) 394.
McManus, F., "Culpa and the law of Nuisance", 1995 J.R. (note) 462.
Malcolm, A.C. (The Hon. David K.), "The High Court and Informed Consent: The Bolam Principle Abandoned" (1994) 1 Tort L. Rev. 81.
Markesinis, B.S., "Negligence, nuisance and affirmative duties of action", (1989) 105 L.Q.R. 104.
Norrie, K., "Informed consent and duty of care", 1985 S.L.T. (News) 289.
P.F., "Nuisance and Negligence", 1986 J.R. 107.
Rodger, A., "Spuilzie in the Modern World", 1970 S.L.T. (News) 33.
Steele, J., "Private law and the environment: nuisance in context", 1995 L.S. 236.
Stein, P., "*The actio de effusis vel dejectis* and the Concept of Quasi-Delict in Scots Law" (1955) 4 I.C.L.Q. 356.
Stewart, W.J., "Lawburrows: Elegant Remedy or Absurd Form", 1988 S.L.T. (News) 181.
Stuart, S., "Bad Neighbours", 1984 S.L.T. (News) 45.
Watchman, P., "What the Law Says About Burst Pipes", 1987 SCOLAG 10.
Whittey, N., "Nuisance", *Stair Memorial Encyclopaedia*, Vol. 14.

---

[5] s. 2.
[6] See *Mustard v. Paterson*, 1923 S.C. 142 (*Casebook*, Ext. 30).

CHAPTER 3

DELICTS WITH NAMES II

This next section deals with a number of delicts, some of which have 3.1
been described in England as economic torts. This is by no means a
closed nor a clearly identified category. However, what these delicts do
have in common is that they all define the limits of legal trading and so
are usefully considered together.

Fraud

This delict protects the infringement of many different interests. It 3.2
may, for example, cause someone nervous shock[1] or result in their
becoming involved in some dangerous escapade.[2] Often it is encountered in commerce. Fraud involves the making of a false representation of fact without belief in its truth, intending that the person to
whom it is made should act in reliance thereon, which causes a
consequent loss.[3]

Frequently it is encountered in connection with contracts—the
fraud inducing a contract either with the person perpetrating the
fraud or with another party. Damages are recoverable whether or not
the contract can be rescinded, emphasising the independent nature of
the delict.[4] Fraud can be carried out in an infinite number of ways, and
in particular it is possible to commit the delict without words but to do
so by actions or deeds. A good recent example is *Hillcrest Homecare
Services v. Tartan Home Care Ltd.*[5] The pursuers alleged that the
defenders had induced them to purchase a nursing home by arranging

---

[1] *Wilkinson v. Downton* [1897] 2 Q.B. 57.

[2] See *Burrows v. Rhodes* [1899] 1 Q.B. 816, which arose from the Jameson raid. Sir
Leander Starr Jameson led a raid against the Transvaal to support rebels (mainly
British) to advance Cecil Rhodes' colonial ambitions. Jameson was captured and
handed over to the British. The reasoning might be a little coloured by the
circumstances.

[3] See generally *Boyd & Forrest v. Glasgow & South-Western Ry*, 1912 S.C. (H.L.) 93.

[4] *Thin & Sinclair v. Arrol* (1896) 24 R. 198; and see *Post Office v. Morton*, 1992
G.W.D. 26–1492.

[5] 1996 G.W.D. 4–215.

matters so that they and their surveyor were fooled into thinking there were more occupants than actually there were!

Breach of confidence

3.3   This was not, until very recently, a well-defined delict. The Scottish Law Commission stated that the position was obscure, not least because the decisions in some earlier cases, while bearing strong similarities to a delictual approach, were in fact decided on principles of common law copyright, which extended to unpublished material.[6] Common law copyright was abolished by the Copyright Act 1911, s. 31. Breach of confidence probably covers cases where information which should not be divulged is disseminated causing loss or distress. The authorities reviewed by the commission do support a delictual duty not to reveal confidential information causing loss, injury or damage, but it is not clear whether the obligation has to emanate from a recognised relationship involving confidentiality preceding the obtaining of the information (such as doctor and patient), or whether it can arise out of the particular circumstances.[7] The commission recommended that if legislation were to be introduced the common law should be supplemented rather than replaced. The obligation proposed was delictual in nature, arising *ex lege* from one person obtaining information in certain circumstances: either (1) by agreement or undertaking, the contract thereby bringing the persons into the necessary relationship, or (2) in circumstances where a reasonable man in the defender's position would have regarded himself as being bound to treat the information as confidential.[8]

3.4   The law has now to be considered in the light of recent cases in the House of Lords and in the Court of Session which do support an obligation of confidence. The first is the celebrated *Spycatcher* litigation.[9] So far as the case in the House of Lords is concerned the essential facts were that a former secret service operative, Mr Peter Wright, published a book in Australia which revealed information which he had obtained while working for the British security service.

---

[6] Scottish Law Commission, No. 90, Cmnd 9385 (1984), p. 8.

[7] *Brown's Trs v. Hay* (1898) 25 R. 1112; *Levin v. Caledonian Produce (Holdings) Ltd*, 1975 S.L.T. (Notes) 69; *Roxburgh v. Seven Seas Engineering Ltd*, 1980 S.L.T. (Notes) 49.

[8] Scottish Law Commission, *op. cit.*, p. 55. For a full analysis of the nature of the obligation, see Wei, "Surreptitious Takings of Confidential Information", 1992 L.S. 302.

[9] *Att.-Gen. v. The Observer Ltd and Others*; Att.-Gen. v. Times Newspapers and Others [1988] 3 W.L.R. 776. For the background to this case and an enjoyable read see Turnbull, *The Spycatcher Trial* (Heinemann, London, 1988). See also Jones, "Breach of Confidence after Spycatcher" [1989] C.L.P. 49.

The Crown sought to restrain publication in the United Kingdom by injunction.

In the House of Lords, Lord Keith took the view that the law had long recognised an obligation of confidence arising out of relationships such as doctor and patient, priest and penitent, solicitor and client, and banker and customer. Presumably from the standpoint of English law, Lord Keith said: "The obligation may be imposed by an express or implied term in a contract but it may also exist independently of any contract on the basis of an equitable principle of confidence." In his opinion an invasion of personal privacy was sufficient to justify the law's interference. In stating this he referred to the granting of an injunction in England arising out of the Scottish divorce between the Duke and Duchess of Argyll.[10] This case was also cited to justify the proposition that "It is a general rule of law that a third party who comes into possession of confidential information which he knows to be such, may come under a duty not to pass it to anyone else." The obligation may be quite wide: "Further as a general rule it is in the public interest that confidences should be respected and the encouragement of such respect may in itself constitute a sufficient ground for recognising and enforcing the obligation of confidence even where the confider can point to no specific detriment to himself."

In the Wright case, the *Sunday Times* newspaper sought to justify its 3.5 publication of the material it knew well was confidential, on the basis that it was to be published in America. The House of Lords did not regard this as acceptable: according to the House, "[t]he fact that a primary confidant [Wright], having communicated the confidential information to a third party [*Sunday Times*] in breach of obligation, is about to reveal it similarly to someone else [U.S. publishers], does not entitle that third party to do the same." Accordingly, *Times* Newspapers were held to be in breach of an obligation of confidence in publishing the information and were liable to account for the profits resulting from the breach.

The second case is *Lord Advocate v. The Scotsman Publications* 3.6 *Ltd.*[11] In this case another secret service agent wrote a book. *The Scotsman* among others wanted to print details of the book. By the time the case reached the Inner House the issue was whether the mere fact of publication was sufficiently contrary to national interests (represented by the Crown), regardless of the nature of the actual material in the book, to be prohibited—*i.e.* the emphasis was not on anything actually said in the book. It was not surprising, therefore, that interdict was refused, apparently on the basis of the lack of interest of the Crown in restraining non-prejudicial matters. However,

---

[10] *Duchess of Argyll v. Duke of Argyll* [1967] Ch. 302.
[11] 1988 S.L.T. 490 (*Casebook*, Ext. 9).

the court was of the opinion that confidential information did not cease to be confidential merely because it had been disclosed in breach of obligation. Further, the Inner House considered that there was probably an obligation in Scots law to prevent a third party obtaining and publishing confidential information and knowing it to be so. The obligation may be based on equity, as it is in England. Nothing was said about damages.

The House of Lords dismissed the Lord Advocate's appeal.[12] Nevertheless, it was made clear that if the book had contained prejudicial matter and there had been no previous publication, the result would probably have been different.

While the cases discussed involve the state, confidentiality also applies in relation to private individuals, and commercial contracts often include confidentiality clauses which could provide the necessary foundation for a case against a third party.

Passing off

3.7   This well-recognised and often utilised delict can be used to obtain an interdict or damages or both where one party has represented his goods or services as being those of another in a way calculated to deceive the public, divert custom and cause loss of business to the other. Sometimes, as we shall see, this element of calculating to deceive will easily be inferred from the circumstances. It can result in damages or a restitutionary remedy for the wrong of an account of profits.[13]

3.8   In *Haig v. Forth Blending Co.*[14] the court reviewed the existing authorities and provided a useful set of propositions applicable to these cases.

> (1) It is not permissible to sell goods in such a way that the public may be confused into thinking that the goods are those of the complainer.
> (2) A trader must show that his goods are recognised by the public or a particular section of it and that any name, mark or get-up is associated in their minds with his goods alone.
> (3) The trader must show a likelihood of confusion although he need not actually show that any particular member of the public has been confused—certainly where the remedy sought is interdict.
> (4) There is no right of property in any name, mark or get-up: the essence of the delict is the defender's attempt to appropriate the pursuer's goodwill.

---

[12] *The Times*, July 7, 1989.

[13] It has been held that a pursuer must claim either an account of profits or damages: *Treadwell's Drifters Inc. v. RCL Ltd*, 1996 S.L.T. 1048 (decided in 1993).

[14] 1954 S.C. 35 (*Casebook*, Ext. 21).

(5) "Get-up" includes design, labels and generally the way the thing is packaged for the public—a special design of a useful part of an article may form part of the get-up.

(6) In considering whether the public has been deceived, a member of the public is "a person of reasonable apprehension and proper eyesight."

(7) A bottle may be part of the get-up and it may be associated with a single trader.

(8) If the goods of a trader have, from a peculiar mark or get-up, become known by a particular name, the adoption by another of any mark or get-up which will cause his goods to attain the same name is actionable.

(9) An innocent manufacturer may have to answer for a dishonest retailer if the manufacturer provides a weapon for the dishonest retailer.

(10) Even if there is no intention to deceive on the part of a retailer, he may be interdicted if the public are being misled.

The *Haig* case was an action by a whisky company against blenders and retailers. The complainers were trying to prohibit the use of a bottle of triangular shape similar to one they had used for a long time. There was material before the court which indicated that barmen and customers were confused, thinking that the defenders' product was the complainer's "Dimple". Interdict was granted.[15]   3.9

A more recent statement of the nature of the delict in the House of Lords casts some doubt on the possibility of an innocent trader being held liable and tries to focus less on the appropriation of goodwill and more on the elements of loss and misrepresentation. It constitutes an attempt to find a broader principle behind the rules of passing off. In doing so it admits of the possibility of an expansion of the rules. Lord Diplock, in *Erven Warnink v. Townend*[16] indicated that the following five elements would have to be present to support an action: 3.10

(1) a misrepresentation,[17]

(2) made by a trader in the course of a trade,

(3) to prospective customers of his or ultimate consumers of goods and services supplied by him,

(4) which is calculated to injure the business or goodwill of another trader (in the sense that this is a reasonably foreseeable consequence), and

---

[15] See *Casebook*, para. 6.2.4. for comment.

[16] [1979] A.C. 731.

[17] It has been held in Scotland following this authority that a mere misrepresentation is not sufficient: *Treadwell's Drifters Inc. v. RCL Ltd*, 1996 S.L.T. 1048 (decided in 1993).

(5) which causes actual damage to the business or goodwill of the trader by whom the action is brought, or which will probably do so.

3.11 Thus it is not even permissible to use one's own name in trade if used fraudulently or to create avoidable confusion.[18] Interdict might be available if it can be shown that one's own name has attached to some particular product.[19] It is usually permissible to use a word or name which is part of the English language for a product and so it is essential for the complainer to show that any word has become associated with his product alone. For this reason, a trader is well advised to register any new word he has invented under the Trade Marks Act 1938 (as amended). If this is not done there is a danger that a concocted word may lose its distinctiveness, becoming by enthusiastic marketing a generic term for products of that kind. Browsing through the *Concise Oxford Dictionary of Current English* (9th ed.) one can find "Sellotape: transparent cellulose or plastic tape" and "Hoover: a vacuum cleaner", showing this process in action.[20]

3.12 Cases tend to turn on different issues and to an extent the principles set out in the *Forth Blending* case are not exhaustive. In deciding whether there is a likelihood of confusion, the territory in which the parties operate may be important. Thus, in the case of the *Dunlop Pneumatic Tyre Co. Ltd v. Dunlop Motor Co. Ltd*,[21] although both companies had similar names, it was held that the citizens of Kilmarnock were unlikely to be confused between the pursuers, the Dunlop

---

[18] *Baume & Co. Ltd v. Moore* [1958] Ch. 907; *O'Briens v. Watts*, 1987 S.L.T. 101.

[19] *Parker Knoll v. Knoll International* [1962] R.P.C. 265. See Clive, "Goods by Any Other Name", 1963 S.L.T. (News) 106.

[20] Although it is equally interesting to note that among much erudite philological information in the introduction to the dictionary the following also appears: "This dictionary includes some words which have, or are asserted to have, proprietary status as trade marks or otherwise. Their inclusion does not imply that they have acquired for legal purposes a non-proprietary or general significance, nor any other judgement concerning their legal status. In cases where the editorial staff have some evidence that a word has proprietary status this is indicated in the entry for that word by the abbreviation *propr.*, but no judgement concerning the legal status of such words is made or implied thereby." Both "Sellotape" and "Hoover" are so marked. See *Re Gramophone Co.'s Application* [1910] Ch. 423. Further researches reveal the position to be even more interesting. It transpires that "Proprietary terms are of more than usual concern to lexicographers since such terms are often the subjects of protracted correspondence or even threatened litigation": Burchfield, "Controversial Vocabulary in the Oxford English Dictionary" in *Unlocking the English Language* (Faber, 1989), p. 96. His further exposition indicates that passing-off would be unlikely to be successful against a dictionary as the publisher is not trying to sell the product. It is the use of dictionaries by Trade Marks registrars and the like that gives the proprietor of a mark an interest in the publication of the word with a lower case first letter indicating generic use.

[21] 1907 S.C. (H.L.) 15.

tyre company from England, and the defenders, a family business in Kilmarnock. In any event the sort of work carried out by the two companies was, in the main, different. That the market sector is quite often crucial can be seen from the case of *Scottish Milk Marketing Board v. Drybrough & Co. Ltd*[22] where the pursuers, who had sold butter under the name "Scottish Pride" for some considerable time, tried to prevent the defenders from selling a lager by the same name. They were unsuccessful on the basis that confusion was unlikely to result. They were also unsuccessful in a slightly more subtle argument. The dairy company had been sponsoring sporting events to associate, in the public mind, their product with health. They complained that the defenders' actions would damage that advertising. This did not seem to carry much weight at the interim hearing.

Where the market area is narrow confusion is much more likely, as where the International House of Heraldry were able to restrain the use of "International Art of Heraldry".[23] In *Dash Ltd v. Philip King Tailoring*,[24] it was argued that the confusion which was said to exist in the case was only such as to amount to the possibility of confusion, whereas the *Haig* case required a likelihood of confusion. Lord McDonald, giving the opinion of the court, stated that the *Haig* case dealt with the similarity of goods rather than names. The court did, however, consider that in the case before it, if the test were likelihood, it had been met. There seems to be no reason why the principles expounded in *Haig* should not apply to names as much as get-up—the test should be the same whether a trader obtains another's sale by using a name or a get-up. "Likelihood", it is submitted, is still the better verbal formulation.[25]

It seems to be the case that a narrow approach is not taken with this delict in that the pursuer is permitted to claim in circumstances where the defender, rather than actually pretending to sell someone's goods, pretends that his goods are in some way the same as the pursuer's or by his actions tries to appropriate exclusiveness and style. The Scottish case of *John Walker & Sons Ltd v. Henry Ost & Co. Ltd*[26] supports this broader view in that the court accepted that a producer was entitled to protect his product from sales of non-Scotch whisky on the basis that there would be damage to his sales where someone tasted the inferior 3.13

---

[22] 1985 S.L.T. 253.

[23] *International House of Heraldry v. Grant*, O.H., Lord Marnoch, Apr. 23, 1991 (1991 G.W.D. 23–1352).

[24] 1989 S.L.T. 39.

[25] And see *John Walker & Sons v. Douglas Laing & Co.*, 1993 S.L.T. 156 in which likelihood as opposed to probability was considered sufficient in breach of interdict proceedings. This case, although reported in 1993, was decided in 1976.

[26] [1970] 1 W.L.R. 917; and see *Lang Brothers v. Goldwell*, 1982 S.L.T. 309 (*Casebook*, Ext. 22).

product and decided not to try the real thing. This case need not be restricted to mere geographic appropriation but applies to the whole image of a product.

Wrongful refusal to contract

3.14 Usually it is not a delict to refuse to contract. But for a long time it has been recognised that persons in certain occupations were compelled to contract, namely the carrier of goods and the innkeeper. An innkeeper, for example, must provide accommodation, food and drink unless: (a) no security for the bill is proffered if requested; (b) the "guest" is accompanied by an animal causing alarm to other guests; (c) the complainer is not actually on a journey; (d) the traveller refuses to pay or is of undesirable character; or (e) there is no available accommodation.[27] The rules relating to carriers are now usually considered as part of the law relating to carriage of goods.[28] It has been suggested that this delict, "should be kept apart from the economic torts as they develop".[29]

CONSPIRACY, INTERFERENCE IN CONTRACT AND INTIMIDATION

3.15 These are strictly speaking three separate delicts but, as the leading modern cases often involve more than one, they may usefully be considered together. They are frequently found in cases of industrial conflict. It has to be said that these delicts are becoming ever more interrelated, so much so that some writers have begun to speak of a general delict of wrongful interference with trade, or causing loss by unlawful means. They have been joined by the English legal profession. The existence of such a tort was pled and conceded in the House of Lords in *Lonrho plc v. Al-Fayed*.[30] It was accepted in the House that the tort exists but that its definition is as yet uncertain. It was briefly considered in a Scottish case which appeared to recognise the wider tort: *Shell U.K. Ltd v. McGillivray*.[31]

Each of them should be viewed against the background that the law in England, and probably the law of Scotland, generally prefers to leave people free to participate in a competitive free market. Thus, in *Mogul Steamship Co. Ltd v. McGregor, Gow & Co.*[32] it was held not to

---

[27] See *Rothfield v. N.B. Ry*, 1920 S.C. 805.
[28] See Gloag and Henderson, 10th ed., Chaps 26 and 27.
[29] Carty (1988), p. 284.
[30] [1991] 3 W.L.R. 188.
[31] 1991 S.L.T. 667.
[32] [1892] A.C. 25.

be actionable for the defendants to put the plaintiffs out of business by undercutting their competitors, offering rebates to those exclusively dealing with them and restricting their own agents from dealing with competitors. Shortly afterwards, in *Allen v. Flood*,[33] a union official was held not to be liable for telling his employers that if certain workers were not dismissed, the union workers would not work. The workers were employed on a daily basis and were under no obligation to sign on for work the next day.

On the other hand, the law of Scotland recognises a doctrine, from the civil law of *aemulationem vicini*[34] which would generally suggest that the malicious infliction of harm would be actionable, even if the conduct complained of is, on the face of it, lawful. A similar line has been taken in the United States.[35] The European Court of Justice has held that not all price competition can be regarded as legitimate and has penalised predatory pricing.[36]

The following interrelated delicts should therefore be seen as exceptions to a general approach that permits harm to others as a result of the lawful conduct of business.

Conspiracy

The most significant Scottish case is *Crofter Hand Woven Harris Tweed Co. Ltd v. Veitch*,[37] a decision of the House of Lords which is now considered to be the leading authority in this area in both Scotland and England. The facts are quite complicated. The Crofter company marketed cloth woven by the Isle of Lewis crofters using yarn imported from the mainland. Yarn was also spun on the island itself. The island spinners were members of the TGWU. The union tried to get a higher rate of pay for its members who spun yarn on the island. The island employers said they could not afford to pay their members more money; the TGWU ordered its members not to handle the yarn of the mainland producers. The House of Lords held that this conduct was not actionable but a number of propositions can be taken from it:

3.16

---

[33] [1898] A.C. 1.

[34] See para 2.20 and see Bowen L.J. in *Mogul Steamship*, cited above. Johnston, D.E.L., "Owners and Neighbours: From Rome to Scotland" in *The Civil Law Tradition in Scotland* (Evans-Jones ed., Stair Soc. Sup. 2, 1995).

[35] *Tuttle v. Buck* (1909) 119 N.W. 946. But see the comments on the case in Weir, *Economic Torts* (Oxford, 1997), pp. 72–74.

[36] *AKZO Chemie B.V. v. Commission of the European Communities* (C 62/86), 1991 T.L.R. 432.

[37] 1942 S.C. (H.L.) 1 (*Casebook*, Ext. 23). For a review of the case and conspiracy generally see J.M. Thomson, "An Island Legacy – the Delict of Conspiracy" in *Comparative and Historical Essays in Scots Law* (Carey Miller & Mayers, eds, Butterworths, 1992), p. 137.

(1) Conspiracy of one variety consists in the agreement of two or more to do an unlawful act or to do a lawful act by unlawful means so long as the acts are actually carried out in pursuance of the conspiracy to the damage of the pursuer.

(2) Conspiracy of the other variety consists in a "conspiracy to injure" with a predominant purpose to injure where injury is actually caused even where there are no unlawful means or unlawful acts. This differs from a "set of acts dictated by business interests" which is not actionable.

(3) There is nothing unlawful in giving a warning or intimation that if the party addressed pursues a certain course of conduct, others may act in a manner he will not like, so long as nothing unlawful is threatened or done.

(4) It is possible for something which would not be actionable if done by one person to be actionable if he conspires to do it with another. This may be anomalous but it is said to be firmly entrenched in the law.

(5) It is not conspiracy (absent unlawful means) if the predominant motive is not unlawful. It was this last proposition which proved decisive in the *Crofter* case: the union's predominant motive was to advance the members' interests.

A distinction has been made between cases where the conspiracy is to use unlawful means which, if harm results, will be actionable regardless of motive, and "simple" cases, where, as in *Crofter* there are no unlawful means and where only the absence of a legitimate predominant motive will make conspiracy to do something not in itself illegal, actionable.[38]

3.17 Another development which may make simple cases less common is Lord Diplock's view that breach of the competition provisions of the EEC Treaties amounts to a breach of duty which is actionable. If so it would be actionable for an individual or group of individuals to unduly restrict competition within the common market or to abuse a dominant position within the common market.[39]

3.18 There are proposals to introduce a new Competition Act in the United Kingdom modelled on the European Union Treaty provisions. These may in time replace some of the existing remedies or at least take away the pressure for the separate delicts to become a

---

[38] A speech by Lord Diplock was interpreted in the Court of Appeal as meaning that a justifiable predominant purpose would excuse even an unlawful means conspiracy (*Lonrho v. Shell Petroleum Co. Ltd (No. 2)* [1982] A.C. 173; see also *Metall und Rohstoff A.G. v. Donaldson Lufkin and Jenrette Inc.* [1990] Q.B. 391). This error was set right by the House of Lords, the leading speech being by Lord Bridge who had sat with Lord Diplock on the Appellate Committee in the *Lonrho v. Shell* case: *Lonrho Ltd v. Al-Fayed* [1991] 3 W.L.R. 188.

[39] *Garden Cottage Foods v. Milk Marketing Board* [1984] A.C. 130.

general control of trade. It is too early to comment on this development.[40]

Inducing breach of contract

It is an actionable wrong knowingly to induce a person to break his 3.19 lawful, valid and subsisting contract with another. This was apparent from some dicta in *Crofter* but was applied in the case of *British Motor Trade Association v. Gray*[41]:

> After the second world war there was a shortage of motor vehicles. The BMTA was formed, consisting of manufacturers and their distributors. They developed a scheme whereby every purchaser of a new car signed an agreement undertaking not to resell the car within a specified period. It was alleged that the respondent had purchased such vehicles within the specified period knowing full well that a covenant had been executed, *i.e.* he had induced the original purchaser of the car to break his covenant with BMTA.

The court allowed the case to proceed: "if damage results, it is an actionable wrong for a third party knowingly and unjustifiably to induce a breach of a lawful contract." Lord President Cooper said that although such conduct had never been stated as a delict in the law of Scotland that was just a coincidence. Cases where people were held liable for enticing employees away from their employers[42] were just examples of this broader principle. In any event, it was assumed that there was such a delict in *Crofter*.

It is clearly established that the defender must be aware that there is 3.20 a valid contract.[43] That said, the courts will judge the defender by the standard of knowledge he ought to have had: thus a defender cannot say that he was unaware that the men working in a factory were under a contract with the factory owner simply because the specific contracts are not known to him.[44] On the other hand, in the Outer House it has been held that there had to be knowledge on the part of the defender of the existence of the contract and that recklessness or turning a blind eye was not sufficient unless it was tantamount to intention.[45] There must be loss before there can be liability but this will easily be inferred. It is, as in cases of conspiracy, a defence to have a legitimate interest in

---

[40] See Middleton, K.G., "Reform of U.K. Competition Law", 1998 S.L.T. (News) 47.
[41] 1951 S.C. 586.
[42] See, for example, *Belmont Laundry Co. Ltd v. Aberdeen Steam Laundry Co. Ltd* (1898) 1 F. 45.
[43] *British Homophone v. Kunz* [1935] All E.R. 627.
[44] See *Stratford v. Lindley* [1964] 3 All E.R. 102.
[45] *Rossleigh Ltd v. Leader Cars Ltd*, 1987 S.L.T. 355 at 360, *per* Lord Mayfield.

inducing the breach and this is illustrated by the case of *Findlay v. Blaylock*[46] where a woman failed in an action against the father of the man to whom she had been engaged. At the time the case was decided engagement was a legal contract, breach of which would sound in damages. The father was held entitled as the curator of his minor son to look after his interest by persuading the son to break off the engagement with the pursuer, whom he considered to be unsuitable.

In the English case of *D.C. Thomson v. Deakin*[47] three ways of committing the delict were set out: (1) direct persuasion, which covers cases such as the defender enticing the pursuer's contracting partner[48]; (2) direct intervention by striking at the other contracting partner (for example, if the defender imprisoned the pursuer's contracting partner)—it is not clear whether the interference need be unlawful to be actionable because the interference in this case is direct[49]; (3) finally, indirect intervention, in the sense that it is not the other contracting partner who is interfered with directly, will be actionable where loss is caused if, but only if, the means used are unlawful. This could be where the defender destroys the pursuer's contracting partner's machinery. "Unlawful means" for the purposes of this delict may be conduct in breach of the criminal law, a statutory provision, or indeed a breach of some other contract.

It has been said in England that there is no tort of inducing an unfair dismissal under the statutes as opposed to a wrongful dismissal at common law.[50]

3.21   This area of liability may be extending to unlawful interference in contract, whether or not there is a breach, but it is too early to say whether it will go so far.[51]

Intimidation

3.22   In *Rookes v. Barnard* [52] the plaintiff was a skilled draftsman working in a closed shop for BOAC. He left his union and eventually his workmates intimated that if he was not removed in three days they would withdraw their own labour. In view of this and the possibility that other workers would come out in sympathy, BOAC suspended and then dismissed Mr Rookes. As between BOAC and Rookes the dismissal was lawful. The jury found that a conspiracy existed, that the

---

[46] 1937 S.C. 21.
[47] [1952] 2 All E.R. 361.
[48] Often described in England by reference to the first major case on the subject: *Lumley v. Gye* (1853) 2 E. & B. 216.
[49] See *Stratford v. Lindley* [1964] 3 All E.R. 102.
[50] *Wilson v. Housing Corporation* [1996] T.L.R. 733.
[51] *Torquay Hotel Co. Ltd v. Cousins* [1969] 1 All E.R. 522, *per* Lord Denning; *Merkur Island Shipping Corp. v. Laughton* [1983] 2 A.C. 570 at 608.
[52] [1964] A.C. 1129.

defendants were a party to it and that it had caused his dismissal. Because there was a "no strike" agreement the threat to withdraw their labour was a threat by the employees to breach their contracts with BOAC. It was held in the House of Lords that the threat to breach their contracts amounted to intimidation and that Rookes could sue his workmates for the loss of his job. Intimidation included not just threats to commit a tort but also threats to breach a contract.

It is worth noting that the union were protected from liability for strikes which broke contracts in pursuance of a trade dispute (under the Trade Disputes Act 1906) but were not given immunity to intimidate. The effect of *Rookes* was altered by the Trade Disputes Act 1965 which gave immunity for one form of intimidation—the threatening to procure a breach of contract.

Rookes is clear authority for a delict of intimidation. Stair himself considered it a delict following the Roman law:

"Extortion signifies the act of force, or other means of fear, whereby a person is compelled to do that which of their proper inclination they would not have done. It doth also imply the obligation of the injurer to the injured, to repair his loss and damage by such acts."[53]

It has to be said, though, that he may not have had in mind the threat to commit a breach of contract.

Rookes is an example of what is called three-party intimidation: A 3.23 threatens B in order to hurt C. There is no clear authority, other than the statement by Stair, and certain *obiter* remarks in *Stratford v. Lindley*[54] for the existence of two-party intimidation, *i.e.* where A threatens B causing him loss. While it seems reasonable where the intimidation is criminal or delictual, to permit a delictual remedy where the threat is to break a contract would have potentially profound effects upon the law of contract. Weir[55] argues that such behaviour does constitute actionable intimidation (standing that often there will be a remedy for the breach of the contract itself) whereas Wedderburn[56] considers that this upsets the object of the law. Finally, if the intimidation is to make someone enter a contract it may be the case that the Scottish courts would uphold the concept of economic duress as vitiating the contract and permitting of restitution.[57]

If the threat is not complied with in a two-party situation then there is the possibility that the conduct, if carried out, may amount to some

---

[53] Stair, I, ix, 8.
[54] [1964] 3 All E.R. 102.
[55] [1964] C.L.J. 225.
[56] (1964) 27 M.L.R. 257.
[57] Woolman, *Contract*, 2nd ed., p. 77.

other delict. If the threat is not complied with in a three-party situation then the intended victim is unlikely to have suffered loss and the issue would not arise.

Further reading

Adams, J., "Is There a Tort of Unfair Competition?" 1985 J.B.L. 26.

Cameron, J.T., "Intimidation and the Right to Strike", 1964 S.L.T. (News) 81.

Capper, D., "Damages for breach of the Equitable duty of Confidence", 1994 L.S. 313.

Carty, H., "Intentional Violation of Economic Interests: the Limits of Common Law Liability" (1988) 104 L.Q.R. 242.

Ewing, K., "Interdicts in Labour Law", 1980 S.L.T. (News) 121.

MacQueen, H.L., "Wee McGlen and the Action of Passing Off", 1982 S.L.T. (News) 225.

MacQueen, H.L., "The Wee McGlen case: Representations of Scottishness— Passing off and Unfair Trading" (1983) 5 E.I.P.R. 18.

Phillips, J. and Coleman, A., "Passing Off and the Common Field of Activity" (1985) 101 L.Q.R. 242.

Reid, C.T., "Damages for Deliberate Abuse of Power", 1988 S.L.T. (News) 121.

Russell, P., "The Commercial Exploitation of Fictitious Names" (1980) 130 N.L.J. 256.

Stewart, Q., "The Law of Passing-Off—A Scottish Perspective" (1983) 5 E.I.P.R. 64.

Thomson, J., "An Island Legacy – the Delict of Conspiracy", in *Comparative and Historical Essays in Scots Law* (Carey Miller and Meyers, eds, Butterworth, 1992), p. 137.

Wadlow, C., *The Law of Passing-Off* (Sweet & Maxwell, 1990).

Waelde, C., "Wet? Wet – a little mystery unresolved", 1996 S.L.T. (News) 1.

Wei, G., "Surreptitious Takings of Confidential Information", 1992 L.S. 302.

CHAPTER 4

LIABILITY FOR UNINTENTIONAL HARM I: AN OUTLINE ACCOUNT

INTRODUCTION

This chapter is an attempt to set out the main principles, rules and 4.1
themes applying to most ordinary cases of liability for unintentional
harm. It is presented on the basis of what commentators have regarded
as the law for the last 50 years or so. The judges hardly ever set out a
coherent theory of liability. They do not have to. If recovery is allowed
that is usually the end of the matter because most decisions depend
upon the facts of the case. If liability is denied the court need only
focus on whatever element of the case failed to satisfy the court—*e.g.*
no duty, no breach, no loss, no fault, lack of foreseeability, no
causation or that the loss was too remote. Once the reader has a
grasp of the general issues and can follow the way in which courts and
commentators consider and discuss the subject, it is then possible to
examine, in some detail, some problem topics. These topics, of interest
in themselves as being a series of rules applying to particular activities
or losses or injuries, are very important because they either now
question, or have in the past questioned, the very elements which
constitute the generally accepted framework.

What most of the instances of liability discussed in Chapters 2 and 3 4.2
above and 7 and 8 below have in common is that they are well-
established instances of where loss has been wrongfully caused. Loss
wrongfully caused is the basis of liability in Scotland, derived from the
liability under the *lex Aquilia* for *damnum* (loss) *injuria* (wrongfully)
datum (caused). Wrongfulness is very easily apparent where there is an
intention to cause harm or the act itself is such that a person is treated
as having intended the harm. However, an act can easily be wrongful
for these purposes when it is done without due care.

A common example of the sort of liability discussed in this and the
next chapter is that which attaches where a pedestrian pursuer is
inadvertently run down by the motorist defender. In England such

problems are dealt with by what can be seen as a separate tort of negligence. In Scotland liability is based on the damage caused by the infringement of an interest (*e.g.* the pedestrian's physical integrity) occurring through the lack of due care. The result is almost always the same in both jurisdictions.

4.3   Many scholars have written well on the history and development of liability generally, and in this area in particular. [1] While it is impossible to summarise the different views and the detailed history here, there are some propositions which are worth noting. The first is that the current law in Scotland is that which has been decided in the House of Lords in the twentieth century, in English as well as Scottish appeals. If the net effect of these is to impose a system or framework which is not the same as would have resulted from an unimpeded development of native Scots law and practice that may be unfortunate, but the law is what the House says it is. [2]

The main issue is the concept of a duty of care. There is no liability for a failure to take reasonable care unless there was a duty to take care in the first place. This was not necessarily the Scots view. [3] However, after clearly demonstrating this, Black, [4] in a particularly penetrating historical analysis of the law, accepted that the duty of care concept is part of the law of Scotland.

4.4   Secondly, *culpa* (see Chapter 1), is still discussed in Scottish cases, but usually in the negative sense of there being no liability without fault. *Culpa* itself is something of a compromise notion involving a question very like that of a notional duty of care. *Culpa* may have been an application, a more detailed expression, of *injuria*, the wrongfulness, in the sense of "against the law" of the *lex Aquilia* upon which the Scottish law was undoubtedly modelled. Kamba's conclusion for South African law, "[t]hat the English law concept of notional duty of care is in substance the equivalent of the Roman-Dutch law requirement of wrongfulness (injuria) but the approach in the two systems of law is significantly different", may well be valid for Scots law.

4.5   It was one decision, *Donoghue v. Stevenson*, [5] which launched liability for unintentional harm as one of the most frequently litigated instances of delictual liability. [6] That case is clearly established

---

[1]   See further reading section.

[2]   See Rodger, "Lord MacMillan's Speech in *Donoghue v. Stevenson*" (1992) 108 L.Q.R. 236 for an earlier "Scottish" draft of the *Donoghue* speech.

[3]   See Lord Kinnear in *Kemp & Dougall v. Darngavil Coal Co. Ltd*, 1909 S.C. 1314 at 1319 and Lord President Dunedin in *Clelland v. Robb*, 1911 S.C. 253 at 256 for the language of duty: Rodger, *op. cit.*, p. 249.

[4]   Black, *Historical Survey*, p. 326. See also discussion of *Bourhill v. Young* [4.10 and 11].

[5]   1932 S.C. (H.L.) 31; for the whole story, see Rodger, 1988 C.L.P. 1.

[6]   Although it should be appreciated that both jurisdictions allowed recovery for negligence before it.

authority in both Scotland and in England but controversy still exists over what exactly is its *ratio decidendi*. As well as clearly establishing the head of liability for unintentional physical harm, it has provided a workable conceptual framework for handling most cases.

> It all began in a café in Paisley. Mrs Donoghue had gone along to the café with a friend who bought her an opaque bottle of ginger beer. The shopkeeper poured some ginger beer over ice cream in a glass from which Mrs Donoghue drank. Then her friend poured out the remainder which was when Mrs Donoghue alleged she saw a decomposed snail in the bottle and as a result (she alleged) she suffered a serious illness. As this was an example of a case proceeding only upon legal debate, the averments are assumed to be true. Mrs Donoghue did not have a contract with the seller nor with the manufacturer of the goods and so her only possible remedy was in delict against the manufacturer on the basis of his fault in not taking care in the production of the product.[7]

The House of Lords held that the case was one which could proceed to   4.6
a proof before answer (which means that it was sound in law).

One thing which should be mentioned first is that at the time the most important thing the case did was to avoid the so-called heresy that there could be no delictual liability upon a defender if he had supplied goods under a contract—that in effect he was only liable to the customer. Instead the manufacturer of the product was held to owe a duty to take care because of the relationship between himself and the ultimate consumer—a relationship of proximity or neighbourhood. This principle of liability is sometimes known as the neighbourhood principle after the following celebrated passage in Lord Atkin's speech. Although not a definition, this passage is often considered to express the principle upon which delictual liability for unintentional harm proceeds:

> "The rule that you are to love your neighbour becomes in law, you must not injure your neighbour; and the lawyer's question, Who is my neighbour? receives a restricted reply. You must take reasonable care to avoid acts or omissions which you can reasonably foresee would be likely to injure your neighbour. Who, then, in law, is my neighbour? The answer seems to be—persons who are so closely and directly affected by my act

---

[7] This case is justly famous and was celebrated recently by the Canadian Bar Association. The resulting "Paisley Papers" are a valuable collection of essays on negligence but also reveal some interesting background to the case: see further reading. See also Rodger, "Mrs Donoghue and Alfenus Varrus", 1988 C.L.P. 1 and (1992) 108 L.Q.R. 236.

that I ought reasonably to have them in contemplation as being so affected when I am directing my mind to the acts or omissions which are called into question."[8]

4.7 From the speeches in *Donoghue* and the treatment of it in later cases, it is possible to set out something of a formula for working out whether there may be an action for unintentional harm. (Difficulties inherent in this framework are discussed in the next chapter.)

(1) There must be a duty of care owed by the defender to the pursuer.
(2) There must be a breach of the duty.
(3) The breach must cause a loss.

Within each of these essential components there are other issues which have to be addressed. In so doing it must be appreciated that there is no such thing as negligence in the air—every case turns on its own facts—and that the categories of negligence are never closed: except in cases where the courts have actually excluded recovery as a matter of policy or precedent, it is always possible to argue that there is a ground of action.

1. DUTY OF CARE

4.8 From Lord Atkin's dictum, it can be seen that very much depends upon whether the defender should reasonably have foreseen that his acts or omissions would cause harm to the pursuer. At this stage it should be made clear that "acts or omissions" is not a phrase devoid of difficulty. Generally there is no liability for a pure omission—that is a failure to do anything to prevent harm where there is no duty owed—as where I see you about to walk off the edge of a cliff.[9] What is or is not reasonably foreseeable depends upon the foreseeability of the reasonable man. The reasonable man has a place in many areas of the law but certainly now spends most of his time as a legal device for determining whether or not there is liability for unintentional harm. The reasonable man is not the average man for quite often he is far more rigorous in the conduct of his affairs than is the average man.

---

[8] *Donoghue*, per Lord Atkin at 44.
[9] See paras 5.40; Logie, "Affirmative Action in the Law of Tort: the Case of the Duty to Warn" (1989) 48 C.L.J. 115; Markesinis, "Negligence, Nuisance and Affirmative Duties of Action" (1989) 105 L.Q.R. 104. The other difficulty is characterisation: if I accidentally park my car on your foot and do not move it when you shout "Ouch, my foot!" is that an act or an omission? See *Fagan v. Metropolitan Police Commissioner* [1969] 1 Q.B. 439.

Reasonable foreseeability is partly an objective test—we do not ask: 4.9
did this defender foresee the harm; but neither do we assume a
completely objective approach and say the reasonable man does or
does not foresee X or Y. Instead we ask whether a reasonable man in
the position of the defender would have contemplated the harm—a
technique which might conveniently be described as defender objec-
tivity—we put the reasonable man in the defender's position and ask
him what he can see. What is required is the application of reason and
not prophecy.

A duty owed to a particular pursuer

Shortly after *Donoghue* the conceptual framework for negligence cases   4.10
was developed further. *Bourhill v. Young*[10] (which is discussed again
[5.25] in the context of nervous shock cases) highlights these points.

> A motorcyclist who overtook in a way that a reasonable road user
> would not have done was sued by a woman who suffered nervous
> shock as a result of seeing the aftermath of the resulting accident.
> She had gone to see what had happened.

It was held that she could not recover. While the motorcyclist was
careless in his actions and owed a duty not to be careless to, for
example, other road users, he did not owe a duty of care to, and thus
could not be said to be legally negligent towards, this particular
pursuer. This was because she was outwith the ambit or the scope
of the duty of care. The motorcyclist would not, in the Atkinian sense,
have had her in his contemplation. He could have contemplated harm
to people he might have struck with his cycle or even, perhaps, people
who might have been struck by debris from a collision because they
were in the vicinity, but not persons who only later came to the scene.

This case was significant for Scots law because a civilian approach   4.11
would be to achieve the same result by saying the motorcyclist was at
fault, sufficient in itself for liability, but that the harm was too remote.
The House, however, dealt with the matter on the basis that the
deceased motorcyclist had not owed a duty to the pursuer. The
remoteness issue is, however, a legitimate one in considering whether
or not there is a duty of care at all. This is because the reasonable man
would not contemplate an injury too remote from the act or omission.
Thus remoteness of injury (as contrasted with the entirely different
problem of remoteness of damage [4.40]) is part of the duty inquiry.[11]

---

[10] 1942 S.C. (H.L.) 78. This case has now had its human dimension explored. See
   McBryde, "*Bourhill v. Young*: the Case of the Pregnant Fishwife" in *Comparative
   and Historical Essays in Scots Law* (Carey Miller and Meyers, eds, Butterworth,
   1992), p. 66.
[11] And see the discussion at para. 4.3.

4.12   Negligence is therefore something different from carelessness, which is often used as a legally neutral word.[12] It is dangerous to use the word negligence other than in the sense of legally actionable carelessness. There must be a duty owed to the particular pursuer by the actual defender.

What is to be foreseen?

4.13   Just as it is from *Donoghue* that liability is judged on the basis of the use of reason, so too from *Donoghue* it can be taken that what is to be foreseen is the injury to the pursuer. "Injury" is not a helpful word in this context because as liability is based on *damnum injuria datum*, injury might be thought to relate to *injuria* whereas actually it is related to *damnum* (loss), often in the shape of personal injury (injury to the person in body or feelings). "Harm" signifies more accurately the object of foreseeability.

Foreseeability is just like crystal ball-gazing. Courts who look at these problems after they have happened (*ex post facto*) are in the same position. If one had the gift of foresight one might see the following sequence of events:

(1) Post office workers uncover a manhole in a public road.
(2) They erect a canvas shelter.
(3) They stop for a tea break.
(4) They remove the ladder from down the hole.
(5) They close the shelter with a tarpaulin.
(6) They place paraffin fuelled red warning lamps around the shelter and leave.
(7) Two young children remove the tarpaulin.
(8) They take up a paraffin lamp.
(9) They enter the shelter.
(10) One knocks the lamp over.
(11) The paraffin unexpectedly vaporises and bursts out in a rush of flame.
(12) The boy loses his balance and falls, burning himself.

Looking at these events it is clear that a line could conceivably be drawn at any event. One could say: you must not open manholes or you pay if someone gets harmed, or going on to number (3) you must not open a manhole and leave it unattended, and so on. In this case the foresight which reason would permit us (as opposed to crystal ball-gazing) might fade around number (6) or (7) or (8) and certainly reason is strained at about (10), (11) and (12): it could be said that almost everything is

---

[12] Lawyers tend to use the word "accident" to cover incidents where there is loss or damage but no fault—the layman does not discriminate. He says, "I have had an accident—it was your fault."

foreseeable but not everything reasonably foreseeable. The facts set out above are basically those of *Hughes v. Lord Advocate*.[13] The House of Lords decided that while the explosion might have been unforeseeable the danger of an explosion and the harm it might cause was not different in kind to the harm which actually resulted. There was a reasonably foreseeable danger of harm by fire in some form if an open manhole, lamps and equipment were left about which were obvious allurements to young children. So in assessing what is reasonably foreseeable (or put another way, what is too remote to be reasonably foreseen) we are to look at the harm which actually occured. In this case then, as the harm which occurred was injury by fire, the foreseeability required need only extend to about number (6) above. It should be appreciated that this is significantly different from saying that one must reasonably foresee what actually happened: that places the point of foresight at number (12) and would deny recovery, unlike *Hughes* where recovery was allowed.

The full subtlety of this approach can be appreciated by looking at another problem. Imagine the following situation: 4.14

(1) There is a cauldron of molten liquid.
(2) It has a loose cover.
(3) The cover falls into the molten liquid.
(4) It unexpectedly reacts chemically with the liquid and explodes injuring someone.

In this case the reasonable man (as opposed to the soothsayer) foresees up to number (3). The question then is whether that is sufficient. The answer given in a case on these facts[14] was "No". The harm to which foreseeability would extend would be harm by splashing molten liquid as the lid fell into the cauldron, not harm caused by eruption as a result of chemical reaction.

Such cases may therefore often involve fine distinctions, but if the   4.15 distinction were not made the overall picture would be distorted— people at fault would escape liability simply because the mechanism of the calamity differed from the usual.

The test is particularly difficult to apply in cases which involve a third party, largely because there is then the possibility of saying that the third party was the cause of the harm rather than the defender. This involves the question of causation which is discussed below but is usually approached, at least as a first step, by asking if there is a duty or whether harm of the kind which actually resulted should reasonably have been foreseen. Again, imagine our soothsayer consults the crystal ball and sees the following:

---

[13] 1963 S.C. (H.L.) 31. For a background account of the case, see Walker, "Reflections on a Leading Case" (1992) 37 J.L.S.S. 394.
[14] *Doughty v. Turner Manufacturing Co.* [1964] 1 Q.B. 518.

(1) Some borstal boys are working on an island.
(2) They are being supervised by borstal officers.
(3) The supervisers go to bed instead of supervising the boys.
(4) Seven of the boys escape.
(5) They go on a yacht and crash into another yacht damaging it.

The owner of the second yacht sues the persons legally responsible for the supervision of the boys. The problem in this case is that as between the pursuer and the defender the defender himself has not actually done anything to the pursuer. But that does not matter—we ask if there is a duty of care. It is reasonably foreseeable that borstal boys, if not guarded, will escape and that they, being on an island, will damage a yacht. The reasonable man foresees as far as number (4) and that is enough to establish the duty. And so the House of Lords held in a case on (basically) these facts. [15]

4.16   It can therefore be said that before there can be a duty of care the defender must be held to have been able reasonably to foresee that his acts or omissions would result in harm occurring of the kind which did actually result, it being unimportant that the actual harm resulted partly by the agency of the pursuer himself (*Hughes*) or by a third party (*Dorset Yacht*).

4.17   Often it is not necessary to take such a rigorous analytical approach to resolve such problems. If no ordinary reasonable man would be aware of the risk he cannot be held reasonably to have foreseen it. Thus where patients developed spastic paraplegia caused by phenol entering molecular cracks in ampules containing local anaesthetic, it was held that as this was not a known hazard at the time it could not reasonably be foreseen: "We must not look at the 1947 accident with 1954 spectacles."[16] This emphasises that although the court has the benefit of hindsight and can see the whole series of facts, reasonable foreseeability may well stop before any harm can be foreseen.

Developments in the concept of the duty of care

4.18   The existence of a duty of care has been recognised in an ever widening set of circumstances but so, too, has it been recognised that in new cases care must be taken and it cannot be assumed in establishing new duties that reasonable foreseeability of harm or proximity alone will suffice. So while *Donoghue* is seen as establishing a general duty to take reasonable care to avoid foreseeable physical injury or damage to property, other cases have gone further, notably so in *Hedley Byrne & Co. Ltd v. Heller & Partners Ltd* [17] [5.5]. The

---

[15] *Home Office v. Dorset Yacht Co.* [1970] A.C. 1004.

[16] *Roe v. Minister of Health* [1954] 2 Q.B. 66.

[17] [1964] A.C. 465.

court held that there was a duty not to cause foreseeable economic loss even where there was no damage to the pursuer's person or property, if the pursuer received information from a person who knew that if it was wrong and reliance was placed upon it, and reliance was reasonably placed upon it, the pursuer would suffer loss. The position had eventually come so far that Lord Wilberforce was able to say, in *Anns v. Merton London Borough Council* [18] that,

> "[t]hrough the trilogy of cases in this House, *Donoghue v. Stevenson, Hedley Bryne & Co. Ltd. v. Heller & Partners Ltd.* and *Home Office v. Dorset Yacht Co. Ltd.*, the position has now been reached that in order to establish that a duty of care arises in a particular situation it is not necessary to bring the facts of that situation within those of previous situations in which the duty of care had been held to exist. Rather the question has to be approached in two stages. First one has to ask whether, as between the alleged wrongdoer and the person who suffered the damage, there is a sufficient relationship of proximity or neighbourhood such that, in the reasonable contemplation of the former, carelessness on his part may be likely to cause damage to the latter—in which case a prima facie duty of care arises. Secondly, if the first question is answered affirmatively, it is necessary to consider whether there are any considerations which ought to negative, or to reduce or limit the scope of the duty or the class of person to whom it is owed or the damages to which a breach of it may give rise."

In the Scottish appeal *Junior Books v. The Veitchi Co.* [19] a duty was found to exist in a case where the defenders, who had no direct contract with the pursuers, did some work on the pursuers' property which was defective as opposed to dangerous: *i.e.* it was not within the principle of *Donoghue*, there being no harm to person or property. Since the case proceeded on the basis that there was no physical damage to his property, effectively the pursuer recovered a pure economic loss. Such a decision could have had enormous implications for the law relating to contracts generally, and consumer contracts in particular, so the House of Lords were careful to limit the decision to the special facts of the case. These matters are considered in more detail in the next chapter.   **4.19**

In the next chapter it will also be seen that the law has refused to extend the duty of care established in *Junior Books. Junior Books* owned the building, the floor of which was defectively laid. In a later case the House of Lords preferred to follow a long line of precedent

[18] [1978] A.C. 728 at 751.
[19] 1982 S.L.T. 492.

stating that someone who did not own goods at the time they were damaged could not sue in delict.[20] Then in two cases where consideration had been given to the duty of care, the Privy Council advised that reasonable foreseeability of economic loss was not itself a sufficient basis for establishing a duty of care; there has to be a close and direct relationship between the pursuer and the defender, such as was explicitly held to exist in *Junior Books*.[21] The House of Lords in one English appeal indicated that in future the two-stage test in *Anns* was not to be regarded in all circumstances as a suitable guide to the existence of a duty of care.[22] In two subsequent English appeals heard consecutively, the House of Lords departed from *Anns*.[23] In cases where a completely new kind of duty is sought to be imposed,the favoured test is now to ask if it is "fair, just and reasonable" so to do.

2. BREACH OF A DUTY

4.20 Once a duty is established a breach of that duty must also be present. Again the reasonable man is to the fore. This time he is asked what he would or would not have done had he been in the defender's position, to eliminate the risk which in the exercise of his reasonable foreseeability he had identified. The nature of this requirement was examined in the Scottish case, *Muir v. Glasgow Corporation*.[24]

> A church party obtained permission to use the defenders' tearoom. The tea-urn was carried by two men, McDonald and Taylor. For some unexplained reason the urn was dropped and young Eleanor Muir was severely burned. The action was based on the fault of the manageress in allowing the urn to be carried through the tearoom or for not clearing the children out of the way.

4.21 It was accepted that the defenders owed a duty to the pursuer: the question was whether or not there had been a breach of this duty. The House of Lords made it clear that the standard to be used was the conduct of the reasonable man. This was said to be an impersonal test.

---

[20] *Leigh and Sillavan Ltd v. Aliakmon Shipping Co. Ltd (The Aliakmon)* [1986] 2 W.L.R. 902.

[21] *Yuen Kun Yeu v. Att.-Gen. Hong Kong* [1988] 1 A.C. 175; *Wallace Edward Rowling et al. v. Takaro Properties Ltd* [1988] 2 W.L.R. 418.

[22] *D. & F. Estates Ltd v. Church Commissioners for England* [1989] A.C. 177.

[23] See para. 5.16; *Murphy v. Brentwood D.C.* [1991] 1 A.C. 398; *Department of the Environment v. Bates* [1991] 1 A.C. 499—the effect for general theory being that the trilogy of cases [4.18] still stands, as does *Junior Books*, but the reasonable foreseeability prima facie test is seriously disapproved as a mode of determining new duties.

[24] 1943 S.C. (H.L.) 3.

"It eliminates the personal equation and is independent of the idiosyncrasies of the particular person whose conduct is in question." However, Lord MacMillan went on to add an important qualification: "but there is a sense in which the standard of care of the reasonable man involves in its application a subjective element. It is still left to the judge to decide what, in the circumstances of the particular case, the reasonable man would have had in contemplation, and what, accordingly, the party sought to be made liable ought to have foreseen."

There is one comment which should be made about this reappearance of the reasonable man. In this context, the focus is not simply on whether it is possible for some harm of the kind suffered to result; instead "[t]he court must be careful to place itself in the position of the person charged with the duty, and to consider what he or she should have reasonably anticipated as a natural and probable consequence of neglect."[25] In the circumstances of *Muir*, it was held that the manageress had taken reasonable care: her duty was only to take reasonable care, not to prevent all accidents occurring in the premises.

The issue of breach of duty is usually considered in a more practical way by assessing the various options which the reasonable man considers relevant. 4.22

The most scientific way of going about this task is to apply a calculus of risk—assessing the probability of injury against the difficulty, expense and other factors involved in preventing or avoiding the injury. This, after all, is the sort of thing the reasonable man would do when directing his mind to the acts or omissions which are called into question—particularly so if "he" is a legal person like a large employer or a railway operator. It has to be said that it is seldom that judges actually or, rather, explicitly decide cases in this way. It may be that what follows reasonably represents the mechanism of their intuition or unarticulated thoughts. So, for example, when a seaman on a grain ship was sent below to fetch some timber and fell from a stair, he alleged breach of duty to provide a handrail. His employers stated that no other employers in that business erected such rails. The reasonable man is not, however, the average man and the court said:

> "If a real risk is one which would occur to the mind of a reasonable man and which he would not brush aside as far fetched . . . then surely he would not neglect such a risk if action to eliminate it presented no difficulty, involved no disadvantage and required no expense."[26]

---

[25] *per* Lord Thankerton at 8.
[26] *Overseas Tankship (U.K.) v. Miller* [1967] 1 A.C. 617, *per* Lord Reid at 642.

4.23   Again in *Morris v. West Hartlepool Steam Navigation Co. Ltd*[27] it was said that in considering whether some precautions should be taken against a foreseeable risk, the duty is, "to weigh on the one hand the magnitude of the risk, the likelihood of an accident happening and the possible seriousness of the consequences if an accident does happen, and on the other hand the difficulty and expense and any other disadvantage of taking precautions." A modern formulation of the factors to be considered in taking such a scientific approach[28] is as follows:

> "First, the degree of probability that damage will be done by the conduct which is challenged; secondly, the magnitude of the harm which is likely to be done if the risk unfortunately materializes; thirdly, the value or utility of the object to be achieved by the conduct in question; and fourthly, the burden in terms of cost, time and trouble, of taking precautions against the risk of damage."[29]

This calculated approach is apparent in a number of cases, particular factors being thought to weigh heavily in the calculation.

1. The degree of probability

4.24   In *Bolton v. Stone*,[30] for example,

> a woman was struck by a ball hit for six out of a cricket ground. She was walking on a quiet road adjacent to the park. The ball went over a 17-foot fence which was about 80 yards from the batsman. The victim herself was about 100 yards from the batsman. Such a stroke had been played only some six times in 30 years and no one had been hit.

The plaintiff failed to recover.[31]

---

[27] [1956] A.C. 552 at 574.

[28] The scientific approach is often called the "Learned Hand formula". It is called this after the U.S. judge whose name was Learned Hand and who set it out in *United States v. Carroll Towing Co.* (1947) 159 F (2d) 169 at 173: "If the probability [or harm] be called P; the [gravity of] injury L; and the burden [of adequate precautions] B; liability depends upon whether B is less than L multiplied by P; *i.e.* whether $B < PL$."

[29] Atiyah, *Accidents, Compensation and the Law* (3rd ed., 1980), p. 44.

[30] [1951] A.C. 850.

[31] A claim in nuisance also failed. Prior to *Bolton*, but in different circumstances, a claim in nuisance had been successful where golf balls had regularly been hit out of bounds (*Castle v. St Augustine's Links and Anor* (1922) 38 T.L.R. 615) and recently another similar claim based on negligence was successful in Scotland: *Whitefield v. Barton*, 1987 S.C.L.R. 259, in which *Bolton* was considered and the sheriff principal appeared to be following *Castle*. See also the similar case of *Lamond v. Glasgow Corp.*, 1968 S.L.T. 291.

2. The magnitude of the harm

This factor is well illustrated by *Paris v. Stepney Borough Council.*[32]   4.25

> The plaintiff was blind in one eye as a result of enemy action during the war but this was not known by his employers until discovered by the firm's medical officer. He was given notice. Before leaving the firm he hit a bolt with a steel hammer and a piece of metal hit his good eye and he lost his sight in it, leaving him blind.

The court accepted that there was a duty to supply goggles to this particular employee, taking into account the employer's knowledge of his disability, the seriousness of the injury and the likelihood of total blindness occurring. There would have been no breach of duty, on the evidence of practice at the time, if the pursuer had had two good eyes.

3. The value of the activity

If there is some extraordinary benefit which can be achieved this will   4.26
allow an abnormally high risk to be assumed. In *Daborn v. Bath Tramways Motor Co.,*[33]

> the defendants were responsible for the driving of an ambulance with a defective signalling system. There was, however, a sign at the back of the vehicle which said: Caution left hand drive. The court held that in wartime there was a necessity of using all possible vehicles and said it was necessary to "balance the risk against the consequences of not assuming that risk and in the present case that calculation seems to me to work out in favour of the plaintiff".

4. Knowledge of, availability of, or expense involved in taking, precautions

This factor may allow fewer precautions to be taken. For example: 4.27

> a large factory was flooded by an unusually heavy rainstorm. The water mixed with an oily liquid usually gathered in channels. The company spread sawdust on the floor but they did not have enough to cover the whole area. The plaintiff slipped and a barrel he was rolling went over his leg. The only precaution which would actually have prevented the injury was to close the factory at great expense, when the risk had not been that likely.

---

[32] [1951] A.C. 367; see also *McKinlay v. British Steel Corp.,* 1987 S.L.T. 522; 1988 S.L.T. 810.
[33] [1946] 2 All E.R. 333.

The court held that there was insufficient evidence that a reasonable employer would have closed the factory.[34]

4.28   A related issue is that of usual practice. Once this was very important: if the defender could show that he followed usual practice this would indicate, as a matter of law, that he had not breached his duty.[35] The courts have, however, rectified that approach and usual practice is now simply a factor, albeit quite a significant one, in assessing whether the duty has been breached. In *Cavanagh v. Ulster Weaving Co.*,[36]

> a labourer sued his employer. He had been wearing rubber boots provided by his employers and had fallen from a crawling ladder, which had no handrail, on to a glass roof while carrying a bucket of cement. The rubber boots had become wet and slippery. Expert evidence (which was unchallenged) was led to the effect that the system was perfectly in accord with good practice.

The House of Lords held that on the evidence the jury had been entitled to find for the worker since the evidence as to trade practice alone could not be treated as conclusive in favour of the defendants. The other side of the coin is that simply not to follow a common practice will not constitute negligence if it is otherwise clear that reasonable care has been taken.[37] Overall, the issue is a practical one and the "scientific" or economic approach is only of use as a guide in identifying relevant factors.

Finally, professional persons or persons exercising special skill have to reach a different standard of performance to avoid breaching a duty. This is dealt with in Chapter 5.

3. CAUSATION

4.29   The alleged breach of duty must in fact have been the real predominant or effective cause of the occurrence which resulted in the pursuer's loss, injury or damage — *i.e.* it must be the *causa causans* and not simply the *causa sine qua non* of the accident. This element of

---

[34] *Latimer v. AEC Ltd* [1953] A.C. 643.

[35] This approach was often called the "Dunedin formula": "Where the negligence of the employer consists of what I may call a fault of omission, I think it absolutely necessary that the proof of that fault of omission should be one of two kinds, either to shew that the thing which he did not do was a thing which was commonly done by other persons in like circumstances, or to shew that it was a thing which was so obviously wanted that it would be folly in anyone to neglect to provide it." *Morton v. Wm Dixon*, 1909 S.C. 807. See also Professor Black's comments in *Introduction to Pleading*, p. 28.

[36] [1960] A.C. 145.

[37] *Brown v. Rolls Royce Ltd*, 1960 S.C. (H.L.) 22; 1960 S.L.T. 119.

the claim for unintentional harm has been severely criticised and should be looked at as simply another method of controlling potential liability. The determination of causation is a mixed question of fact and law.

The law states what can or cannot be a legally effective cause and the inquiry into the fact is whether or not the breach of duty or wrongful act actually did cause the loss.[38] This issue is also intimately connected with the issue of remoteness of damage.

The breach of duty must at least be a cause or part of the causation   4.30
mechanism — in a factual or real sense. If the harm would have occurred without the breach of duty then the breach is not even a *sine qua non* and is legally irrelevant. In *Barnett v. Chelsea and Kensington Hospital Management Committee*[39]:

> the plaintiff's husband had a cup of tea. Then he vomited persistently for three hours. A hospital doctor was contacted, who told the man to go home and see his own doctor. The plaintiff's husband died and indeed had been murdered!

The action against the doctor for not treating the man failed because it was not shown that if treated immediately he would have lived — because of the nature of the poison introduced into the tea he would have died anyway. The failure to treat, although a breach of duty, did not in any sense cause the harm. This is often called the "but for" test. The test applies in most cases but it has been pointed out[40] that in the case of omissions and in the case of harm arising from multiple causes, the test is not so useful: in the case of a person shot in the head by two gunmen, neither is a cause utilising the "but-for" test.

Once the breach of duty is established as at least a *causa sine qua non*   4.31
it has to be elevated to a *causa causans* — the legal cause. It has been well said that "[t]he choice of the real or efficient cause from out of the whole complex of the facts must be made by applying common-sense standards. Causation is to be understood as the man in the street, and not as either the scientist or the metaphysician would understand it."[41] The breach, therefore, need not be only the whole complete cause — it

---

[38] There is a full discussion of the disguised policy in both the factual and legal issues in Hart and Honore, *Causation in the Law* and Atiyah, *Accidents, Compensation and the Law*, Chap. 4; an up-to-date but idiosyncratic discussion can be found in Stapleton (1988).

[39] [1969] 1 Q.B. 428.

[40] Atiyah, pp. 116–121.

[41] *Yorkshire Dale S.S. Co. v. MOWT* [1942] A.C. 691 at 706. See Mullany, "Common-sense Causation — an Australian View", 1992 O.J.L.S. 431. This article concludes that "modern psychological research indicates that it is unlikely that there is any consistant common-sense notion of what constitutes a 'cause'.": p. 436.

is sufficient that it has materially caused the harm. This was discussed in *McGhee v. NCB*.[42]

> A labourer whose normal duties were in a pipe kiln was sent to work in a brick kiln where the working conditions were hotter and dustier. The workman later contracted dermatitis and sued, *inter alia*, on the basis that his employers failed to provide showering facilities at the work place.

By the time the case reached the House of Lords it was admitted that there had been a breach of a duty of care. The House found that as the breach of duty had materially increased the risk of the harm this was sufficient to make it a *causa causans*.

4.32   However, a more recent case, *Kay's Tutor v. Ayrshire and Arran Health Board*[43] shows the limitations of the *McGhee* case. It also profoundly illustrates how causation is a legal concept. Apart from the Lord Ordinary, every judge seized of the case — the unanimous Inner House and the unanimous House of Lords — denied recovery. As Lord Ackner said, "if sympathy alone could be a valid basis for awarding [damages] to the appellant's son . . . to compensate him for his many and serious disabilities, then this claim would have given rise to no argument."

> The pursuer's son went to hospital suffering from meningitis. By a mistake in the treatment, the child was given a massive overdose of penicillin. As an immediate result the child suffered convulsions and hemiparesis. However, as a result of prompt remedial action the child soon recovered from these effects and recovered from the meningitis but turned out to be deaf. Evidence that the penicillin itself would damage the hearing nerve was rejected. Indeed, there was no known case where deafness had been caused by a penicillin overdose and very many where deafness had been caused by meningitis.

The defenders admitted that the doctor was negligent (*i.e.* had breached his duty) and accepted responsibility for the convulsions and hemiparesis. The issue then was whether the overdose was a cause at all, *i.e.* even a *causa sine qua non*, of the child's deafness. The answer was in the negative. It could not be a cause at all.[44] In the House of Lords, attempts were made to rely on *McGhee*. This was held, by the House of Lords, not to be possible:

---

[42] 1973 S.C. (H.L.) 37.

[43] 1987 S.L.T. 577.

[44] In a relatively recent case a lady who suffered a stroke six days after starting a course of contraceptive pills could not establish that they were the cause and *absolvitor* was granted: *Ingram v. Ritchie*, 1989 G.W.D. 27–1217.

"The principle in *McGhee* would only fall for consideration if it was first proved that it was an accepted medical fact that penicillin in some cases caused or aggravated deafness. The question would then arise whether when there are two competing causes of deafness, namely meningitis and penicillin, the law should presume in favour of the plaintiff that the tortious cause was responsible for the damage."[45]

Novus actus interveniens

This phrase identifies a particular type of causation problem — that   4.33
which arises when another cause (often but not necessarily an act of a third party) results in harm to the pursuer after the defender has breached his duty. For example, Marcel pushes Albertine on to the road where she stumbles and falls. She is then run over by Robert who is driving blindfold. Has Robert's action broken the chain of causation thus relieving Marcel of liability, *i.e.* is it a *novus actus interveniens*?

Generally, there is a presumption against a subsequent act being a   4.34
novus actus. This is because if it is treated as a *nova causa* the original wrongdoer is completely discharged. There are no definite rules of law fixing what is or is not a *novus actus*:

"There are certain propositions that I think are well established and beyond question in connection with this class of case. One is that human action does not per se sever the connected sequence of acts . . . The question is not whether there was new negligence but whether there was a new cause . . . It must always be shown that there is something which I will call ultroneous, something unwarrantable, a new cause coming in disturbing the sequence of events, something that can be described as either unreasonable or extraneous or extrinsic. I doubt very much whether the law can be stated more precisely than that."[46]

The courts take a flexible approach to such questions and the rather   4.35
rigid, last opportunity rule,[47] which ascribed causality to the actor who had the last opportunity to avoid an accident, is only of use as a guide, if at all, to cases where one of the participants is stationary. The proper approach is that taken in *The "Boy Andrew" v. The "St Rognvald"*[48]:

A steamship was doing nine knots trying to overtake a drifter doing eight knots. The ships were apart by a lateral distance of

[45] *per* Lord Griffiths at 581. In the later case of *Wilsher v. Essex Area Health Authority* [1988] 2 W.L.R. 577 the House seemed to go even further in restricting the scope of *McGhee*.
[46] *The Oropesa* [1943] P. 32; 1 All E.R. 214.
[47] *Davies v. Mann* (1842) 10 M. & W. 546.
[48] 1947 S.C. (H.L.) 70.

100 feet. The stern of the steamship was nearly level with the stern of the drifter. The drifter, without warning, made a move to starboard which immediately became a sharp swerve. The master of the steamship gave the order "hard astarboard" and rang the engine room to stop. Unfortunately the drifter was struck aft and 15 feet from the stern killing the whole crew.

What was the cause of the loss of the life? Was it the drifter in turning off its course? Was it the steamship for trying to overtake without leaving the other vessel a wide berth? It was held that both ships' actions were causes of the loss. The last opportunity rule was therefore not applied and said to be of a very limited value. Indeed the next case shows it to be inapplicable even in a case where one of the participants in an accident is not in motion.

4.36   *Rouse v. Squires,*[49] it is submitted, shows the appropriate modern approach.

Mr Allen was driving along a three-lane motorway. His lorry jack-knifed blocking the slow and middle lane. A Morris 1100 collided with it. Mr Rouse, driving his lorry, saw the other vehicle and parked in front of Mr Allen's vehicle to see if assistance was required. Then a Mr Franklin came along and parked at the rear of Mr Allen's lorry so that the light from his headlights could cast some light on the affair. Then Mr Squires came on the scene. He thought the vehicles in front were moving but noticed that the vehicle in the slow lane (Franklin's) was not moving. He moved into the centre lane to find yet another obstruction (the Morris). He tried to avoid the vehicles but skidded, striking the Morris and the lorry. Unfortunately, Mr Allen's jack-knifed lorry then ran forward killing Mr Rouse, who had been standing in front of it.

In the lower court it had been held that the fault was all that of Squires as the obstruction was well enough lit and a driver should have spotted it. The court was really resolving the issue between Squires (the defendant) and Allen (the third-party driver). The Court of Appeal held that if a driver (such as the third-party driver) negligently obstructed a highway and created a danger to other road users then his actings contributed to the causation of an accident of which the immediate cause was the negligent driving of another driver (in this case the defendant) but which would not have occurred but for the continuing danger from the obstruction. Accordingly, while the immediate cause of the accident was the defendant's negligence, there had been no break in the chain of causation between the third party's negligence and the accident and the third-party driver was accordingly one-quarter to blame.

---

[49] [1973] Q.B. 889.

It is open to the court then to find a *novus actus* as a result of the 4.37
actings of a third party and thereby exonerate the defender. At this
stage the inquiry resembles and overlaps the remoteness of injury
question. In short, the intervention of a third party will not operate as
a *novus actus* if it is the very kind of thing that the defender was
supposed to take reasonable care to prevent. The position on this
point is not absolutely clear, particularly as to the degree of likelihood
of the intervention — this, it would seem, is a matter of fact to be left
to the tribunal of fact. Two divisions of the Inner House had taken
fixed and divergent views, one holding that the intervention had to be
very likely, the other that it was sufficient if it were likely.[50] The House
of Lords indicated that the position is more fluid:

> "Unless the judge can be satisfied that the result of the human
> action is highly probable or very likely he may have to conclude
> that all that the reasonable man could say was that it was a mere
> possibility. Unless the needle that measures the probability of a
> particular result flowing from the conduct of a human agent is
> near the top of the scale it may be hard to conclude that it has
> risen sufficiently from the bottom, to create the duty reasonably
> to foresee it."[51]

This leaves the matter quite at large for the fact-finding tribunal. The
broader issues involved in the intervention of third parties are
discussed in the next chapter.

Another aid to flexibility is the Law Reform (Miscellaneous 4.38
Provisions) (Scotland) Act 1940, s. 3, which provides:

> "(1) Where in any action of damages in respect of loss or damage
> arising from any wrongful acts or negligent acts or omissions two
> or more persons are . . . found jointly and severally liable in
> damages or expenses, they shall be liable inter se to contribute to
> such damages or expenses in such proportions as the jury or the
> court . . . may deem just . . .
> (2) Where any person has paid any damages or expenses . . . he
> shall be entitled to recover from any other person who, if sued,
> might also have been held liable in respect of the loss or damage
> on which the action was founded, such contribution, if any, as the
> court may deem just."

The effect of this is to allow the sort of apportionment which was
apparent in *Rouse v. Squires*, above [4.36].

---

[50] *Squires v. Perth & Kinross District Council*, 1986 S.L.T. 30; *Maloco v. Littlewoods
Organisation Ltd*, 1986 S.L.T. 272; and see also *Bell v. Scottish Special Housing
Association*, 1987 S.L.T. 320 and the English case *Maloco (Smith) v. Littlewoods*,
1987 S.L.T. 425, *per* Lord Mackay at 433.

[51] *Maloco (Smith) v. Littlewoods*, 1987 S.L.T. 425, *per* Lord Mackay at 433.

4.39   The pursuer's own actings may be such that he has caused his own loss despite some breach of duty by the defender, and so a claim will fail. This is the result where, for example, a worker does not use or would not have used a safety device which the employer has failed to provide in breach of duty and which the workman alleges would have prevented his injuries.[52] If his conduct falls short of being causative to the exclusion of the defender's liability then it may be sufficient lack of care for his safety to amount to contributory negligence [11.21].

REMOTENESS OF DAMAGE

4.40   Remoteness of damage (as opposed to remoteness of injury) operates throughout the law of damages and is essentially a method of preventing a wrongdoer having to pay for all the results of his wrongdoing. It operates to protect someone in breach of contract as much as someone who has been in breach of a delictual duty. One thing, and possibly only one thing, is clear: the precise rules on remoteness of damage are different in contract and delict.[53] Accordingly, the issue of remoteness of damage in delict can only come into play once it has been established that a legal wrong has taken place, *i.e.* that some loss or injury has occurred.

4.41   An *obiter* remark of Lord Kinloch is often cited in this area. He said:

> "The grand rule on the subject of damages is, that none can be claimed except such as naturally and directly arise out of the wrong done; and such, therefore, as may reasonably be supposed to have been in the view of the wrongdoer."[54]

Although quite pithy, this statement does not set out one clear test. In the first part it espouses a direct and natural consequences test but in the second part it introduces the reasonable foresight of the wrongdoer. As it turns out there has been a long-running controversy as to which test applies and most commentators have favoured one or the other of these approaches, although quite often some hybrid is urged.

4.42   In England particularly the issue has been litigated and the view there has been reached that reasonable foreseeability is the test, except in cases where there is an aggravation of a person's physical condition as a result of the wrong [4.46]. The position is not settled in Scotland

---

[52] *Donaghy v. NCB*, 1957 S.L.T. (Notes) 35.

[53] *Koufos v. Czarnikow* [1969] 1 A.C. 350 ("*The Heron II*"): note the *Heron I* is presumably another ship and not, so far as the author is aware, the subject of any litigation.

[54] *Allan v. Barclay* (1864) 2 M. 873 at 874; for a more recent application see *Runciman v. Borders R.C.*, 1988 S.L.T. 135.

and so the English cases may well be persuasive.[55] What it is important to realise is that the law on liability has itself moved in the course of the twentieth century. Cases such as *Hughes v. Lord Advocate* have restricted the possibility of liability arising at all for especially unforeseeable events.[56] Thus, it is not often that situations will arise where someone would have to rely, as once was the case, on remoteness rules in the event of an unusual occurrence, for that will have been resolved at the preliminary stage of asking whether harm of the kind was reasonably foreseeable.

There have been several cases in Scotland since Lord Kinloch's 4.43 *obiter dictum* but two English cases have to be mentioned. They each involve a high-level discussion of the issues and have become almost a kind of shorthand used by lawyers for the tests used in the cases. The first is *Re Polemis and Furness, Withy and Co. Ltd* (known as "*Polemis*").[57] In this case, a decision of the Court of Appeal, the charterers of a ship had loaded it with, *inter alia*, petrol. While docked at Casablanca, Morocco, servants of the charterers — Arab stevedores — allowed a plank to fall into the hold of the ship, which led to a fire which destroyed the ship. The mechanism of the loss was that the stevedores were negligent (in the sense of not having taken the care of a reasonable stevedore) and dropped a plank. The plank struck something and caused a spark. The spark ignited petrol vapour in the hold. It was expressly held as a fact that the causing of the fire could not reasonably have been anticipated from the falling of the board, though some damage to the ship might reasonably have been anticipated. The arbitrators awarded full damages. The Court of Appeal agreed with them. Warrington L.J. stated:

> "The presence or absence of reasonable anticipation of damage determines the legal quality of an act as negligent or innocent. If it be thus determined to be negligent, then the question whether the particular damages are recoverable depends only on the question whether they are the direct consequence of the act."

It was considered by the Court of Appeal that because the plank could have caused damage, for example, to the cargo, it was sufficient to make the actual damage which had occurred recoverable.

This case is often contrasted with a Privy Council decision in which 4.44 its reasoning was expressly criticised: *Overseas Tankship (U.K.) Ltd v. Morts Dock & Engineering Co.* (known as "*The Wagon Mound (No. 1)*").[58] This case also took place at a dock but this time in

---

[55] In the case of *Lafferty v. Alex Snowie*, 1987 G.W.D. 19–743, it was agreed that the test of remoteness in tort set out in *The Heron II* should apply!

[56] See also *Maloco (Smith) v. Littlewoods*, 1987 S.L.T. 425.

[57] [1921] 3 K.B. 560.

[58] [1961] A.C. 388.

Sydney, Australia. The ship was being loaded with oil. As a result of
the lack of care of the servants of Overseas Tankship, some of the oil
was spilt on to the water. Workmen from Morts were welding. When
the spillage happened, work was suspended for a while but then was
allowed to continue. However, later some molten metal fell from the
wharf and set fire to a piece of rag floating on the oil atop a piece of
debris. The oil caught fire and the whole wharf was engulfed in flames,
resulting in considerable losses. It was found that Overseas Tankship
did not, and could not reasonably be expected to, know that the oil
could be set on fire in such a way. (The oil was particularly thick and in
respect of its flammability quite unlike petrol or paraffin.) It was also
held that some damage had been caused by the oil as a direct
consequence, namely fouling of the wharf slipway, although no
damages were claimed for that.

This finding and these facts squarely raised the issue of remoteness.
The Privy Council allowed an appeal against the full court of the
Supreme Court of Australia which had followed *Polemis*. In so doing,
it effectively, although not formally, overruled *Polemis* and also cast
doubt on the difference between culpability and compensation. One
possible red herring which should be noted is that Viscount Simonds
refers to *Polemis* as having been rejected with determination by the
Scottish courts. Professor Walker[59] points out that that statement is
unwarranted.

4.45   Thus, tension exists between the authorities, although it has to be
said that the law of England seems to have settled for a foreseeability
test.[60] In Scotland the position is not settled and there is some
authority, principally in *Kelvin Shipping Co. v. Canadian Pacific
Ry*[61] that a direct and natural consequences test is appropriate:

> The defenders admitted being responsible for the collision be-
> tween their ship, the *Metagama*, and the pursuers', *Baron Vernon*.
> What they disputed was subsequent damage to the ship. She had
> been tied to the beach at position no. 1 but slipped off and ended
> up on the opposite bank at position no. 2. She was tied up there
> under the supervision of a third party. Later, the *Baron Vernon*
> was carried away by the tide into the navigable channel and sank
> there.

The first thing that has to be said about this decision of the House of
Lords is that it is an example of the sort of remoteness case which can
be dealt with equally as a matter of causation. All three judges

[59] See generally *Delict*, pp. 242–283.
[60] See *Koufos*, above.
[61] Often known by the names of the ships: *Baron Vernon v. Metagama*, 1928 S.C.
(H.L.) 21.

considered the issue of *nova causa*. However, the leading speech of Viscount Haldane includes the following statement:

> "The damage is recoverable . . . if it is the natural and reasonable result of the negligent act, and it will assume this character if it can be shown to be such a consequence as in the ordinary course of things would flow from the situation which the offending ship had created."[62]

This looks like a direct and natural consequences test but again does mention reasonableness.

All that can be said is that almost always the result will be the same in practice no matter what verbal formulation is used and especially so now that the test of liability in negligence involves excluding harm of an unforeseeable kind.

Notwithstanding the controversy over principle sketched above, the law in both jurisdictions adheres to a "thin-skull" rule.[63] This holds that a wrongdoer must take his victim as he finds him. So if harm results which is much worse than would normally naturally be expected, the wrongdoer is still liable. This would apply where, for example, a person slaps a person who, because he has a rare disease, dies instead of merely bruises. The matter was considered (*obiter*)[64] in Scotland in *McKillen v. Barclay Curle & Co. Ltd.*[65] Lord President Clyde denied that foreseeability was relevant and adopted the Lord Kinloch dictum. Lord Guthrie, who came to the same result, also founded on Lord Kinloch's dictum, and seems to have been of the view that even if foreseeability were an issue, it would, in the "thin-skull" cases, be irrelevant: "There is no ground for holding that a reasonable man would have assumed that the pursuer had a sound pair of lungs."[66] The spectrum is complete with Lord Migdale, who also accepted Lord Kinloch's dictum but expressly rejected *Polemis* and adopted a test of reasonable foreseeability. He came to the same result as the others because the defender "ought to have had in contemplation that his victim might be a sickly person whose health was such that a fall would start off complications which would not be likely to afflict a person in normal health."[67] For him, personal injuries cases are an exception to the applicable *Wagon Mound* rule. Lord Cameron said nothing of relevance to the dispute but

4.46

---

[62] at 25.

[63] For England, see *Smith v. Leech Brain & Co.* [1962] 2 Q.B. 405, an exception to *Wagon Mound*; and *Thurogood v. Van den Berghs and Jurgens* [1951] 2 K.B. 537.

[64] *Obiter* because there was a failure to establish causation by medical evidence.

[65] 1967 S.L.T. 41, and see *Gilchrist v. D.B. Marshall (Newbridge) Ltd*, 1991 S.L.T. 842.

[66] at 44.

[67] at 45.

took the view that Lord Kinloch's dictum was the beginning and end of the matter.

4.47   Lord Cameron applied a "natural and direct consequences" test to allow a proof before answer of a claim of the loss of opportunity to participate in a redundancy scheme, suggesting some small East-coast judicial support for what is sometimes called "the West of Scotland heresay" of pro-*Polemis* thinking.[68]

Further reading

Bates, F., "What must be foreseen?" 1970 S.L.T. (News) 97.

Davies, M., "The Road from Morocco: *Polemis, Donoghue*, No Fault" (1982) 45 M.L.R. 534.

Fleming, J.G., "Tort in a Contractual Matrix" (1995) 3 Tort L. Rev. 12.

Kidner, R., "Resiling from the *Anns* principle: the variable nature of proximity in negligence" (1987) 7 L.S. 319.

Kidner, R., "Remoteness of Damage: the Duty Interest Theory and the Re-interpretation of *The Wagon Mound*", 1989 L.S. 1.

McBryde, W.W., "*Bourhill v. Young*: The Case of the Pregnant Fishwife" in *Comparative and Historical Essays in Scots Law* (Carey Miller and Meyers, eds, Butterworth, 1992), p. 66.

McKenzie, D.W. and Evans-Jones, R., "The Development of Remedies for Personal Injuries and Death" in *The Civilian Tradition in Scots Law* (Evans-Jones, ed., Stair Soc., 1995).

Mullany, N.J., "Common-sense Causation – An Australian View", 1992 O.J.L.S. 431.

Rodger, A., "Mrs Donoghue and Alfenus Varrus", 1988 C.L.P. 1.

Walker, D.M., "Remoteness of Damage and *Re Polemis*", 1961 S.L.T. (News) 37.

Walker, E.D., "Reflections on a Leading Case: *Hughes v. Lord Advocate*" (1992) 37 J.L.S.S. 394.

Wright, "Causation in Tort Law" (1985) 73 Cal. L. Rev. 1735.

---

[68] *Campbell v. F. & F. Moffat (Transport) Ltd*, 1992 S.L.T. 962, albeit that the authority referred to was *Allan v. Barclay* (above).

Chapter 5

LIABILITY FOR UNINTENTIONAL HARM II: DIFFICULT TOPICS

In this chapter consideration is given to some topics which do not fit 5.1 neatly into the outline account given in the last chapter. There are two objectives. First, to consider topics which have in the past, or still do, raise difficult questions as to the existence of a duty of care. Usually these topics are difficult because they involve some element of policy. Secondly, the opportunity is taken to mention special rules which apply to some of the topics under consideration. However, they are not really all that difficult at all. Students and some practitioners find economic loss in particular awesome. The learning in the judgments and the volume of academic literature contribute to this feeling. The secret is not to panic and to relax. There is no answer—the student and the practitioner can only know the cases[1] and formulate arguments and the judge need only, for his part, referee. The House of Lords which has in recent years appointed itself not so much a court of last resort as the ultimate seminar room troubles itself over these issues far too much. The best thing that has come out of the last decade or two is the cross-citation of cases from each of these enclaves of the law (and others). That is most conducive to justice so far as treating like cases alike. But if it is necessary to achieve a synthesis after the analysis then it will be heavy going indeed—as, it shall be seen, it has been.

It has become harder in this edition to separate liability for 5.2 professional conduct and economic loss; because professional liability is a hybrid problem encompassing economic loss duty and standard issues it is now better dealt with at the end after the five other topics which are essentially duty matters.[2] One case has necessitated the creation of a new category of difficult case. Treating this as a new category effectively means taking a position on the case: the main difficulty is that the restrictive nature of the decision is not

---

[1] Note for student—if you do not know the cases, panic and do not relax.
[2] Pedagogically it was better treated as a whole for some business law students but they must now carefully consider the entire economic loss section.

universally appreciated. The order of treatment is as follows. (1) Economic loss—because reasonable foreseeability does not provide the test of liability and because the rules as they stand are not capable of a simple single principled exposition. (2) Nervous shock because historically it has tested the law of negligence and remarkably still does. The present rules also require a more extensive exposition than any broad statement of principle would allow. Foreseeability is not the simple test here either. (3) Liability of defenders who, although not protected by immunity, while they are perhaps amenable to private law, are also characters in public law. Here, foreseeability is again not the sole test and the rules applicable require fuller exposition. (4) Cases of intervention of other parties are apparently not so exciting but the issue of foreseeability is tested and there are issues of policy and theory at stake. Depending on the view taken there may be some more special rules to appreciate. (5) Indirect physical damage. (6) Professional liability is a hybrid. There are special rules about the standard of care. There is a special immunity for one profession. The economic loss cases have applied to professions and professional cases have extended the economic loss jurisprudence. Where possible the duty issues are dealt with under the economic loss section.

It would be possible to have another section on pre-personality cases. It is possible, and it has been the case, that actions raised by, or on behalf of or derived from a foetus can be so treated. However, it is still the case that these are usually dealt with by the courts either under the appropriate section of the Damages (Scotland) Act 1976 or as "title to sue" matters and they are so dealt with in this book.

ECONOMIC LOSS

5.3 When delicts and torts were first growing wealth was in land and in the person's ability to sell his labour. So the law had delicts and torts that protected land and the person. The shift of wealth to contract and to capital is a shift to the less tangible. While a contract may be written on paper it need not be and its worth can be more than the largest estate. The ostensible castle may be mortgaged to the turret and the shares in the company holding that mortgage worth more than the castle. Other aspects of life begin to seek protection. The other pressure is that negligence as a ground of liability has caught on. Once lack of care is actionable in many situations it is then asked why should it matter what the loss is? Once people are being made to pay for their bungles they should pay for them all. I break the tip of your little finger by accident and I have to pay; what if I accidentally ruin you by giving you poor advice? In one case the loss is bearable although—strictly speaking and for the ancient Romans—irreparable, whereas the other is reparable simply by paying money. Yet the law baulks.

Now we turn to the rules and themes and "principles" to see what the law says. The present writer does not consider that the law has yet "settled", regardless of what the House of Lords has said, and so to state the law as it is or will be in the next big case requires not a dogmatic statement of a view or any particular dicta but, so far as is in keeping with the concise mission of the text, an exposition of the rules and themes and such principles as have emerged.

TYPES OF CASES

The law quite happily awards damages for what could be called   5.4
economic loss in many cases. What is easily compensated is a person's loss of wages while he is injured, or the loss of use of an item while it is being repaired. These are economic losses but losses which are well recognised as beyond dispute. The law has no difficulty with such claims because they are closely derived from previously legally recognised interests—a person is injured or property damaged and other losses follow. Such consequential loss is quite easily and reasonably foreseeable and likely to be limited to an amount of money bearing some proportional relationship to the person or thing damaged.

After that the law scatters and principle is difficult to synthesise. It is possible to detect two sets of cases which may or may not reflect some form of complex principle—they do offer predictive value.[3] There are then other cases! For the purposes of this concise exercise it is hoped that no serious injustice is done to the complexity of the subject if these are treated as follows:

(1) *Hedley Byrne* liability (assumption of liability/special relationship cases).
(2) *Simpson v. Thomson* bright line non-liability cases (economic loss derived from non-pursuer).
(3) *Henderson v. Merrit* liability (expanded *Hedley Byrne* liability).
(4) *White v. Jones* liability.

---

[3] I am obliged to Wilkinson and Forte's article at 1985 J.R. 1 which clearly identified for me at least these two lines of cases. Students should still find the article helpful once they have surveyed the main cases. Two other key analytical articles which will help with the current law are Hogg, "Relational Loss, the Exclusory Rule and the High Court of Australia" (1995) 3 Tort L. Rev. 26; Cane, "Contract Tort and the Lloyd's Debacle" in *Consensus in Idem* (Oxford, 1996).

1. *Hedley Byrne* liability (assumption of liability/special relationship cases)

5.5   The foundation case, as important as *Donoghue*, is *Hedley Byrne & Co. Ltd v. Heller and Partners*.[4] It established that there could be liability for a negligent mis-statement and at the same time clarified a number of other matters.

> The plaintiffs were a firm of advertising consultants. They booked advertising for clients on the basis that they (*Hedley Byrne*) themselves would be contractually liable to the advertiser. Accordingly, it was important for them to make inquiry into the credit-worthiness of their customers. In this case they did so by contacting their own bankers, who in turn contacted the defenders, who were the bankers of the client company, Easipower. In reply the defendants said Easipower were believed to be "respectably constituted and considered good for its normal business engagements" and that it "would not undertake any commitments they were unable to fulfil." A later inquiry obtained a similar response by letter with a statement that the letter was "without responsibility"

The actual decision in the case was that there should be no recovery because of the effect of the disclaimer in the letter but that decision implied that the court accepted the following propositions:

> (1) There can be liability for words as much as for deeds.
> (2) Despite the absence of a contract there can be liability in respect of negligent mis-statements if a special relationship exists.
> (3) There can be recovery for a pure economic loss even where it does not arise from damage to the pursuer's property.

5.6   It is the existence or otherwise of this special relationship that filters cases out. Not every loss through a mis-statement will attract liability. Whether or not a special relationship exists will depend on each case. Sometimes this will be very obvious, especially if there is an existing relationship such as in the case of solicitor and client. But *Hedley Byrne* is authority for recognising a non-contractual special relationship where two factors are present:

> (1) the pursuer reasonably relies on the statement made by the defender, and
> (2) it was reasonable that the defender should know that the pursuer would rely on the statement.

It is this element of reliance which allowed the disclaimer to be effective. At the very time the statement was made there was a

[4] [1964] A.C. 465.

disclaimer made which would prevent the reasonable man in the position of the recipient taking advantage of it. The relevance of this formulation of the duty of care to the professions is that quite often they will exhibit or profess a certain skill and in so doing will almost automatically engender reliance.

In the many years that have passed this case has been interpreted 5.7 and reinterpreted. Following *Yuen Kun Yeu*[5] it was, and sometimes still is, interpreted more from the defender's point of view, the question asked being simply, "Has the defender assumed responsibility for the statement complained of?"

It should be added here, parenthetically, that doubts that *Hedley Byrne* might not extend to Scotland or that it might be restricted to certain particular trades or professions were set aside by the case of *Martin v. Bell-Ingram*,[6] which both established *Hedley Byrne* liability in Scotland and made it clear that surveyors could be liable to persons other than those who instructed them. Surveyors in that case were held liable to a disappointed purchaser who bought on the basis of the survey and found that he had purchased a property worth far less than the surveyor had indicated. The complicating factor had been the fact that the survey had been prepared on the instructions of the building society who were lending money to the purchaser, not the purchaser himself. There was no contract and so only delict could provide a remedy. Liability was established on the basis that a reasonable purchaser would rely on the report given to the lender. In *Martin* a disclaimer was issued, just as in *Hedley Byrne*,[7] except the disclaimer came in writing after the initial mis-statement and after the pursuer had suffered his loss by contracting to buy the house. The disclaimer was held ineffective.

This idea of the foreseeability of the mis-stator that the statement would be relied upon by the actual pursuer harmed reached the House of Lords in *Caparo Industries plc v. Dickman*[8]:

> Accountants were auditors to a company. There are statutory requirements for such an audit. The plaintiffs alleged that on the basis of the accounts they bought more shares and took over the company. The accounts, they alleged, were negligently prepared and they suffered loss.

---

[5] [1988] W.L.R. 175; and see also *Rowling v. Takaro Properties Ltd* [1988] 2 W.L.R. 418; and *D. & F. Estates Ltd v. Church Commissioners for England* [1988] 3 W.L.R. 368.

[6] 1986 S.L.T. 575.

[7] *Harris v. Wyre Forest D.C.* [1988] 2 W.L.R. 1173 and on appeal [1989] 2 W.L.R. 790. See also Stewart, "Ten Years of Fair Contracts in Scotland?" 1987 S.L.T. (News) 361; "Fifteen Years of Fair Contracts in Scotland?" 1993 S.L.T. (News) 15.

[8] [1990] 1 All E.R. 568; see the discussion and application of the case in *Al Nakib Investments v. Longcroft* [1990] 3 All E.R. 321 and in the Scottish case *Bank of Scotland v. 3i plc*, 1992 G.W.D. 6–321.

The House of Lords held that there was no duty of care between the accountants and potential purchasers of shares. The accountants owed a duty to the shareholders as members of the company to prepare the accounts properly to the extent that the shareholders could utilise the accounts to judge the health of their company; they did not owe a duty to potential purchasers of shares. The difficulty of this distinction can be illustrated by the example of the shareholder who sells his shares as a result of wrongly prepared accounts. Lord Bridge distinguished the two types of investment decision in such a way that, although not decided, the case of sale might be decided differently. If specific representations are made to a potential acquirer with the intent to induce reliance then a case is statable on the basis of this proximity, the potential pursuer being identifiable.[9]

In yet another reformulation the Court of Appeal laid down some marks for cases such as these, the following factors being significant:

    (1) the purpose for which the statement was made;
    (2) the purpose for which it was communicated;
    (3) the relationship between the parties;
    (4) the size of any class to which the person receiving the advice belonged;
    (5) the state of knowledge of the adviser;
    (6) reliance by the person in receipt of the advice.[10]

5.8   The high point of liability based on *Hedley Byrne* is measured by a Scottish case, *Junior Books v. The Veitchi Co.*[11]

> The pursuers, who owned a factory, entered into a contract with Ogilvie (Builders) Ltd for the laying of a floor in the production area. Ogilvie sub-contracted to the Veitchi Co. as specialist sub-contractors. Junior Books sued for the losses due to bad workmanship which they said resulted in them obtaining a floor which was defective, although not dangerous, and which would involve expense in being put right.

Lord Fraser summarised the legal issue:

> "The appeal raises an important question on the law of delict, . . . which is not precisely covered by authority . . . whether the appellants having . . . negligently laid a floor which is defective, but which has not caused danger to the health or safety of any person nor risk of damage to any other property belonging to

---

[9] *Morgan Crucible Co. plc v. Hill Samuel* [1991] 1 All E.R. 148.
[10] *James McNaughton Paper Group Ltd v. Hicks Anderson & Co.* [1991] 1 All E.R. 134; see also *Grampian Regional Council v. Cowan & Linn*, 1989 S.L.T. 787.
[11] 1982 S.L.T. 492.

the owner of the floor, may in the circumstances . . . be liable for the economic loss caused to them by having to replace the floor."

This case has been much analysed and discussed. It raised a very large number of points, the most important of which can be set out as follows:

(1) Is there liability for carelessly done work which will fore-seeably cause economic loss as a result of its defective condition?
(2) Is there a difference between houses and goods?
(3) Is the fact that the defender has or may have contractual exemptions a relevant factor in formulating his duty to the pursuer who was not a party to the contract?

The answers given in the case were: (1) yes, in certain circumstances but not by any means all; (2) yes; (3) possibly, but the point did not require to be decided.

These answers decided very little save the point in the case, 5.9 particularly because of the terms of the leading speech. However, the attitude to the first and primary question made and makes the case of the first significance. In achieving that positive answer, considerable doubt was again cast upon the floodgates argument: that if the case were successful there might be, in Cardozo's phrase, "liability in an indeterminate amount for an indeterminate time to an indeterminate class." Rejecting those fears both Lord Fraser and Lord Roskill were in accord with the view of Lord Wilberforce in the nervous shock case *McLoughlin* [5.26]. In addition, for Lord Roskill, Lord Wilberforce's dictum in *Anns* [4.18, 5.31], now considered to be overstated and infelicitously so, was of help in indicating when a duty might be established—the two main indicators being proximity and foresee-ability. Lord Russell concurred.

Answers (2) and (3) above can be seen in the speeches of the "nearly dissenter" Lord Keith and the "dissent" of Lord Brandon of Oak-brook. Lord Keith agreed with the majority decision, but expressed considerable reservations. First, he considered that the case could not and should not be used to develop a liability for defective products generally; and secondly, he agreed with Lord Brandon that there might be difficulties in formulating the duty of care where there are exemption clauses in the contract under which the work is done initially. Lord Brandon dissented and would have allowed the appeal resulting in the case being dismissed. The majority refused the appeal and allowed the case to proceed to a proof before answer.

The decision is clearly right and is so on the expressed basis, that of the proximity of the parties. That is little justification for it depends upon what is meant by proximity. That inquiry, for the majority, is essentially a relational, factual matter. Lord Roskill came to his conclusion based on eight points of proximity which included factors such as that the potential pursuer was known precisely by the defender and that the pursuer relied upon the defender and that the defender was aware the pursuer was relying upon him.[12]

5.10   The case was quickly taken up by litigants and almost as quickly denounced by commentators and courts.[13] It was called a damage to property case, which clearly it was not.[14] It was said to depend very largely on its own facts, said (with respect rather exaggeratedly) to be unique, and unable to lay down any principle in the law of delict.[15] It has been suggested that the House succumbed too easily to a proximity test.[16] However, the case is now even more secure than it has been in view of the decision in *Henderson* noted below.[17]

The scope of cases falling within the arguments relating to primary economic loss has expanded because the House of Lords correctly reclassified certain losses as economic losses rather than damage to property cases. In *D. & F. Estates v. Church Commissioners*[18]:

> plaster was incorrectly applied by sub-contractors (Hitchins) to a wall. The court at first instance held the main contractor (Wates) liable for a series of losses resulting from the defect.

Both the Court of Appeal and the House of Lords disagreed. The loss was held to be pure economic loss which is not itself recoverable under *Donoghue*. That was correct. In another landmark case, *Murphy v. Brentwood District Council*,[19] the House of Lords departed from *Anns* on the fundamental question of the duty owed by a local authority and this aspect of the case is dealt with below [5.31–5.39].[20] The importance of the case in this context is that it firmly established a line between economic loss and physical damage. A building which falls down and causes damage is dangerous and covered by *Donoghue v. Stevenson*. The collapse of the building is not actionable damage under *Donoghue* because it does not damage other property; it is damage to the thing-in-

---

[12] *Casebook*, Ext. 41 and para. 12.3.20.

[13] See, generally, Logie, "The Final Demise of *Junior Books*", 1989 J.R. 5 (*Casebook*, Ext. 42).

[14] *Tate & Lyle Foods v. Greater London Council* [1983] 2 A.C. 509.

[15] *D. & F. Estates v. Church Commissioners* [1988] 3 W.L.R. 368, *per* Lord Bridge.

[16] *Maloco v. Littlewoods Organisation Ltd*, 1987 S.L.T. 425, *per* Lord Goff.

[17] See 5.46. For a recent Scottish consideration after *Henderson*, see the valuable discussion of recent authorities in *Strathford East Kilbride Ltd v. HLM Design Ltd*, 1997 Rep. L.R. 112, decided on the basis of an absence of an assumption of liability.

[18] [1988] 3 W.L.R. 368.

[19] [1990] 3 W.L.R. 414. *Al-Nakib Investments v. Longcroft* [1990] 3 All E.R. 321.

[20] The decision was instantly applied to the case of a builder: *Department of the Environment v. T. Bates Ltd* [1990] 3 W.L.R. 457. This case was argued before *Murphy* but decided immediately after it.

itself. The error in *Anns*, which itself originated in the judgment of Lord Denning in *Dutton v. Bognor Regis UDC*,[21] was to say that imminent danger to health or safety meant that money spent in preventing such was recoverable under *Donoghue* as preventing physical injury.

In an independent development the doctrine has shown its strength 5.11 in the overall picture of the law in the House of Lords decision in *Spring v. Guardian Assurance plc*[22] in which by a 4–1 majority it was held that the *Hedley Byrne* principle applied to an employment reference notwithstanding that if the case had been brought in defamation a defence of qualified privilege could have been run successfully. Abbreviating the facts, the plaintiff was unsuccessful in gaining employment because of a bad reference—a kiss of death. As a result of inadequate investigation into the material in the reference, information had been given which was untrue. The economic loss caused was reasonably foreseeable and so *Hedley Byrne* was applicable. This decision was arrived at notwithstanding the long-standing rule in the law of defamation that references were entitled to qualified privilege. *Spring* has been applied in Scotland by the Inner House.[23]

Fair, just and reasonable

Anns had been used by teachers, students, practitioners and judges 5.12 for some time as a guide at least. An important court full of jurists, removing that guide, had to offer something else. The answer was based on some efforts that had been canvassed in other cases: in cases of new duties—like those to take care not to cause economic losses—it has to be fair, just and reasonable to impose a duty. This test is now extensively used. As noted in the preceding chapter, it was applied in a physical damage case, *Marc Rich*, and the implications of that are dealt with below [5.44]. However, while in a new type of primary economic loss case it might be appropriate to consider this test, a case falling within *Hedley Byrne* does not require such an exercise.

Excursus: disclaimers

The actual decision in *Hedley Byrne* was that the disclaimer prevented 5.13 actionable reliance. That is perfectly in accord with principle. Until I say "put all your money on black, the odds of winning are 100–1 in your favour"[24] I have no liability at all as your roulette adviser. If I then say at the same time, "but I don't accept any liability for saying that", there seems to be a symmetrical justice about denying the person relying on the advice and suing for it. It was generally considered that disclaimers would

---

[21] [1972] 1 Q.B. 373.
[22] [1995] 2 A.C. 296.
[23] *Donlon v. Colonial Mutual Group (U.K. Holdings)*, 1997 S.C.L.R. 1088.
[24] Note for the uninitiated—the odds are evens, so the advice is bad.

usually work and that is still the starting point. As explained above in discussing the *Martin* case, the disclaimer has to come into the transaction as close to the roulette example as possible to be potentially effective in preventing reliance—if it comes after reliance ('faites vos jeux, s'il vous plaît, messieurs, mesdames'), it is too late.

Parliament decided some time ago that some disclaimers of liability had to be prevented or prohibited under the Unfair Contract Terms Act 1977. As the name suggests, this was about contract rather than delict but contracts can exclude delictual liability. The English provisions clearly covered non-contractual disclaimers but it did not appear that the Scottish provisions did so too. Lord Weir in *Robbie v. Graham & Sibbald*,[25] expressed regret that he had no control over the disclaimers in the case as would have been the case if the English provisions applied. The Act was amended by the Law Reform (Miscellaneous Provisions) (Scotland) Act 1990.[26] The Act now applies to matters other than contracts and covers notices and disclaimers. It must be fair and reasonable to rely on the provision. The time at which this is tested is the time when the liability arose or would apart from the notice or disclaimer have arisen.[27]

The House of Lords in two joined English cases analysed the issues and rejected the view that disclaimers can completely destroy a duty arising at all and thus prevent the possibility of applying the Unfair Contract Terms Act 1977.[28]

2. *Simpson v. Thomson* bright line non-liability cases (economic loss derived from non-pursuer)

5.14   Wilkinson and Forte identified this category of case[29]:

> "By secondary, or derivative loss is meant loss which arises as a consequence of physical injury to the person or property of another [*i.e.* someone other than the pursuer]."

Scots law had for a long time refused to allow damages in delict for an economic loss resulting from a person's contractual losses—that is, losses which are losses because the pursuer has the right to another person's services or another person's property. So it had been held that an employer could not recover for the loss of his employee's services when

---

[25]   1989 S.L.T. 870.

[26]   See *Casebook*, Ext. 95 and para. 12.2.5.

[27]   See *Melrose v. Davidson & Robertson*, 1992 S.L.T. 395, on appeal 1993 S.L.T. 611 for a case where it was held that the unamended Act could control terms in a contract to which the party complaining was a party but the party complained against was not (that party being sued and being the beneficiary of the exclusion).

[28]   By then applying the Act it was possible for a disclaimer not to apply in relation to advice concerning the purchase of a dwelling as opposed to a commercial transaction: *Smith v. Eric S. Bush* and *Harris v. Wyre Forrest D.C.* [1989] 2 W.L.R. 790.

[29]   1985 J.R. 1 at p. 8.

he had been injured by the defender.[30] The House of Lords refused to allow recovery where a person suffered loss as a result of damage to property but where the pursuer did not own that property.[31]

The decisions in *Donoghue* and *Hedley Byrne* obviously required 5.15 that rule to be reconsidered for it was clear after *Hedley Byrne* that there was no absolute rule against the recovery of pecuniary loss. Such a reconsideration took place in *Dynamco Ltd v. Holland, Hannen and Cubitts (Scotland) Ltd.*[32]

> Occupiers of a factory raised an action against contractors who were working nearby and had cut the electricity cable leading to the factory. The claim was one for a purely financial loss on the ground that the plant was unable to operate for over 15 hours. The cable belonged to the SSEB.

The court preferred to follow a traditional analysis, expressing the view that even if a duty of care did exist, the loss was too remote. While this may be satisfactory, it is submitted that the court did not fully take into account cases like *Donoghue* and *Hedley Byrne* which bring into the duty question all or most of the limiting factors. The same result obtained in a substantially similar English case, *Spartan Steel & Alloys Ltd v. Martin & Co. (Contractors) Ltd.*[33]

The same process of cross-argument took place in England bringing 5.16 about an unsuccessful challenge in which the non-recovery rule was supported.[34] The decision in *Anns*, among other cases, brought two successful challenges at first instance suggesting that the distinction between economic losses might collapse.[35] By the time the secondary economic loss issue came to the House of Lords the reaction to *Junior Books* and Lord Wilberforce's dictum in *Anns* (discussed above) had begun to set in. The bright line non-recovery rule in secondary economic loss was re-emphasised and further entrenched in *Leigh and Sillivan Ltd v. Aliakmon Shipping Co. Ltd.*[36] The legal background

---

[30]   *Allan v. Barclay* (1864) 2 M. 873 and *Reavis v. Clan Line Steamers*, 1925 S.L.T. 538. The point is still being (unsuccessfully) argued: *D'Amato v. Badger* [1996] D.L.R. (4th) 129.

[31]   *Simpson & Co. v. Thomson* (1877) 5 R. (H.L.) 40.

[32]   1972 S.L.T. 38.

[33]   [1973] Q.B. 27. Ironically, in a recent cable case it is arguable there was far too much reanalysis of basic principles: *Coleridge v. Miller*, 1997 S.L.T. 487.

[34]   *Margarine Union GmbH v. Cambay Prince Steamship Co.* [1969] 1 Q.B. 219 (*The Wear Breeze*).

[35]   *Schiffahrt & Kohlen GmbH v. Chelsea Maritime Ltd (The Irene's Success)* [1982] Q.B. 481 (now overruled); *The Nea Tyhi* [1982] 1 Lloyd's Rep. 606 (*obiter*) (now disapproved).

[36]   [1986] 2 W.L.R. 902. The actual law applicable to cases like this one and those cited above, nn. 34e35, has to be read against the repeal of the Bills of Lading Act 1855 and its replacement by the Carriage of Goods by Sea Act 1992—a measure introduced to the Lords by Lord Goff of Chieveley based on a report of the Law Commissions.

was extremely complicated and depends upon a good knowledge of the law relating to the carriage of goods by sea or at least the law of sale of goods. Suffice it to say that normally the risk (the economic burden) of accidental destruction of property passes from the seller to the buyer when ownership passes. Under the Sale of Goods Act 1979 there is no need to transfer the goods to transfer ownership. Commercial dealers will therefore make sure they do not carry the risk or will obtain insurance cover. In *Aliakmon*, due to some alterations being made in a complex contract, the net effect of these was that buyers of a cargo of steel coils did not acquire property nor a possessory title to the goods. The goods were damaged due to the negligence of the shipowners or their servants. The effect of this was that the plaintiffs fell within the aforementioned authorities which stated that there was no right to sue for a loss as a result of damage to property if the plaintiff did not own the property or have a similar proprietary title to it at the time it was damaged. Despite the precedent against the plaintiffs, they argued that the cases like *Hedley Byrne*, *Anns*, and *Junior Books* had so changed the law that the old cases should be ignored and the plaintiffs should recover from the parties who caused the loss. The unanimous decision of the House of Lords was to refuse the claim. Lord Brandon, who had dissented in *Junior Books*, made the only reasoned speech. Passing over *Junior Books* as not being in point, he held that the policy of the law had been to refuse such claims and this generated certainty in the law which is of value to commerce. He pointed out that cases where this problem arose were unusual.

However, the urge to do justice between the parties where there appears to be no water behind the floodgates continues and the right to recover was allowed in a case heard after *Aliakmon* where the pursuer was the hirer of a helicopter.[37] In yet another case a proof before answer was allowed in respect of damage done to mussels. However, it appears that the case is right on the border, for the pursuers had no property in the mussels until settled on ropes. Their loss, at least to some extent, was to their contractual right to be able to attract mussel larvae.[38] In another case (Inner House), no recovery was allowed where the damage was done to a pipe owned by a third party, upon which the pursuers were working, and for which they were contractually responsible.[39] These decisions turn on the interpretation of an *obiter dictum* of Lord Penzance which stated that an action could

---

[37] *United Technologies Corp. Inc. v. North Scottish Helicopters Ltd*, 1988 S.L.T. 77; and (*No. 2*) at 778.

[38] *Mull Shellfish Ltd v. Golden Sea Produce Ltd*, 1992 S.L.T. 703.

[39] *Nacap Ltd v. Moffat Plant Ltd*, 1987 S.L.T. 221. See Young, "Rights of Relief", 1992 S.L.T. (News) 225 for comment on the use of assignation in such cases.

only be raised by someone having ownership of or possession of the property—for example, a lien or hypothec.[40]

In secondary economic loss cases involving one item of damaged   5.17 property where the only reason the case becomes an economic loss case is the separation of property from risk, there is a way of allowing the wrongdoer to compensate the victim without opening any floodgates. The control is the principle of transferred loss enunciated by Goff L.J. (as he then was) in the Court of Appeal decision in *Aliakmon*.[41] It is as follows:

> "There is a recognisable principle underlying the imposition of liability, which can be called the principle of transferred loss. Furthermore, that principle can be formulated. For the purposes of the present case, I would formulate it in the following deliberately narrow terms, while recognising that it may require modification in the light of experience. Where A owes a duty of care in tort not to cause physical damage to B's property, and commits a breach of that duty in circumstances in which the loss of or physical damage to the property will ordinarily fall on B but (as is reasonably foreseeable by A) such loss or damage by reason of a contractual relationship between B and C, falls upon C, then C will be entitled, subject to the terms of any contract restricting A's liability to B, to bring an action in tort against A in respect of such loss or damage to the extent that it falls on him, C."

This argument failed in the House of Lords in *Aliakmon*, which is unfortunate because it seems to be a sensible rule that would not distort the law.

In other jurisdictions the *Hedley Byrne, Junior Books, Anns* ap-   5.18 proach has swept into these secondary cases. In *Caltex Oil Ltd v. The Dredge Willemstad*[42]:

> the dredger negligently broke a pipeline owned by the Australian Oil Refining Ltd which crossed Botany Bay. Caltex sued for the extra cost of having to transport oil around the bay.

They were held entitled to recover. The basis was that there was no floodgates fear in this case because those in charge of the dredger knew whose pipe it was and where it went—it was not like a general electricity cable. There were many other factors, one of the most significant being that the skipper of the dredger was given a chart showing the pipe so that he might avoid it. Put another way, the class

---

[40] In *Simpson & Co. v. Thomson* (1877) 5 R. (H.L.) 40.
[41] [1985] Q.B. 350 at 399, quoted by Lord Brandon of Oakbrook in [1986] 2 W.L.R. 902 at 917.
[42] (1976/77) 136 C.L.R. 529, known both as the *Caltex* case and as *The Willemstad*.

of possible plaintiffs was ascertainable and not general. This case was not followed in this country when it could have been in *Aliakmon*, having been disposed of as virtually without a *ratio decidendi* by Lord Fraser in *The Mineral Transporter; Candlewood Navigation Corp. Ltd v. Mitsui Lines.*[43]

5.19   The Supreme Court of Canada, too, has relaxed. In *Norsk Pacific Steamship Co. Ltd v. Canadian National Ry*[44]:

> a tug, *The Jervis Crown*, owned by the defendants, was towing a barge down the Fraser River when, through its admitted care-lessness, it collided with and damaged the New Westminster Railway Bridge. The bridge was owned by Public Works Canada and used by four railway companies including the plaintiffs, Canadian National Railway. The railway company sued for costs incurred because of the closure of the bridge.

The plaintiffs' case was upheld by the Supreme Court.[45] The basis was the proximity. The trial judge's finding of proximity, based on a checklist not unlike that of Lord Roskill in *Junior Books*, was upheld. While some of the dicta adopt a reasoning wider than that of *Caltex*, the basis is very similar—that of the identifiability of the plaintiff. Again, in this case the defendant actually knew the plaintiff would suffer loss by his carelessness.[46]

3. *Henderson v. Merrit* liability

5.20   This is founded on *Hedley Byrne* to the extent that it would never have happened without it. The case was between Lloyds names and those whom they said had negligently caused them to lose on their Lloyds investment.[47] Superficially the scheme operates by the "name" agreeing to be responsible to an unlimited amount, being worth a certain sum and depositing a fraction of it. Normally this was easy money and becoming a Lloyds name carried a cachet. Bad weather in the United States and large damages claims—ironically probably based on tort—brought about enormous losses. The names case, at its most honourable, was that they did not mind losing but the way their involvement was handled by their agents and sub-agents was negligent—lacking all care for their

---

[43] [1986] A.C. 1.

[44] (1992) 91 D.L.R. (4th) 289.

[45] Albeit by a 4–3 decision.

[46] Lord McLean considered, it is submitted unnecessarily, that the *Murphy* departure from *Anns* meant that in cases not covered by the ratio of *Murphy*, commonwealth authority including *Norsk* should not be considered: *Strathford East Kilbride v. HLM Design*, 1997 S.C.L.R. 877 at 887A.

[47] The background is very complex and there have been exponential developments: see Cave, P. "Contract, Tort and the Lloyd's Débâcle" in *Consensus ad Idem* (Rose ed., Sweet & Maxwell, 1996), p.5.

interests. Liability was established on the basis of *Hedley Byrne* but on at least one view[48] went a step further by accepting that liability extended to careless or dilatory omissions as well as to careless acts. It imposes liability for the underlying professional conduct rather than any particular manifestation of it in words. It accordingly helps justify the decision in *Junior Books*.

4. *White v. Jones* liability

A says he wants to leave his money to P (ursuer). His lawyer 5.21 D (efender) goes and leaves it to B. A dies. B gets the money. P finds out. In *White v. Jones*[49] D had to pay P. How does this fit into the main division into two categories of case? It simply does not and attempts to do so make any theoretical framework impossible.

This is not an obvious economic loss case because there has economically been no loss—the same money exists in the pursuer's hands at the end of the story as at the start. No one is out of pocket. *Hedley Byrne* cannot apply save by extension. It is thus quite clear that it was necessary for the decision that the defendants were solicitors and if there were no imposition of liability the bunglers would get off.

Excursus: a statutory case

There is a statutory intervention which allows the recovery of an 5.22 economic loss—the Administration of Justice Act 1982, ss 7 to 10, which provide that services rendered to an injured person by a relative, unless it is expressly agreed that no sum shall be payable, will be a head of loss allowing recovery of reasonable remuneration and repayment of reasonable expenses. This Act reversed the common law.[50] However, the title to sue approach is respected by refusing the relative who suffers the economic loss title to sue. Instead the loss is recovered in a claim made by the injured person, who is placed under an obligation to account to the person suffering the loss. This, incidentally, is an example of how procedure can remedy some of the concerns on some economic loss cases. One of the worries is that if a non-owner is compensated, the wrongdoer can be met with a double liability if later sued by an owner, an example being *Blackburn v. Sinclair*.[51] The 1982 Act offers one model and the Damages (Scotland) Act 1976 another. A Rule of Court which ordained a person claiming secondary economic loss to aver the identity of the owner at the time of the

---

[48] That of Lord Mustill (dissenting) in *White v. Jones*.
[49] [1995] 2 A.C. 207.
[50] *Robertson v. Turnbull*, 1982 S.L.T. 96.
[51] 1984 S.L.T. 368 (*Casebook*, Ext. 96).

damage and to show evidence of intimation of proceedings might meet some of the worries of those who oppose the recovery of economic loss in cases where another person's property is damaged.

NERVOUS SHOCK

5.23 Nervous shock is a medical condition. It is something different and more serious than simply getting a fright. While it may be that the same accident results in some people suffering a fright and others a nervous shock, only the latter are eligible to be compensated in either the Scottish or English courts. A clear illustration of this is apparent in the case *Simpson v. ICI*[52]:

> There was an explosion at the pursuers' place of work. It was a big one: there were flames, breaking glass and a wall fell down. The defenders admitted responsibility for the accident.

The Inner House held that some of the claims could not be sustained. Lord Robertson said: "It is not enough . . . for the pursuers in each case to show simply that they got a fright and suffered an emotional reaction, if no visible disability or provable illness or injury followed."

5.24 Simply proving such an eligible injury is not sufficient. The reason is that over the years the courts have been circumspect in allowing recovery, probably on the basis that it might impose a very wide liability on a wrongdoer and his insurers. There are two justifications for this fear. First, quite a number of people may sustain nervous shock as the result of the one accident. Secondly, there is a possibility that claims might be fabricated sufficiently well to overcome the first eligibility hurdle and so increase the number of persons claiming.

5.25 All of the issues were considered in an important Scottish appeal to the House of Lords, *Bourhill v. Young*[53] [4.10].

> A motorcyclist was driving carelessly, collided with a motor car and was killed. The pursuer was a pregnant fishwife who heard the collision and later saw the bloodstained road, but she had not actually seen the accident. She alleged that she suffered shock and later miscarried.

The difficulty in this case was that undoubtedly the motorcyclist owed a duty of care to other road users to drive carefully. He had not driven with due care. The court held that the fishwife could not recover.

Thus this case helped to shape the general law itself but it did not

---

[52] 1983 S.L.T. 601 at 605.
[53] 1942 S.C (H.L.)78. See footnote 10 to para. 4.10 above for reference to an article setting out the "story" of this case.

solve the particular problem of nervous shock. In a later case, *Boardman v. Sanderson*[54] there was a decision which is interesting to compare with *Bourhill*:

> A young boy and his father were travelling with the defendant in a car. All three were going away together on holiday. Unfortunately, while the father was paying a garage attendant, the defendant reversed his car over the child's foot. His father did not see the incident but he heard the child scream, saw the resulting injury and suffered shock.

In the English Court of Appeal an award to the father was upheld on the basis that he must have been in the car driver's contemplation, and was thus owed a duty of care.

Other cases denied recovery, the themes discussed usually involving 5.26 the ideas of closeness to the impact, or presence at the aftermath— factors which might indicate that a pursuer was in some way more likely to be in the contemplation of the defender.[55] Effectively the court was looking at proximity in the sense of foreseeability more than in any much narrower way of asking, for example, whether the pursuer could himself have been harmed by the defender's acts.

This whole area of the law was examined by the House of Lords in an English appeal, *McLoughlin v. O'Brian*.[56]

> The plaintiff's husband and three children were involved in a road accident. The accident took place at 4 p.m. The wife heard about the accident from a neighbour about 6 p.m. and was taken to the hospital. She was told that her youngest daughter had been killed and learned the nature and extent of the injuries to the rest of her family. She was able to see her relatives. Subsequently she suffered severe shock followed by a psychiatric illness.

At first instance it was held that there was no duty owed as the possibility of the plaintiff suffering nervous shock was not foreseeable. The Court of Appeal held that it was reasonably foreseeable that she would suffer nervous shock but that on the authorities it was settled law that, as a matter of policy, the duty was limited to persons or owners of property at or near the scene of an accident and directly affected by the negligence. The House of Lords reversed the Court of Appeal. Lord Wilberforce considered all of the themes. He dismissed the fear that there might arise "an industry of lawyers and psychiatrists who will formulate a claim for nervous shock" on the basis that courts should be able to deal with unmeritorious claims in this sphere as in any other.

[54] [1964] 1 W.L.R. 1317.
[55] See *Hambrook v. Stokes Bros* [1925] 1 K.B. 141; *King v. Phillips* [1953] 1 All E.R. 617; *Bain v. Kings & Co. Ltd*, 1973 S.L.T. (Notes) 8.
[56] [1983] A.C. 410.

5.27   This case established that foreseeability of shock is generally sufficient,[57] subject to three possible control mechanisms. First, the class of persons may be a restriction: claims might not be successful if an injury is to some stranger as opposed to a member of a person's family. Secondly, pursuers should generally be close in time and space to the accident. Thus the aftermath doctrine is acceptable.[58] Thirdly, the medium by which the shock is caused may be relevant to restrict liability, the main emphasis here being that normally knowledge of the event causing the shock should come directly to the pursuer. *McLoughlin* undoubtedly made the law clearer and swept away any notions of impact theory in favour of reasonable foreseeability.

A tragedy at the Hillsborough football ground produced a series of cases which must have produced the last word in detailed factual situations to test the theoretical boundaries of nervous shock. *Alcock et al. v. Chief Constable, South Yorkshire*[59] involved some 16 actions raised by people who were not at the actual incident: some were in the stadium, some saw it on television and one actually saw it on television but on a bus just outside the ground.[60]

The issue was said to be proximity with reasonable foreseeability as the guide. The court was forced to consider Lord Wilberforce's markers. It was held that the category of plaintiff was not limited to husband and wife and parent and child. The closeness of tie has to be proved by the plaintiff although it can be assumed in many cases. Thus it was held that in the case of brothers and sisters-in-law there was no special tie of affection. A parent and a fiancé were within the close ties. Three members of the House would consider the claim of a bystander who was not within the special class of rescuer which has for some time been within the bounds of proximity largely to encourage rescuers.[61]

On the communication point the House considered that, in general, presence was required and more distant communication was not sufficient. People who saw the incident on the television and not the actual loved ones were not sufficiently proximate, this being even more restrictive than the first instance decision which allowed live television as a mode of communication, although not recorded highlights nor radio.

---

[57] See *Brice v. Brown* [1984] 1 All E.R. 997.
[58] But in *Alcock* [1991] 4 All E.R. 907, discussed below, the viewing of a corpse eight hours after was not within the aftermath.
[59] [1991] 4 All E.R. 907; reported below as *Jones v. Wright* [1991] 2 W.L.R. 814; [1991] 3 All E.R. 88.
[60] The 16 were test cases for some 150 similar claims; only 10 went on appeal to the House.
[61] *Chadwick v. BRB* [1967] 1 W.L.R. 912. A unanimous first Division excluded bystanders and the argument that fellow employees fell within an actionable relationship (about the pursuer having put the defender in danger) *Robertson v. Forth Road Bridge Joint Board*, 1996 S.L.T. 263.

This decision is difficult in many ways. The relationship point is well made—there is no reason why a wife-beating husband on the point of being divorced who hated his wife should recover from the wrongdoer and a fiancé should not. The means of appreciation of the incident point is not so convincing.

Primary and secondary victims

In *Page v. Smith*[62] a teacher who had for some years suffered from a condition at the time of the case called M.E. was in a collision of moderate severity with the defender. He was not physically injured but within about three hours his condition returned in a virulent way preventing him from working. The leading speech is that of Lord Lloyd of Berwick, in whose speech the 3–2 majority concurred. He accepted a factual distinction between primary and secondary victims and that this distinction should have legal consequences.[63] The primary victim is directly involved but others who suffer through what they see or hear are secondary victims. The previous big cases—*Bourhill, McLoughlin* and *Alcock*—were secondary cases. Lord Lloyd followed the judge at first instance and tried to treat the case simply. It is recognised that drivers owe a duty to other road users and that the defender was in breach of that duty in the sense that he drove carelessly. Had he so much as bruised the plaintiff he would have been liable for some damages and there would have been no question of reopening the question of duty. It thus goes against common sense (which is often mentioned as a touchstone of proximity or duty[64]) that just because (luckily) he was not physically injured he could not recover. There was one more critical point dividing the House. That is the question of reasonable fortitude or the customary phlegm. For Lord Keith, who accepted that there was foreseeability of physical injury and proximity, the key point was that shock was not foreseeable to a normal person. With respect that view is not correct if proximity exists. The victim must be taken as found. A haemophiliac in the car would have been compensated if a minor collision had caused him to bleed to death. It must always be remembered, too, that duties among road users were established well before *Donoghue v. Stevenson*. The only difference in this case from cases decided in the nineteenth century is the recognition of the injury. A final point in favour of the *dissent* is that the majority view bears a worrying resemblance to the *Anns/Dutton* heresy that economic loss can be treated as property damage even although the property did not actually fall down and hurt anyone. That logic was clearly persuasive at the time and for some time. Is the majority in *Page* guilty of the same logical error, *viz.* mental illness = physical injury? No, if it can be accepted that the interest in one's mental health is equivalent to the security of one's arms and legs.

5.28

---

[62] [1996] 1 A.C. 155.
[63] Following Lord Oliver in *Alcock* p410–411.
[64] Although it is not that common and seldom is it sensible.

Page was followed by a 2–1 majority in *Frost*[64a] in the Court of Appeal to allow the claim of a policeman who suffered shock in the Hillsborough disaster. Lord Justice Rose saw the policeman as a primary participant. This was because the police were employees in the course of their employment and because they were rescuers. Dissenting, Lord Justice Judge could not see the mopping up exercise as involving participation. The same kind of argument had been unsuccessful in the First Division, in *Robertson v. Forth Road Bridge Joint Board*,[64b] in which workmen claimed when, while working, one saw a colleague blown off the defendant's bridge and another heard a loud noise and then noticed the deceased was missing. Even had a *Frost* approach been taken it is unlikely that the Division would have accepted that, on the facts, these employers were participating enough.

5.29   In *Haggerty v. E.E. Caledonia*[65] the Court of Appeal had to revisit the issue in the case of an off-duty worker on a supply ship who witnessed the Piper Alpha disaster. It seems he was some 500 m away and a fireball fizzled out some 50 m in front of him. It was held that the decision that he was not a primary victim was correct—his fear for his own life was not a rational one.

5.30   Finally, before the recent flourish of activity, further development had in any event taken place as a result of the decision of the Court of Appeal in *Attia v. British Gas*.[66]

> In this case the plaintiff witnessed her home (with its contents) burning down as a result of the defendants' alleged negligence. The plaintiff suffered nervous shock.

The court accepted that a claim could be made in such circumstances and that it was not essential that the shock resulted from witnessing damage to property as opposed to persons, or as a result of fear for one's own safety.

PUBLIC LAW

5.31   As has been demonstrated above, there are difficulties enough with the concept of the duty of care in the context of private law—that is, the law between persons. However, the matter becomes even more complicated when there is an element of public law involved. Public law, of course, concerns the relationship between the individual and the state. Sometimes—indeed perhaps quite often—public authorities

---

[64a] *Frost v. Chief Constable South Yorkshire* [1997] 1 All E.R. 540.
[64b] 1996 S.L.T. 263. Lord Cowie nearly dissented: 271. Rose L.J. thought it doubtful in *Frost*. Henry L.J. would have accepted that view of the case in *Frost*.
[65] [1997] T.L.R. 69.
[66] [1987] 3 All E.R. 455.

cause loss to individuals through their actings or their failure to act. Sometimes the matter is not difficult, as where the authority is under a statutory duty to act or refrain from acting (see Chapter 6). However, it can be difficult to deal with a case where the authority has failed to act because often there may be very good political reasons for not acting—such as a lack of resources. While *Anns v. Merton LBC*[67] became famous for the so-called Wilberforce dictum on the scope of liability generally, the actual *ratio* was concerned with the liability of a public authority. The essential facts were that a builder was under a statutory duty to notify the council before the foundations of a house were covered up. The council were alleged to have been negligent in failing to inspect the foundations to ensure they were of sufficient depth, and in breach of duty imposed under byelaws to ensure that the building was built in accordance with the plans. The court considered that:

> "it must be in the reasonable contemplation not only of the builder but also of the local authority that failure to comply with the byelaws' requirement as to foundations may give rise to a hidden defect which in future may cause damage to the building affecting the safety and health of owners and occupiers. And as the building is intended to last, the class of owners and occupiers likely to be affected cannot be limited to those who go in immediately after construction."[68]

The reasonable foreseeability which, generally, is so important in the establishment of liability, is apparent here. But that is not, in such cases, the end of the matter.

Lord Wilberforce in *Anns* identified a difficulty which had not been properly considered in the lower courts: that the powers and duties of the council were definable in terms of public rather than private law. He said: "The problem which this type of action creates is to define the circumstances in which the law should impose, over and above, or perhaps alongside, these public law powers and duties, a duty in private law towards individuals such that they may sue for damages in a civil court."

The court noted one common distinction made in public authority 5.32 cases: namely that between a discretionary area (where the authority has a discretion to do or not to do something) and an operational area (where it is doing something it has decided to do—for example, where a council decides to have five lorries grit roads but then forgets to send a memo to the appropriate department sending the gritting lorries out). Lord Wilberforce issued a caution:

---

[67] [1978] A.C. 728.
[68] [1985] A.C. 210.

> "Although this distinction between the policy area and the operational area is convenient, and illuminating, it is probably a distinction of degree, many 'operational' powers or duties have in them some element of discretion. It can safely be said that the more 'operational' a power or duty may be, the easier it is to superimpose on it a common law duty of care."

However, that is not the end of the matter. According to the House of Lords in *Anns*, even where a discretionary power or duty is in question the council must avail itself of the discretionary power whenever and as often as they may be of the opinion that the public interest will be promoted by its exercise. Thus in the example of the gritting lorries, if empowered to spend money on lorries and grit and drivers for them, on the basis of the *Anns* formulation there could be a case made out if the council did nothing at all during an extended period of icy, snowy weather.

The framework set out in *Anns* was criticised, distinguished and eventually departed from in a later House of Lords decision.

5.33   In *Rowling v. Takaro Properties Ltd*[69] a property developer was refused damages for the delay of a Minister in dealing with an application in connection with the financing of a development. In the lower court it was held that there was a duty but no breach. While Lord Keith said it was unnecessary to decide if there was a duty because no breach had been established, his *obiter* comments are of interest. In particular he dealt with the discretion/operational distinction:

> "this distinction does not provide a touchstone of liability, but rather is expressive of the need to exclude altogether those cases in which the decision under attack is of such a kind that a question whether it has been made negligently is unsuitable for judicial resolution, of which notable examples are discretionary decisions on the allocation of scarce resources or the distribution of risks . . . If this is right, classification of the relevant decision as a policy or planning decision in this sense may exclude liability; but a conclusion that it does not fall within that category does not . . . mean that a duty of care will necessarily exist."

Instead he suggested that courts should just look at all the circumstances.[70] In *Yuen Kun Yeu v. Att.-Gen. Hong Kong*[71] a commissioner registered a company as a deposit-taking company under an ordinance, the company went into liquidation and an action was brought

---

[69] [1988] 2 W.L.R. 418.
[70] See generally Feldthusen, "Failure to Confer Discretionary Public benefits: The Case for Complete Negligence Immunity", 1997 Tort L.Rev. 17.
[71] [1988] 1 A.C. 175.

by plaintiffs who had lost money as a result of relying on the company's status. Lord Keith, giving the advice of the board, refused to allow the claim. First he disposed of the wider *ratio* of *Anns*: "for the future it should be recognised that the two stage test in *Anns* is not to be regarded as in all circumstances a suitable guide to the existence of a duty of care." This time, however, Lord Keith was more constructive and gave guidance as to how cases like these and, indeed, any novel cases, should be considered. It was necessary that a close and direct relationship between the parties be established before liability in tort could arise. All circumstances had to be taken into account including reasonable contemplation of harm, although foreseeability of injury by itself is insufficient to create a duty. In the case before the board it was held that there had not been sufficient close and direct relationship between the official and the disappointed investors. *Obiter*, cases like *Hedley Byrne* were explained on the basis of a voluntary assumption of liability.

In *Murphy v. Brentwood*[72] the House of Lords departed from its previous decision in *Anns* on the particular finding of a duty being encumbent upon the council, in the particular case of its implementation of building control.[73] A strong theme in the decision was to restrict recovery for economic loss generally and to preserve the so-called logic that if *Anns* were right then there would be liability in respect of chattels or goods, which is something the law must not allow. Nonetheless, a major part of the decision was also that the building legislation did not intend to create or found such a liability. Later English cases have emphasised an enthusiasm for protection of public bodies. The most recent reaffirmation in the House of Lords is *Stovin v. Wise*.[74]

5.34

> Stovin, on his motor bike, collided with Mrs Wise who was not keeping a good lookout. She settled with him but called the council as third parties due to the state of the crossroads where the accident took place. There had been three previous accidents. The council's surveyor examined the site and agreed it was dangerous and that work should be done. This was approved by the council providing the owners of the land would agree to the work being done. Nothing was achieved but if the council had not delayed the works could have been done because the owners would have agreed to the work without the need for the council to exercise its statutory powers.

---

[72] [1991] 1 A.C. 398.

[73] It overruled *Dutton v. Bognor Regis UBC* [1972] 1 Q.B. 373 and all cases subsequent to *Anns* decided on the basis of it.

[74] [1996] A.C. 923. See also the important *X. v. Bedfordshire C.C.* [1995] 3 All E.R. 353.

By a 3–2 majority the House of Lords denied recovery. For the majority this was a case involving omissions. Lord Hoffmann left open the question whether the *Anns* decision was wrong—that the courts could impose common law duties. It was, however, clear that the policy/operational distinction was inadequate to be a guide to liability.[75] On an examination of the facts of the case, there are certainly grounds for thinking this not to be one crying out for a finding of liability. Despite the decision having been taken that the work ought to be done, there was no time-scale for it. It could have been done in one, two or three years. That would put it in a different budgetary cycle. The cost had not been ascertained. The judge at first instance did not make a finding that the decision was irrational. There was a computer system which identified black spots. This was not such a black spot.[76] It should, however, be appreciated that in dissenting Lord Nicholls praised the decision in *Anns*. It liberated the law from the unacceptable yolk of the rigid rule against liability in English law.[77]

5.35   The whole topic hardly appeared in Scotland at all. It is hard to say why. The propositions expounded in *Anns* were adopted for Scots law by Lord Dunpark in *Hallett v. Nicholson*.[78] The case concerned the acts and alleged omissions of a fire authority. The statutory framework was set out and the discretion/operation distinction noted. Lord Dunpark set out three propositions which he took from *Anns* and *Dorset Yacht Co. v. Home Office*:

> "(1) Acts or omissions committed by a statutory authority in the proper exercise of its statutory duties or powers do not found a cause of civil action . . . (2) Acts or omissions which are committed by a statutory authority in the course of an improper exercise of its statutory duties or powers and which infringe the rights of third parties may be actionable at civil law. (3) For such an exercise to be improper, it must be either (a) not authorised by statute or (b) not made bona fide in the interests of the public within the limits of any statutory discretion."[79]

5.36   In *Bonthrone v. Secretary of State for Scotland*,[80] a fourth proposition was put forward.

> "When the exercise of a statutory power confers a discretion on the authority entitled to exercise it as to the manner in which, or the means by which it is to be exercised, then if the discretion is

---

[75] at 951.

[76] at 956.

[77] at 931.

[78] 1979 S.C. 1.

[79] 1979 S.C. at 9.

[80] 1987 S.L.T. 34; *Casebook*, Ext. 56; and see also *Lamont v. North East Fife D.C.*, 1987 G.W.D. 37–1310.

exercised within the ambit of the power, and in bona fide, albeit the exercise of it can be shown to display an error of judgement, a person who suffers loss as a result of the exercise of the power will not have an action of damages against the authority which exercised it . . . the taking of reasonable care in connection with the exercise of a statutory power . . . does not arise until the discretionary stage of its exercise has ceased and the executive stage has begun."[81]

The *Hallett/Bonthrone* formulation—different in style and perhaps in substance than the formulations presently discussed in England— has formed the basic framework in Scottish cases for some time.[82] No reference was made to this line in *Ward v. Chief Constable*,[83] but probably for the good reason that this was a case where action was implemented on the ground and the police were protected by the need for the pursuer to prove malice and want of probable cause. It is not, therefore, a Scottish equivalent of *Hill v. Chief Constable*,[84] in which there was no liability for a failure to properly investigate crime.

In *Duff v. Highlands and Islands Fire Board*,[85] the fire brigade left   5.37 after they thought they had put out a fire. It broke out again and burnt down the property and one beside it. Lord Macfadyen rejected arguments of public immunity. While on the evidence the brigade were assoilzied, the fact that the brigade had gone into action meant that ordinary principles of liability applied. It is respectfully submitted that this decison is correct. Interestingly, the anti-liability approach of the House of Lords in recent years has been reinforced in the English Court of Appeal in a series of cases involving the fire brigade refusing liability, mainly on the rationale that liability would cause defensive practices.[86]

Forbes v. Dundee Council,[87] represents the arrival in Scotland of the   5.38 rhetoric culmination of the issues in a Scots court, albeit it will not be the last word. It is, for the present, required reading. *Hallet* and *Bonthrone* are no longer even discussed but the principal English cases like *Stovin* are.

A woman lost her footing when leaving a large shop. She did not trip on a dangerous step but her rhythm of walking was broken

[81] 1987 S.L.T. at 41.
[82] *Johnstone v. Traffic Commissioner*, 1990 S.L.T. 409; *Ross v. Secretary of State*, 1990 S.L.T. 13; *Wilson v. McCaffrey*, 1989 G.W.D. 1–37.
[83] 1991 S.L.T. 292.
[84] [1987] 1 All E.R. 1173.
[85] 1995 S.L.T. 1362.
[86] *Capital and Counties v. Mapshire Council*; *John Munroe v. London Fire Authority*; *Church of Jesus Christ of Latter-Day Saints v. West Yorkshire Fire Authority* [1997] T.L.R. 141. See also *Nelson Holdings Ltd v. British Gas* [1997] T.L.R. 122; *Oll Ltd v. Secretary of State for the Home Dept*, unreported, Q.B., June 16, 1997.
[87] 1997 S.L.T. 1330.

by the irregular spacing of the steps, not conforming in this regard (it was alleged) to the building regulations which the defenders were charged by statute to apply.

Lord Nimmo-Smith dismissed the action. He accepted that the issue of reasonable foreseeability of harm of the kind which happened was sufficiently stated to entitle the pursuer to a proof before answer. There was no duty following the English cases.[88] Timorously, but fairly, his lordship considered that the trend was away from imposing civil liabilities on local authorities. He did not think that there was enough in *Duff* to support the dicta in favour of liability in that case.

The decision in *Forbes* cannot be justified by the cases mainly relied upon. The injury was a physical injury. As explained in more detail below,[89] *Marc Rich* is not correctly understood as overruling *Donoghue*, not even for property damage.[90] Leaving that essential point aside, it is correct in its application of the *Murphy* principle and without a doubt also correct on the *Pullar* line.[91]

The fact that the Scots courts have kept the essence of *Anns* closely in view may mean that they are closer to a truer analysis. Feldthusen has expressed the view that Lord Wilberforce in *Anns* intended immunity from civil action to apply to all bona fide exercise of discretion at any level.[92]

5.39   Looking around the common law world, it is notable that members of the judicial committee of the House of Lords sitting as the Board of the Privy Council on an appeal from New Zealand, on a case very like *Murphy*, declined to follow it on the immunity point: *Invercargill City Council v. Hamlin*.[93] It was said that conditions and expectations in New Zealand were different in this area of building control, which can be seen as involving some degree of public protection. *Murphy* itself was based on an anti-liability decision from Australia.[94] Canada which, as has been seen in relation to economic loss, is much more like the House of Lords in its *Junior Books* phase in its approach to liability, has none the less respected the immunity.[95] Commonwealth cases are extremely influential in the House of Lords and Privy Council.[96]

---

[88] *X. v. Bedfordshire* being expressly mentioned.

[89] 5.44.

[90] Lord Nimmo-Smith may have been deflected by the argument noted at 1335, which it is submitted is erroneous.

[91] See Chap. 6.

[92] Feldthusen, "Failure to Confer Discretionary Public benefits: The Case for Complete Negligence Immunity", 1997 Tort L. Rev. 17 at 20.

[93] [1996] A.C. 624.

[94] *Sutherland Shire Council v. Heyman* (1985) 157 C.L.R. 424.

[95] *Just v. British Columbia* (1990) 64 D.L.R. (4th) 689.

[96] But did not attract Lord Maclean in *Strathford East Kilbride Ltd v. HLM Design Ltd*, 1997 Rep. L.R. 112 at 27–07.

Finally, it must not, however, be forgotten (as often it is) that *Hedley Byrne* liability is independent and at the very least authorities can be vicariously liable for the failures of their professional or skilled staff.[97]

THIRD PARTY INTERVENTION

This is another difficult area where the law has to reconcile the desire 5.40 to compensate individuals who have suffered harm with other compelling interests. It will occasion no surprise that this is done by using the duty of care to determine who shall and who shall not recover. The cases also raise questions as to the significance of reasonable foreseeability in determining the existence of a duty of care.

The root of the problem is that English law has for a long time had a general rule that there is no liability for what is called a pure omission—a failure to prevent a person coming to harm in the absence of a duty to prevent it.[98]

The *Dorset Yacht* case [4.15] made it clear that a defender could be liable for the acts—even the criminal acts—of a third party.[99] Foreseeability of harm to the yacht owners if the boys went unsupervised was enough to create the necessary duty—there was no pre-existing relationship between the yacht owner and the employers of the probation officers. Add to that the pre-*Dorset Yacht*, *Hughes* case, [4.13] where all the law required was that the reasonable foreseeability sufficient to establish a duty is foreseeability of harm of the kind that actually occurred, and there is a framework which can allow a pursuer to recover damages from a person who has in some way culpably allowed other people to cause him harm.

The issue was sharply raised in Scotland by *Squires v. Perth and* 5.41 *Kinross D.C.*[1]

> A burglar robbed the pursuer's jewellers shop. Contractors employed by the district council were working on flats above the pursuer's premises. They neglected the security of the building and the flats were left unsecured. They put up scaffolding. It had been removed before the theft but it had alerted the thief (who himself gave evidence!) to the possibility of a burglary.

---

[97] *Lambert v. West Devon* [1997] T.L.R. 167; *Phelps v. Hillingdon LBC* [1997] T.L.R. 502.

[98] See Logie, "Special Relationships, Reasonable Foreseeability and Distinct Probabilities: the Duty to Prevent Damage to the Property of Others", 1988 J.R. 77.

[99] Although the Scots law had recognised a similar liability in *Scott's Trs v. Moss* (1889) 17 R. 32.

[1] 1986 S.L.T. 30.

The Inner House found the council liable on the basis that the theft was reasonably foreseeable. That the thief did not carry out the theft in a foreseeable way was unimportant because of the decision in *Hughes v. Lord Advocate* [4.13]. The court, in allowing the claim, had held that the third party intervention had to be "very likely to" occur. However, in the later case of *Maloco v. Littlewoods*,[2] the Inner House held that it was sufficient that the intervention be likely. The facts of the case were that some third parties, probably young children, set a fire which burnt down a derelict cinema which Littlewoods had purchased. The fire spread to damage Mr Maloco's café and the church in the charge of Mr Smith, who also sued Littlewoods. As indicated above [4.37], when that case came to the House of Lords, Lord Mackay settled that point by indicating that it is essentially a question of fact and that the intervention should be high on a scale of probability before there can be liability.[3]

5.42   In the *Maloco* case, while it was perhaps likely that vandals could gain entry and that they might start a small fire, it was not likely that they would start a conflagration which would engulf an entire building. So far as the court was concerned the building did not contain readily combustible materials, at least in the sense that they would set fire to this particular building.[4] It would have been very difficult for the court to hold that harm of the kind which did occur was foreseeable: it is a matter of comparing the flammability of the materials with the material of the building—the result would perhaps have been different if the building had been made of wood or if there had been drums of petrol lying about in a concrete building. Nor is it entirely accurate to suggest that Lord Mackay equated reasonably foreseeable in this context with highly probable—instead the pursuers had failed to establish that harm of the kind which had occurred was reasonably foreseeable. The focus of the reasonable foreseeability test is on harm of the kind which results—the acts of third parties should be thought of as mere cogs in the mechanism of liability.

5.43   There is a tremendous tension between the speeches of Lord MacKay and Lord Goff.[5] In later cases the divergence has often followed national lines. In *Fry's Metals Ltd v. Durastic Ltd*,[6]

> a company entered into a lease with another company of factory and office premises for the six-month period to March 23, 1984.

---

[2] 1986 S.L.T. 272.

[3] Substantial parts of the speeches appear in the *Casebook*, Ext. 39.

[4] See the Lord President, 1986 S.L.T. at 276J: "There was nothing about the building, so far as we know, . . . to suggest that it could easily be set alight"; and Lord Mackay, 1987 S.L.T. at 429B: "The type of film used in the cinema was non-inflammable"; see generally Logie, 1988 J.R. 77.

[5] Lord Keith agreed with both!

[6] 1991 S.L.T. 689.

Two separate alarm systems protected the premises: a conventional bell system mounted on an exterior wall manually set by a key, and a private system installed by a security company at the request of the tenants, connected to the offices of the security company by landline. The tenants notified the security company that cover would not be required after March 30. On April 2 the tenants sought to hand over the keys to the landlords. The keys were refused because electricity and gas meters required to be read before the handover was complete. This took place on April 9. On April 7 the premises were broken into and vandalised. Both alarm systems failed to operate. The landlords sued the tenants for loss caused by the failure of the private alarm system.

It was argued, on the basis of Lord MacKay's speech, that there is a duty in delict to take care in respect of the occupation of premises to prevent damage by the action of a third party, which arises if, but only if, the injury or damage by third parties arising from the act or omission of the person against whom the duty of care is alleged is highly probable. Lord Dervaird held that test met.

In Scotland in *Gillon v. Chief Constable*[7] a police officer who was told to stand with her back to the ground was "run-down" by a footballer. She sued her employer and lost on the basis of *Bolton v. Stone* unlikeliness. But it is an example of the fact that, although there was another human being (in this case a footballer) in the chain of events, a case could be made out.

In England, in *Topp v. London Country Bus Ltd*[8] the owners of a minibus stolen by unknown persons were held not to be liable to the husband of a person run down by the bus. The case was argued on the basis of allurement: the ignition key was left in the lock and the vehicle left unattended. The court held that foreseeability was not enough. The fact that the allurement and danger argument was taken shows the influence of Lord Goff's speech—the attempt was to bring the case within his catalogue of situations in which there could be liability. Lord MacKay's test could, however, bring about the same decision because the need for the needle to be high might rule this case out—it is not like untrained borstal boys trying to sail boats. Even if it was foreseeable that the car would be stolen, the next stage—driving such as to injure another—is not perhaps probable: most people, most of the time do not run people down. On the other hand, there are car thieves and there are car thieves—some are excellent and careful drivers who safeguard their booty; others may be young "neds" who may never actually have learned to drive. The harm of the kind

---

[7] 1996 Rep. L.R. 165.
[8] [1991] T.L.R. 552.

which resulted was not the harm reasonably to be foreseen, namely car theft.

However, in another English case a decision was reached, albeit against the background of the Occupiers' Liability (Scotland) Act 1960, which fits more into the "foreseeability with high probability" model. In *Cunningham and Others v. Reading Football Club Ltd*[9] the plaintiffs were injured at a football match by bits of terracing thrown at the police. Four months earlier concrete had been thrown. The club knew it was a local derby and knew that trouble might arise. The club were held liable.

INDIRECT PHYSICAL LOSS

5.44   This could be a very large category but it is restricted to one relatively new category which it is submitted has been ill understood. In *Marc Rich & Co. A.G. and Others v. Bishop Rock Marine Co. Ltd and Others (The Nicholas H)*[10]

> a tanker developed a crack in its hull carrying a cargo incorporating the Hague-Visby rules. It was inspected by a surveyor acting for the vessels classification society. The surveyor recommended permanent repairs in dry-dock there and then but was persuaded to change his mind, allowed temporary repairs and the vessel to sail. The Nicholas H sank as a result of the temporary welding failing. After sundry claims the cargo owners were still carrying a loss and sued the classification society.

For the purposes of the legal argument on duty the parties accepted that the plaintiffs had title to sue, it was foreseeable that lack of care was likely to expose the cargo to physical damage, that the damage suffered was physical damage and that the damage was as a result of the carelessness of the surveyor. At first instance the plaintiffs were successful. The Court of Appeal allowed an appeal on the basis that the cargo having been sent under the Hague-Visby rules meant that the shipowner (and not the defendants) was under a duty. The House of Lords decided by a 4–1 majority to agree with the Court of Appeal and refused the appeal.

The importance of the case is that the new duty ("fair, just and reasonable" test) was used in a case where it appears the loss was damage to property rather than economic loss.

This case looks a little like a primary economic loss case and it also has features of the public authority cases. It would have been better if

---

[9] [1991] T.L.R. 153.
[10] [1995] 3 All E.R. 307.

it had been decided on these two lines. In Scotland it has been taken as allowing theoretical issues from primary economic loss cases to be brought to bear on a property damage case. In *British Telecom v. Thomson*[11] a sub-contractor's work caused property damage (in this respect unlike *Junior Books*), yet the case was argued as if it were an economic loss case. The claim was refused and upheld on appeal by a 2–1 majority. In *Coleridge v. Miller*[12] there was another case of simple property damage which is burdened by a consideration of what it is thought *Murphy* did to the law. Once the defender has damaged the pursuer's property in a reasonably foreseeable way, causing harm of the kind which was envisaged, only remoteness of damage can save the wrongdoer. *Marc Rich* does, however, require *indirect* property damage cases to be given more consideration than a simple *Donoghue* analysis.

PROFESSIONAL LIABILITY

There are two main reasons why it is appropriate to treat professional 5.45 liability separately. The first is that the existence of a duty of care in certain professional areas has been the subject of decision. The second is that the standard of care differs—the reasonable man, although he might be prepared to give it a try, will not make a very successful attempt at brain surgery. One thing which has to be made clear immediately is that the word "profession" is used here as a matter of convenience. As will be seen, the legal considerations do not depend upon the defender being a member of a professional body as opposed to, say, a trade association: "If I engage a man to exercise his expertise on my behalf . . . it matters not whether he is to prepare a conveyance of land or to drive a straight furrow across it."[13]

The delictual duty

Professional liability can, of course, occur contractually. The 5.46 existence of a contract does not, however, preclude the existence of a delictual duty. That was clear in Scotland even before *Donoghue*.[14]

---

[11] 1997 Rep. L.R. 23.

[12] 1997 S.L.T. 487.

[13] *Arenson v. Casson Beckman* [1977] A.C. 405, *per* Lord Kilbrandon at 430.

[14] *Edgar v. Lamont*, 1914 S.C. 277. Resistance in England in relation to concurrent liability (*Tai Hing Cotton Mill Ltd v. Lin Chong Hing Bank* [1986] A.C. 80; *National Bank of Greece v. Pinios Shipping Co. (No. 1) (The Maria)* [1989] 1 All E.R. 213; *Greater Nottingham Co-operative Society Ltd v. Cementation Piling and Foundations Ltd* [1988] 3 W.L.R. 396 and *Pacific Associates Inc. v. Baxter* [1990] Q.B. 993 yielded to the House of Lords' decision in *Henderson v. Merrett Syndicates Ltd*, [1994] 3 W.L.R. 761

Generally, the standard of care required is the same in contract as in delict but it is always possible as a matter of express contract for a party to bind himself to a higher standard of care or agree a lower standard. Sometimes there will be professional liability based on duties other than that to take care to prevent foreseeable harm. Thus, often the delict of fraud will provide a remedy if there has been the necessary intention to deceive. As we shall see later, there may, in respect of medical treatment, be liability based on assault. However, in the main liability is usually in issue because of unintentional harm due to a lack of the care required by law: professional people are generally trying to assist the recipient of their skills and not to cause harm. A complicating factor is that professional services are often rendered on the basis of oral or written advice rather than doing or omitting to do something.

5.47   Perhaps the best place to start is with physical injury caused by a lack of due care. It is clear from the cases like *Hunter v. Hanley*[15] that there is a duty to take care to prevent such harm by acts or omissions. There was authority in England that there was also a duty not to cause foreseeable physical harm by the giving of negligent advice. In *Clayton v. Woodman & Son (Builders) Ltd*[16]:

> An architect gave instructions direct to a bricklayer. The architect knew the instructions would be promptly obeyed and should have realised that they could result in serious injury. In fact the wall on which the plaintiff was working collapsed, injuring him.

The court at first instance held that there was a breach of duty but the decision was reversed on the facts, in that the Court of Appeal did not accept the finding that the architect had given any direct order.

However, the greatest difficulty was with negligent advice which did not cause damage to property or injury to person, as has been seen above.

The standard of care

5.48   The professional person is judged by the standard of his profession, not that of the reasonable man. This was established in the case of *Hunter v. Hanley*,[17] a case where a doctor used an inappropriate needle in treating a patient. Lord President Clyde said (at 217):

> "In the realm of diagnosis and treatment there is ample scope for genuine difference of opinion and one man clearly is not negligent

[15] 1955 S.L.T. 213.
[16] [1962] 2 Q.B. 533.
[17] 1955 S.L.T. 213; and see *Bolam v. Friern Hospital Management Committee* [1957] 1 W.L.R. 582. See also *Moyes v. Lothian Health Board*, 1990 S.L.T. 444; "Medical Negligence: *Hunter v. Hanley* 35 Years On", 1990 S.L.T. (News) 325; *Casebook*, paras 8.31–8.48 and cases cited therein.

merely because his conclusion differs from that of other professional men . . . The true test for establishing negligence in diagnosis or treatment on the part of a doctor is whether he has been proved to be guilty of such failure as no doctor of ordinary skill would be guilty of if acting with ordinary care."

So the ordinary practitioner is not judged by the standard of the consultant. However, the person who holds himself out as possessing a higher degree of skill may well be held liable in delict if he fails to reach that higher standard.

The basic test refers to what it is other professionals do. In England 5.49 the test was put in a different way (intended to have similar effect) in *Bolam v. Friern Hospital Management Committee*,[18] McNair J. stating that the professional would not be liable if he has acted in accordance with a practice accepted as proper by a responsible body of medical men skilled in that particular art. That has been interpreted as meaning that even a small group of practitioners can constitute a responsible body of opinion.[19] The English courts have also addressed another very important question—whether the courts have the final say in what is or is not negligent in professional cases. There were some indicators that the court retained an overall locus to adjudicate on the evidence or indeed to declare a professional practice negligent.[20] However, in *Bolitho v. City and Hackney Health Authority*[21] the House of Lords retreated from interference.

> A senior nurse conveyed her serious concerns about a child's treatment but no doctors came. Eventually his respiratory system collapsed and in trying to revive the child, he suffered serious brain damage. Breach of duty was established on the failure of the senior doctor, called regularly by the nurse, to have the boy treated. It was common ground that intubation so as to provide an airway in any event would have ensured that the respiratory failure which occurred did not lead to cardiac arrest. The judge had evidence from eight medical experts, all of them distinguished. Five for the plaintiff said neglect and three for the defendants said no negligence.

The defendants won on the *Bolam* test even although the judge had a feeling that the defendants' evidence did not make sense. The House of Lords retained a very limited place for the courts:

---

[18] [1957] 2 All E.R. 118.
[19] *De freitas v. O'Brien* [1995] T.L.R. 86.
[20] *Hucks v. Cole* [1993] 4 Med. L.R. 393; *Edward Wong Finance Co. Ltd v. Johnson, Stokes & Master* [1984] 1 A.C. 296; *Sidaway v. Governors of the Bethlem Royal Hospital* [1985] 1 All E.R. 643.
[21] [1997] 3 W.L.R. 1151.

"the court is not bound to hold that a defendant doctor escapes liability for negligent treatment or diagnosis just because he leads evidence from a number of medical experts who are genuinely of opinion that the defendant's treatment or diagnosis accorded with sound medical practice . . . The use of 'responsible, reasonable and respectable' all show that the court has to be satisfied that the exponents of the body of opinion relied upon can demonstrate that such opinion has a logical basis. In particular in cases involving, as they so often do, the weighing of risks against benefits, the judge before accepting a body of opinion as being responsible, reasonable or respectable, will need to be satisfied that, in forming their views, the experts have directed their minds to the question of comparative risks and benefits and have reached a defensible conclusion on the matter."

This does not go far enough. In the ordinary case it may well be right that a professional who has done what his brethren do is free of liability but there will be other cases where, based on the evidence, the community through the court decides on evidence that that practice is simply wrong. It could only happen where there is a conflict and the essence of the conflicting positions is capable of expression in a way comprehensible to laypeople. Logic alone cannot be the only test a harmful professional practice must pass.

Some particular problems in professional liability cases

1. Medical cases

5.50   Medical cases have raised some difficult problems which are worth special consideration. The professional error must still cause the loss. If after medical treatment someone is worse off than when they went into hospital they still have to show that it was the doctor's fault which caused the loss. This was re-emphasised in the case of *Kay's Tutor v. Ayrshire and Arran Health Board*[22] [4.32]. Although the hospital admitted administering a huge overdose of penicillin, the pursuer failed because he could not show that the child's deafness was caused by the overdose rather than the meningitis that had taken the child into hospital in the first place. If there are a number of possible causes it must be shown that the breach of duty, on the balance of probabilities, was an operative cause of the loss.[23]

5.51   Another issue is the interrelation of liability based on negligence and liability based on assault [2.2]. The House of Lords has refused to accept the so-called informed consent doctrine as part of English law. This doctrine is based upon the law of assault— *i.e.* in England,

---

[22] 1987 S.L.T. 577.
[23] *Wilsher v. Essex Area Health Authority* [1988] 2 W.L.R. 557.

trespass to the person. It will result in a doctor being held liable if the whole procedure and risks are not explained to the patient. The basis of the doctrine is that the patient cannot be touched unless he gives his full consent. In theory the consent that the patient gives is not effective unless the consent is informed—that is, based on all the relevant available information. Instead, the House of Lords held that the general rule in *Hunter* is applicable in this area of medical work and the issue is now resolved by asking whether the risk is one which the ordinary doctor exercising ordinary care would reveal to the patient. This question will generally be answered by considering the views of medical witnesses.[24]

A particularly interesting case is *Gold v. Haringey Health Authority*,[25] in which the failure complained of was to advise of an alternative and more efficient method of contraception. The case was decided on the basis of the *Hunter* test, but it might be thought that the other view which was argued—that the doctor was giving contraceptive advice and should have been judged by the standard of, say, a family planning adviser—is at least as attractive. However, the court was reluctant to dissect a doctor's work functionally: it refused to accept that there was a different standard of care in giving advice as opposed to carrying out medical treatment.

2. Legal advisers

In the House of Lords case of *Robertson v. Fleming*,[26] a solicitor   5.52
prepared documents for his client but which were to be useful to his client's creditors in the event of the client's insolvency. When the client became insolvent it was found that the solicitor had failed to take necessary steps to make the security documents effective. The creditors suffered a loss. They were held unable to recover in delict but were allowed to recover on the basis of an implied contract, or a *jus quaesitum tertio*. It was thought to be clear that a solicitor could only be liable to his own client. This is a House of Lords case in a Scottish appeal and is thus, to the extent that its *ratio* is in point, binding. However, it is entirely at odds with the neighbour principle. It is also contrary to the principle that the professional should answer for his lack of skill.

Liability for economic loss based on *Hedley Byrne* in particular seems clearly applicable to solicitors if they have assumed responsibility or come within the special relationship. In *Weir v. J.M. Hodge*[27] Lord Weir felt himself bound by *Robertson*. *Robertson* was also

---

[24] *Sidaway v. Governors of the Bethlem Royal Hospital* [1985] 1 All E.R. 643; and see *Moyes v. Lothian Health Board*, 1990 S.L.T. 444 for a Scottish "Warning of risks" case; see, too, *Cameron v. Greater Glasgow Health Board*, 1993 G.W.D. 6–433.

[25] [1987] 3 W.L.R. 649.

[26] (1861) 4 Macq. 167.

[27] 1990 S.L.T. 266.

followed by Lord Cameron of Lochbroom in *MacDougall v. Clydes-dale Bank Trustees*.[28] In *Bolton v. Jameson & Mackay*[29] Lord Wylie took the view that *Robertson* had been overtaken and allowed proof before answer on the averments that solicitors had acted improperly in paying a sum to their own client without, in the special circumstances, taking account of the pursuer's interests.

A statement of the scope of a solicitor's liability by Lord Jauncey (as he then was) outlines four factors which are relevant in answering the question whether a solicitor owes a duty to a third party:

> "(1) the solicitor must assume responsibility for the advice or information furnished to the third party; (2) the solicitor must let it be known to the third party expressly or impliedly that he claims, by reason of his calling, to have the requisite skill or knowledge to give the advice or furnish the information; (3) the third party must have relied upon that advice or information as a matter for which the solicitor has assumed personal responsibility; and (4) the solicitor must have been aware that the third party was likely so to rely."[30]

It is submitted that it is correct to say that *Robertson* is still in force and binding, albeit (if that is correct) doomed to being departed from in a Scots appeal. However, other views on this particular decision are tenable and Professor Norrie's strongly expressed view that the decision is *obiter* does indeed have support by inference from *White v. Jones*,[31] discussed above, where (as he points out) Lord Goff did not consider that the case required the use of the practice direction.[32] It must be noted, too, that the case, being Scottish, was not binding in *White* in any event. Whatever one's view, the case is a dead letter save for the significant theoretical point that obligations similar to delictual obligations can be accomodated within contract itself by virtue of the doctrine *jus quaesitum tertio*.[33]

5.53   There is, however, one apparently unusual exception to liability for professional negligence and that is in the case of the lawyer who is conducting a court action.

> *Rondel v. Worsley*[34] was an action raised by a criminal against the dock brief (a barrister who appears without prior instruction to

---

[28] 1993 S.C.L.R. 832.

[29] 1987 S.L.T. 291, reversed on other grounds 1989 S.L.T. 222.

[30] *Midland Bank plc v. Cameron, Thom, Peterkin & Duncans*, 1988 S.L.T. 611 at 616.

[31] See 5.21 above.

[32] Norrie, "Disappointed beneficiaries, the House of Lords and Scots Law", 1995 Rep. L.R. 3–2—because the case was *obiter* and irrelevant.

[33] See Woolman (2nd ed.) pp. 160 *et seq. Strathford East Kilbride Ltd v. HLM Design Ltd*, 1997 S.C.L.R. 877.

[34] [1969] 1 A.C. 191.

act for anyone who might instruct him) who appeared for him at the Old Bailey. He claimed his defence had been badly run and that if it had been done properly he would not have been convicted.

The House of Lords held that barristers (in Scotland, advocates) were immune from suit in respect of their conduct and management of a cause in court and the preliminary work connected therewith such as the drawing of pleadings. It also seemed to be the case that the immunity would extend to a solicitor carrying out advocacy work.

Such a statement in favour of lawyers by lawyers required some justification. The immunity was not, said the court, based on the absence of contract but upon policy and long usage and there were three good reasons for it: a barrister had to be able to carry out his duties fearlessly and independently; there would be a retrying of the original action if actions were allowed—to see if with the right conduct the case would have been won; barristers are compelled by their own professional rules to accept clients. An opportunity arose shortly afterwards to examine the extent of the immunity. In *Saif Ali v. Sydney Mitchell & Co.*[35] it was held that a barrister could be liable for advice which was not intimately connected with the actual conduct of a case such as the giving of opinions. Interestingly, the two Scottish law lords dissented on this point, preferring that there be a blanket immunity for all work, even work where litigation was only in contemplation. In this particular case the barrister had left the plaintiff with no one to sue and was himself sued.

In *Kelly v. Corston*,[36] it was held by the Court of Appeal that the immunity extended to settlements which required to be approved by the courts. The same applied to settlements at the door of the court. With respect this takes the immunity much too far. Both of these matters are advice simple and the lawyers who give it should be potentially liable for it, recalling that it will still have to be shown that no other responsible barrister would have settled or agreed the settlement to attach liability.

3. Negligent mis-statements and contracts

If a negligent mis-statement induces a contract then it may well be a negligent misrepresentation. In the law of contract if one party to the contract misrepresents facts to the other deliberately, negligently, or innocently, there may be a remedy by way of rescission of the contract.[37] However, for a long time the rule in *Manners v.* 5.54

---

[35] [1978] 3 All E.R. 1033.
[36] [1997] T.L.R. 466.
[37] See Woolman, pp. 72–85.

Whitehead[38] held sway. Even although there had been a negligent misrepresentation, if it were made by the other contracting party then damages in delict were only available if there was proof of fraud. The position was changed by the Law Reform (Miscellaneous Provisions) (Scotland) Act 1985, s. 10(1) which provides that:

> "A party to a contract who has been induced to enter into it by negligent misrepresentation made by or on behalf of another party to the contract shall not be disentitled, by reason only that the misrepresentation is not fraudulent, from recovering damages from the other party in respect of any loss or damage he has suffered as a result of the misrepresentation; and any rule of law that such damages cannot be recovered unless fraud is proved shall cease to have effect."

It goes without saying that the pursuer must still prove the existence of a duty to take care towards him in the particular circumstances of the transaction.

5.55   Professional liability is developing all the time. This is partly because many activities are being organised along professional lines with codes of self discipline and an element of holding out to the public on behalf of members. While it is clear that there are two general themes running through the cases—that of the need for the special relationship based upon reliance in cases of mis-statements and that of the higher standard of care once the issue is perceived of as a "professional" case—it should be remembered that it may be the reliance and the holding out elements which are at the heart of liability: it may not be that courts will always take the *Gold* approach[39] and refuse to look behind the profession to the function carried out by the defender. The opening up of financial services and the existence of multi-disciplinary practices might, unfortunately, make this an issue.

Further reading

5.56 The topics considered in this chapter each attract considerable academic interest—often well beyond the frequency of cases in the law office or the court. Most of the cases discussed above or even many of those simply noted are texts longer than this whole book. But as should by now be clear these areas are all in some way or another either about challenging the very basis of the law or at the least mapping out its boundaries. If it is the case, as suggested in the first chapter, that the law of delict can be as much about social, cultural,

---

[38] (1988) 1 F. 171.
[39] See *Philips v. William Whiteley Ltd* [1938] 1 All E.R. 566.

economic and political issues, then it is proper that more wide-ranging investigations are made and comparative examinations conducted. The student, teacher and practitioner researcher should find many interesting arguments canvassed in many of these articles. This section is accordingly one of the longest in this book. The Scottish courts do in difficult cases look at the law from the Commonwealth and elsewhere; this explains the many comparative or foreign articles referred to in this list. Practitioners may find these references helpful in novel cases

Adams, J. and Brownsword, R., " '*The Aliakmon*' and the Hague Rules", 1990 J.B.L. 23.

Allen, D., "Local Authority Liability for Defective Premises" (1985) 274 E.G. 657.

Amin, S.H., "Extending the Neighbourhood", 1982 S.L.T. (News) 61.

Arnott, J.M., "Defects in Building and Pure Economic Loss" (1989) 34 J.L.S.S. 183.

Bailey, S.H. and Bowman, M.J., "The Policy/Operational Dichotomy—a Cuckoo in the Nest", 1986 C.L.J. 430.

Blaikie, J., "Negligent Solicitors and Disappointed Beneficiaries", 1989 S.L.T. (News) 317.

Blaikie, J., "The Dilatory Solicitor and the Disappointed Legatee", 1993 S.L.T. (News) 329.

Blaikie, J., "Nervous Shock: Traumatised Fellow workers and Bystanders", 1994 S.L.T. (News) 297.

Blaikie, J., "Professional negligence: the dilatory solicitor and the disappointed legatee", 1996 S.L.P.Q. 245.

Brodie, D., "Public Authorities and the Duty of Care", 1996 J.R. 127.

Cane, P., "Economic Loss in Tort: is the Pendulum Out of Control?" 1989 M.L.R. 200.

Cheer, U., "New Zealand Court of appeal rejects the 'Murphy' approach to tort liability for defective buildings" (1995) Tort L. Rev. 90.

Clarke, H., "Civil Liability of Public Authorities" (1986) 136 N.L.J. 435, 495.

Clifford, P. and Sharp, C., "Negligence, Duty, Economic Loss and Policy" (Note), 1995 Tort L. Rev. 169.

Craig, P.P., "Negligence in the Exercise of a Statutory Power" (1978) 94 L.Q.R. 428.

Davidson, F.P., "Insurers—Duty of Disclosure and Duty of Care", 1988 S.L.T. (News) 73.

Doyle, J.J., "The Liability of Public Authorities (1994) 1 Tort L. Rev. 189.

Duff, P., "Criminal Injuries Compensation, Nervous Shock and Secondary Victims", 1992 S.L.T. (News) 311.

Duncan Wallace, I.N., "Negligence and Defective Buildings: Confusion Confounded?" (1989) 105 L.Q.R. 46.

Duncan Wallace, I.N., "Negligence and Economic Loss: A view of the Future (1993) 1 Tort L. Rev. 152.

Duncan Wallace, I.N., "No Somersault after *Murphy*: New Zealand follows Canada" (1995) 111 L.Q.R. 285.

Duncan Wallace, I.N., "*Murphy* rejected: The *Bryan v. Maloney* Landmark", 1995 Tort L. Rev. 231.

Feenan, D.K., "Medical Negligence; *Hunter v. Hanley*, 35 years on: a reply", 1991 S.L.T. 321.

Fleming, J.G., "Economic Loss in Canada" (1993) 1 Tort L.Rev. 68.

Fleming, J.G., "Once More: Tort Liability for Structural Defects" (1995) 111 L.Q.R. 362.

Fleming, J.G., "Tort in a Contractual Matrix" (1995) 3 Tort L.Rev. 12.

Forte, A.D.M., "Disclaiming Liability for Negligent Property Surveys", 1986 S.L.T. (News) 293.

Forte, A.D.M., "Negligent Misrepresentations" (1988) 33 J.L.S.S. 93.

Giles, M., and Szyszczak, E., "Negligence and Defective Buildings: Demolishing the Foundations of *Anns*?" 1991 L.S. 85.

Griffiths, J.R., "Medical Negligence", 1995 S.L.P.O. 25.

Grubb, A., "Contraceptive Advice and Doctors—a Law Unto Themselves?" 1988 C.L.J. 12.

Hill, J., "Litigation and Negligence" (1986) 6 O.J.L.S. 183.

Hogg, K., "Relational loss, the exclusory rule and the High Court of Australia" (1995) 3 Tort L. Rev. 26.

Holyoak, J., "Accountancy and Negligence", 1986 J.B.L. 120.

Holyoak, J., "Economic Loss in Product and Premises Liability Cases", 1988 J.B.L. 139.

Holyoak, J., "Raising the Standard of Care", 1990 L.S. 201.

Holyoak, J. and Mazzocchetti, F., "The Legal Protection of Economic Interests" (1993) 1 Tort L. Rev. 185.

Honore, T., "*Hedley Byrne & Co. Ltd. v. Heller & Partners*" (1965) 8 J.S.P.T.L. 284.

Howarth, D., "My Brother's Keeper? Liability for Acts of Third Parties", 1994 L.S. 88.

James, M.F., "Professional Negligence and the Reasonableness Test", 1987 J.B.L. 286.

Kidner, R., "Resiling From the *Anns* Principle: the Variable Nature of Proximity in Negligence" (1987) 7 L.S. 319.

Logie, J.G., "Proof of Causation in Medical Negligence Cases", 1988 S.L.T. (News) 25.

Logie, J.G., "Rethinking Negligence", 1988 S.L.T. (News) 185.

Logie, J.G., "Special Relationships, Reasonable Foreseeability and Distinct Possibilities", 1988 J.R. 77.

Logie, J.G., "Affirmative Action in the Law of Tort: the Case of the Duty to Warn", 1989 C.L.J. 115.

Logie, J.G., "The Final Demise of *Junior Books*?" 1989 J.R. 5.

Logie, J.G., "Liability in Negligence of Company Accountants and Auditors", 1991 S.L.T. (News) 169.

McBryde, N.J. and Hughes, A., "*Hedley Byrne* in the House of Lords", 1995 L.S. 376.

McGrath, M., "The Recovery of Pure Economic Loss" (1985) 3 O.J.L.S. 350.

McLean, S.A., "Compensation and Medical Injury" (1981) 63 SCOLAG Bul. 361.

McMillan, A., "Scotland—Last Colony of the Empire?" 1996 S.L.T. (News) 159.

MacQueen, H.L., "Latent Defects, Collateral Warranties and Time Bar", 1991 S.L.T. (News) 77, 91, 99.

Markesinis, B.S., "The not so Dissimilar Tort and Delict" (1977) 93 L.Q.R. 78.

Markesinis, B.S., "An Expanding Tort Law—the Price of a Rigid Contract Law" (1987) 103 L.Q.R. 354.

Markesinis, B.S., "Negligence, Nuisance and Affirmative Duties of Action" (1989) 105 L.Q.R. 104.

Mullany, N.J., "Recovery for Psychiatric Injury by Report: Another small step forward" (1996) Tort L. Rev. 96.

Murphy, J., "Negligently inflicted psychiatric harm: a reappraisal", 1995 L.S. 415.

Norrie, K., "Informed Consent and Duty of Care", 1985 S.L.T. (News) 289.

Norrie, K., "Liability for Failed Sterilisation", 1986 S.L.T. (News) 145.

Norrie, K., "Liability of Solicitors to Third Parties", 1988 S.L.T. (News) 309, 317.

O'Brien, L.S., "The Validity of the Diagnosis of Post Traumatic Stress Disorder", 1994 J.P.I.L. 257.

O'Carroll, M., "Nervous Shock: Proposals for Reform" (1995) 40 J.L.S.S. 231.

Oughton, D., "Liability in Tort for Economic Loss Suffered by the Consumer of Defective Goods", 1987 J.B.L. 370.

Phillips, A.F., "Further Reflections on Medical Causation", 1988 S.L.T. (News) 325.

Phillips, A.F., "Medical Negligence and No-fault Compensation" (1989) 34 J.L.S.S. 239.

Rennie, R., "Negligence Instructions and the Lender's Need to Know" (1994) 39 J.L.S.S. 135.

Shearer, A., "Delictual Liability for Economic Loss", 1983 S.L.T. (News) 157.

Slater, C., "House Valuations and Surveys" (1988) 33 J.L.S.S. 89.

Smith, J.C. and Burns, P., "*Donoghue v. Stevenson*—the Not so Golden Anniversary" (1983) 46 M.L.R. 147.

Sopinka, J., "The Liability of Public Authorities: Drawing the Line" (1993) 1 Tort L. Rev. 123.

Stapleton, J., "The Gist of Negligence" (1988) 104 L.Q.R. 213, 389.

Stapleton, J., "Duty of Care: Peripheral Parties and Alternative Opportunities for Deterrence" (1995) 111 L.Q.R. 301.

Stephenson, I.S., "Goodbye *Junior Books*" (1988) 138 N.L.J. 483.

Stewart, W.J., "Economic Loss from Damage to Others' Property", 1987 S.L.T. (News) 145.

Thomson, J., "Delictual Liability between Parties to a Contract", 1994 S.L.T. (News) 29.

Thomson, J., "Delictual Liability for Pure Economic Loss: recent developments", 1995 S.L.T. 139.

Stuart, S.L., "Title to Sue in Respect of Damage to Property", 1986 S.L.T. (News) 257.

Teff, H., "Liability for Negligently Inflicted Nervous Shock" (1983) 99 L.Q.R. 100.

Todd, S., "Negligence Liability of Public Authorities: Divergence in the Common Law" (1986) 102 L.Q.R. 370.

Todd, S., "Defective Property: The turn of the Privy Council (1996) Tort L. Rev. 91.

Waddams, S.M., "Further reflections on economic Loss: A Canadian Perspective (1994) 1 Tort L. Rev. 116.

Wilkinson, A.B. and Forte, A.D.M., "Pure Economic Loss—a Scottish Perspective", 1985 J.R. 1.

CHAPTER 6

STATUTORY DUTY AND "EUROREP"

This general chapter deals with cases where an Act of Parliament has 6.1
imposed a duty upon someone to do or refrain from doing something.
The question then arises whether a person can sue another for a failure
to implement the statutory duty. So far every head of delictual liability
examined has been imposed by the common law. Now we examine
to what extent there can be liability which stems from a statute. The
fundamental position in Scotland was set out some time ago, albeit on
the basis of many English authorities:

> It has long ago been decided that the mere fact that a duty has been
> created by a statute will not entitle a person injured by the breach of
> that statutory duty to claim damages from the person upon whom
> the duty is imposed (*Atkinson v. Newcastle Waterworks Co.* (1877) 2
> Ex. D. 441 per Lord Cairns, L.C., at p. 448), and the Courts have
> frequently had to determine whether a particular statutory obliga-
> tion does or does not confer a right upon a person injured by its
> breach to damages for that injury. The solution in each case must
> depend upon what the intention of Parliament was in enacting the
> obligation in question, and what persons consequently have a right
> to enforce it or to found upon it as a basis for a claim of damages.[1]

Professor Walker says that there are two ways of looking at this
type of liability: the one, that it is an instance of common law delict,
the only difference being that the duty is imposed by Parliament
instead of by the common law; the other, that the statute creates the
entire obligation and the delict system of the common law merely
provides the mechanism for its enforcement. Walker prefers the
second view on the persuasive basis that sometimes Parliament
imposes duties which do not accord with the common law and
sometimes it imposes duties which are not civilly actionable.[2] This
chapter also deals with what is called by some in England, Eurotorts,

---

[1] *Pullar v. Window Clean*, 1956 S.L.T. 18, *per* Lord President Clyde at 21.
[2] Walker, *Delict*, pp. 296–297.

for some, a new or emerging tort. These new wrongs are well placed here if Professor Walker's second line is correct, for they are expressly obligations imposed by European Community law but the delict system is expected to provide mechanisms and remedies. The name chosen here reflects the origin of the obligation—European law—and the nature of the remedy—reparation.

6.2   There are three types of statutory duties with which this chapter is not concerned. The first is where Parliament clearly intends for there to be civil liability, examples being the Occupiers' Liability (Scotland) Act 1960, the Animals (Scotland) Act 1987 and Part I of the Consumer Protection Act 1987. Secondly, there are statutes which impose duties but which expressly declare that there is no intention of creating civil liability, for example the Health and Safety at Work etc. Act 1974 [see 7–42 *et seq.* for the leading section in this regard], the Guard Dogs Act 1975 and the Medicines Act 1968. The third category is cases where a statute imposes some duty on a public authority, in which case the element of public law has to be taken into account [5.31–5.35].

6.3   Instead we are concerned with the more difficult case where Parliament has said nothing at all about civil liability. This is therefore a specialised area of statutory interpretation.[3] It is a difficult area to understand and so at the outset it is as well to look at a case to put the subject into perspective. *Cutler v. Wandsworth Stadium Ltd (in liquidation)*[4] was an action raised by a bookmaker for damages against a licensed dog track for their refusal to allow him space on their premises to carry on bookmaking. The bookmaker founded on the Betting, Gaming and Lotteries Act 1934, s. 11(2) which provided that so long as a totalisator (state bookmaking system) was being lawfully operated from a licensed dog track, the occupier:

> "(a) shall not . . . exclude any person from the track by reason only that he proposes to carry on bookmaking on the track; and (b) shall take such steps as are necessary to secure that . . . there is available for bookmakers space on the track where they can conveniently carry on bookmaking . . . and every person who contravenes or fails to comply with, any of the provisions of this subsection shall be guilty of an offence."

Now, while it is clear that Parliament was imposing a duty on the stadium proprietor it is not clear from reading the Act when, if at all, and in what circumstances, a person might be able to sue in the civil courts for a failure to carry out the duty. In the House of Lords, Lord Reid identified certain issues which can help to determine the question. He asked: "For

---

[3] Walker, D.M., *The Scottish Legal System*, (7th rev. ed.), 1997 at 395 *et seq.*

[4] [1949] 1 All E.R. 544. This case was influential and approved in *Pullar*, above.

whose benefit was this sub-section intended?" And, as Law Lords usually do, he provided an answer to his own question: "I think that it was primarily intended for the protection of those members of the public who might wish to bet on these tracks." Not for bookmakers. The idea was to provide competition for the state-run totalisator. Another factor for Lord Reid was that, "If the legislature had intended to create such [civil] rights, [one] would expect to find them capable of reasonably precise definition." This the bookmaker was unable to do since, for example, there were many answers to the question, "How many bookmakers must be allowed in?"— all that ask, or just enough to leave enough space for the dogs? Lord Reid concluded by pointing out that the statute imposed a criminal penalty which was "appropriate and sufficient for the general obligation imposed." Indeed it can be said that where protection of a specific class is clear, and there is no mention of a civil or criminal sanction, that is the very kind of case where a civil action is necessarily upheld to give effect to the duty.[4a]

That, then, is the sort of issue with which this head of liability deals. Other issues arise in other cases and it is possible to set out a list of requirements the presence of which might lead to success, and the absence of which are likely to bring defeat for the pursuer.

1. There must be a statutory duty in force and applicable to the defender

The statute must tell the defender to do or refrain from doing some- 6.4 thing—it is not enough that it permits or allows the defender to do or refrain from doing something. It must also be applicable to the facts of the case, so where an Act imposed a duty relevant to a "factory" it was held not to cover a trawler. This decision was not as obvious as at first it might seem. Initially the court's attention was directed to a definition section which included drydocks within the definition of "factory". Another example, and a case of interest on other points, is *ICI v. Shatwell*.[5]

> ICI employed the respondent plaintiff George Shatwell and his brother James as shotfirers. There was in force at that time regulation 27(4) of the Quarries (Explosives) Regulations 1959 (SI 1959 No. 2259) which stated that "No shotfirer shall fire any round of shots . . . at a quarry . . . unless he has tested the circuit for continuity . . . A shotfirer shall not make any such test unless all persons in the vicinity have withdrawn to a place of safety and he himself has taken proper shelter." The brothers tested the explosives with short leads without taking proper shelter and were blown up.

It was held, among other things [11.19], that the employers were not in breach of statutory duty since the duty was clearly incumbent upon the plaintiff and his brother themselves.

[4a] Lord Browne-Wilkinson in *X v. Bedfordshire County Council* [1995] 3 All E.R. 353.
[5] [1965] A.C. 656.

2. The duty must be intended to protect the pursuer

6.5   This point is illustrated by *Cutler* above, where although there may have been some intention by Parliament to help bookmakers general-ly, it was essentially members of the public who were being protected. In *McMullan v. Lochgelly Iron and Coal Co.*[6] the court held that section 49 of the Coal Mines Act 1911 protected a workman on the basis that the section occurred in Part II of the Act, the heading of which was "Provisions as to Safety", and the purpose of section 49 was to ensure the safety of the workmen employed in the mine.

3. It must be a duty which the statute intends to be enforced by civil action

6.6   Again *Cutler* is an illustration of this point in that the obligation was one regulated by the criminal law. There are no fixed rules in these matters. Sometimes some sections of an Act have been held civilly actionable whereas others have not. If there is another remedy in the Act or clearly envisaged by the Act then that will usually exclude an action based on the statute. In the case of *J. Bollinger v. Costa Brava Wine Co. Ltd*,[7] there was an attempt by French champagne producers seeking an injunction against a Spanish company using the name "champagne", to found on the Merchandising Marks Act 1887 which provided penalties against persons for false trade descriptions and the like. However, the Act preserved the right of a party to proceed with a passing-off action [3.7–3.13] and accordingly could not be used in support of a civil action based on breach of the statute. It is also worth noting that the statute was held intended to protect the public from false trade descriptions rather than offering a protection to rival traders.

4. The intention must be to guard against the harm that has occurred

6.7   This is another particular application of statutory interpretation. It may be that the pursuer is the sort of person who is supposed to be protected by the Act and the defender may have a duty incumbent upon him which Parliament intends to give rise to civil liability, but no action will lie if the harm is not within the scope of the protection offered by the Act. *Carroll v. Andrew Barclay and Sons Ltd*[8] demon-strates the point:

> The Factories Act 1937 provided that every part of the transmis-sion machinery should be securely fenced. A workman was

---

[6] 1933 S.C. (H.L.) 64.
[7] [1960] Ch. 262.
[8] 1948 S.C. (H.L.) 100.

injured when a belt forming part of the transmission machinery broke. One of the ends hit his head. The belt had been enclosed but not fenced.

It was held that the employers were not in breach of section 13 as that provided only for fencing which would prevent persons from coming into contact with the machinery but not fencing which would protect them from broken parts of the machinery coming out to strike them.[9]

5. Breach of duty

The pursuer must still show a breach of the duty imposed. The content of the duty is a matter of interpretation of the legislation. This is a specialised matter of pleading. Sometimes the standard required will be reasonable care as in common law liability but other standards exist, mainly because statutes have usually been passed to impose a higher degree of care. Thus, sometimes there is absolute liability[10] or cases where something must be achieved "so far as it is reasonably practicable", or an Act may allow a defence of impracticality only, regardless of how unreasonable it would be to take certain steps. Examples of these can be seen in the treatment of the Factories Act [7.38–7.43]. In *Edwards v. NCB*,[11] the following formulation of reasonable practicability was offered: 6.8

> "Reasonably practicable is a narrower term than physically possible and seems to me to imply that a computation must be made by the owner in which the quantum of risk is placed in one scale and the sacrifice involved in the measures necessary for averting the risk (whether in money, time or trouble) is placed in the other, and that, if it be shown that there is a gross disproportion—the risk being insignificant in relation to the sacrifice—the defendants discharge the onus on them . . . The questions he has to answer are: (a) what measures are necessary and sufficient to prevent any breach . . . (b) are these measures reasonably practicable?"

If the duty is an absolute one then only the happening need be proved.

6. Causation

Normally it is essential to show that the harm was caused by the breach of the statutory duty.[12] A statute can make proof of causation unnecessary. 6.9

---

[9] See also *Gorris v. Scott* (1874) L.R. 9 Ex. 125.

[10] See *Summers v. Frost* [1955] A.C. 740.

[11] [1949] 1 K.B. 704.

[12] *Wardlaw v. Bonnington Castings*, 1956 S.C. (H.L.) 26.

7. Damages

6.10 There seems to be no authority on remoteness of damage in statutory liability cases.[13] Probably the same approach would be taken as in the general law.

8. Defences

6.11 There remains only one more speciality of liability for breach of statutory duty and that is that the defence of *volenti non fit injuria* [11.19] does not normally apply, on the basis that if Parliament had intended a duty to be so restricted it would have said so. This is well illustrated by the case of *Wheeler v. New Merton Board Mills Ltd*[14]:

> A boy was employed to clean the blades of a machine. There was a lever which he was to use to stop the machine to let him do this. Either through pressure of work or over eager application to his task his practice was to try to clean the blades while the machine was still in operation. Scrutton L.J. takes up the story: "He went on for three months taking shaving out of the knives while the machine was still working, and by good luck he did so for three months without having his fingers cut off, but at last the evil day came when he lost his hand and fingers."

> The court held that he was not defeated by the plea of *volenti*. The case of *ICI v. Shatwell*, mentioned above, shows that so long as the injury complained of has not been caused by a breach of statutory duty by the defender the plea of *volenti* is still open. In that case there was a statutory duty but it was incumbent upon the injured man himself. It should be noted that Parliament can include such a defence should it so wish, as it has in the Occupiers' Liability (Scotland) Act 1960 and the Animals (Scotland) Act 1987. That Parliament does this indicates that the inapplicability of the *volenti* defence is not restricted to cases under the Factories Acts.

> It is possible for conduct to amount to contributory negligence reducing or completely excluding liability [11.21].

EUROREP

6.12 This head of liability has been described as a new and emerging tort. It is included here because it bears great similarity to statutory liability in

---

[13] See *Delict*, p. 323.
[14] [1933] 2 K.B. 669.

that there may be no express provision for damages and in that it is the national system of law, particularly that dealing with compensation in the civil courts, that gives effect to the right of damages on breach.

The first manifestation was in relation to the competition policy of the European Community.[15] It was suggested in one case that a breach of these provisions might be actionable in the United Kingdom courts for damages.[16]

The next development is in relation to the enforcement of Com- 6.13 munity law generally. The methods provided by the Treaty, mainly Article 169, have not been adequate. The decision in the landmark case *Van Gend en Loos v. Nederlandse Tarief Commissie*[17] declared that certain Treaty Articles could have direct effect[18] in the Member States and later decisions declared that regulations and directives[19] can have this effect too. That is not the end of the matter, for the problem with directives is that, as they are frequently addressed to a Member State with instructions to achieve an objective, there is the possibility, and in some states the probability, that the Government will not implement or will improperly implement the directive. This failure heretofore had been thought only challengeable at the supranational level of the Commission suing the Member State before the European Court of Justice.

Some directives, indeed many directives, allow the Member State 6.14 some considerable discretion. If it is not exercised then there is a gap in the Community enforcement mechanism.[20] This was plugged in a decision which will produce volumes of litigation in all sorts of areas.

Directive 80/987 was intended to provide workers with a minimum level of protection in the event of the insolvency of their employers. The deadline for implementation was October 23, 1983. The Italian Government failed to implement the directive and was sued by the Commission, who obtained a ruling against Italy.[21] Nonetheless, nothing had been done by May 1991. *Francovich* is in fact two cases, raised separately and later joined, whereby workers who were uncompensated sought damages against the State for payment of wages as provided by the directive or alternatively for compensation for the loss as a result of the failure of the State to implement the

---

[15] For Community law generally, see "European Community Law and Institutions", *The Laws of Scotland: Stair Memorial Encyclopaedia*, Vol. 10.

[16] *Garden Cottage Foods v. Milk Marketing Board* [1984] A.C. 130.

[17] [1963] 1 C.M.L.R. 105.

[18] See *Stair Memorial Encyclopaedia*, Vol. 10, para. 81.

[19] *ibid.* paras 89–93.

[20] What follows is indebted to G.H. Downie, "New Right to Damages in Community Law" (1992) 37 J.L.S.S. 424; see also C. Boch and R. Lane, "A New Remedy in Scots Law: Damages from the Crown for Breach of Community Law", 1992 S.L.T. 145.

[21] *Commission v. Italian Republic* [1989] E.C.R. 143.

directive.[22] On a preliminary ruling[23] it was held that the directive just failed to meet the twin criteria for direct effect as the State had a considerable discretion.

6.15   The court did allow the compensation claim: "The full effectiveness of rules of Community Law would be undermined and the protection of the rights which they create weakened if individuals were unable to obtain reparation when their rights were infringed as a result of Member State's violation of community law."[24] There are three conditions for such a case:

(1) the result prescribed by the directive must involve the attribution of rights to individuals;
(2) the content of those rights must be identifiable from the provisions of the directive;
(3) a causal link must exist between the violation of the Member State's obligation and the damage suffered by the injured person.[25]

It is for the national courts to decide the form of the reparation process. However, the national systems must designate the competent courts and forms of proceedings which may be used to pursue such "Eurorep" cases. Downie helpfully points out that the effect is retroactive—all past failures to implement directives are now potentially actionable. Downie argues, too, that the reach of the two decisions mentioned above has been extended by the *Francovich* case. This case dealt with a directive and so it was arguable that it applied only to directives and not other European Union legislation. It was also a case of a failure to legislate.

6.16   The European Court of Justice took the law a stage further in two joined cases.[26] In *R. v. Secretary of State for Transport, ex parte Factortame Ltd*[27] companies owned and operated by Spanish citizens sought judicial review complaining of the illegality of a United Kingdom statute and related regulations. A first ECJ reference declared that any national rules precluding remedies enforcing Community law were inapplicable and so injunctions could be brought against the Crown and national courts could declare United Kingdom legislation inapplicable. In the second reference the United Kingdom legislation was ruled to have been contrary to European Union law. It

---

[22] C–6/90 and C–9/90, *Andrea Francovich v. Italian Republic; Danila Bonifaci & Others v. Italian Republic* [1992] I.R.L.R. 84.

[23] See *Stair Memorial Encyclopaedia*, Vol. 10, paras 239–244.

[24] para. 34.

[25] para. 40.

[26] For a detailed analysis see Upton, "Crown Liability in Damages under Community Law [Parts 1 & 2]", 1996 S.L.T. (News) 175 and 211.

[27] [1990] 2 A.C. 85, HL; [1991] 1 A.C. 603, ECJ (C–48/93).

was changed by the United Kingdom Parliament as a result. The plaintiffs then sought the damages they had claimed in the original judicial review—they had, after all, been precluded (they said) from fishing by what had been declared to be illegal legislation. It was held that such a right to damages did arise. In *Brasserie du Pecheur S.A. v. Germany*[28] French brewers complained that the German law on beer duty was contrary to EU law and that they had sustained a loss as a result. They, too, were entitled to recover.

The ECJ based its rules for establishing liability on its existing rules on non-contractual liability of the Community. Community law confers a right to reparation where three conditions are met:

(1) the rule of law infringed must be intended to confer rights on individuals;
(2) the breach must be sufficiently serious;
(3) there must be a direct causal link between the breach of the obligation resting on the state and the damage sustained by the injured parties.

In deciding whether the matter was sufficiently serious the decisive test is whether the Member State had manifestly and gravely disregarded the limits on its discretion. Certain factors can be taken into account (so can others not listed by the Court) in approaching that question:

(a) the clarity and precision of the rule breached;
(b) the measure of discretion left to the Member State;
(c) whether the infringement and any damage caused were intentional or voluntary;
(d) whether any error of law was excusable;
(e) the contribution, if any, a Community institution might have made;
(f) the adoption or retention of national measures.

Where there has been (a) a judgment finding an infringement established; (b) a preliminary ruling; or (c) an established body of ECJ jurisprudence, then the breach is sufficiently serious.

A number of practical points were also laid down in the joint cases. The obligation to make reparation did not depend on a condition based on any concept of fault (intentional or negligent) beyond that of a serious breach of community law. The extent of reparation must be commensurate. The local system may set the criteria but they must not be less favourable than those applying to similar claims based on domestic law and must not be such as in practice make it impossible or excessively difficult to obtain reparation. Damages for loss of profit could not be ruled out as many cases involve commerce. Exemplary

6.17

---

[28] C–46/93; [1996] 2 W.L.R. 506.

damages, where they apply nationally, could not be ruled out either. The date from which damages would be payable was not cut off at the date of a decision—there was no temporal limitation.

6.18   Perhaps the best example of the current position and one more like those that might be expected to concern the ordinary practitioner in the future is *Dillenkofer v. Germany*.[29] The plaintiffs lost money when their holiday companies went bust. They sued the state for failure to have implemented the directive on package travel swiftly enough to have covered their cases. The Court referred to the *Brasserie* criteria and the *Francovich* criteria. The Court explained that although *Francovich*, another non-transposition case, did not expressly mention the need for serious breach, it was implied within it. Thus failure to transpose within the set time-limit is *per se* a serious breach. In this case the rights conferred and the persons on whom they were conferred was clear.[30]

This head of liability will increase as the years go by.[31] The challenge now is to guess which European legislation will found *Brasserie* claims. Students studying delict and European Union law have ready-made dissertation topics.

Further reading

Boch, C. and Lane, R., "A New Remedy in Scots Law: Damages from the Crown for Breach of Community Law", 1992 S.L.T. 145.

Buckley, R., "Liability in Tort for Breach of Statutory Duty" (1984) 100 L.Q.R. 204.

Downie, G.H., "New Right to Damages in Community Law" (1992) 37 J.L.S.S. 424.

Upton, M. "Crown Liability in Damages under Community Law", 1996 S.L.T. (News) 175, 211.

---

[29] 1996 T.L.R. 564,.

[30] The U.K. joined the case to argue that late transposition should not be a matter of liability *per se* and that it would have to be shown that it was a manifest and grave breach. The directive was implemented by the U.K. in the The Package Travel, Package Holiday and Package Tours Regulations 1992 (S.I. 1992 No. 3288).

[31] See also *R.v. Ministry of Agriculture and Fisheries, ex p. Hedley Lomas (Ireland) Ltd* [1996] T.L.R. 353; *R. v. H.M. Treasury, ex p. British Telecommunications plc* [1996] 3 W.L.R. 203.

CHAPTER 7

SPECIAL AREAS OF ACTIVITY

This chapter deals with certain very common instances of liability. 7.1
Most are special because of statutory intervention. The common
factor is that while common law applies to some extent, many of
the most usual incidents are covered by some statutory provision.
Simple road traffic cases are accordingly not dealt with here.[1] Note
should, however, be taken of the differences in the standard of care
required under the various statutes and the different terminology
employed. Each of these instances of statutory liability is subject to
the general law of statutory interpretation and the principles set out in
Chapter 6. This chapter deals with occupiers' liability, product
liability, liability in respect of animals and employer's liability.

OCCUPIERS' LIABILITY

The liability of an occupier is now mainly a matter of statutory 7.2
liability (see Chapter 6), in particular the Occupiers' Liability (Scotland) Act 1960. The Act was passed to alter the Scots common law
which had been strongly influenced by English principles imposed by
the House of Lords.[2] It is submitted that this is now a matter of legal
history; but in reading pre-Act decisions, it should be borne in mind
that the classification of the injured person, as either licensee, invitee
or trespasser, was crucial. Although that is no longer the case it is still
a circumstance which must be considered as affecting what care a
reasonable occupier would actually take.[3]

The broad purpose of the Act is to provide that occupiers must take 7.3
reasonable care for persons entering on their premises. It does not

---

[1] For a review see Stewart, "Reparation: Road Traffic Cases" (1994) 39 J.L.S.S. 211.
[2] *Dumbreck v. Addie & Sons*, 1929 S.C. (H.L.) 51. The position in England has
recently changed, although not so far as to make it identical to the law in Scotland:
see Occupiers' Liability Act 1984.
[3] See *McGlone v. BRB*, 1966 S.C. (H.L.) 1.

create a general liability upon an occupier of the property to take any care for persons who have not entered on the property, such as adjoining proprietors or passers-by. Such individuals are protected by general principles of liability for unintentional harm (see Chapters 4 and 5) and nuisance [2.12–2.19] and other related delicts. One of the most common errors made by party litigants and inexperienced solicitors is to plead such a case in such a way that it infers a duty of insurance "to ensure" as opposed to "to take reasonable care to ensure".

7.4   The first question is usually to determine who is the occupier. Here we gain some assistance from the Act.[4] It defines "occupier of premises" as "a person occupying or having control of land or other premises."

However, we still require to know what is meant by occupying or having control. To resolve this question regard is had to the law as it applied before the Act. This is still effectively determined by the common law which is expressly saved in the statute.[5] The test is a matter of possession and control and will be a matter of fact in each case. An example is *Telfer v. Glasgow D.C.*[6]:

> The Co-operative Society were in the course of selling property to Glasgow District Council. Both the council and the society were sued in respect of an injury sustained on the property. It was held, *inter alia*, that the society were the occupiers. They had the keys and the *de facto* power to exclude others.

7.5   The next question is to ask what is meant by premises ("land" being apparently self explanatory). This is not defined in the Act and is a matter to be determined in each case. The Act also imposes liability for certain areas which (as they have been separately described) are not premises and may be described as notional premises.[7] So the following are covered by the Act: fixed or moveable structures, including any vessel, vehicle or aircraft. This provision in its terms covers most modes of transport and it will be a question of statutory interpretation whether, for example, a hoist or a ski-tow fall within the statutory definitions.

An open area of land attracted liability when Mrs Cairns, a grandmother, tripped in a concealed hole at a Butlins camp. The defenders denied the existence of a hole on the basis of regular inspections. The court held there was a hole and because they had

---

[4] Occupiers' Liability (Scotland) Act 1960 (the "1960 Act"), s. 1(1).

[5] 1960 Act, s. 1(2).

[6] 1974 S.L.T. (Notes) 51. See also *Feely v. Co-operative Wholesale Society*, 1990 G.W.D. 4–221. And see also for an independent contractor pursuer himself being in control: *Poliskie v. Lane*, 1981 S.L.T. 28.

[7] 1960 Act, s. 1(3).

regular inspections they must have been negligent and missed it![8] It covers a workshop on a caravan site.[9]

Gloag and Henderson state: "The Occupiers' Liability Act does not apply to public roads, streets or footpaths which at common law or by public or private Acts are the responsibility of public bodies."[10] The passage has been approved in a recent case.[11] However, it is difficult to find any authority for this proposition, which is contrary to the plain meaning of the Act.[12] It is true that, historically, liability in respect of roads developed separately from occupiers' liability, while liability for premises was subject to the older "English" tripartite system. It is also the case that even if prima facie the Act could be said to apply to a road, the requirement of occupation of a road may be hard to establish. Control might not be so difficult to establish.

In practice, despite a brave attempt by the sheriff principal at Glasgow to state the law properly in *King v. Strathclyde R.C.*,[13] the Inner House balkanised pavement cases in the daily cited case of *Gibson v. Strathclyde R.C.*[14]

The following, sometimes obvious, practical propositions can be extracted from that case.

(1) Liability is for fault.
(2) The general rule applies that a pursuer's personal injury case should not be dismissed on relevancy unless it is bound to fail if proved, the onus of establishing that being on the defender.[15]
(3) A daily inspection case cannot *normally* be supported by a bald averment it would be reasonable and practicable to do that.[16]
(4) It is possible to establish a daily inspection case without averments of proper practice giving rise to an inference of negligence although the circumstances should be, on one view, special, exceptional and obvious,[17] or perhaps better the subject of averment.[18]

---

[8] *Cairns v. Butlins*, 1989 G.W.D. 40–1879.
[9] *Morley v. The Most Noble Ian Campbell*, 1997 G.W.D. 18–844.
[10] *Introduction to the Law of Scotland* (9th ed., 1987), p. 568.
[11] *Lamont v. Monklands D.C.*, 1992 G.W.D. 4–200.
[12] *Stair Memorial Encyclopaedia*, Vol. 20, para. 614, "Roads", indicates that the Act applies to private roads and many cases of general negligence in respect of public roads are set out (para. 611) but no view is expressed on this point.
[13] Glasgow, Jan. 8, 1991.
[14] 1993 S.L.T. 1243.
[15] Lord Justice-Clerk Ross at 1245 H–K.
[16] Lord Justice-Clerk Ross at 1246A; Lord Weir at 1248B.
[17] Lord Weir at 1248A
[18] Lord Justice-Clerk Ross at 1246H.

The arguments often made by pursuers were made in this case and largely rejected, particularly the point that the pursuer seldom has the knowledge of what is reasonable or practicable, the daily burden of roads administration being beyond their knowledge and in the absence of private or public funding, that of their professional advisers. On the other hand, it is regularly suggested by defenders that the pursuer must specify which council takes which particular precautions. That, it is submitted, goes far too far. As public authorities are involved in roads and pavement cases, it should not be forgotten that general principles of liability apply, albeit the "great" cases are not cited and discussed.[19] The same requirements of specification have been carried over to all cases, perhaps unnecessarily.[20]

7.6   The duty and the standard of care are laid down by the Act. To succeed the pursuer must bring himself within the terms of the Act[21]:

> "The care which an occupier of premises is required, by reason of his occupation or control of the premises, to show towards a person entering thereon in respect of dangers which are due to the state of the premises or to anything done or omitted to be done on them and for which the occupier is in law responsible shall, except in so far as he is entitled to and does extend, restrict, modify or exclude by agreement his obligations towards that person, be such care as in all the circumstances of the case is reasonable to see that that person will not suffer injury or damage by reason of any such danger."

While this provision can be summarised to the effect that the occupier must take such care as is reasonable in all the circumstances, it is nevertheless a statutory duty and it is important to try to fit specific cases into the statutory definition of the duty. Despite the positive formulation of the duty, it seems now to be settled that it imposes no evidentiary burden upon the occupier. The pursuer will still have to show the circumstances which give rise to the duty; a pursuer cannot merely aver that he has suffered an accident on premises and put the onus on the defender to prove that he took reasonable care.[22]

---

[19] *Stovin v. Wise* [1996] A.C. 923, although an English House of Lords case is still important but is not in point where there is already a duty of care recognised in Scotland by an authority. *Forbes v. Dundee*, 1997 S.L.T. 1330 imports these *Stovin* arguments into a Scots discussion but on the facts the basis of the case may have merited such an argument.

[20] See Kinloch, "Slippery Substances", 1995 Rep. B. 4–7.

[21] 1960 Act, s. 2(1).

[22] See *Wallace v. City of Glasgow D.C.*, 1985 S.L.T. 23; *Walker v. Eastern Scottish Omnibuses Ltd*, 1990 G.W.D. 3–140; *Miller v. City of Glasgow D.C.*, 1989 G.W.D. 29–1347. For notes on the law in practice see Kinloch, "Slippery Substances", 1995 Rep. B. 4–7.

Previously decided cases can illustrate what the rule set out in the 7.7
statute means. It certainly would cover many a derelict building.[23] An
injury due to the "state of the premises" can result from less obvious
circumstances. There is no reason to think that facts similar to a case
decided before the Act would not support liability: an action by a father
in respect of the death of his son as a result of his eating poisonous berries
in the Botanic Gardens in Glasgow was held to be relevant.[24] Leaving a
bucket which was usually filled with water, filled instead with petrol
might be something "done on the premises".[25] Poor lighting indicates
that the state of the premises is inadequate.[26] A weather bar over which
people often tripped and which could have been replaced by a safer one
affected the state of the premises.[27] Allowing a house to become damp
such that it affected a child's asthma has fallen within the Act.[28]

As a result of there being no express categories of victim it does not 7.8
matter, in principle, whether someone is on the premises by invitation or
as a trespasser: the standard of care, in both cases, is still reasonable care.
These points were considered in *McGlone v. British Railways Board.*[29]

> A boy aged 12 climbed up a transformer belonging to the board.
> It was surrounded on three sides by a large fence and on the other
> by the railway. A gap between the fence and a wall was restricted
> by barbed wire in a fan shape. There were signs saying,
> "Danger—overhead live wires." The boy was badly burned as
> a result of an electric shock sustained when he came into contact
> with one of the wires high up the transformer.

The court held that although the barrier was not impenetrable it
indicated to the victim that he would be in danger and that was enough
to implement the duty of care. Lord Reid expressed the view that the
degree of care to be shown could vary depending on whether the
person was trespassing or not. Lord Reid's opinion has not in any way
resulted in an under-the-table categorisation of victims: instead it
usefully serves to make courts and advisers remember that the Act
refers every case back to its own circumstances. This area of the law
and the case of *McGlone* were considered again by the House of Lords
in *Titchener v. British Railways Board.*[30]

> A girl was struck by a train as she crossed a busy railway line. She
> was aware that it was such and usually looked both ways. She

---

[23] *Telfer v. Glasgow D.C.* (cited, n. 5).
[24] *Taylor v. Glasgow Corp.*, 1922 S.C. (H.L.) 1.
[25] *Ross v. McCallum's Trs*, 1922 S.C. 322.
[26] *Millar v. Fife R.C.*, 1989 G.W.D. 40–1880.
[27] *McMillan v. Ministry of Defence*, 1990 G.W.D. 5–271.
[28] *Guy v. Strathkelvin D.C.*, 1997 S.C.L.R. 405.
[29] 1966 S.L.T. 2.
[30] 1984 S.L.T. 192; followed in *Devlin v. Strathclyde R. C.*, 1993 S.L.T. 699.

alleged the board should have inspected for gaps in the fence and repaired them. It was held that the existence and extent of a duty to fence will depend upon the circumstances of the case including the age and intelligence of the particular person entering on the premises. Thus the board owed no duty to that particular pursuer in these particular circumstances to repair the fence.

Indeed, Lord Fraser said that if it had been necessary to do so, he would have held that the board owed her no duty to provide a fence at all. This applies generally so that an obvious danger does not require to be fenced or signposted.[31]

7.9   It is possible to exclude the duty by agreement but not by a simple notice or warning. However, such notice or warning will be a circumstance to be accorded whatever weight is appropriate.[32] Further, there is statutory control of agreements where premises are used as business premises. Section 16 of the Unfair Contract Terms Act 1977 provides:

> "Where a term of a contract purports to exclude or restrict liability for breach of duty arising in the course of any business or from the occupation of any premises used for business purposes of the occupier, that term—
>
> (a) shall be void in any case where such exclusion or restriction is in respect of death or personal injury;
> (b) shall in any other case, have no effect if it was not fair and reasonable to incorporate the term in the contract."

The 1960 Act does not relieve an occupier of any higher duty of care incumbent upon him[33] such as the employer's duty to provide for his employees under the Factories Act [7.38–7.43].

7.10   There is no obligation to a person entering on the premises in respect of a risk which that person has willingly accepted as his.[34] In *Titchener* (above) it was reiterated that the part of the Act which deals with acceptance of risk merely put into words the principle expressed by the maxim *volenti non fit injuria* [11.19]. In *Titchener* it was stated that if there had been a duty of care this "*volenti*" subsection would have applied to exclude liability. In evidence, the pursuer had said that she had known she was "taking a chance".

7.11   The Act makes special provision for cases involving landlord and tenant. This is important, for the tenant is the person in actual occupation and would seem to be the occupier for the purposes of

---

[31] *Stevenson v. Glasgow Corp.*, 1908 S.C. 1034.
[32] *McGlone*, above.
[33] 1960 Act, s. 2(2).
[34] 1960 Act, s. 2(3).

the Act. The landlord under a lease may, however, be the one who has the responsibility for certain aspects of the state of the premises. While the tenant is entitled to pursue a claim against the landlord for a breach of an obligation under the lease, this is a contractual right which would not be available to his guests or members of his family. Accordingly, the Act makes the landlord liable instead of the tenant, if under the lease the landlord is responsible for the maintenance or repair of the premises.[35]

The most important question is, of course, whether the landlord is responsible in the first place: this will be determined by the contract of lease. Apart from any special terms in the lease there are two major implied conditions:

> (1) There is an implied warrandice that the subjects let are fit for the purpose for which they are let. In an urban lease the landlord is impliedly obliged to maintain the subjects in a tenantable and habitable condition, having put them in such a state at entry.
>
> (2) There is a statutorily implied condition that subjects are and will be maintained reasonably fit for human habitation.[36]

Accordingly, in most cases where someone is injured in a council house they will have a possible delictual remedy against the landlord even if they do not have a contractual right under the lease. Lord Johnston has recently decided in the Outer House that section 3 of the Act effectively overruled the effect of the existing common-law rule which relied upon privity to deny the tenant's claim.[37]

PRODUCT LIABILITY

This area like many others now involves the application of both the common law and statute. It is another area which usually involves unintentional harm. The general common-law duty to take reasonable care has been supplemented by a special statutory form of strict liability by the Consumer Protection Act 1987.[38] Not all cases are covered by the Act so the common law is still relevant.

7.12

---

[35] 1960 Act, s. 3(1).

[36] Housing (Scotland) Act 1987, Sched. 10, and see *Haggarty v. Glasgow Corp.*, 1963 S.L.T. (Notes) 73; 1964 S.L.T. (Notes) 95.

[37] *Guy v. Strathkelvin D.C.*, 1997 S.C.L.R. 405—the common-law rule was in *Cameron v. Young*, 1908 S.C. (H.L.) 7.

[38] This only applies to damage attributable to defective products arising after March 1, 1988, where the product has been supplied after that date.

The common law

7.13   Mention has already been made of the case of *Donoghue v. Stevenson* in the context of liability for unintentional harm generally.[39] However, while that case has a wide *ratio* establishing proximity as a basis of liability, it also has a narrow *ratio* which is a suitable beginning from which to look at product liability. That narrow *ratio* is apparent from a dictum of Lord Atkin:

> "a manufacturer of products, which he sells in such a form as to show that he intends them to reach the ultimate consumer in the form in which they left him, with no reasonable possibility of intermediate examination, and with the knowledge that the absence of reasonable care in the preparation or putting up of the products will result in an injury to the consumer's life or property, owes a duty to the consumer to take that reasonable care."[40]

It has been accepted that the principle could apply to services as much as goods.[41]

The intermediate examination point requires some clarification. In *Donoghue* the seller of the ginger beer could not be expected to open the bottles to check for decomposed snails. However, if the bottle had been translucent, the retailer might have been expected to check for obvious impurities. In the case of *Grant v. Australian Knitting Mills Ltd*[42] the issue was whether it was possible to recover in respect of dermatitis contracted as a result of injurious chemicals being present in the plaintiff's underwear. The difference between this case and *Donoghue* was that the retailer took the underpants from their pack and placed them on his shelves, whereas the alleged snail in *Donoghue* remained in its bottle all the time. The Privy Council refused to accept the significance of that distinction. There was no need for the product to remain as it had been put out. On the other hand, it was stated that the defect in the product has to remain "hidden and unknown to the consumer". The *Grant* case is also of interest because it was held that the plaintiff did not have to prove the mechanism of the harm—it was possible to establish the cause by an inference from the proven facts [12.2–12.8]. This matter of intermediate examination makes warnings and instructions all the more important:

---

[39] 4.6 above.

[40] 1932 S.C. (H.L.) 31 at 57. Lord Rodger has traced the legal ancestry of the *Donoghue* snail back to a cigar stub in a Coca-Cola bottle in Tennessee: "Lord Macmillan's Speech" (1992) 108 L.Q.R. 236 at 244.

[41] *Haseldine v. C.A. Daw & Son Ltd* [1941] 3 All E.R. 156.

[42] [1935] All E.R. 209.

In *Kubach v. Hollands*[43] a science teacher (employed by the first defendant, the proprietrix of the school) bought some chemicals for an experiment from the second defendants. The second defendants had purchased the chemicals from the third party. Unfortunately, the chemical supplied was mixed with another chemical which caused an explosion when used. So far as the second defendants' supply to the school was concerned, they were held liable—the defect was latent and there was no reason for the teacher to test the substance. The issue was between the third party and the second defendants. The third party's invoice stated that the chemicals should be "examined and tested by user before use."

The court held for the third party on the basis that the second defendants "had ample and repeated opportunity of intermediate examination, and, if they had taken the simple precaution which the invoice warned them to take, no mischief would have followed."

The issue of intermediate examination and the general question of 7.14 causation are interrelated. The issue of intermediate examination can be analysed as whether the cause of the accident was the fault of the manufacturer or due to another cause.[44] The case of *Evans v. Triplex Safety Glass Co. Ltd*[45] illustrates this.[46] It is also a convenient example of how the common law fails to offer what many consider to be adequate protection for the consumer.

Mr Evans bought a car. The manufacturers of the car fitted a windscreen manufactured by the defenders. When Mr Evans was driving his car the windscreen disintegrated and injured people in the car. The accident could have been due to faulty fitting of the windscreen or could have been due to other causes such as faulty manufacture of the windscreen. Because Evans failed to prove fault on the part of the manufacturer either of the car or of the windscreen, he lost his case.

It was such difficulties which led to calls for liability independent of fault, to which we now turn.

---

[43] [1937] 3 All E.R. 907.
[44] For a discussion of the modern relevance of intermediate examination, see *Murphy v. Brentwood D.C.* [1990] 3 W.L.R. 414.
[45] [1936] 1 All E.R. 283.
[46] And see also *Diamantis Pateras* [1966] 1 Lloyd's Rep. 179, *per* Lawrence J. at 188.

The Consumer Protection Act 1987, Part I

7.15   This statute implements an EEC directive[47] and it is expressly stated in the Act that it has to be construed to comply with the directive.[48] For some time there had been moves to introduce some form of strict liability but no domestic solution had come to fruition.[49] There are many matters of policy reflected in such a system. In the main, liability is placed on the person most able to prevent an accident in the first place—the producer. Secondly, the cost of an accident is removed from the consumer, who generally would find it expensive to insure, and passed to someone else more likely to be able to obtain insurance cover on reasonable terms.

7.16   The Act provides a limited form of strict liability for defective products which does not, however, replace any existing liability in delict.[50] Broadly speaking, there is strict liability on a producer for damages caused by a defective product. Each of the key elements in this liability is defined by the statute. The following treatment is intended to give a broad view of the Act but does not deal with every aspect of it.

Product

7.17   "Product" means any goods or electricity and includes any goods comprised in another product whether by virtue of being a component part or raw material or otherwise.[51] Thus both the car and the windscreen in a case like *Evans* would be products. "Goods" is further defined as including "substances, growing crops and things comprised in land by virtue of being attached to it and any ship, aircraft or vehicle."[52] for Scotland the reference to "attached" means becoming heritable by accession to heritable property.[53] There is no liability in respect of any defect in any game or agricultural produce, which is defined as being any produce of the soil or stock farming or fisheries so long as the supply was at a time when it had not undergone an industrial process.[54]

---

[47] Dir. No. 85/374/EEC.

[48] s. 1(1). This is no platitude. It had been anticipated that the Commission might challenge the U.K.'s implementation of the directive as being too restrictive to liability in places. Such a case did emerge, *Commission v. U.K.* [1997] All E.R. (EC) 481, and this very provision convinced the Court that the U.K. had complied, for if this provision were given effect to the U.K. law would comply with E.C. law. That is an optimistic view of the approach of U.K. courts to legislation!

[49] The Strasbourg Convention: Dir/Jun (76) 5; the Scottish and English Law Commissions: Cmnd 6831 (1977); the Pearson Commission: Cmnd 7054 (1978).

[50] s. 2(6).

[51] s. 1(2).

[52] s. 45 (1).

[53] s. 45(5).

[54] ss. 2(4) and 1(2).

Defect

The Act provides a definition of "defect", which exists "if the safety 7.18
of the product is not such as persons generally are entitled to
expect."[55] Realising that this would not answer every problem or
might lead to diverging judicial opinions, the Act provides that while
all the circumstances of the case should be taken into account, the
following must be considered:

"(a) the manner in which and purposes for which, the product has
been marketed, its get-up, the use of any mark in relation to
the product and any instructions for, or warnings with respect
to, doing or refraining from doing anything with or in
relation to the product;
(b) what might reasonably be expected to be done with or in
relation to the product; and
(c) the time when the product was supplied by its producer to
another."[56]

This is sometimes referred to for convenience as a consumer expectation test. Only experience in the courts will reveal the scope of the test.
A case like *Kubach* (above) would fall easily within the Act. The
product, to be within the consumer's expectation of safety, would have
to have the instruction sheet which warned the user to test the product
before use. The interesting question will be to see how far the courts
will allow otherwise dangerous products to be supplied simply because
they are supplied with warnings.

Producers and suppliers

In the first place, liability is on the producer. This includes the 7.19
manufacturer but may also include the person who wins or abstracts
raw materials. Someone who processes agricultural products is a
producer. Someone who simply packages goods is not a producer.[57] As well as the producer, other persons may be liable in respect
of the same product,[58] namely any person who holds himself out as the
producer by putting his brand on the goods (sometimes known as an
"own brander") and a person who imports goods from outside the
European Community in the course of his business to supply them to
another (an "importer").[59] Further, in addition to those liable above

---

[55] s. 3(1).
[56] s. 3(2). See Stoppa, "The Concept of Defectiveness in the Consumer Protection Act
1987: a critical analysis", 1992 L.S. 210.
[57] s. 2(2) (a), although he may be liable under another head.
[58] s. 2(2) (b); s. 2(2) (c).
[59] It goes without saying that students must be familiar with the membership of the
European Community.

as producers, there is liability too on the supplier of goods, for example, a retailer, but only if: (a) the victim requests that the supplier reveal one or more of the producers; (b) that request is made within a reasonable time after damage occurs, and at a time when it is not reasonably practicable for the victim to identify all of the producers himself; and (c) the supplier fails to identify the producer or the person who supplied to him.[60] The value of this provision is to encourage the supplier to reveal the person who produced the article. Once the provision is appreciated in the business community it is likely that steps will be taken to record the source of products and components so that liability can be avoided by a supplier by complying with the request and naming the person who supplied to him. Any persons who are liable are liable jointly and severally.[61] These provisions make it likely that a person in the position of the plaintiff in *Evans* (above) would recover. He could sue either the car manufacturer or the windscreen manufacturer, both of whom are prima facie liable.

Damages

7.20   The damages recoverable are limited by the Act. Damages are recoverable for personal injuries, death or damage to the pursuer's property. Damage to the product itself or damage to a product caused by one of its defective component parts, is not recoverable.[62] Damages can only be recovered in respect of property which is:

> "of a description of property ordinarily intended for private use, occupation or consumption; and intended by the person suffering the loss or damage mainly for his own private use, occupation or consumption."

In any event, even if not a business asset, the value of the property damaged must exceed £275. However, it should be noted that this limit does not apply to personal injuries or death.

Defences

7.21   It is crucial to know the defences for they affect the scope of liability significantly. They are:

1. Compliance with any requirement imposed by or under any enactment or with any Community obligation. This is self explanatory.

---

[60] s. 2(3).
[61] s. 2(5).
[62] s. 5(1) and (2).

2. The defender did not supply. This covers a situation where someone takes the product away from the defender, as by theft or mistake.

3. The supply is not in the course of a business by someone who is not one of the producer class or, if he is, he is so by virtue of things not done with a view to a profit. Blaikie has well explained this provision by saying, "the commercial producer who gives his product away for nothing . . . cannot rely on this defence. However the lady who makes confectionery for the cake and candy stall at the church sale of work would not be liable."[63] In the same way it is perfectly permissible to make a present for a person's birthday, without attracting strict liability.

4. The defect did not exist at the relevant time. Generally the relevant time is the time of supply. This will allow a defence where it can be shown that someone else has tampered with the product.

5. The state of scientific and technical knowledge at the relevant time was not such that a producer of products of the same description as the product in question might be expected to have discovered the defect if it had existed in his products while they were under his control. This is often known as the development risks defence. The directive provided that the Commission would review in 1995 whether Member States should be allowed to continue to permit this and other provisions.[64] There are arguments for and against it. Not to have it inhibits entrepreneurs and inventors or at least puts their costs up.[65]

6. Defect in a product in which the defender's product is comprised. This is a defence only if the defect is wholly attributable to the design of the subsequent product or to compliance by the defender with instructions given by the final producer. Again this would cover cases like *Evans*. It is a valuable protection for component makers who do not know what their product is to be used for—where bolts are subjected to inordinate stress and strains by the "assembling" manufacturer.

7. Contributory negligence is recognised.[66] It can be seen then that it is impossible to understand fully the scheme of strict liability without

---

[63] Blaikie, "Product Liability" (1987) 32 J.L.S.S. 325 at 328.

[64] Nothing has been done as a result of the review at the time of writing. The other two provisions are a limitation on maximum damages never adopted by the U.K. and the option to include primary agricultural products and game within "product"—an option not taken up by the U.K. See Hodges, "The European Commission's 1995 Review of the Product Liability Directive" [1996] J.P.I.L. 135.

[65] See Goldberg, "The Development Risk Defence and Medicinal Products" (1991) 36 J.L.S.S. 376. See n. 48 above for the challenge by the Commission on the U.K. formulation.

[66] s. 6(4), and see [11.21].

comprehending the defences, a postion which obtains equally in the other new strict liability scheme under the Animals (Scotland) Act 1987 [7.23–7.33].

7.22 There are complicated time-bar provisions providing broadly that there shall be a limitation period of three years from the time the victim was aware, or it was reasonably practicable for him to be aware, of the essential facts to ground an action. There is a long-stop prescriptive period of 10 years.

LIABILITY FOR ANIMALS

7.23 The law was extensively reformed by the Animals (Scotland) Act 1987.[67]

Strict liability before the 1987 Act

7.24 A person in charge of a wild animal or an animal which could be shown to have vicious propensities was strictly liable for the harm which it caused. The fact that reasonable care was taken was not a sufficient defence—effective precautions had to have been taken. So when a dog with vicious propensities managed to break its chain and then bit a passer-by, it was not sufficient to show that the chain looked strong and usually held the dog.[68] Certain animals were deemed to have the vicious propensities required to attract the strict liability and were described as *ferae naturae* (such as lions, tigers, elephants, bears and boars). This was in distinction to animals *domitae naturae* (such as dogs, cats, and cattle including bulls!),[69] whose damage did not attract strict liability unless they could be shown to have previously exhibited dangerous propensities. These categories were categories of law and it was not competent to show that a particular animal *ferae naturae* was as a matter of fact domesticated.

7.25 Defences were available to a defender who could show (1) that the beast was provoked by the complainer, (2) that the beast was actually still under control, (3) that the animal was improperly loosed by a third party, or (4) *damnum fatale* [11.18].

7.26 The Dogs Act 1906 rendered the owner of a dog liable in damages for injury done to cattle including horses, sheep, goats and swine without proof of negligence or vicious propensities.[70]

---

[67] The Act applies only in relation to injury or damage caused on or after June 10, 1987.

[68] *Burton v. Moorhead* (1881) 8 R. 892.

[69] *Clark v. Armstrong* (1862) 24 D. 1315.

[70] The Winter Herding Act 1686 survived and was used until the new legislation came into force.

The Guard Dogs Act 1975 was expressly stated not to create any civil liability but is now to an extent incorporated in the 1987 Act.

Common law: negligence

Whether or not we are concerned with the new statutory liability, 7.27 the general principles of negligence are still relevant. This was certainly the case where there was strict liability at common law. In *Henderson v. John Stuart (Farms) Ltd*[71]:

> A farmworker who was an experienced stockman was fatally injured by a Friesian dairy bull. He had been cleaning out its box which was not fitted with baffles or escape gaps. It was not averred that the bull (which is, of course, *domitae naturae*) had dangerous propensities. It was held that there was no need to aver dangerous propensities to state a relevant case. The action was founded on the employer's breach of duty to his employee [7.34–7.37] by failing to follow normal practice in relation to looking after bulls.

The Animals (Scotland) Act 1987

The Act covers many matters relating to animals and only the parts 7.28 dealing with liability for animals are dealt with in this book. It creates a new form of strict liability, specifically replacing that set out above[72] while preserving any liability under the general law relating to negligence.[73] Like any other instance of statutory liability (see Chapter 6 above) it is important to ask first of all—upon whom does liability fall? The Act imposes liability on a "keeper of an animal". The meaning of this is defined by the Act.[74]

A person is a keeper if he owns the animal or has possession of it, or 7.29 he has actual care and control of a child under the age of 16 who owns the animal or has possession of it.

If the animal has been abandoned or has escaped, liability is not avoided until another person acquires ownership or comes into possession of it.[75] The Crown does not acquire ownership of an animal if it is abandoned.

---

[71] 1963 S.C. 245; and see also *Hill v. Lovett*, 1992 S.L.T. 994.

[72] s. 1(8) (a). The argument that essentially fault was required and that the Act had been intended to simplify the previous law rather than radically alter it was (it is submitted, rightly) rejected in *Foskett v. McClymont*, (1998) Rep.L.R. 13, discussed at 7.31 below.

[73] A negligence case was run in parallel to a statutory case in *Fairlie v. Carruthers*, 1995 S.L.T. (Sh. Ct) 56.

[74] s. 5.

[75] Contrast this with the common law position where a strict liability case was not allowed where a bullock had escaped from the custody of its owner: *Stilie v. Wilson*, 1988 S.C.L.R. 108. However, the Inner House held that the facts should be established first: 1990 S.L.T. 145.

A person is not liable as a keeper if he is detaining a stray animal under section 3 of the Act, nor if he is otherwise temporarily detaining it with a view to restoring it as soon as is reasonably practicable to its owner or a possessor of it.

Beware the Queen's corgis for, although the Act expressly binds the Crown, proceedings cannot be brought against Her Majesty.[76]

Types of animals

7.30   Reading the Act as a whole it is possible to put animals into three categories:

(1) Animals belonging to a species whose members generally are by virtue of their physical attributes or habits likely (unless controlled or restrained) to injure severely or kill persons or animals, or damage property to a material extent.

(2) Dogs and dangerous wild animals (as defined by the Dangerous Wild Animals Act 1976).[77]

(3) Cattle, horses, asses, mules, hinnies, sheep, pigs, goats and deer.[78]

7.31 These are not distinct categories. The first category is the general category and the other two are specific statutory examples of animals which will fall within the Act. Thus animals in the second category are "deemed to be likely (unless controlled or restrained) to injure severely or kill persons or animals by biting or otherwise savaging, attacking or harrying." That is not to say that other animals not listed in the Dangerous Wild Animals Act might not yet fall within the first category. This view is now confirmed by the decision in *Foskett v. McClymont*,[79] a case in the best tradition of the *Dandy*.

> The pursuer, a research student, siting a radar installation with permission, was returning from his work. He said he met an animal that would not let him past. He said the defender had told him how to deal with such an eventuality—he waved his arms at it, shouted at it and tapped it on the nose twice. The bull (as it turned out to be) charged him and tossed him over a wall on to stinging nettles.

There was no argument about a common-law case. The argument that because cattle are deemed to damage land meant that a bull could not

---

[76] s. 6.

[77] s. 1(3) (a). The Act was applied to a dog without difficulty in *O'Neil v. Coyle*, 1995 G.W.D. 21–1185.

[78] s. 1(3) (b).

[79] (1998) Rep.L.R. 13.

cause personal injury was rightly rejected. More difficult was the decision that an averment that a bull is a species of animal whose members are by virtue of their physical attributes or habits likely severely to injure persons, etc., was held sufficiently specific. While it was appreciated that some bulls are docile and some not, it is not clear whether this was thought to be as a result of genetics (which is the foundation of the language of "species"). The defenders were probably entitled to more specification. The Act incorporates the Dangerous Wild Animals Act 1976. That Act, in its Schedule (and see Dangerous Wild Animal Act 1976 (Modifications) Order 1984, s.1, S.I. 1994, No. 1111), makes zoological Linnaen descriptions of species authoritative and so it might reasonably be assumed that the proper course was to plead a zoological species. The defender's experts would really need to know what animal was being discussed. Similarly, animals in the third category are "deemed to be likely (unless controlled or restrained) to damage to a material extent land or the produce of land, whether harvested or not."

The phrase "attack or harry" was considered in *Fairlie v. Car-* 7.32 *ruthers,*[80-81] and was held not to include a case where a frisky dog knocked a person over while it was being exercised. It was not harrying as it was one single incident. Attack was more difficult because it seemed to require some form of intent and it would not be appropriate to look into the mind of a dog! With respect, the decision is correct but there is no question of looking for intent—if objectively the act is an attack that is the end of the matter. What the sheriff really did was to look objectively at the evidence and see whether he was satisfied that it was an attack or an accident.

Once a keeper of an appropriate animal has been found it need only be 7.33 shown that the injury or damage complained of is "directly referable" to (as opposed to "caused by") the physical attributes or habits of the animal. However, the nature of the liability cannot be fully understood without some reference to the defences and exclusions which are provided by the Act.[82]

(1) There is no liability for injury in the form of a disease transmitted by means unlikely to cause severe injury. Thus, if your panther licks my hand and I acquire some hideous disease I do not have the benefit of the strict liability.

(2) The mere presence of an animal does not incur strict liability where, for example, I ski into a reindeer in the Cairngorms, or

---

[80-81] 1995 S.L.T. (Sh.Ct.) 56; *Casebook*, Ext. 69.
[82] Set out in s. 2.

again, where I trip over the proverbial sleeping dog lying on the pavement or drive into it.[83]

(3) There can be apportionment of liability between owner and possessor.

(4) The fault of the pursuer is a defence, in effect allowing the defence of contributory negligence.[84]

(5) There is statutory provision to allow for the voluntary assumption of risk [11.19]. If you stick your head in the lion's mouth and you lose your head you have probably taken a chance that will leave the keeper free of liability. (If he said, as owners of animals tend to say, "It's all right, he'll not hurt you", that might affect the nature of the risk which was accepted and might in any event be a negligent mis-statement [5.22].)

(6) There is a defence if the person (or other animal) injured had been on the land where the beast was without authority, *unless* the animal was kept wholly or partly for the purpose of protecting persons or property, in which case there is no defence *unless* the keeping of the animal and the use made of it was reasonable and, if the animal is a guard dog within the terms of the Guard Dogs Act 1975, there has been compliance with section 1 of the Act. The Guard Dogs Act 1975 penalises the use of a guard dog unless its handler (being a person who is capable of controlling the dog) is present and the dog is under his control, if not actually tied up. Notice of the dog's presence must be displayed at every entrance to the property. The Dangerous Wild Animals Act 1976 forbids the keeping of any dangerous wild animal as defined in the Act without a licence. The keeper must insure against third party liabilities, which seemed to imply a right of action (now confirmed by the 1987 Act). The list of dangerous animals includes: wolf, jackal, foxes and dogs (except the domestic dog and the common red fox), cassowary, old world monkey, mangabey, baboon or mandrill, alligator, emu, cobra or mamba, lions, tigers, cheetahs, gibbons and gila monsters,

---

[83] Although such may be actionable in negligence: see *Davies v. Mann* (1842) 10 M. & W. 546; *Swan v. Minto & Son*, unreported, Lanark Sheriff Court, May 19, 1997. There is, however, much authority which might be considered based on the facts or culture of the time, supporting the view that there was no liability for escaping farm animals—mainly the Inner House decision in *Fraser v. Pate*, 1923 S.L.T. 457. That case relied on the English case, *Heath's Garage Ltd v. Hodges* [1916] 2 K.B. 370 which became even more entrenched in English law for some time only to be abolished by statute: Animals Act 1971, s. 8(1).

[84] Such a plea was taken but not argued and would not have found favour in *Fairlie v. Carruthers*, 1995 S.L.T. (Sh.Ct.) 56. For the defence, see below [11.21].

orang-utans and chimpanzees, ostriches and grizzly bears, vipers and rattlesnakes.[85]

When all of the above is taken into account, this new liability places liability without proof of fault on the keeper of the appropriate type of animal for injury or damage (providing it is referable to the category of beast) unless the claimant is at fault, has assumed the risk or failed to take care for his own safety. It is not a defence to show *damnum fatale* [11.18], nor the intervention of a third party.

EMPLOYER'S LIABILITY

For some time an employer has been held to have a personal duty 7.34 to take reasonable care for his employees' safety.[86] At an early stage in the industrial revolution, it was appreciated that the common law did not adequately provide for the victims of industrialisation and so there has been a long series of statutory interventions creating various forms of absolute liability.[87] Nonetheless, the common law developed to a stage where it was held that an employer personally owed a duty of reasonable care to his workmen—a duty which was not fulfilled by entrusting it to a competent foreman. The classic statement of the duty is in *English v. Wilsons & Clyde Coal Co.*[88]:

> "To take reasonable care, and to use reasonable skill, first, to provide and maintain proper machinery, plant, appliances, and works; secondly, to select properly skilled persons to manage and superintend the business; and thirdly, to provide a proper system of working."

So, where a plaintiff was injured when a piece of a drift (a kind of chisel) broke and entered his eye, a claim was made under the first head. As the drift had been purchased from a reputable supplier, this was held sufficient to discharge the employer's duty of reasonable care—the employer is not, at common law, an insurer of his workman's safety.[89] However, the result of that particular decision was changed by the Employers' Liability (Defective Equipment) Act 1969 which deems the negligence of the supplier to be the negligence of the

---

[85] Note that the common names, such as those listed, are not definitive—that is only the case with the zoological terms listed in the Schedule.

[86] See *Hislop v. Durham* (1842) 4 D. 1168.

[87] See the Employer's Liability Act 1880 and the Workmen's Compensation Act 1887.

[88] 1937 S.C. (H.L.) 46.

[89] *Davie v. New Merton Board Mills* [1959] A.C. 604.

employer, while allowing the employer to maintain a claim against the supplier.[90]

7.35   The second head comprises the duty to provide the employee with competent fellow workers, a duty breached in the case of *Hudson v. Ridge Manufacturing*[91] where an employee, well known to the employer as a practical joker, tripped up a fellow employee, who was a cripple, causing him injury. That the duty is, however, still one of reasonable care is illustrated by a contrasting Scottish case of *McLean v. Remploy Ltd*[92] in which the pursuer tripped over a length of yarn tied across her path by fellow employees. There was no liability as such conduct could not be expected.[93]

7.36   Finally, the third head demands that the working system should be reasonably safe. For example, an employer was held liable where he failed to provide a window cleaner with blocks which would prevent the window he was cleaning falling on his fingers.[94] On the other hand, in a recent Scottish case an employer was absolved when a workman used the top end of a ladder, which had wheels at the top, upside down so that the wheels were on the ground. Worse, the pursuer ordered the apprentice (who was holding the foot of the ladder) to move away. The pursuer fell.[95] Another ladder case further illustrates the wide scope of "system". In *McGregor v. AAH Pharmaceuticals*,[96] the employee did not use the stepladders provided but clambered up shelves, despite a booklet instructing that this ought not to be done. The employee won. The ladders were not close enough and, although there had been reprimands for a failure to use ladders, there had been no disciplinary proceedings.

7.37   Nonetheless, merely because a case does not fall within one of these three heads does not signify that it is of no merit. It might still fall within the general obligation to take reasonable care for the workman's safety.[97]

Perhaps the most interesting line of cases in recent years, giving substance to the general category, are those where the injury has not

---

[90] See *Casebook*, Ext. 92. There are grave difficulties in applying the Act, particularly in England, but the Inner House applied it in its proper strength in *Edwards v. Butlins Ltd*, 1997 G.W.D. 21–1052.

[91] [1957] 2 Q.B. 348.

[92] 1994 S.L.T. 687.

[93] And see the similar but more gruesome English case, *Smith v. Crossley Bros Ltd* (1951) 95 Sol. Jo. 655.

[94] *General Cleaning Contractors v. Christmas* [1953] A.C. 180.

[95] *Russell v. Motherwell Bridge Fabricators Ltd*, 1992 G.W.D. 14–827; see now reg. 16 of the Workplace (Health, Safety and Welfare) Regulations 1992 (see para. 7.45 below).

[96] 1995 G.W.D. 32–1656.

[97] *Longworth v. Coppas International (U.K.) Ltd*, 1985 S.L.T. 111, although see *Forsyth v. Lothian Regional Council*, 1995 G.W.D. 4–204.

been physical. In *Walker v. Northumberland C.C.*[98] a local authority were held liable for failing to relieve the pressure of work on an employee who then had a nervous breakdown. However, he had already had one. So far as the first breakdown was concerned, it had not been reasonably foreseeable. After that it was foreseeable.[99] It should be said that it appears that an attempt was made to bring this case within the category of a safe system. There is no Scottish authority as such but a similar case was settled for a substantial sum of money.[1] It may be that the safe system category has expanded to become a residual category.

Statutory liability

Introduction

Recent years have seen the start of a revolution in the statutory protection of workers. As was the case in product liability [see 7.12–7.22] the impetus came from the European Union. The Single European Act included a new Article 118A to the Treaties with a view to improving health and safety law across Europe. There then followed a large number of European Union directives which compelled the Member States to achieve the effect they desired.[2] Next, the United Kingdom chose to implement the directives by bringing into effect regulations under the Health and Safety at Work etc. Act 1974.[3] The Health and Safety Executive take about two hundred and forty pages to set out and explain the new regime, so what follows must be taken as at best an attempt to set out the broad approach of the law and some of the details most likely to be of relevance to the lawyer studying or practising the law of delict.[4] 7.38

As a result of the law on limitation, cases under the previous law will still arise and trouble practitioners, potentially for very many years in the future. But the proportion of such cases is already shrinking and,

---

[98] [1995] 1 All E.R. 737.

[99] See also *Petch v. Customs and Excise Commissioners* [1993] I.C.R. 789.

[1] *Ballantyne* v. *SRC* noted by McLean, "When Stress Fractures—part 1", Rep. B. 12–3; "part 2", Rep. B. 13–4.

[2] For example, the Provision and Use of Work Equipment Regulations 1992 (S.I. 1992 No. 2932) to an extent implemented Council Directive 89/655/EEC ([1989] O.J. L393).

[3] Management of Health and Safety at Work Regulations 1992; Workplace (Health, Safety and Welfare) Regulations 1992; Provision and Use of Work Equipment Regulations 1992; Personal Protective Equipment at Work Regulations 1992; Health and Safety (Display Screen Equipment) Regulations 1992; Manual Handling Operations Regulations 1992.

[4] The new laws applied as at January 1, 1993 but their effect was delayed in some instances (most importantly, old workplaces until January 1, 1996 and old work equipment until January 1, 1997).

by the time the student reader of this book himself or herself personally represents a client, cases will be very few.[5] For the proper understanding of what follows only a few points are made from the old law.

The Factories Act 1961 was the culmination of a long series of Acts designed to make employers liable for injuries due to their workmen. How far the interpretation of the 1961 Act will be successfully prayed in aid in relation to the new regulations made under the 1974 Act cannot be guessed. The European provenance of the laws is likely to require a *communautaire* approach to interpretation. But it is the case that the drafting of the United Kingdom legislation has largely followed and built upon judicial interpretation of the pre-existing United Kingdom law, which to that limited extent is still of value in interpreting the new law so long as that interpretation is indeed in accord with the European Union legislation.

Where the previous legislation did not mention reasonable care, the duties could be very strict and indeed absolute. A case which makes that very clear is *John Summers v. Frost*,[6] in which a maintenance fitter, grinding metal on a grinding machine, injured his thumb. It was held that the duty to fence, imposed by the 1937 equivalent of section 14(1), was an absolute one. The machine was not fenced so the employer was liable despite the uncontroverted evidence that the machine could not be used if it were fenced and that it was fenced so far as was reasonably practicable.[7]

7.39 Under the old law a workman could only benefit from it if it was interpreted in his favour. The new regulations are on first blush United Kingdom law and the same rule applies. There were many cases under the old law where workmen failed to recover because their accident did not quite fit the statutory provisions. So, for example, a labourer on the way to the lavatory was injured by some hot slag which fell from a bogie. The employers admitted that they had to answer a common-law case but the court upheld the submission that there was no statutory case: the Act provided for a safe means of access to every place of work—a lavatory was not a place of work.[8] The new legislation is more generous in such cases and, interestingly, judicial attitudes to interpretation may also have changed.[9]

---

[5] Accordingly, for such cases the reader needs be referred to specialist texts and perhaps old editions of the same. See Munkman on *Employers Liability* (12th ed., Hendy and Ford, Butterworth, 1995); Redgrave's *Health and Safety* (2nd ed., Hendy and Ford, Butterworth, 1993; Supplement 1996).

[6] [1955] A.C. 740.

[7] The practical solution to this problem now is that any individual machine can be exempted by the appropriate government minister.

[8] *Rose v. Collvilles Ltd*, 1950 S.L.T. (Notes) 72.

[9] Compare *Cavanagh v. Godfreys of Dundee*, 1997 S.L.T. (Sh. Ct.) 2.

As may generally be the case in statutory liability, *volenti non fit* 7.40
injuria is not a defence.[10] Causation is still an issue and even in cases
of absolute liability it has to be shown that the breach of the
statutory duty was the cause of the loss. So, even although the
defence of *volenti non fit injuria* might not be available, it is
sometimes possible to show that the workman was the cause of
his own injuries, or that he was 100 per cent contributorily
negligent.[11]

Quite often an injured workman will base his case on both the 7.41
common law and breach of statutory duty. These two different
cases have to be pled separately and considered separately notwithstanding that they may be based on the same or similar facts. Thus,
sometimes there may be a common-law case even where there has
been no breach of a statutory duty[12] and, even more significantly,
the fact that an employer has complied with all his statutory duties
may not absolve him from his duty at common law.[13] And there
may be a breach of statutory duty where there has been no breach
of the common law duty, as where an employer has taken all
reasonable care but has failed to meet the higher standards
demanded by the statute. The student, whether undergraduate or
not, may sometimes wonder on reading a report why the learned
lawyers for the pursuer have not spotted some whizz-bang statutory
point and champ at the bit to show them how it is done. Damages
tend to be higher from juries and statutory or regulation cases may
seem to be more complicated and allow the defenders to have the
court exercise its power to refuse the more lucrative jury trial — so
if there is a simple common-law case, it might be better to leave
aside the "fancier" case.[14]

The new regulations

As the purpose of this book is to deal with the law of delict and 7.42
this subject is being examined from the point of view of breach of
statutory duty, it is difficult at this stage to decide how much of the
new regulations need be treated. The regulations, after all, are
designed mostly to prevent injury in the first place—they are made
under the Health and Safety at Work etc. Act 1974 which utilises
the Health and Safety Executive and their inspectors to prevent
injury and to prosecute those who infringe the rules whether or not

---

[10] *Wheeler v. New Merton Board Mills* [1933] 2 K.B. 669.
[11] *McWillams v. Sir William Arrol & Co. Ltd* [1962] 1 W.L.R. 295.
[12] See *Rose v. Collvilles*, above.
[13] *Franklin v. Gramophone Co. Ltd* [1948] K.B. 542.
[14] A brave decision for those such as Hugh Campbell, Q.C. who made this interesting
point at a Law Society Update Conference.

anyone has actually been hurt. The Act itself has this to say about civil liability:

"**47.**—(1) Nothing in this part shall be construed—

(a) as conferring a right of action in any civil proceedings in respect of any failure to comply with any duty imposed by sections 2 to 7 or any contravention of section 8; or

(b) as affecting the extent (if any) to which breach of a duty imposed by any of the existing statutory provisions is actionable; or

(c) as affecting the operation of section 12 of the Nuclear Installations Act 1965 . . .

(2) Breach of a duty imposed by health and safety regulations . . . shall, so far as it causes damage, be actionable except in so far as the regulations provide otherwise.

(3) No provision made by virtue of section 15(6) (b) shall afford a defence in any civil proceedings, whether brought by virtue of subsection (2) above or not; but as regards any duty imposed as mentioned in subsection (2) above health and safety regulations . . . may provide for any defence specified in the regulations to be available in any action for breach of that duty.

(4) Subsection (1) (a) and (2) above are without prejudice to any right of action which exists apart from the provisions of the Act, and subsection (3) above is without prejudice to any defence which may be available apart from the provisions of the regulations there mentioned.

(5) Any term of an agreement which purports to exclude or restrict the operation of subsection (2) above, or any liability arising by virtue of that subsection shall be void, except in so far as health and safety regulations . . . provide otherwise.

(6) In this section 'damage' includes the death of, or injury to, any person (including any disease and any impairment of a person's physical or mental condition)."

On the face of it there will be little in the new regulations which will not be actionable. They are also examples of modern drafting at its most distant from ordinary clear language: "In calculating the number of males or females who work in any workplace . . . any number not itself divisible by 25 without fraction or remainder shall be treated as the next number higher than it which is so divisible." Thus, 26 equals 50!

As stated above, the European provenance should be respected in interpretation but the language used is in some respects familiar and the starting point should be to construe the provisions in harmony with the Health and Safety at Work and the Factories Acts. There are Approved Codes of Practice which may be founded upon in criminal proceedings. They are not excluded from civil proceedings and might be expected to be of considerable evidential value.

Finally, it must not be forgotten that there remains the separate 7.43 scheme of liability against the Government for Eurorep, discussed above.[15] One of the most likely occurrences of such liability may well be in employer's liability for the reason that much of the activity of the European Union is directed towards labour conditions across the market. It is not enough, therefore, when representing an employee merely to see if there is a case under the domestic regulations; it is necessary, too, to know whether the Government has failed to give the protection desiderated by European Union legislation.

Management of Health and Safety at Work Regulations 1992

By virtue of regulation 15, breach of a duty imposed by these 7.44 regulations must not confer a right of action in any civil proceedings. But recently the Government chose to compel us to pay attention to this document by using it to implement another European directive. The non-applicability is dis-applied in relation to any duty imposed by the regulation on an employer to the extent that it relates to work of a kind which could involve risk to the health and safety of a new or expectant mother[16] or her baby from any processes or working conditions, or physical, biological or chemical agents, including those specified in the directive.[17]

Workplace (Health, Safety and Welfare) Regulations 1992

The regulations apply immediately to a "new workplace", which is 7.45 one used for the first time as a workplace after December 31, 1992. A "workplace" is defined in a complicated fashion[18] but the basic definition is:

> "Any premises or part of premises which are not domestic premises and are made available to any person as a place of work, and includes—
> (a) any place within the premises to which such person has access while at work; and
> (b) any room, lobby, corridor, staircase, road or other place used as a means of access to or egress from the workplace or where

---

[15] Chap. 6.

[16] An employee who is pregnant; who has given birth within the previous six months; or who is breastfeeding: Management of Health and Safety at Work (Amendment) Regulations 1994 (S.I. 1994 No. 2865).

[17] The 1994 Amendment Regulations.

[18] See reg. 2.

facilities are provided for use in connection with the workplace other than a public road [as defined in the Roads (Scotland) Act 1984, s. 151]."[19]

Certain building operations are excluded, as are ships as defined, and installations such as oil exploration rigs.[20]

The duty is placed on an employer to ensure that any workplace under his control complies with any applicable provisions of the regulations. Every person who is deemed to be the occupier of a factory under section 175(5) of the Factories Act 1961 has to ensure the premises comply with these rules.

Regulations 12 may be chosen as an example of the new regulations and can be compared with the Factories Act provisions:

"(1) Every floor in a workplace and the surface of every traffic route in a workplace shall be of a construction such that the floor or surface of the traffic route is suitable for the purpose for which it is used.

(2) Without prejudice to the generality of paragraph (1), the requirements in that paragraph shall include requirements that—

(a) the floor, or surface of the traffic route, shall have no hole or slope, or be uneven or slippery so as, in each case, to expose any person to a risk to his health or safety;

(b) every such floor shall have effective means of drainage where necessary.

(3) So far as is reasonably practicable, every floor in a workplace and the surface of every traffic route in a workplace shall be kept free from obstructions and from any article or substance which may cause a person to slip, trip or fall.

(4) In considering whether for the purposes of paragraph (2) (a) a hole or slope exposes a person to a risk to his health or safety—

(a) no account shall be taken of a hole where adequate measures have been taken to prevent a person falling;

(b) account shall be taken of any handrail provided in connection with any slope.

(5) Suitable and sufficient handrails and, if appropriate, guards shall be provided on all traffic routes which are staircases except in circumstances in which a handrail cannot be provided without obstructing the traffic route."

---

[19] reg. 2(1).

[20] The Construction (Health, Safety and Welfare) Regulations 1996 now define out of the regulations under discussion workplaces where the only activity being undertaken is construction work as defined unless excluded by those regulations!

It can be seen at once that this is a wider protection than the existing law: "slip, trip or fall"[21] and "traffic routes" being two clear examples.

The workplace equipment, devices and systems must be maintained in an efficient state (from a health and safety point of view), in an efficient working order and in good repair.[22] Other regulations provide for ventilation,[23] for the temperature being reasonable,[24] for suitable and sufficient light which, so far as is reasonably practicable, shall be by natural light,[25] for cleanliness and freedom from waste,[26] free space to work and move about in,[27] for a suitable workstation with a suitable seat, suitable referring as much to the person actually using it as the task in hand. Yet others provide against falls or falling objects, which should be prevented other than by providing hard hats and the like.[28] So far as is practicable (note, not reasonably), every tank, pit or structure where there is a risk of a person in the workplace falling into a dangerous substance (as defined) in the tank, pit or structure, must be securely covered or fenced.[29] Where necessary, for reasons of health or safety, windows or other translucent surfaces in a wall must be of safety material and be marked to make them apparent.[30] Windows, skylights and ventilators must be capable of being opened and closed and cleaned safely.[31] Every workplace must be organised in such a way that pedestrians and vehicles can circulate in a safe manner and the traffic routes must be suitable, but the duty is only to the standard of reasonable practicality for a workplace which is not a new workplace, modification, extension or conversion.[32] Doors and gates must be suitably constructed.[33] Escalators and moving walkways must function safely.[34] Suitable and safe sanitary conveniences must be provided at readily accessible places and they must thus be ventilated and lit, clean and orderly.[35] Suitable and sufficient

---

[21] See W.C.G., "Tripping and Slipping", 1963 S.L.T. (News) 65; and see Kinloch, "Slippery Substances", 1995 Rep. B. 4–7 and 1995 Civ. P.B. 1–9.
[22] reg. 5.
[23] reg. 6.
[24] reg. 7.
[25] reg. 8.
[26] reg. 9.
[27] reg. 10.
[28] reg. 13.
[29] reg. 13.
[30] reg. 14.
[31] regs 15 and 16.
[32] reg. 17.
[33] reg. 18.
[34] reg. 19.
[35] reg. 20.

washing facilities must be available at readily accessible places.[36] An adequate supply of wholesome drinking water must be provided which must be readily accessible at suitable places and provided with cups unless supplied in a convenient jet.[37] Suitable and sufficient accommodation must be provided for clothing and facilities for changing.[38] Suitable and sufficient rest facilities must be provided and facilities to eat meals.

Provision and Use of Work Equipment Regulations 1992

7.46   There are three important preliminary definitions:

"use" in relation to work equipment means any activity involving work equipment and includes starting, stopping, programming, setting, transporting, repairing, modifying, maintaining, servicing and cleaning, and related expressions shall be construed accordingly[39];

"work equipment" means any machinery, appliance, apparatus or tool and any assembly of components which, in order to achieve a common end, are arranged and controlled so that they function as a whole[40];

"suitable" means suitable in any respect which it is reasonably foreseeable will affect the health or safety of any person.[41]

There is a general duty to ensure work equipment is maintained in an efficient state, in efficient working order and in good repair.[42] In *McTighe v. East & Midlothian NHS Trust*,[43] a nurse in a lifting case failed in a case based on regulations 5 and 6 of the Provision and Use of Work Equipment Regulations 1992. The equipment in question was the bed in which the patient was positioned, a part of which gave way. Interestingly, too, the pursuer argued without objection that regulation 5, in allowing suitability to be judged by reference to reasonable foresight, did not comply with the foundation European Directive, allowing the pursuer to claim against the defenders on that basis, their being an emanation of the state.

---

[36] reg. 21.

[37] reg. 22.

[38] regs 23 and 24.

[39] reg. 2; mowing a lawn with a lawnmower is use: *Mitchell v. Inverclyde D.C.*, 1997 G.W.D. 31–1593.

[40] reg. 2. An example is a lawnmower: *Mitchell v. Inverclyde D.C.*, 1997 G.W.D. 31–1593

[41] reg. 5.

[42] reg. 6.

[43] (1998) Rep. L.R. 21.

Where the use of work equipment is likely to involve a specific risk to health or safety the employer must ensure that its use and repair is restricted to those designated.[44] Information, instruction and training must be given.[45] Work equipment must conform to European Community standards.[46]

The following regulation replaces some of the previously familiar sections of the Factories Act 1961.

"**11.**—(1) Every employer shall ensure that measures are taken in accordance with paragraph (2) which are effective—

(a) to prevent access to any dangerous part of machinery or to any rotating stock-bar; or

(b) to stop the movement of any dangerous part of machinery or rotating stock-bar before any part of a person enters a danger zone.

(2) The measures required by paragraph (1) shall consist of—

(a) the provision of fixed guards enclosing every dangerous part of rotating stock-bar where and to the extent that it is practicable to do so, but where or to the extent that it is not, then

(b) the provision of other guards or protection devices where and to the extent that it is practicable to do so, but where or to the extent that it is not, then

(c) the provision of jigs, holders, push-sticks or similar protection appliances used in conjunction with the machinery where and to the extent that it is practicable to do so, but where or to the extent that it is not, then

(d) the provision of information, instruction, training and supervision.

(3) All guards and protection devices provided under sub-paragraphs (a) or (b) or paragraph (2) shall—

(a) be suitable for the purpose for which they are provided;

(b) be of good construction, sound material and adequate strength;

(c) be maintained in an efficient state, in efficient working order and in good repair;

(d) not give rise to any increased risk to health or safety;

(e) not be easily bypassed or disabled;

(f) be situated at sufficient distance from the danger zone;

(g) not unduly restrict the view of the operating cycle of the machinery, where such a view is necessary;

---

[44] reg. 7.
[45] regs 8 and 9.
[46] reg. 10.

(h) be so constructed or adapted that they allow operations necessary to fit or replace parts and for maintenance work, restricting access so that it is allowed only to the area where the work is to be carried out and, if possible, without having to dismantle the guard or protection device.

(4) All protection appliances provided under sub-paragraph (c) of paragraph (2) shall comply with sub-paragraphs (a) to (d) and (g) of paragraph (3).

(5) In this regulation—

'danger zone' means any zone in or around machinery in which a person is exposed to a risk to health or safety from contact with a dangerous part of machinery or a rotating stock-bar;

'stock-bar' means any part of a stock-bar which projects beyond the head-stock of a lathe."

Special hazards must be prevented especially by using appropriate measures to minimise the effect of the hazards as well as to reduce the likelihood of them occurring, those hazards being parts falling or being ejected from the work equipment; rupture or disintegration of equipment parts; equipment catching fire or overheating; or its discharging gas or liquids which are used or stored in the equipment; the explosion of the equipment or article or substance produced, used or stored in it.[47] Employers must ensure protection from things at a very high or low temperature.[48] Equipment must have controls to start, vary and stop equipment and in many cases provide an emergency stop control.[49] All control systems shall, so far as reasonably practicable, have safe (as defined) control systems.[50] Equipment is to be isolated from all its sources of energy and it should be stable.[51]

Suitable and sufficient lighting must be provided.[52] So far as reasonably practicable, maintenance must be possible when the machine is stopped. In a delightful conundrum, regulation 24 declares: "Every employer shall ensure that work equipment is marked in a clearly visible manner with any appropriate [warnings] for reasons of health and safety."[53]

Personal Protective Equipment at Work Regulations 1992

7.47   Personal protective equipment means all equipment (including clothing affording protection against the weather) which is intended

---

[47] reg. 12.
[48] reg. 14.
[49] regs 14, 15, 16 and 17.
[50] reg. 18.
[51] regs 19 and 20.
[52] reg. 21.
[53] The draughtsman does not give (or has no idea how to give) an example.

to be worn or held by a person at work and which protects him against one or more risks to his health or safety, and any accessory designed to meet that objective.[54] The Health and Safety Executive call the object of these regulations "P.P.E." but, preferring English, "personal protective equipment" will be called "safety kit" in the text that follows. The regulations take effect from January 1, 1993. Quite a lot of commonly encountered safety kit is excluded from the regulations as being dealt with by existing regulations including, for example, ear protectors already provided for by the Noise at Work Regulations 1989. The attitude of the whole scheme is that safety kit is a kind of last resort—the idea is not to have a very dangerous factory with heavily armoured workers; better to have workers in shorts and T-shirts with the risks otherwise eliminated.

Every employer must ensure that suitable safety kit is provided unless the risk is otherwise controlled. The kit is not suitable unless it is appropriate for the risks involved, it takes account of ergonomic requirements and the state of health of the person who wears it, it fits, so far as reasonably practicable it is effective, and it complies with the law.[55] The kit is all to be compatible.[56] Before choosing the kit the employer has to carry out an assessment which, in all but the most routine cases, ought to be recorded.[57] The kit must be maintained in an efficient state, in efficient working order and in good repair.[58] Accommodation has to be provided for the kit.[59] Happily this does not mean that every employer must buy a semi-detached house for every pair of tackety boots but might mean as little as a peg for a hard hat. The employee is to be instructed in the use of the kit. Presumably the tying of the tackety boot laces can be assumed (but perhaps not) but things like welding masks and the like will require more help. The code indicates that the help is extensive including theoretical and practical training.[60] Reasonable steps must be taken to ensure that the kit is properly used.[61] The employee is himself under a duty to use the kit and report its loss or defective condition.[62]

At the time of writing the only example is that an employer was found liable where a workman required to mow grass with a lawn-mower on wet grass did not have suitable non-slippy shoes.[63]

---

[54] reg. 2.
[55] reg. 4.
[56] reg. 5.
[57] reg. 6.
[58] reg. 7.
[59] reg. 8.
[60] reg. 9.
[61] reg. 10.
[62] regs 10 and 11.
[63] *Mitchell v. Inverclyde* D.C., 1997 G.W.D. 31–1593.

Health and Safety (Display Screen Equipment) Regulations 1992[64]

7.48   These regulations have come to the attention of the public more than the others. This is because they are new, not only like the other regulations in the sense of being newly expressed, but in the sense that there was barely any regulation at all in this field before the regulations. The key definitions are:

> "display screen equipment" means any alphanumeric or graphic display screen, regardless of the display process involved (in what follows, such are called screens);
>
> "use" means use in or in connection with work;
>
> "user" means an employee who habitually uses display screen equipment as a significant part of his normal work;
>
> "workstation" means an assembly comprising—
>
> > (i)   display screen equipment (whether provided with software determining the interface between the equipment and its operator or user, a keyboard or any other input device);
> >
> > (ii)   any optional accessories to the display screen equipment;
> >
> > (iii) any disk drive, telephone, modem, printer, document holder, work chair, work desk, work surface or other item peripheral to the display screen equipment; and
> >
> > (iv)   the immediate work environment around the display screen equipment.[65]

The guidance indicates that an ordinary television screen is outside the rules but that microfiche readers are within the rules. The guidance also shows that there may be some difficulty in ascertaining who is a user. The courts will accordingly be busy in due course. The guidance offers seven criteria which can be weighed up in making a decision: they are dependency, discretion, training, prolonged spells of over one hour, daily use, fast information transfer and criticality of errors. Drivers, cabs, screens on board a means of transport, portables (not in prolonged use), calculators and window typewriters are excluded from the regulations. A suitable assessment must be carried out.[66]

Very detailed provisions[67] are made for workstations first put into

---

[64] These implement Directive No. 90/270/EEC, May 29, 1990. For an analysis of the directive, and the draft of the U.K. regulations, see Lloyd and Simpson, "The Computer at Work", 1992 S.L.T. (News) 177.

[65] All four definitions in reg. 1.

[66] reg. 2.

[67] See the Schedule.

service on or after January 1, 1993. Others must be brought up to that standard by December 31, 1996.

Daily work on screens is to be planned to provide interruptions to reduce the workload. In the guidance it is pointed out that short, frequent breaks are better than occasional, long breaks.[68] The employer must provide eye tests.[69] Adequate health and safety training in relation to the equipment used is to be given.[70] The users must be told about all aspects of health and safety relating to their workstations and the measures taken by the employer to comply.[71]

Manual Handling Operations Regulations 1992[72]

This regulation came into force on January 1, 1993:   7.49

"Manual handling operations" means any transporting or supporting of a load (including the lifting, putting down, pushing, pulling, carrying or moving thereof) by hand or by bodily force;

"load" includes any person and any animal.

A patient probably is a "load".[73] A bundle of laundry is a load,[74] as is a bale of hay.[75] Remarkably a bracket type flap on a door was considered a load—this is possible and in the case perhaps just right but it is certainly at the boundary of the penumbra of the word.[76] Regardless of the result, this case is one of the best at the time of writing for a display of Euro-centred argument by counsel and an awareness of this interpretive background and thus a valuable read for the student. A lawnmower, while being pushed, is not a load.[77]

Importantly, the familiar word "injury" is subject to a restricted definition:

"Injury" does not include injury caused by any toxic or corrosive substance which
   (a) has leaked or spilled from a load;

---

[68] reg. 4.
[69] reg. 5. "Eye test" is further defined in other U.K. legislation.
[70] reg. 6.
[71] reg. 7.
[72] This implements Directive No. 90/269/EEC.
[73] *Fraser v. Greater Glasgow Health Board*, 1996 Rep. L.R. 62 but there was no liability in that it was thought, it is submitted wrongly, that the sudden nature of the need to lift in this case was not within the duties imposed by the regulations.
[74] *Anderson v. Lothian Health Board*, 1996 Rep. L.R. 88.
[75] *Nicolls v. City of Glasgow*, unreported, Glasgow Sh. Ct, Dec. 23, 1996.
[76] *Divit v. B.T.*, 1997 G.W.D. 12–530.
[77] *Mitchell v. Inverclyde D.C.*, 1997 G.W.D. 31–1593.

  (b) is present on the surface of a load but has not leaked or spilled from it; or

  (c) is a constituent part of a load.[78]

Each employer must, so far as reasonably practicable, avoid the need for his employees to do any manual handling which involves a risk of their being injured. In *Cullen v. North Lanarkshire Council*[79] a case failed because the employee lost his footing while lifting and it was thought, it is submitted wrongly, that the regulations were only directed towards strain injuries.[80]

If manual handling is necessary then the employer must assess the risks according to the details in the Schedule to the regulations. Where it is not reasonably practicable to avoid the need for employees to undertake any manual handling operations at work which involve a risk of their being injured, the employer must take appropriate steps to reduce the risk to the lowest level reasonably practicable and must give general indications and, where possible, precise indications on the weight of each load and the heaviest side of any load whose centre of gravity is not positioned centrally.[81]

7.50   Despite some familiar language,[82] this is a completely new regime and one informed by technicians in the field of ergonomics and safety rather than general common sense and humanity. They really are about making work safe in an absolute sense. Although at first sight they seem exceptionally onerous to the lawyer used to reasonable care and a few specific instances of strict liability, their rationale is unimpeachable. The other thing to remember is that, first, these are primarily preventative measures, secondly, criminal measures and, thirdly (perhaps) matters of civil liability. It is better for everyone, other than reparation lawyers, that people do not get hurt than that they have a right to damages if they do.

---

[78] All three definitions in reg. 2.

[79] 1996 Rep. L.R. 87. N.B. Reversed 1998 G.W.D. 400.

[80] The HSE guidance talks of "the transporting" of loads (p. 1) not just straining at lifting. At p. 6, para. 15 it seems clear that manual handling is accepted as involving moving, steadying or positioning in. Paragraph 16: "Manual Handling also includes the intentional dropping of a load and the throwing of a load whether into a receptacle or from one person to another". It was found that there was no risk of injury. Paragraph 62 states: "Additionally, because of the way in which pushing and pulling forces have to be transmitted from the handler's feet to the floor, the risk of slipping and consequent injury is much greater. For this reason pushing or pulling a load in circumstances where the grip between foot and floor is poor—whether through the conditions of the floor footwear of both—is likely to increase significantly the risk of injury". This makes it clear that risk of injury is a wider concept than just strain. N.B. The Inner House reversed, preferring the analysis in *Anderson*, n.74 above: 1998 G.W.D. 400.

[81] reg. 4.

[82] The High Court of Justiciary has held that the approach to "so far as reasonably practicable" taken in the Factories Act case of *Nimmo v. Alexander Cowan & Sons Ltd*, 1967 S.L.T. 277 should be followed in a criminal case under the Health and Safety at Work etc. Act 1974: *Lockhart v. Kevin Oliphant Ltd*, 1993 S.L.T. 179.

Many lawyers raising a Factories Act case would consult an expert on health and safety. Now it seems as if an expert report on many of these matters would be de rigueur. Indeed, the other side of the coin is that a favourable report may well prove to be a pre-litigation *coup de grâce*. The health and safety guidelines are likely to be of use in arguing whether or not many of these regulations have been implemented, while of course they do not determine the result in any legal sense.

Further reading

Anon, "Medical Negligence: *Hunter v. Hanley* 35 years On", 1990 S.L.T. (News) 325.

Blackie, J., "The Provoking Dogs Problem 2" (1993) 38 J.L.S.S. 148.

Blaikie, J., "Product Liability" (1987) 32 J.L.S.S. 325.

Carey Miller, D.L., "A Statutory Substitute for *Scienter*", 1973 J.R. 61.

Carey Miller, D.L., "The Scottish Institutional Writers on Animal Liability", 1974 J.R. 1.

Clark, A., "Product Liability: The New Rules", 1987 S.L.T. (News) 257.

Clark, A., *Product Liability*, Sweet & Maxwell, 1989).

Conway, R., "The Manual Handling Regulations: The story so far", 1996 Rep. L.B. 12–2.

Ervine, W.C.H., "Product Liability and Part 1 of the Consumer Protection Act 1987", 1988 SCOLAG 21.

Feenan, D.K., "*Hunter v. Hanley* 35 years on: a reply", 1991 S.L.T. (News) 321.

Fergusson, Pamela R., "Pharmaceutical Products Liability", 1992 J.R. 226.

Fergusson, P.W., "Liability in Negligence for Trespassing Criminals", 1987 S.L.T. (News) 233.

Goldberg, R., "The Development Risk Defence and Medical Products" (1991) 36 J.L.S.S. 376.

Ingman, T., "Rise and Fall of the Doctrine of Common Employment", 1978 J.R. 106.

Jackson, B.S., "Liability for Animals in Scottish Legal Literature", 1977 J.R. 139.

Newdick, C., "The Future of Negligence in Product Liability" (1987) 103 L.Q.R. 288.

Newdick, C., "The Development Risk Defence", 1988 C.L.J. 455.

Norrie, K., "Common Practice and the Standard of Care in Medical Negligence", 1985 J.R. 145.

Oughton, D., "Liability in Tort for Economic Loss Suffered by the Consumer of Defective Goods", 1987 J.B.L. 370.

Spink, P., "The Consumer Protection Act—the State of the Art Defence" (1997) 42 J.L.S.S. 416.

Stapleton, J., "Product Liability Reform—Real or Illusory" (1986) 6 O.J.L.S. 392.

Stoppa, A., "The Concept of Defectiveness in the Consumer Protection Act 1987: a critical analysis", 1992 L.S. 210.

CHAPTER 8

VERBAL INJURIES

Introduction

8.1 Actions for verbal injuries have been permitted in the Scottish courts for a very long time. Indeed, there is a record of a case of slander coming before the Court of Session as early as 1542.[1] That, however, was exceptional, for at that time the Church courts had jurisdiction in such matters. Stair considered fame, reputation and honour to be among the interests which the law protects and described them, somewhat enigmatically, as being "in some way reparable".[2] The examples he cites indicate a form of compensation for the infringement of the interests. Unfortunately our law of verbal injuries is not clear and the reason is that damages have been given over the centuries, not just for the loss to reputation wrongfully caused (following the *lex Aquilia*) but also (this time following the Roman *actio injuriarum*) for insult, affront or (as it is sometimes known) *contumelia*. The history of the subject—that it was dealt with by Church courts—makes it likely that it has become something of a mixture of doctrines. Quite often the same words will attract damages under both civilian heads but damages will be payable if there is loss without insult or insult without loss. It would be misleading to suggest that these two heads are clearly separated—rather the Scots law relating to verbal injury is a native creation which incorporates elements of both types of liability. Because of the *actio injuriarum* element in verbal injury, proof of fault is not essential.

As cases are rare there is little pressure among the profession for change or rationalisation. The excitement is more directed towards considering whether the structure which exists can be extended towards the protection of privacy. The terms used by the writers and the courts cause problems not only of description but of analysis.

---

[1] Stair Society, Vol. 20, "Delict", p. 268.
[2] I, ix, 4.

The main difficulty, as in many areas of the law, is terminological: the term verbal injury has been used in various senses. However, for the purpose of the present exposition, Professor Walker's classification is still adopted and the reader is referred to the further reading section for comment: "verbal injury is the genus, and it comprises three species, convicium, defamation (or libel or slander) and malicious or injurious falsehood."[3] This analysis is no longer universally accepted by the commentators. It is a fascinating area of the law but as legal aid is not available[4] for such actions it is usually only seen in disputes between public figures and celebrities from the entertainment industry against newspapers and broadcasting organisations. It appears in a student book and in practitioner texts because (i) it has a constitutional role in determining what it is a person may say or write; and (ii) it is doctrinally the main manifestation of the *actio injuriarum* strand of delictual liability.

DEFAMATION

Communication

The statement must have been communicated to someone: "You   8.2
can shout a slander to the waves."[5] In Scotland it is sufficient that the
statement has been communicated to the pursuer alone, as in the case
of *Ramsay v. Maclay*[6]:

> A former debt collector sued because his former associates wrote
> asking why he had not accounted for some money he had
> collected. The letter said there would be serious consequences
> and that the matter would be reported. The court agreed the case
> could proceed even though the letter had been seen only by the
> pursuer.

The methods or means of communication are various. For example, a wax effigy has been held sufficient means of communication,[7] as has a cinema film.[8] Most cases turn on spoken or written communication. In England this distinction is technically important, spoken defama-

---

[3] pp. 729–847, at p. 732: note the discussion of the case which follows, and see 1970 J.R. 157; for a different view, see T.B. Smith (1962), pp. 724–732. For a complete examination of the whole terminological problem, see Norrie, 1985 J.R. 163; Norrie, *Defamation and Related Actions in Scots Law* (1995).

[4] In one English case an action was raised on the basis of malicious falsehood which did attract legal aid: *Joyce v. Sengupta* [1992] T.L.R. 453.

[5] McKain, Bonnington and Watt, *Scots Law for Journalists* (6th. ed., 1995), p. 164.

[6] (1890) 18 R. 130.

[7] *Monson v. Tussauds* [1894] 1 Q.B. 671.

[8] *Youssoupoff v. MGM* (1934) T.L.R. 581.

tion being slander and written defamations being libels. Anyone who transmits a defamation is liable for it.[9] But innocent dissemination (other than by authors, editors and publishers as defined) have a statutory defence.[10] A broadcaster with no effective control over a live programme is entitled to the defence.[11] An Internet service provider (as opposed to Internet publisher) is also entitled to the defence.

For convenience, in this book the term "statement" is used to cover all communications.

Falsity

8.3   The statement complained of must be a false statement. The law in this area is intimately connected with procedural issues. If the statement is defamatory it is assumed to be untrue and the defender must prove that it is true, if necessary by putting a counter-issue to a jury. In effect, if the defender does not positively prove the truth of the statement his defence will fail even if the pursuer fails to prove it was false. For that reason the matter is better examined from the defender's point of view and so is dealt with under the defence of *veritas* (truth) [8.13], known in England as justification.

The statement must be defamatory

8.4   The distinction between fact and law here is important.[12] Whether words are reasonably capable of being defamatory is a question of law; it is then a matter of fact (perhaps for a jury to determine) whether in all the circumstances the statement is actually defamatory. That said, there is no strict legal definition of what is or is not defamatory. A phrase used in the English law conveys the idea inherent in the cases: the statement can be defamatory if it tends to lower the plaintiff in the estimation of right-thinking members of society generally. The authorities fall roughly into more or less identifiable categories.

8.5   Statements imputing immorality or criminality[13] can be defamatory as where it is suggested that someone has committed a crime or behaved less than decorously. Perhaps the most extreme case (in the sense of being favourable to a pursuer) is *Cuthbert v. Linklater*.[14]

Mrs Cuthbert raised an action against the author Eric Linklater

---

[9] *Hayforth v. Forrester-Paton*, 1927 S.C. 74.

[10] Defamation Act 1996, s. 1

[11] s. 1(3). For the kind of facts this might in future cover, see *Prophit v. BBC*, 1997 S.L.T. 745.

[12] Not least because defamation cases may still be heard by a jury, unless special cause is shown: see *Shanks v. BBC*, 1991 G.W.D. 27–1641; *McCabe v. News Group Newspapers Ltd*, 1992 S.L.T. 707.

[13] *Leon v. Edinburgh Evening News*, 1909 S.C. 1014.

[14] 1935 S.L.T. 94. For background to this case, see *Casebook*, Ext. 82.

in respect of the publication of his novel, Magnus Merriman. One of his characters, Beaty Bracken, removed a Union Jack from a castle and placed it in a public urinal. Mrs Cuthbert was a famous Scottish Nationalist who had come to the public attention when she had removed a Union Jack from Stirling Castle and tossed it to a guard (which is not the same as putting it in a public urinal). Her action was allowed to proceed.

Another quite clear category is where a statement is made about 8.6 someone's fitness for their occupation or profession as where a solicitor was accused of conducting cases for his own benefit rather than that of his clients,[15] or a football manager said to treat his players like dirt, break promises and to be parsimonius in paying wages.[16] Accusing a councillor of sheer lunacy and gross maladministration was not defamatory[17] but malicious misuse of public money was.[18]

Finally, imputations about solvency have produced considerable 8.7 litigation.

A solicitor in a county town, who held a number of important positions involving trust in the community, brought an action against a local manufacturer. It was alleged that the manufacturer had said that the solicitor had "been cleaned out and lost his all".[19]

The court allowed the case to proceed on the basis that the words could affect the solicitor's reputation and credit. Interestingly, the Lord President opined that, "If the pursuer had been living on his private means the statement in a railway carriage that he was reported to have 'lost his all' might have excited compassion, but it would not have injured him in his public reputation or purse." In that hypothetical case, the remedy open to the pursuer would be to try to make out some other head of verbal injury such as convicium [8.26].

Innuendo

Sometimes words may not on their face be defamatory. It is 8.8 permissible to allege facts extrinsic to the statement to illuminate the words used and show that as used they are able to convey a defamatory imputation. The innuendo has to be averred and proved. In short an innuendo makes clear the defamatory point of an apparently non-defamatory statement. In *Boal v. Scottish Catholic Printing Co. Ltd,*[20]

---

[15] *McRostie v. Ironside* (1849) 11 D. 74.
[16] *Peat v. News Group*, unreported, O.H., Mar. 8, 1996.
[17] *Brooks v. Lind*, 1997 Rep. L.R. 83.
[18] *ibid.*
[19] *AB v. CD* (1904) 7 F. 22.
[20] 1908 S.C. 667.

Samuel Boal, a journalist and lecturer, brought an action against the defenders for alleged defamation in their newspaper. A report of a charitable home being founded and in which the pursuer was involved asked, "what guarantee is there that the money subscribed does not go to the private profit of . . . the scribbling Boal."

Now it is possible to answer that question by saying: "there is none, for none is needed, Boal is an honest man." But it was held that the statement was capable of a defamatory meaning, namely that the pursuer was the kind of person who would swindle a charity in some way. Once allowed, it is for the jury to decide which of the two possible interpretations the words were intended to have. "Stranger to the truth" has been held a clear enough way of saying "liar" such as not to require an innuendo.[21] The technical nature of innuendo is illustrated by the fact that it is essential to innuendo a statement made in a foreign language.

Damages and interdict

8.9 Damages will always be awarded for a defamatory statement. Either there will be damages based on the *lex Aquilia* action for loss of business or damage to reputation, or there will be an award of solatium for the hurt feelings following the *actio injuriarum*, or both. The more difficult problem in this area is that certain factors are treated as increasing the award which should be made and others as decreasing or mitigating the damages.

The award may be aggravated where the statement has been repeated after a warning that it was false.[22] Walker, relying on English authority, states that a failed attempt to sustain a *veritas* plea may go to aggravation.[23] It is inappropriate to attempt to make a direct comparison between an award of solatium for pain and suffering caused by physical injury and an award of solatium for injury to feelings and reputation.[24] While it is proper for a court to take account of levels of award made in Scottish defamation cases, no assistance can be derived from a consideration of English cases in which awards are assessed on very different principles.[25]

Professor Walker considers that interdict against making a particular

---

[21] *Carroll v. BBC*, 1997 S.L.T. (Sh.Ct.) 23, albeit it was held by the sheriff principal not to be defamatory of a solicitor.
[22] *Morrison v. Ritchie* (1902) 4 F. 645.
[23] at p. 786.
[24] *Winter v. News (Scotland) Ltd*, 1991 S.L.T. 828.
[25] *ibid.*

statement of a defamatory character is doubtless competent, without citing authority.[26]

The English permit an exception where the publication is part of a conspiracy to injure[27] but this exception is narrowly construed.[28]

The recent Scottish case, *McMurdo v. Ferguson*,[29] seems to show a much more favourable attitude to a pursuer and a correspondingly more worrying attitude to freedom of speech. Lord Murray appears to have asked only whether or not the statement was prima facie defamatory. The approach to freedom of speech on the other side of the border might usefully be considered. Read plainly, this could be a considerable restraint on freedom of speech. In the earlier case of *Waddell v. BBC*,[30] the Inner House clearly also considered an application competent but the balance of convenience was in favour of the publisher publishing in the public interest. Walker's earlier statement is not, however, objectionable: "interdict against repetition of a given statement, already held defamatory, is quite competent."[31]

The English rule, as stated by Salmond and Heuston, seems to balance the competing interests properly: "But an interlocutory injunction to restrain the publication of a libel will be granted only in the clearest cases (and probably not at all when justification or fair comment or perhaps even privilege are pleaded), in which any jury would say the matter was defamatory, and in which, if the jury did not so find, their verdict would be set aside on appeal as unreasonable."[32]

Certain factors may mitigate the award of damages. In defamation 8.10 cases, malice is irrelevant unless qualified privilege is pleaded or unless it has increased the injury, but damages may be reduced if it is shown that there was indeed no malice in making the defamatory statement. That the statement was repeated as a general report or that an offer of apology was made may also mitigate. Provocation may mitigate. Section 12 of the Defamation Act 1952 allows the unsuccessful defender to lead evidence of damages already awarded to the pursuer in mitigation—as where someone defamed by the "Moon" newspaper is also defamed by the "Looking-Glass" newspaper and has received compensation from the "Moon" newspaper. Most dramatically, it is possible to show that the pursuer's character is such that it did not

---

[26] *Delict*, p. 457.
[27] *Gulf Oil Ltd v. Page* [1987] Ch. 327. Tony Weir has recently described this case as egregious and disgraceful: Weir, *Economic Torts* (Oxford, 1997), pp. 19–20.
[28] *Ferris-Bank (Anguilla) Ltd v. Layar and Others* [1991] T.L.R. 68, injunction refused.
[29] 1993 S.L.T. 193.
[30] 1973 S.L.T. 246.
[31] *Delict*, p. 453; Salmond and Heuston (21st ed.), p. 567.
[32] Salmond and Heuston, p. 555; injunction refused in *Kaye v. Robertson* [1991] F.S.R. 62. Weir, *Casebook* (8th ed.), p. 22.

suffer damage from the statement. The court keeps this line within close bounds and the evidence of bad character must be bad character in relation to the matter in issue. In *Plato Films v. Speidel*[33]:

> The plaintiff was at the time of the action the Supreme Commander of Allied Land Forces in Central Europe, but had held a number of important positions in the German army before and during the Second World War. The defendants were Plato Films and Stanley Forman. The action concerned a film called *Operation Teutonic Sword*. The defendants admitted that they had said that the plaintiff had been privy to the murder of King Alexander of Yugoslavia and others and that he had betrayed Field Marshal Rommel. They pled justification (or *veritas*). But, alternatively, in mitigation, they claimed that the film accused him of lots of other things including being a war criminal and if he was not prepared to deny these allegations he could not have much of a character.

The House of Lords allowed the allegation that "the plaintiff had a bad reputation as a man who was party to and/or responsible for acts which were war crimes and/or against humanity and/or atrocities" to remain in the pleadings, *i.e.* the House did not say it was inadmissible. At the same time, it was stated that the suggestion that the plaintiff had to complain of every libel in a given work or be held to have admitted it was said to be wholly improper. However, the court held that in this case the allegation involved character in relation to the matter at issue. On the other hand, the good character of the pursuer does not aggravate damages for every pursuer is presumed to be of good character. Previous malice is irrelevant and, as already indicated, bad character in an area not relevant to the issue before the court is not considered.[34] As Lord Radcliffe put it in *Plato Films*, "Life not being a morality play or a Victorian Melodrama, men do not enjoy reputations for being bad or good simpliciter."[35]

Under the European Convention of Human Rights a system must make sure that damages awards are necessary and that there are suitable controls on excess.[36]

Defences to defamation actions

8.11   Many "defences" are simply denials of elements of the delict—for example, to deny that the words were used or that the words were issued with the defender's authority; others are more specialised, applying only to this area of the law.

---

[33] [1961] A.C. 1090.
[34] *C v. M*, 1923 S.C. 1.
[35] [1961] A.C. 1090 at 1130.
[36] English law fell foul: *Tolstoy v. U.K.*, unreported, ECHR, July 13, 1995.

1. *In rixa*

The essence of this defence is that the words were uttered in the heat 8.12
of an argument as an angry retort or as mere abuse. This is especially
so if the words are such as are usually uttered in this context. *Christie
v. Robertson*[37] is an example:

> The parties were at an auction sale at a farm. Each thought a
> particular horse had been knocked down to him. The pursuer saw
> the defender walking away with the horse and made insinuations
> to the effect that the defender was trying to steal the horse. The
> pursuer went to fetch a policeman. The defender then said words
> to the effect that the pursuer should have been in the hands of the
> police 20 times during the last five years.

The pursuer was awarded £1 damages in the Outer House but lost
completely on appeal. However, the court made each party pay his
own expenses, perhaps to discourage others from taking similar
action.

2. *Veritas*

This is a complete defence. The defender simply proves what he said 8.13
was true—the onus of proof, on balance of probabilities, in this
respect being upon the defender.[38] The position at common law
was that the defender had to prove the truth of all material statements, thus justifying everything in the alleged defamatory communication. The position is now regulated by the Defamation Act 1952,
s. 5 which provides:

> "In an action for defamation in respect of words containing two
> or more distinct charges against the pursuer, a defence of *veritas*
> shall not fail by reason only that the truth of every charge is not
> proved, if the words not proved to be true do not materially injure
> the pursuer's reputation having regard to the truth of the
> remaining charges."[39]

Another major statutory intervention is contained in the Rehabilitation of Offenders Act 1974, s. 8. The Act sets out to allow certain
offences to be treated as not having taken place after a period of time
has past and they have become "spent" and the offender accordingly
rehabilitated. The general rule is that the circumstances surrounding

---

[37] (1899) 1 F. 1155.

[38] For a modern example of a successful plea of *veritas*, see *Gecas v. Scottish
Television*, 1992 G.W.D. 30–1786.

[39] As verbally altered by the Scottish section 14. See *Casebook*, App. Ext. 5; and
Gecas, above.

the offence cannot be used against a rehabilitated person but the Act does allow the defence of *veritas* to be pled in defamation actions so long as the original publication was not made with malice.[40]

3. Absolute privilege

8.14   As a matter of law, deriving from public policy, certain statements, although affecting someone in their reputation or causing them dreadful loss, are just not actionable.

8.15   **Parliament.** Statements in either House and reports in *Hansard* are completely protected in the interest of free speech in the chambers. As a corollary, repetition outside the Houses is not so privileged. The protection may be waived by an M.P. for a particular case, allowing the defenders to plead *veritas*.[41] Reports and proceedings published under the authority of either House are, however, protected.[42]

8.16   **Judicial proceedings.** Absolute privilege attaches to all statements made in judicial proceedings whatever the court or the rank of the person sued. It also extends to proceedings in tribunals if the procedures are similar in essence to a court.[43] Fair and accurate reports of judicial proceedings are probably absolutely privileged at common law,[44] and are given statutory absolute privilege if contemporaneous (as defined).[45]

4. Qualified privilege

8.17   In certain circumstances, a defender enjoys what is known as qualified privilege. The defender will have a defence unless it can be shown that the statement was motivated by express or actual malice. Since people are presumed to act honestly, the pursuer must have sufficient evidence to infer malice.

Qualified privilege attaches to circumstances as opposed to any particular person. The list of privileged categories is not closed but changes with time.

---

[40] s. 8(3), (5) and (8); the Act, in allowing publication, interestingly reflects a sentiment expressed in the *Digest* (47, 10, 18): "It is not right or just to condemn anyone for bringing a wrongdoer into disrepute, for it is necessary and proper for the offences of wrongdoers to be known."

[41] Defamation Act 1996, s. 13.

[42] Parliamentary Papers Act 1840.

[43] *Trapp v. Mackie*, 1979 S.C. (H.L.) 38.

[44] *Wright v. Outram* (1889) 16 R. 1004.

[45] Defamation Act 1996, s. 14(1). A court includes any tribunal or body exercising the judicial power of the state, all U.K. courts, the ECJ and the ECHR.

The general rule. A statement is protected if honestly made by a person in the discharge of a public or private duty of some kind or in his own affairs in a matter where his interest is concerned.[46] Categories which are well established are as follows.

Discharge of a duty. A proper complaint to the appropriate authority 8.18 will attract qualified privilege. Thus, for example, it was held that there could be qualified privilege when a complaint was made to a chief constable about the conduct of a sergeant.[47] The privilege extends to statements made about candidates in elections.[48]

The House of Lords has considered the effect and extent of privilege and in particular in relation to a complaint against the police. Mirza complained that he was arrested by Fraser because he was a Pakistani and a justice of the peace. What Mirza intended to convey by this was that he had been arrested on no reasonable grounds, something which it had been held Mirza knew to be untrue. However, the statement only supported an innuendo of prejudice in respect of which no malice could be shown. The House held that the existence of the knowing falsehood was sufficient to evidence malice albeit not in relation to the actual defamatory statement. The malice was enough to constitute a misuse of the occasion giving rise to the qualified privilege.[49] Something more than negligence is required for the defence to be lost—the occasion of complaint must not be misused: *Hamill v. Lord Advocate*.[50] A complaint needs to be directed towards the proper source to have the privilege. So a complaint about a nursing home might have been protected if made to the Health Board rather than to a BBC documentary.[51]

Protection of the interests of another. If someone asks for information 8.19 or a character reference about another individual then that is an occasion which attracts qualified privilege to the extent that the reply deals with relevant matter.[52]

Between persons having a common interest. Qualified privilege at- 8.20 taches where a communication is made between parties, one who has an interest in making it and the other having an interest to receive

---

[46] *Dunnet v. Nelson*, 1926 S.C. 764.

[47] *Cassidy v. Connachie*, 1907 S.C. 1112.

[48] *Bruce v. Leisk* (1892) 19 R. 482. Note the Representation of the People Act 1983, s. 106, which makes it an offence to make a false statement about a candidate's personal character or conduct for the purpose of affecting the candidate's return at an election.

[49] *Fraser v. Mirza*, 1993 S.L.T. 527, reversing 1992 S.L.T. 740.

[50] 1994 G.W.D. 33–1960.

[51] *Baignet v. McCulloch*, 1997 G.W.D. 16–737

[52] *Dundas v. Livingstone* (1900) 3 F. 37.

it, so long as they are in good faith and the statement is not published more widely than is necessary.[53]

8.21 **Protection of one's own interests.** This heading permits statements replying to attacks on oneself so long as pertinent.[54] A recent case provides a very practical example of what this defence is about. *Chapman v. Barber*[55] is a case between two company directors.

> Chapman sent Barber draft minutes of a board meeting. Barber thought the minutes suggested that Barber had been conducting himself improperly and responded by accusing Chapman of acting against company policy and misleading the board with a malicious and inaccurate minute. Chapman pointed out that Barber's version had been seen by non-director staff.

The court held that the statements were covered by qualified privilege and the fact of others seeing the document which had, after all, been marked private and confidential and sent in the usual way did not result in the privilege being lost. Rules like this prevent storms in teacups.[56]

8.22 **Published reports.** This is a recognised head of qualified privilege at common law and includes reports about parliamentary proceedings, the court or quasi-judicial bodies so long as fair and accurate.[57] The Defamation Act 1952, s. 7, however, expressly provides for "Qualified privilege of newspapers":

> "The publication in a newspaper [any paper containing public news or observations thereon or consisting wholly or mainly of advertisements, which is printed for sale and is published in the United Kingdom either periodically or in parts or numbers at intervals not exceeding 36 days] of any such report or other matter as is mentioned in the Schedule to this Act shall be privileged unless the publication is proved to be made with malice."

This necessitates consideration of the Schedule, which divides newspaper statements into two categories. The reason for this is that Part 1 statements are entitled to qualified privilege without explanation or contradiction, whereas Part 2 statements do require explanation or contradiction to obtain qualified privilege. If the statement is a Part 2 matter then the Act is not a defence if the paper has refused to publish

---

[53] *Leitch v. Lyal* (1903) 11 S.L.T. 394.
[54] See *Shaw v. Morgan* (1888) 15 R. 865; *Adam v. Ward* [1917] A.C. 309.
[55] 1989 S.L.T. 830.
[56] The defence was also held applicable where there was an entry in company accounts "defalcation by director": *May v. Teague Homes*, 1996 G.W.D. 23–1344.
[57] See, generally, *Allbutt v. GMC* (1899) 23 Q.B.D. 400.

a reasonable explanation or contradiction. Generally, too, the statement must not be unlawful or of no public benefit. Part 1 matters
cover, *inter alia*: legislative acts; international organisations; courts
martial; courts; and official notices. Matters set out in Part 2 cover,
inter alia: transactions of public associations for business sports and
the like; public meetings, whether the audience is public or restricted;
local authorities; and tribunals.

The defence is an aid to free speech, allowing honest mistakes to be 8.23
made on these important occassions. This policy was strong enough to
allow the English Court of Appeal to refuse to apply the law relating to
negligent mis-statements to a reference which was "so strikingly bad as
to amount to . . . 'the kiss of death' " to the plaintiff's career. There had
been no malice in the preparation—the defendant was a fool and not a
rogue.[58] However, in the house of Lords the view was taken that as there
could be liability for making mistaken good reference, as in *Hedley
Byrne*, there was no reason why a mistaken bad reference should not be
actionable too. That decision has now been applied in Scotland by an
Extra Division in *Donlon v. Colonial Mutual Group (UK Holdings) Ltd*.[59]

5. *Fair comment*

This is a defence in its own right although it is closely related to 8.24
qualified privilege. Unlike qualified privilege, the facts stated have to
be truly stated. The protection is against the innuendo or inference
which can arise from the stated facts. The protected statement must
therefore be a comment and not a statement of fact. The defence arises
from the individual's interest in commenting upon public matters and
so the matter discussed must be to do with the public interest. It is also
essential that the comment be honestly and fairly made as opposed to
being inspired by malice. A good example is *Merivale v. Carson*.[60]

> The plaintiff and his wife were authors of a play called *The Whip
> Hand*. A review appeared in the *Stage* magazine: "The Whip
> Hand . . . gives us nothing but a hash-up of ingredients which
> have been used ad nauseam, until one rises in protestation against
> the loving, confiding, fatuous husband with the naughty wife and
> her double existence, the good male genius, the limp aristocrat,
> and the villainous foreigner." The innuendo alleged was that the
> review suggested that the play was immoral.

The court said that every latitude should be allowed to comment on a
matter of public interest (which included the play as it was being
performed to the public) even if opinionated or prejudiced, unless

---

[58] *Spring v. Guardian Assurance plc* [1992] T.L.R. 628.
[59] 1997 S.C.L.R. 1088.
[60] (1887) 20 Q.B.D. 275.

the writing was done with an indirect and dishonest intention to injure the plaintiff. In one of the most important Scottish cases *Crotty v. McFarlane*,[61] it was said that criticisms were to be examined to see whether they expressed honest opinions, however unjust, or whether they were couched in language so reckless and exaggerated that no reasonable man could possibly have entertained the opinion or used the language. It was held that the language in the case was acceptable even though it was hostile or even if it was grossly unjust. It has been held more recently that calling a sports administrator a "dictator" might fall within the defence as the phrase no longer had the connotation of murder associated with Hitler or Stalin[62]; "malicious misuse of public money" said of a councillor was fair comment if defamatory.[63]

6. *Offer of amends*

8.25 A person who has published a statement alleged to be defamatory may offer to make amends in relation to the statement generally or in relation to a specific defamatory meaning which the person making the offer accepts that the statement conveys (to be called a qualified offer).[64] The offer must be in writing, expressed to be an offer in terms of the Act, and if it is a qualified offer it must state the defamatory meaning concerned.[65] The offer must be to make a suitable correction and a sufficient apology, to publish the correction and apology in a reasonable manner practicable in the circumstances and to pay the victim compensation and costs.[66] An offer cannot be made after serving a defence.[67] An offer can be withdrawn before acceptance and a renewal is treated as a fresh offer.[68]

Once accepted the victim cannot bring or continue proceedings. If the details are not agreed the court can make the necessary orders and can settle the damages on the common-law basis.[69]

Unless it can be shown that the offeror knew or had reason to believe that the statement related to the victim and was both false and defamatory, the offer is a defence if the publisher wants to use it—but if he does, he may not use any other defence.[70] The offer may be relied on in mitigation of damages whether or not relied on as a defence.[71]

---

[61] Jan. 27, 1891; *Casebook*, Ext. 86.
[62] *Farry v. News Group*, 1996 G.W.D. 2–109.
[63] *Brooks v. Lind*, 1997 Rep.L.R. 83.
[64] Defamation Act 1996, s. 2 (1) and (2). Section 2 is not in force at time of writing.
[65] *ibid.* s. 2 (3).
[66] *ibid.* s. 2 (4).
[67] *ibid.* s. 2 (5).
[68] *ibid.* s. 2 (6).
[69] *ibid.* s. 3.
[70] *ibid.* s. 4
[71] *ibid.* s. 4 (5).

CONVICIUM

The roots of this head of liability are in the *Digest*.[72] The Praetor 8.26
[2.25] says, "Nothing shall be done to bring a person into hatred,
ridicule or contempt." While this is considered by Professor
Walker to be part of the law of Scotland, other commentators
are more doubtful.[73] Convicium consists in maliciously abusing a
person or holding him up to public ridicule or contempt and
causing him loss or hurt to his feelings. An example of the kind
of case which should be described as convicium is *Steele v. Scottish
Daily Record*.[74] Counsel before the Inner House agreed to describe
the action as one for verbal injury and so the Division did not
analyse the matter. The sheriff-substitute treated it as convicium in
the Walker sense.

> This action was based on an article appearing in the "Judge"
> section of the *Sunday Mail*. The paper reported that the pursuer,
> a motor dealer, had insisted upon holding a man to his con-
> tractual obligations. Part of the report stated: "But fair's fair—
> Did your firm have to make him take a car he didn't want, a car
> he can't afford to run? A car that he's going to find very hard to
> sell with the coming of winter? You're in the big time, Mr Steele.
> Probably you didn't know the tough times young Mr McLeod
> was going through. Come on . . . let's show us that the big time
> has a big heart too."

Note that this could not be a defamation case as the facts stated did
not allege dishonourable or immoral conduct. In the event, the court
held the case of convicium was not made out because the pursuer had
not shown that the article intended to have the pursuer ridiculed or
treated with contempt. An alternative test equivalent to that in
defamation—a lowering in public esteem—was rejected.

More difficult is the question whether the maxim *veritas con-* 8.27
vicium non excusat (truth does not excuse convicium) applies. There
were indications in *Steele* that it might not. However, there is old
authority for the proposition that truth is no defence and no clear
authority against. This question of truth as a defence is an area of
controversy: it is practically important for journalists; and if truth
is a defence, then the threefold division of verbal injuries is harder
to maintain. McKain, Watt and Bonnington go so far as to say: "if

---

[72] 47, 10, 15. Or even in the *Twelve Tables*: Smith, "When the Truth Hurts", 1998
S.L.T. (News) 1.
[73] Walker, pp. 736 *et seq.*; see contra, Norrie (1995) note 3 above, at pp. 35 *et
seq*.
[74] 1970 S.L.T. 53.

the remedy of convicium was ever one of the forms of verbal injury recognised by Scots law . . . this is no longer so . . . It is suggested that journalists should proceed on the basis that such a remedy is no longer open to pursuers in Scotland."[75] They take the view that if the rule is *veritas convicium non excusat* then it is an unwarrantable restraint on the freedom of the press. Norrie[76] seems to accept that approach. But it is submitted that this is only one side of the policy arguments. In the present writer's view, there is much to be lost by abandoning the rule. Other jurisdictions have dealt with the problem of balancing freedom of the press and the interests of the individual by developing a tort of unwarranted intrusion of privacy.[77] These jurisdictions take the view that an unrestricted press is not so important that the individual must go unprotected. Scots law has no tort or delict of privacy at present but the *veritas convicium non excusat* rule would prevent infringement of individual privacy.[78]

MALICIOUS FALSEHOOD

8.28 This species of verbal injury is probably an offshoot from the English law of defamation. There is not all that much Scottish authority for it but it seems quite unobjectionable in principle. The requisites are an actually spiteful communication, which is false, and which causes or is calculated to cause damage. It differs from convicium in that the statement must be false, and from defamation in that the statement need not lead to a lowering of the victim's reputation in the estimation of right-thinking subjects. It is known under four heads: slander of title (in the sense of legal ownership); slander of property (in the sense of physical land or buildings); slander of goods (moveables); and slander of business. An example is *Bruce v. Smith*.[79]

> In this case a builder sued in respect of an article in the *Glasgow Evening News* which said, "People . . . in the city have discovered a new distraction in watching the rents which are appearing in the frontage of a new property still unoccupied. A year or so ago the building collapsed due to an insecure foundation, but it has been run up again. Signs of fresh weakness are already evident, and there is much speculation as to the future of the part of small crowds which gather in the evening, and gaze blankly at the

---

[75] McKain, Bonnington and Watt, *Scots Law for Journalists* (6th ed., 1995), p. 202.
[76] Norrie, *op. cit.*, n. 3.
[77] Wacks (1980).
[78] See 8.29, and Further reading.
[79] (1898) 1 F. 327.

building. The master of works may hear that his services are required—when the tenement comes down with a run for the second time."

The building was therefore becoming difficult to sell or to let. The claim was held to be relevant and indeed the court did not require the pursuer to prove malice, merely that the statement was false and calumnious.

PRIVACY

Given the importance of the free exchange of information and 8.29 opinion, the law of verbal injury cannot be left to a compartment of private law, to be developed on a case-by-case basis. In the last decades the most prominent debate centres around privacy. Convicium is especially important in this regard and has been mentioned as a valuable protection of privacy by Blom-Cooper.[80] But it is undeniable that the *actio injuriarum* could not be said to be specifically directed towards privacy and the interest in keeping certain aspects of one's life private is not notable in the institutional writings nor in leading defamation cases.

In 1990 the first Calcutt report was published.[81] It was established as a result of public concern about intrusions into the private lives of individuals by the press. Three criminal offences were proposed which encompassed trespassing for a story, using surveillance devices and taking photographs or recordings without consent with a view to publication. Consideration was to be given to the law of Scotland to see if it required to be extended. No statutory right of reply was introduced. A tort of infringing privacy was not recommended for immediate introduction. The press was given a last opportunity to show that self-regulation worked. The offences proposed have not to date been introduced.

A Government review was published in 1993.[82] It recommended the special offences be introduced in England but said nothing at all about

---

[80] "The Right to be Let Alone" (1989) 34 J.L.S.S. 402.

[81] The *Report of the Committee on Privacy and Related Matters*, Cmnd 1102 (June 1990).

[82] *Review of Press Self-Regulation*, Cmnd 2135 (Jan. 1993). For a discussion, see Carey Miller and Lardy, "Calcutt II: Comments from a Scots Perspective", 1993 S.L.T. (News) 199. The Lord Chancellor's Department and the Scottish Office have (post-Calcutt II) published a discussion paper, *Infringement of Privacy*, July 1993, Central Office. The quotation this time is Milton: "For solitude sometimes is best society, And short retirement urges sweet return." For comment, see Lawrie, 1993 S.L.T. (News) 285. For a full review, see Hogg, "The Very Private Life of the Right to Privacy" (EUP, 1994), Hume Paper Vol. 2, No. 3.

Scotland. The review is an excellent source for the reader keen to consider the various problems which it is argued the law might address. The main interest for this book is recommendation (3), that consideration be given to introducing a tort of infringement of privacy.

The right to privacy is actionable in the United States of America and the action was developed on the basis of English common law rather than the constitution but the constitutional background in the United States might have helped. Thus it can be expected that the establishment of a Scottish parliament and the incorporation of the European Convention on Human Rights might result in an interest being recognised to such an extent that a court might choose to recognise a right of privacy. Alternatively, some terrible scandal might cause Parliament to act in response to public fury, whereupon the various working papers hitherto produced might be dusted down.

Further reading

Blom-Cooper, L., "The Right to be Let Alone" (1989) 34 J.L.S.S. 402.

Bonnington, A.J., "Privacy: Letting the Right Alone", 1992 S.L.T. (News) 289.

Bonnington, A.J., "The Defamation Bill" (1996) 41 J.L.S.S. 102.

Carey Miller, D.L., "Defamation by a Judge", 1980 J.R. 88.

Carey Miller, D.L. and Lardy, H., "Calcutt II: Comments from a Scots Perspective", 1993 S.L.T. (News) 199.

Cassimatis, A.E., "Defamation – The constitutional public officer defence", 1996 Tort L. Rev. 27.

Elliot, R.C., "Recent Developments in English Law: Libel: Free Speech, Privacy and Reputation", 1993 S.L.T. (News) 223.

Hogg, M.A., "Privacy: A Valuable and Protected Interest in Scots Law", 1992 S.L.T. (News) 349.

Hogg, M.A., "The Very Private Life of the Right of Privacy", Hume Paper Vol. 2, No. 3 in *Privacy and Property* (1994).

Kilbrandon, Lord, "The Law of Privacy in Scotland" (1971) 2 Cambrian L.R. 35.

Laurie, G.T., "Privacy, Paucity and the Press", 1993 S.L.T. (News) 285.

Norrie, K., "Hurts to Character, Honour and Reputation: a Reappraisal", 1985 J.R. 163.

Norrie, K., "Defamation, Negligence and Employers' References" (1994) 39 J.L.S.S. 418.

Norrie, K., "The Defamation Act", 1996 S.L.T. (News) 311.

Styles, S.C., "Two Flaws in the Law of Defamation", 1991 S.L.T. (News) 31.

Wacks, R.I., "The Poverty of Privacy" (1980) 96 L.Q.R. 73.

Wacks, R.I., *Privacy and the Law* (Clarendon Press, Oxford, 1989).

Walker, D.M., "Verbal Injury—Convicium or Defamation?" 1970 J.R. 157.

Wilton, G.W., "Reminiscences of the Scottish Bar: Striking Slander Suits" (1944) 56 J.R. 11.

Woolman, S.E., "Defaming the Dead", 1981 S.L.T. (News) 29.

CHAPTER 9

PARTIES

TITLE TO SUE

Title to sue is a curious and ill-defined requirement for a successful 9.1 action. It appears to the present writer to be little more than a procedural device to filter certain claims which are legally irrelevant. This view is strengthened when it is remembered that the requirement of title and interest to sue is present in, *inter alia*, the law of contract and the law of property. Thus, in certain cases it can be said that the pursuer has no title to sue and the claim will be disposed of immediately or after a preliminary proof on the particular point—so, for example, a pursuer generally has no title to sue if someone else is harmed.[1] Title to sue depends upon the existence of a legal right. Thus, in cases where legal rights are well established and clear the idea is perhaps helpful, such as where a person destroys the pursuer's heritable property or assaults the pursuer. Where the law is developing there can be few fixed categories of cases where there is no title to sue. For example, prior to *Junior Books* [5.8], if a person had sought compensation for economic loss deriving from a defective product, he might well have been told that he had no title to sue as the product was not dangerous to person or property. Even after *Junior Books*, a pursuer making a claim for economic loss not directly falling within the *rationes* of *Junior Books* or *Hedley Byrne* [5.5–5.7] has been met with a plea of no title to sue.[2] Once an area of law becomes contentious it is not helpful to consider it in terms of title to sue for the law underlies the plea, not vice versa. However, outside developing areas of delict, it is a valuable and effective plea preventing time, effort and money being wasted on the proof of what must ultimately be a hopeless case.[3]

---

[1] *McLachlan v. Bell* (1895) 23 R. 126.

[2] See *Nacap v. Moffat Plant Ltd*, 1987 S.L.T. 221 and *North Scottish Helicopters Ltd v. United Technologies Corp. Inc.*, 1988 S.L.T. 77; (*No. 2*), 1988 S.L.T. 778.

[3] *William Grant & Son v. Glen Catrine Bonded Warehouse*, 1995 S.L.T. 936 is a case which can be examined to discuss the value of having a distinct plea.

9.2   A pursuer must have title and interest to sue: "interest" means that the pursuer has suffered some loss or infringement of a civil right, protected by law. It is not necessary that there be what is sometimes called a patrimonial interest—a loss to a person's estate in every case.[4] If there is title to sue, interest is usually presumed. The two requirements are closely related.

Other procedural aspects

9.3   The general rule is that a pursuer must sue for all loss in a single action. Thus, if injuries worsen after the pursuer has obtained damages in an action, he cannot recover further compensation unless the special statutory exception for provisional damages in the Administration of Justice Act 1982, s. 12 applies.[5] The Act permits a pursuer to come back to court to make a claim for further compensation if (but only if) in the original action (i) the defender is a public authority or is otherwise indemnified[6] and (ii) it is admitted or proved that the pursuer may develop some serious disease or suffer some serious deterioration in his physical or mental condition.[7] If this is established the court may award damages immediately, on the basis that the injuries will not get worse, and allow a later application should the pursuer's condition deteriorate. The court may specify the period within which the application must be made.[8]

If a number of parties have a claim arising from the same incident they must raise separate actions.[9] However, a joint claim is permissible where two people have suffered the same harm and have a joint interest, such as where common property is damaged.

PARTICULAR PARTIES

The Crown

9.4   At common law the Crown was never vicariously liable (see Chapter 10) for the actings of its agents or employees but the liability of the Crown is now governed by the Crown Proceedings Act 1947, as amended. The Crown is liable both as an employer and as an occupier.[10] The Crown is also bound by statute, expressly or by

---

[4] For a recent review in contract: *Gunstone v. Scottish Women's Athletic Association*, 1987 S.L.T. 611.

[5] See *Casebook*, Ext. 96.

[6] s. 12 (1) (b); statutory instrument may designate a responsible authority, s. 12 (6).

[7] s. 12 (2) (a).

[8] See J. Blaikie, "Provisional Damages: a Progress Report" (1991) 36 J.L.S.S. 109.

[9] *Killin v. Weir* (1905) 7 F. 526.

[10] s. 2 (1) and the Occupiers' Liability (Scotland) Act 1960, s. 4.

necessary implication. The Crown is not vicariously liable for judges or the police. Immunity is preserved for prerogative acts.[11] The Sovereign herself enjoys personal immunity.

There is a special provision in respect of injuries suffered by members of the armed forces. By section 10 (1) of the 1947 Act there was no liability in delict if the injuries were certified as pensionable. This led to hardship in some cases where members of the armed forces considered that they were not properly compensated by the pension. An extreme example was *Adams v. War Office*,[12] where certification was made but no pension was actually awarded! Mounting pressure resulted in the passing of the Crown Proceedings (Armed Forces) Act 1987 which provides:

> "section 10 of the Crown Proceedings Act 1947 . . . shall cease to have effect except in relation to anything suffered by a person in consequence of an act or omission committed before the date on which this Act is passed."[13]

However, the Secretary of State can revive the effect of section 10 if it appears necessary or expedient to do so by reason of any imminent national danger or of any great emergency or for the purposes of any warlike operations in any part of the world outside the United Kingdom.[14]

Actions against the Crown should be raised against the Lord 9.5 Advocate. He must have the prior authority of whomsoever he represents before initiating or defending an action.[15] This is not something which can be challenged by a private party.[16] It is the practice to call the Secretary of State for Scotland as the defender in cases where one of his departments is involved. The "new" right of action based on a failure to implement a European Community directive represents an expansion of liability of the Crown [6.12–6.14].

Corporations

1. Incorporated bodies

The whole range of incorporated bodies whether incorporated by 9.6 royal charter, under the Companies Acts or otherwise, may sue and be sued in their own name so long as the wrong is one done to the

---

[11] s. 11.
[12] [1955] 3 All E.R. 245.
[13] The Act came into force on May 15, 1987.
[14] Consider the application of the Act to Northern Ireland. The Government did not activate the protection on the outbreak of the Gulf War: *Mulcahy v. MOD* [1996] 2 W.L.R. 474.
[15] Crown Suits (Scotland) Act 1857, ss. 1 and 2.
[16] 1857 Act, s. 3.

organisation, not merely to any, or indeed all, of the individuals forming it. Such an action would be bad for want of title to sue. An incorporated body being a legal person cannot have hurt feelings and therefore cannot be awarded solatium.[17] It can, however, be injured in its reputation.[18]

Again because incorporated bodies have no actual physical body, technically they are always vicariously liable. No distinction is made between *ultra vires* and *intra vires* acts.[19] Therefore there is no difficulty arising from the need for a mental element in some delicts.[20]

2. Unincorporated bodies

9.7 Generally speaking an unincorporated body cannot sue in its own right. However, in one case[21] an unincorporated voluntary association would have been allowed to sue for damages if it could have shown its patrimonial interests had been damaged. The case is subject to criticism on the basis that it proceeded by analogy with a case involving an incorporated body (see *Solicitors of Edinburgh v. Robertson*[22]), but in doing so the court refused to accept that in the circumstances some patrimonial damage could be inferred.

An unincorporated body as defender will be liable to the extent of any property held in trust for all the members and to the extent of the members' interest in the body, *e.g.* a club subscription.[23]

9.8 There is not much authority relating to the precise legal position of partnerships—because it is considered in law to have quasi-personality, it may be the case that a firm can only sue if the alleged wrong is done to it as a quasi-person rather than to an individual partner.[24] Partners are jointly and severally liable.[25] They are so liable for the matters set out in the Partnership Act 1890:

"Where, by any wrongful act or omission of any partner acting in the ordinary course of the business of the firm, or with the authority of his co-partners, loss or injury is caused to any person not being a partner in the firm, or any penalty is incurred, the firm is liable therefore to the same extent as the partner so acting or omitting to act."[26]

---

[17] *Waverley Housing Management v. BBC*, 1993 G.W.D. 17–1117.
[18] *Solicitors of Edinburgh v. Robertson* (1781) Mor. 13935.
[19] *Houldsworth v. City of Glasgow Bank* (1880) 7 R. (H.L.) 53.
[20] *Muir v. Glasgow Corp.*, 1943 S.C. (H.L.) 3.
[21] *Highland Dancing Board v. Alloa Printing Co.*, 1971 S.L.T. (Sh.Ct.) 50.
[22] (1781) Mor. 13935.
[23] *Gibson v. Smith* (1849) 21 Sc. Jur. 331.
[24] On the authority of the "peculiar" case of *Melville v. Cummings*, 1912 S.C. 1185.
[25] 1890 Act, s. 12; *Casebook*, Ext. 84.
[26] s. 10. See also the liability under s. 11 relating to misapplication of funds.

The essence of this liability is the scope of the partnership business.[27]

Trade unions are yet another special instance of an unincorporated 9.9
body. It is important to consider trade unions in the context of their
immunities [11.8–11.13]. If it were not for their immunities such
organisations would probably be illegal at common law. A trade
union is an organisation which consists mainly or wholly of workers
whose principal purpose includes the regulation of worker–employer
relations.[28]

A trade union is expressly[29] not an incorporated body. A union
may sue or be sued in its own name and any judgment is enforce-
able against any property which is held in trust for its benefit. It
has been held in England that a trade union cannot sue in its own
name for defamation.[30] Leaving aside the issue of the immunity, an
action for interference with contract, intimidation or conspiracy
can only be brought against the union if (and only if) the act
complained of was authorised or endorsed by the union in the ways
set out in section 20 of the Trade Union and Labour Relations
(Consolidation) Act 1992. The union may repudiate acts and thus
avoid liability.[31]

Families

1. Married women

Married women are in every respect in the same position as married 9.10
men so far as delictual actions are concerned as a result of reforms
over the years.[32] A married woman in minority is no longer under the
curatory of her husband.[33] If one spouse is to be liable for the act or
omission of another, liability must arise from a basis other than
marriage such as agency, employment or as a joint wrongdoer.

While the Law Reform (Husband and Wife) Act 1962, s. 2 removed
the difficulties which formerly existed from the doctrine of the
common law that husband and wife were one person which prevented
them suing each other, it left a residual power with the court.[34] The
court may exercise a discretion to dismiss an action if it is shown that
no substantial benefit would accrue to either party if the action
continued. The Scottish Law Commission have recommended the

---

[27] *Lloyd v. Grace Smith* [1912] A.C. 716.
[28] Trade Union and Labour Relations (Consolidation) Act 1992, s. 1; workers and
employers are defined in ss. 30, 295 and 296.
[29] Trade Union and Labour Relations (Consolidation) Act 1992, s. 10(1).
[30] *Willis v. Brooks* [1947] 1 All E.R. 191.
[31] s. 21.
[32] Married Women's Property (Scotland) Act 1881; Married Women's Property
(Scotland) Act 1920.
[33] Law Reform (Husband and Wife) Act 1984, s. 3. See *Casebook*, Ext. 97
[34] See *Casebook*, Ext. 90.

repeal of section 2(2): it appears not to have been used—on consultation no one could point to a case which was not raised because of it and cohabitants have not flooded the courts with trivial claims.[35] A spouse has no title to sue for the enticement of the other spouse [2.5].

A spouse may be able to claim losses of the nature of personal services caused by injuries sustained by the other spouse, in a claim of the injured spouse,[36] but the spouse suffering the loss has no title to sue.[37] So, if a wife is injured in a car accident, a claim may be made in the wife's action for the cost to her husband of paying for a housekeeper. If, however, the husband is the wrongdoer, the husband has no claim for his services on the basis of authority in Scotland and in England—although it might be doubted whether Parliament intended this generous discount to the shareholders of insurance companies.[38]

2. Parents

9.11 Parents are not liable for the delicts of their children. There is Scottish authority,[39] but a better illustration is the English case of *Newton v. Edgerley*.[40] In this case a gun was actually discharged by a child not party to the action called Antrobus. The court held the father negligent, not so much for allowing the child to have the gun (for that seemed to be normal in the country), but for telling the child only to use it privately. The father should have appreciated that the boy probably would not obey this command. Accordingly, the father had failed to instruct him how to carry a gun in company.[41] It is clear, then, that the liability was personal to the father and not a vicarious liability for his child.

Parents can sue children just as children can sue their parents.[42] Parents and children are "relatives" for the purposes of the Administration of Justice Act 1982. [See para 5.28 and paras 11.30 *et seq.*]

The parents' claim for the death of a child, resulting from injuries caused while *in utero*, has now been judicially considered in terms of the Damages (Scotland) Act 1976. After a divergence of judicial authority, the matter was settled in *Hamilton v. Fife Health Board*.[43] In this case it was accepted by the pursuers that prior to being born a "child" is not a person. It was accepted by the defenders that the *nascituri* principle [see

---

[35] Scot. Law Com. No. 135, 10.1–10.8.
[36] Administration of Justice Act 1982, ss.7–9. *Casebook*, Ext. 96.
[37] s. 8(2) and (4).
[38] *Hunt v. Severs* [1994] 2 A.C. 350; *Kozikowska v. Kozikowski*, 1996 S.L.T. 386.
[39] *Davie v. Wilson* (1854) 16 D. 956.
[40] [1959] 1 W.L.R. 1031.
[41] See, for a different set of circumstances producing a different result, *Donaldson v. McNiven* [1952] 2 All E.R. 691.
[42] *Wood v. Wood*, 1935 S.L.T. 431.
[43] 1992 S.L.T. 1026; 1993 S.L.T. 624.

para. 9.13 for an explanation] is accepted in Scotland, subject to the limitation that the fiction operates "only for the purpose of enabling the child to take a benefit to which, if born, it would be entitled" and cannot be invoked in the interest of any third party. On a close reading of the Act, Lord Prosser concluded that Parliament had not intended a foetus to be a person capable of sustaining personal injuries.[44] The Division held that injuries caused to a foetus are "properly and sensibly" described as "personal injuries" even although when inflicted the "victim" did not enjoy legal personality.

> "To suppose that only one who enjoys legal personality can sustain 'personal injuries' is to attach an artificial legal meaning to the adjective 'personal' in s. 1(1)."

Sadly this is not sufficiently explained. A further comment is offered which may be intended to explain this point:

> "there are many examples in history of adult, sentient human beings being denied human status and legal personality and of limited liability companies and even of non-human animals being accorded rights and responsibilities normally appropriate only to human beings."

However, that can be argued the other way. Slaves in Rome being adult and sentient could not sue for personal injuries—indeed, to flog another's slave was to commit a delict against the slave's owner.[45] Noxal surrender, by which slaves (and at one time children) would be handed over to the victim of their wrongdoing, occurs in an action against the owner or father and is in a way a method of damage limitation for slave owners and fathers. Limited companies generally can sue *because* they have legal personality and so the quotation above is questionable. Animals seldom vindicate any rights they may have in any court. The court stated that the case depended not on a fiction but on the neighbour doctrine of *Donoghue*. This is surprising as there is no neighbour until the foetus is born alive. It would be said of a pregnant single woman living next door that I have one neighbour not two! It is submitted the decision is wrong. It will be appreciated that this decision is relevant to the interpretation of the 1976 Act, discussed below.

3. Children, minors and pupils

The law is now stated in terms of a distinction between children and others but the fundamentals of the law of delict cannot be so easily stated, yet. Professor Walker states that a pupil can be liable in an   9.12

---

[44] This view is preferred in the second edition of this book as against that in *McWilliams v. Lord Advocate*, 1992 S.L.T. 1045.

[45] Gaius, III, 222.

action *ex delicto* on the authority of *Somerville v. Hamilton*.[46] Neither Glegg, nor the *Green's Encyclopaedia* (title "Minors and Pupils"), published well before Walker, considered the position settled, although depending on the circumstances a pupil may be guilty of contributory negligence. *Somerville* was a spuilzie [2.21] case in which a child of six was sued. The report in *Morison's Dictionary* is exceedingly brief but it does appear to support Professor Walker's view. The next case in the *Dictionary*, however, does not seem to support that view. The later case of *Bryson v. Somervill* was equally a case of spuilzie, in which, despite the pursuer's plea that the boy had the intent to do harm, the boy's plea which was simply that he was under the age of 14 was upheld—and quite clearly so, without any inquiry as to his understanding, allowing it to be suggested that a pupil is not liable in delict at all.[47]

Spuilzie is a delict which depends upon the act concerned and is not where the harm is usually unintended. It may be that a pupil's liability for loss wrongfully caused (including unintentional harm) could be established on the basis of the *Digest*, to which Professor Walker also makes reference:

> "Therefore the Aquilian Action will fail . . . if an infant has caused damage, though Labeo says that if a child were over seven years of age he could be liable under the Lex Aquilia in just the same way as he could be liable for theft. I think this is correct, provided the child were able to distinguish between right and wrong."[48]

It should be noted that in Scots criminal law there is no criminal liability until a child is aged eight or over.

The Age of Legal Capacity (Scotland) Act 1991, which came into force on September 25, 1991, did not intend to deal with the liability of under-age persons in delict.[49] It has, however, made a number of changes in relation to claims that they can make, prescription and the conduct of litigation. While accepting that the age of majority is 18, it establishes 16 as the age of legal capacity. Those aged 16 and 17 have full capacity subject to exceptions. Those under 16 have no capacity subject to exceptions. The Act is fully treated in the periodical literature and only the features relevant to delict are mentioned here.[50]

---

[46] (1541) Mor. 8905.
[47] (1565) Mor. 1703, and see Stewart, "A Note on the Liability of Pupils in Delict", 1989 S.L.T. (News).
[48] *Dig.* IX, 2, 5, 2.
[49] s. 1(3) (c).
[50] See Nichols, "Can They or Can't They?" 1991 S.L.T. (News) 395; Norrie, "The Age of Legal Capacity (Scotland) Act 1991" (1991) 36 J.L.S.S. 434; Barr and Edwards, "Age of Legal Capacity: Further Pitfalls", 1992 S.L.T. (News) 77, 91.

Children aged 16 or over can give consent to medical treatment and thus protect the doctor from proceedings for assault.[51] Children under 16 may consent to a procedure or treatment (but not non-therapeutic research) so long as the medical practitioner considers that the child is capable of understanding the nature and possible consequences of the treatment. Informal guidance and medical ethics together make it extremely likely that parents will be brought into such a decision-making process.

A transaction for the purposes of the new Act includes the bringing or defending of, or the taking of any step in, civil proceedings.[52] Thus, those 16 years and over will raise and defend actions in their own names and without a curator *ad litem*. Those under that age, including those who would have been minors under the old law, would have to litigate with their guardian. The new minor's right of setting aside transactions does not apply to civil proceedings.[53] Discharges given on receipt of a settlement payment must be granted by the minor but can be set aside until the minor reaches the age of 21.[54] An application can be made by all parties to the sheriff in summary form asking the court to ratify, in which case it cannot be challenged. The statute does not make clear which of its provisions apply to common forms of conclusion of actions. A minute approved by the court indicating that the action has settled is a step in civil process on the face of it, but in reality the court does not usually know anything about the settlement. Perhaps where a party is *ex facie* a minor a new practice could develop whereby the court does inquire into the settlement prior to interponing authority. A settlement which agrees to an award of damages is in a very similar position, being even more a step in process but nothing can be discovered from the amount settled, save that if it is very close to the sum sued for the tests applied in ratification are virtually met *ex facie*. However, because most pursuers sue for a good bit more than they realistically expect to get, inquiry would be the only way in which the substance of the protection of minors could be met. Nonetheless, the statute has exempted legal proceedings, no doubt for good policy reasons. Barr and Edwards consider that the minor has the protection of the court during a litigation and not at these stages of settlement, and so the setting aside provisions should apply rather than the litigation exclusion. This is debatable. *Ex facie* the court papers are stages in process. The protections Barr and Edwards refer to as being present in litigation—the rules of evidence, proce-

---

[51] s. 1(1) (b); s. 9.

[52] s. 9.

[53] s. 3(3) (d).

[54] On the midnight of the anniversary of birth (or the next day, if a leap year).

dure and natural justice—do not prevent the litigating minor agreeing in the course of proceedings to drop a head of claim, perhaps
worth a very great sum, or, even more problematically, agreeing not
to call a witness who would be essential to establish the whole case let
alone part of it. The court, in an adversarial system, would take no
part in any of these steps which are highly detrimental. Thus, there is
no substantial contrast between the "fought-out" decree and the
settlement by minute with or without settlement figure. In favour of
their approach is that, so far as the statutory right of relief is
concerned, the courts do distinguish between forms of settlement
[see 11.32].

The Children (Scotland) Act 1995 gave effect to the international
desire to protect the rights of children. A person under the age of 16
has legal capacity to instruct a solicitor in connection with any civil
matter where that person has a general understanding of what it
means to do so and a person of 12 years or older is presumed to have
that general understanding.[55] Such a person has legal capacity to sue
in civil proceedings.[56]

4. Unborn children

9.13   The title of the chapter suggests correctly that the law is concerned
with the persons who come before courts. A court is not, in general, a
debating forum, nor is it an advisory centre. So injuries to or the
premature termination of a foetus immediately raises the problem that
there is no party before the court. But the law is equally concerned
with rights and the example of cases involving children shows that if
the right is there someone can be allowed to bring the action. There is
no lengthy train of ancient authority dealing with these issues. It may
be that in relation to some of the issues it might have been assumed
that the answers were obvious. For the purposes of inheritance the
issue had been contemplated a long time ago based on the civilian
maxim. The doctrine is set out in Bankton as follows:

> "A child in the mother's womb is esteem'd as already born, in all
> things that concern its own interest, but is not reckoned among
> children in relation to questions to the advantage of parents from
> a certain number of children. By our law, rights may be granted in
> favour of children *nascaturi* of any particular person, tho' not
> begotten at the time, and upon their existence they are entitled
> thereto, in the same manner as if they had been born at the date of
> rights."[57]

---

[55] s. 2 (4A) of the 1991 Act, inserted by the 1995 Act.
[56] s. 2 (4B).
[57] *Inst.*, I, ii, 7.

The doctrine had already received judicial approval in a succession case.[58] The Scottish Law Commission did not consider it necessary to legislate considering that Scots law would permit recovery in the case of injury to an unborn child.[59] In *Cohen v. Shaw*,[60] the law was considered in detail. The pursuer claimed, *inter alia*, on behalf of a child born alive after the death of his father for damages. Lord Cullen allowed a jury trial. He accepted that the *nascaturi* doctrine could apply unless it were excluded by statute. The 1976 Act did not exclude it. That decision supported the Law Commission's view.[61] In *Kelly v. Kelly*,[62] a husband sought to interdict his wife from aborting their child.[63] It was accepted that interdict would be available to a person's representative to prevent damage being caused to that person if it would result in an award of damages. If abortion had been an actionable wrong the father could have sued. However, as the foetus itself had no right to continued existence while in the womb, it could not be represented as a matter of law.[64]

If a child is born alive and in such a way different from the norm that it will over its life be much more expensive to raise, the parents have a claim for wrongful birth.[65] Indeed, after some debate it has been established in the Inner House that the birth of a healthy child in breach of duty is actionable by the parents for the pregnancy itself and the increased costs involved in having to bring up a child, the overall assessment of damages being at large.[66]

The fact that an abortion might have been allowed does not

---

[58] *Elliot v. Joicey*, 1935 S.C. (H.L.) 57, *per* Lord Macmillan at 70. The Canadian case of *Montreal Tramways v. Leveille* [1933] 4 D.L.R. 337 is often cited.

[59] *Liability for Antenatal Injuries* (Scot. Law Com. No. 30, Cmnd 5371, 1973). The English legislated: Congenital Disabilities (Civil Liability) Act 1976. This was after the report of the English Law Commission (*Report on Injuries to Unborn Children*) (Law Com. No. 60, Cmnd 5709, 1974). The Scottish Law Commission's position was criticised at the time: Rodger, "Ante-natal Injury", 1974 J.R. 83.

[60] 1992 S.L.T. 1022.

[61] It is also supported by earlier cases which made such awards but without discussion: *Moorcraft v. W. Alexander & Sons*, 1946 S.C. 466; *Leadbetter v. NCB*, 1952 S.C. 19; *Riddell v. James Longmuir & Sons Ltd*, 1971 S.L.T. (Notes) 33. See also Norrie, "Liability for Injuries Caused Before Birth", 1992 S.L.T. (News) 65, especially at 66 where it is argued that there is no need for the fiction.

[62] 1997 S.L.T. 896.

[63] Or more accurately, in this context, foetus.

[64] At 901. Reference was made to a number of English and Commonwealth authorities. See, *inter alia*, *Paton v. British Pregnancy Advisory Service* [1979] 1 Q.B. 276; *B. v. Islington Health Authority* [1991] 1 Q.B. 638; *Borowski v. Att.-Gen. for Canada* (1987) 39 DLR (4th) 731; *F. (in utero)* [1988] 2 W.L.R. 1297; *Dehler v. Ottawa Civic Hospital* (1979) 101 D.L.R. (3d) 686.

[65] *Jones v. Lanarkshire Health Authority*, 1990 S.L.T. 19; and more emphatically in *Anderson v. Forth Valley Health Board*, 1997 G.W.D. 39–2016.

[66] *McFarlane v. Tayside Health Board*, 1998 G.W.D. 4–180.

break the causal link.[67] However, where a person is aware that a sterilisation operation has failed and nevertheless continues to have potentially procreative sex, then a second pregnancy is not actionable.[68]

Excursus: wrongful life

9.14   Another, and different, question (as well treated here as anywhere else in the text) is the action of a child born in some way different from the norm to claim in its own right for damages for the failure of the medical practitioner to advise (or advise in sufficient time) the parents to consider seeking a legal abortion. The main difficulty this claim meets is the question of existence itself. Non-existence may well be a peaceful sleep but just as fear of the dreams at the other end[69] make suicide unappealing for the large majority so must it be wondered whether we have been awakened from a nightmare by birth. Phenomenologically, we can agree with Norrie: "There have been times when we all were, in fact, non-existent but we have never experienced that state."[70] Even then, Norrie's verity is based upon testimony and documentary and inferential evidence[71]—I do not know that I once did not exist; I might have existed before and just have forgotten. As soon as one strays into metaphysics or religion, certainty vanishes: Is there a queue of souls begging to be born in any shape or form rather than reside or be consigned to some Hell? Is it better to be born with a disadvantaged limb in a wealthy and fashionable part of Edinburgh or hale and hearty in a famine-ridden part of Africa? Was a now forgotten choice taken to be a disabled child as opposed to a battery chicken? Neither do many of the bodily challenged consider that their normality should be treated as something which should be treated by awarding damages—suggesting that they are damaged instead of different.

Causation is another important issue. The pursuer's difficulties are not caused by the delayed or inaccurate medical advice, nor by the mother's non-application for abortion, but are an aspect of life itself (or caused by a Great Mover, not amenable to the jurisdiction).

Norrie's conclusion, that "a child's action based upon the denial of a 'right' to have had its life prevented has, and ought to have, no chance of success", is sound so long as life itself is valued. In *P's CB v.*

---

[67] *Emeh v. Kensington, Chelsea and Westminster Area Health Authority* [1985] Q.B. 1012.

[68] *Sabri-Tabrizi v. Lothian Health Board*, unreported, O.H., Dec. 17, 1997.

[69] *Hamlet*, Act III, Sc. 1.

[70] Norrie, "Wrongful Life in Scots Law: No Right, No Remedy", 1990 J.R. 217.

[71] Albeit entitled to the very greatest weight: my birth certificate and my mother, who says she was there, tells me.

CICB,[72] it was indeed held that no such case could succeed even in a case where the child suing had been born as a result of rape and with physical and mental abnormalities.

Insane persons

Persons mentally afflicted are thought to have no title to sue. This is 9.15 probably because there is another person with title to sue, namely the guardian of the afflicted person's estate (known as the curator *bonis*). Insanity at the time of the critical act or omission should be a defence if alienation of reason can be established. Again this was anticipated in the *Digest*:

> "accordingly the question is asked whether there is an action under the Lex Aquilia if a lunatic causes damage. Pegasus says there is not, for he asks how there can be any accountable fault in him who is out of his mind; and he is undoubtedly right . . . Therefore the Aquilian action will fail in such a case."[73]

The modern law has adopted a similar course. In *Waugh v. James K. Allan Ltd*[74]:

> The pursuer was struck by a heavy lorry driven by the employee of the defenders. The driver was still breathing when the lorry stopped but died immediately afterwards. The driver had had a heart attack. There was evidence that the driver had said he had been sick before taking his lorry out.

The House of Lords eventually supported the Lord Ordinary and the Inner House's view that there was no reason why—the driver being a reasonable though strong and determined man—he should not have taken his lorry out after having been sick some 15 minutes before.

In the similar English case of *Roberts v. Ramsbottom*[75] a 73-year-old accountant was held liable for a motor accident because he retained some control, even though imperfect (unlike the Scottish driver who had a sudden coronary). This finding was made despite a doctor having given evidence to the effect that the defendant was suffering from automatism at the time. The court held that the medical condition, although described as automatism, was not legally relevant: he had had one collision before the collision in question and should have stopped after the first one.

The common ancestry of delict and crime suggests that, in any delictual case that comes before the courts, serious account should be

---

[72] 1996 G.W.D. 39–2243.
[73] *Dig.* IX, 2, 5, 2.
[74] 1964 S.C. (H.L.) 102; *Casebook*, Ext. 91.
[75] [1980] 1 All E.R. 7.

taken of *Ross v. H.M. Advocate*[76] and its many successors, certainly where automatism is a result of external factors as opposed to sudden illness.

Debtors whose estates are bankrupt[77]

9.16   The debtor has title and interest to sue for personal wrongs such as assault, unintentional personal injury or defamation.[78] The trustee in bankruptcy has no title and interest to sue but if the bankrupt recovers compensation, the damages go to the estate.[79] If, however, the recovery of *solatium* is after the debtor's discharge, and the trustee was never sisted in the action, the debtor keeps the damages.[79a]

In other cases—those involving patrimonial loss—the trustee has title and interest. It may be that a person whose estates are insolvent has no title to sue unless he can show that the trustee and the creditors have abandoned a claim.[80]

Assignees

9.17   This area of law assumes importance because of decisions like *Aliakmon* and *Nacap* [5.17]. If a person does not have title to sue, it is possible to obtain a title to sue before raising the action by obtaining an assignation of the claim from a person who does have title to sue. Naturally this depends upon the person having title to sue being prepared to assign. An example of the stringency of the rule is *Symington v. Campbell.*[81]

> The pursuer purchased a vessel called *Alarm* on May 18, 1893. He sued for damage which had been done to it in January 1893 when it was owned by someone else. The action was raised on June 28, 1893. On June 29, 1893 the pursuer obtained an assignation in his favour. The court held that the assignation came too late and that

---

[76] 1991 S.L.T. 564.

[77] This terminology is required (rather than "bankrupt": Bankruptcy (Scotland) Act 1985).

[78] *Muir's Trs v. Braidwood*, 1958 S.C. 169.

[79] *Jackson v. McKechnie* (1875) 3 R. 130.

[79a] *Coutts Trs (Sharp) v. Coutts*, 1996 S.C.C.R. 1026. See generally Scot. Law Com. Consultation Paper on the law of bankruptcy: "Solatium for personal injury/ Future wage loss" (1994).

[80] *Crindall v. John Mitchell (Grangemouth) Ltd*, 1984 S.L.T. 335; 1987 S.L.T. 137 at 141. The only possible difficulty with this statement is that section 32 of the Bankruptcy (Scotland) Act 1985 allows the debtor to keep his income, placing the onus on the trustee to make a claim upon it. This income is a kind of patrimony and it might be that an action relating to it should not be affected by the rules of title to sue. Some cases may be best left taken by the person making the outlay; see *EIF Enterprise (Caledonia) Ltd v. London Bridge Engineering Ltd* (1997) T.L.R. 607.

[81] (1894) 21 R. 434.

accordingly the pursuer had no title to sue.[82] The value of an assignation as a mode of settlement in cases involving relief and economic loss has been doubted.[83]

Members of the public

A member of the public cannot in general sue just to find out what the law is on any particular topic.[84] But if a member of the public has a right as such member of the public then there is likely to be sufficient title and interest to sue.[85]

Further reading

Barr, A. and Edwards, L., "Age of Legal Capacity: Further Pitfalls", 1992 S.L.T. (News) 77, 91.

Blaikie, J., "Provisional Damages: a Progress Report" (1991) 36 J.L.S.S. 109.

Devereux, J.A., "Actions for Wrongful Birth" (1996) Tort L. Rev. 107.

Dickinson, I., "Still no Interdicts against the Crown", 1994 S.L.T. (News) 217.

Doyle, J.J., "The Liability of Public Authorities" (1994) 1 Tort L. Rev. 189.

Grainger, C.J., "Wrongful Life: A wrong without a remedy" (1994) 1 Tort L.Rev. 164.

Nichols, D., "Can They or Can't They?" 1991 S.L.T. (News) 395.

Mildred, M., "Group Actions Present and Future", 1994 J.P.I.L. 276.

Norrie, K., "Actionability of Birth", 1983 S.L.T. (News) 121.

Norrie, K., "Damages for Birth of a Child", 1985 S.L.T. (News) 69.

Norrie, K., "Wrongful Life in Scots Law: No Right, No Remedy", 1990 J.R. 205.

Norrie, K., "The Age of Legal Capacity (Scotland) Act 1991" (1991) 36 J.L.S.S. 434.

Robertson, E., "Consider the Foetus", 1997 S.L.T. (News) 319.

Rodger, A., "Antenatal Injury", 1974 J.R. 83.

Russell, E.J., "Abortion Law in Scotland and the Kelly Foetus", 1997 S.L.T. (News) 187.

Stewart, A. A., "Damages for the Birth of a Child" (1995) 40 J.L.S.S. 298.

Stewart, A.A., "Live Issue—Damages for Wrongful Birth" (1996) 41 J.L.S.S. 443.

Stewart, W.J., "A Note on the Liability of Pupils in Delict", 1989 S.L.T. (News) 404.

---

[82] The difference between *Aliakmon* (above) and the *Symington* case is that in the *Symington* case the whole damage had been done before the goods were purchased. In *Aliakmon* the damage was done after the contract of sale but before delivery.

[83] See Young, "Rights of Relief", 1992 S.L.T. (News) 225.

[84] *Scottish Old People's Welfare Council*, 1987 S.L.T. 179.

[85] *Sanderson v. Lees* (1859) 22 D. 24.

CHAPTER 10

VICARIOUS LIABILITY

10.1 As the name suggests, this doctrine enables a person who has done no wrong himself to be held liable for a wrong done by another. This type of liability is now clearly established[1] and it satisfies a desire to transfer liability to pay damages to the person who has been gaining, in a general way, from the actings of the actual wrongdoer. Some maxims are often found in connection with it. The most significant is *culpa tenet suos auctores* (fault adheres to its author).[2] This is said to be a fundamental principle of the law to which vicarious liability is an exception.[3] The other maxim which is encountered is *qui facit per alium per se* (he who does something through another does it himself). This can be seen as an exception to the *culpa tenet* maxim or as an application of it! For a time, the law of Scotland followed the English doctrine of common employment. This held that an employer would not be vicariously liable for injury caused to a workman by a fellow workman on the dubious basis that the workman had, in taking the job, assumed the risk of injury by his fellow workers.[4] Eventually, the common employment doctrine was abolished (both in Scotland and in England) by the Law Reform (Personal Injuries) Act 1948.

10.2 Vicarious liability is an example of joint and several liability. Accordingly, if it applies the actual wrongdoer and the person who is vicariously liable for his actings, are both liable. The most common example of vicarious liability is for employees.

---

[1] See *Baird v. Hamilton* (1826) 4 S. 790.

[2] Or more colourfully, "the fox must pay his own skin": *Wood v. Fullerton* (1710) Mor. 13960.

[3] As MacCormack pointed out, "the principle is cited only in cases where one of the issues is: which of two or more persons is the appropriate defender" (1973 J.R. 69).

[4] *Bartonshill Coal Co. v. Reid* (1858) 3 Macq. 266. The existence of this doctrine made it more attractive to a court sympathetic to an injured pursuer to find a duty personal to the employer which had been broken, for then common employment would not apply.

Vicarious liability for agent

The first point relates to the law of contracts. There is a distinction 10.3
between the contract of agency (and mandate (gratuitious agency))
and employment (*locatio operarum*).[5] As a result of the different
nature of these contracts, the delictual consequences differ. The
obligations of the agent depend upon the instructions given to the
agent. In relation to third parties, the agent's ability to affect his
principal depends upon his authority, express or implied; therefore,
the principal's delictual liability is formulated by reference to this
relationship.

While the liability in respect of an agent and the liability in respect 10.4
of an employer can be distinguished, it is quite possible for someone to
be vicariously liable both as an employer of an employee and as the
principal of an agent. This is particularly important, for an act may be
outside the scope of an employee's employment but within the scope
of his authority, express or implied, as an agent.

A principal will be liable for the acts of an agent where:

1. The acts complained of were expressly authorised

For example, where a solicitor writes defamatory letters on the 10.5
instructions of a client, the client will be vicariously liable.[6]

2. The principal ratifies the act after it has been done

There seem to be few cases of this (understandably, for in the 10.6
normal case it would amount to an acceptance of liability for an act
one had not instructed). However, in *Buron v. Denman*[7] a British naval
commander destroyed certain property and released certain slaves
belonging to a Spanish subject resident abroad. The Foreign and
Colonial Secretaries of State ratified the act of the commander. This
was not a charitable act. By ratifying the act it became an act of state
and therefore non-justiciable.

3. The act complained of is within actual or ostensible authority of the agent

This requires an understanding of the contractual position because 10.7
liability is established by reference to the scope of the agent's
authority.[8] However, for the purposes of the law of delict it seems

---

[5] See Gloag and Henderson, paras 22.1–22.4.
[6] *Crawford v. Adams; Crawford v. Dunlop* (1900) 2 F. 987.
[7] (1848) 2 Ex. 167; and see Lord Denning, *Landmarks in the Law*, pp. 223–227; see
also *Att.-Gen. v. Nissan* [1969] 1 All E.R. 629.
[8] *Percy v. Glasgow Corp.*, 1922 S.C. (H.L.) 144. See *Scobie v. Steele & Wilson Ltd*,
1963 S.L.T. (Notes) 45 for a company's liability for a company director.

that the courts will often hold someone vicariously liable as a principal where they would perhaps not hold the "agent" able to bind the principal in contract. In the case of *Launchbury v. Morgans*[9] this area of the law was examined by the House of Lords.

> Mrs Morgans was the owner and registered keeper of a motor car. There were five people in the car: Mr Morgans, Mr Cawfield and three passengers (who were the plaintiffs in the case). Mr Morgans had gone out drinking and passed the keys to Mr Cawfield. They picked up the three plaintiffs. Mr Morgans fell asleep in the back seat. Mr Cawfield, driving without due care, crashed the car at 90 m.p.h. Mr and Mrs Morgans considered the car as "our car".

The issue before the House of Lords was whether Mrs Morgans could be held vicariously liable for the actions of Mr Cawfield. The court rejected this argument. Lord Wilberforce said, "I regard it as clear that in order to fix vicarious liability on the owner of a car in such a case as the present, it must be shown that the driver was using it for the owner's purposes, under delegation of a task or duty." The argument that the car should be treated as a matrimonial car, making the owner liable for its use, was also rejected.

Vicarious liability for employee

10.8   The first matter to be determined is whether in fact the person who committed the delict is an employee and the proposed other defender an employer. In other words, the contract must be one of employment for service (*locatio operarum*) as opposed to, for example, a contract for services (*locatio operis faciendi*).

10.9   "Employee" for the purposes of vicarious liability is not dependent upon any period of continuous employment, which is a distinctive feature of the "employment rights" given to "employees" as variously defined by various statutes.

10.10   The most difficult area is to distinguish between *locatio operarum* (for example, a chauffeur) and *locatio operis faciendi* (for example, a taxi-driver). The element of control is an important factor and solves many of the most common cases. Since a chauffeur must take the precise route given by his employer he is employed *locatio operarum*; whereas the cab driver, who undertakes only to take the "fare" to a destination and himself chooses the route, is "employed" under a contract *locatio operis faciendi*.

    However, in modern society, the control test may not be sufficient to resolve all cases, mainly because of the existence of many highly

---

[9] [1973] A.C. 127.

technical employments where the employer may not understand what it is the employee is doing, let alone control how he performs his task. The courts now look to various factors in resolving the question.[10] It is said that courts would consider the following:

(1) the intention of the parties;
(2) freedom of selection of employees;
(3) duration of the contract;
(4) whether payment is by salary or wages and whether made by the job or by the piece;
(5) whether the tools and equipment belong to the employer or employee;
(6) the nature of the arrangements for termination.[11]

Thus it is now the case that resident doctors working under the NHS scheme are considered to be employees for the purposes of vicarious liability.[12] There is a trend in some recent English cases (mainly dealing with employment rights under various employment statutes) for the court to look for a mutuality of obligations: the one party to make work available and the other to do it.[13]

Once it has been established that the person who committed the delict is an employee, then the question arises whether the employer should be liable. The problem is to decide whether or not the actings complained of were within the scope of the employee's employment: it is well settled that this extends beyond his duties expressed in the contract. The overall thrust of the authorities is summarised by Lord President Clyde in the following passage from *Kirby v. NCB*[14]:

10.11

"But, in the decisions, four different types of situation have been envisaged as guides to the solution of this problem. In the first place, if the master actually authorised the particular act, he is clearly liable for it. Secondly, where the workman does some work which he is appointed to do, but does it in a way which his master has not authorised and would not have authorised had he known of it, the master is nevertheless still responsible, for the servant's act is still within the scope of his employment. On the other hand, in the third place, if the servant is employed only to do a particular work or a particular class of work, and he does

---

[10] See, generally, *Short v. J. & W. Henderson*, 1946 S.C. (H.L.) 24.
[11] See *United Wholesale Grocers Ltd v. Sher*, 1993 S.L.T. 284 for a recent examination of the key factors.
[12] *McDonald v. Glasgow Western Hospitals Board*, 1954 S.C. 453.
[13] *O'Kelly v. Trusthouse Forte plc* [1984] Q.B. 90; *Nethermere (St Neots) Ltd v. Taverna* [1984] I.C.R. 612; *McLeod v. Hellyer Bros Ltd* [1987] I.R.L.R. 232. It is now spreading to ordinary tort cases: *McMeechan v Secretary of State for Employment* [1997] I.R.L.R. 353.
[14] 1958 S.C. 514 at 532–533.

something outside the scope of that work, the master is not responsible for any mischief the servant may do to a third party. Lastly, if the servant uses his master's time or his master's tools for his own purposes, the master is not responsible."

In most cases where an employee is driving to or from his work the employer will not be liable—the act is outwith the scope of his employment. But if he is driving between places of work and in so doing decides to stay overnight at his own home, he will be within the scope of his employment.[15]

10.12 It is cases two and three above which are the trickiest to distinguish and this is done on the basis of distinguishing scope of the employment from mode of execution of the work. This distinction is particularly apparent in the case of *Williams v. Hemphill*[16]:

> A driver, instructed by his employers to drive from Benderloch to Glasgow, was persuaded by some passengers to drive round by Dollar, a considerable deviation. An accident happened as a result of the driver's fault. A passenger who had not instigated the deviation was injured.

It was held that when the accident took place the driver was still acting within the scope of his employment: *i.e.* the driver was still implementing his master's purpose. Interestingly, opinions were reserved as to the position if the action had been raised by one of the passengers who had requested the deviation.

10.13 Cases like *Hemphill* must be distinguished from cases where the driver goes off "on a frolic of his own."[17] But it is important not to be misled by the rhetorical force of the handy phrase "frolic of his own" and, indeed, the Queen's Bench were not in the case of *Harrison v. Michelin Tyre Co.*[18] The plaintiff had been standing on a duck board and a fellow employee tipped up the duck board. Although this was a frolic it was not the employee's own frolic, but was part and parcel of the employment—"a frolic on the job", it could be said. The point is clearly made in *Rose v. Plenty*[19]:

> A milkman was employed by a dairy company to drive a milk float to deliver milk. At his place of work there was a notice prohibiting milkmen using boys to help them or giving boys lifts. In breach of this prohibition, this particular milkman used the

---

[15] *Thomson v. BSC*, 1977 S.L.T. 26.
[16] 1966 S.C. (H.L.) 31.
[17] *Joel v. Morison* (1834) 6 C. & P. 501. Practical jokes by fellow workers were "frolics of the employees for which their employers were not liable": *Mclean v. Remploy*, 1994 S.L.T. 687 at 688.
[18] [1985] 1 All E.R. 918.
[19] [1976] 1 All E.R. 97.

services of a 13-year-old boy and allowed him to ride on the back of the float. Unfortunately the boy was injured when the milkman drove the float without due care.

In the lower court it was held that the acts were outside the scope of the milkman's employment. On appeal the view was taken that the instructions only affected the mode of execution of the job and did not limit or define the scope of the employment. The milkman was effectively still delivering milk, which is what he was employed to do; he was simply doing it in a forbidden way. Accordingly, his employer was vicariously liable.

If the act has nothing to do with the employment, then the employer is not vicariously liable. In *Kirby* itself, a workman on a temporary work break left his place of work and went into adjacent waste ground where he had no business to be and struck a match contrary to certain statutory provisions. It was held that at the time of the accident he was not mining but was smoking and so the act was outwith the scope of the employment. In this case the court contrasted these facts with those in *Century Insurance Co. v. Northern Ireland Transport Board*[20] where a match was struck while petrol was being transferred. This was held to be an incidence of doing a proper act negligently as opposed to doing an act unconnected with the employment.   10.14

Fraud raises difficult issues. In the most recent case, *Taylor v. Glasgow District Council* which eventually came before the Division,[21] Lord Sutherland (giving the opinion of the court) stated that since *Lloyd* it had not been necessary to show that the employer received any benefit from the fraud and that since *Uxbridge Permanent Building Society v. Pickard*[22] it has not been necessary to show that the employers and the defrauded party have been in some contractual relationship.[23] The matter is often considered in relation to actual and ostensible authority. In the Outer House, reliance was placed on the following passage from Lord Keith of Kinkel, the Scots Lord of Appeal in an English appeal *Armagas Ltd v. Mundogas Ltd S.A.; The Ocean Frost*:   10.15

> "At the end of the day the question is whether the circumstances under which a servant has made the fraudulent representation which has caused loss to an innocent third party contracting with him are such as to make it just for the employer to bear the loss. Such circumstances exist where the employer by words or conduct has induced the injured party to believe the servant was acting in lawful course of the employer's business. They do not

[20] [1942] A.C. 509.
[21] *Taylor v. City of Glasgow*, 1997 Rep. L.R. 17; 1996 Rep. L.R. 69.
[22] [1939] 2 K.B. 248.
[23] at 4–07.

exist where such belief although it is present, has been brought about through misguided reliance of the servant himself, when the servant is not authorised to do what he is purported to do when what he is purporting to do, is not within the class of acts that an employee in his position is usually authorised to do and when the employer has done nothing to represent that he is authorised to do it."[24]

Pro hac vice

10.16   There is one last major complication. Quite often in building, engineering or manufacturing, a worker will be sent to a place outwith his own place of employment. He may have tools or machines from his usual employer with him. When he arrives, he may well be ordered about by a third party. If he is negligent and injures someone else, the question will arise—which of the two people who order him around is vicariously responsible? The law is quite clear on this matter, although each case must turn on its own particular facts and will always be a matter of degree. In *Mersey Docks and Harbour Board v. Coggins and Griffith (Liverpool) Ltd,*[25]

> the harbour authority let a mobile crane to Coggins, a firm of stevedores, for loading a ship. They also provided Coggins with a crane man who was employed and paid and liable to be dismissed by the board. However, the agreement between the board and Coggins stated that the craneman should be the servant of the hirers. The craneman negligently injured a workman and the question was which of the two "bosses" (Coggins or the board) was vicariously liable.

The court refused to follow the contractual provision (certainly where the workman himself was not a party to it) and held that the general employer (the board) would be liable unless it could be shown that the temporary employer had intervened to direct how a specific task was to be carried out. Accordingly, there is a heavy onus on the "original" employer who wishes to prove that a workman has been transferred *pro hac vice* to a third party [see para. 10.17 below].

Liability for independent contractor

10.17   Generally, a person is not vicariously liable for the delicts committed by an independent contractor hired to do a job as opposed to an employee under a contract *locatio operarum*.

Having stated that general rule, it is necessary here to pause and

---

[24] [1986] 1 A.C. 717 at 782.
[25] [1947] A.C. 1; and see also *Park v. Tractor Shovels Ltd*, 1980 S.L.T. 94.

consider *Marshall v. William Sharp & Sons*,[26] the most recent pronouncement of the Inner House on the topic. The ninth edition of
Gloag and Henderson carries the following statement:

> "There is no general rule that an employer is not liable for breach
> of his personal duties to an employee injured through the
> negligent work of an independent contractor employed by the
> employer, nor is there any general rule that an occupier of
> premises is not liable for damage to persons or property on
> the premises caused by such faulty work."[27]

The quotation goes on to say that the issue is a matter of fact and
degree. However, Lord Bridge said in the House of Lords: "It is trite
law that the employer of an independent contractor is, in general, not
liable for the negligence or other torts committed by the contractor in
the course of the execution of the work."[28] Notwithstanding that,
Lord Dunpark in *Marshall* states that he could "see no reason to
depart from the statement of law, which I believe that I personally
inserted in the seventh edition (1968) of Gloag and Henderson . . . and
which has been retained in the ninth at p. 579."[29] Both statements are,
in a sense, correct. The passage in the 9th edition (p. 578) in fact comes
after a section which begins, "the exceptions now recognised to the
general rule that an employer is not liable for damages caused by work
done by an independent contractor are as follows . . ." The addition of
the word "therefore" in the first sentence of the "Dunpark" paragraph
(10th ed., p. 548) makes it clearer that there is a general rule to the
opposite effect! In the ultimate legal analysis the issue is a matter of
fact and degree. However, it is correct and useful to speak of a general
rule in relation to independent contractors—because, vicarious liability being an exception to the principle *culpa tenet suos auctores*, some
special facts and circumstances ought to be required to attract
liability.[30]

The actual decision in *Marshall* is, it is submitted, wrong. The facts
were as follows:

> Marshall entered a burner/dryer to see if it was sparking properly.
> An electrician, Dean, was operating the button which made the

---

[26] 1991 S.L.T. 114.

[27] at p. 579.

[28] *D. & F. Estates Ltd v. Church Commissioners* [1988] 3 W.L.R. 368.

[29] 1991 S.L.T. 114 at 125.

[30] The present writer would prefer the statement in the first edition of Gloag and
Henderson (p. 360): "As a general rule, subject to many qualifications, a person
who has a particular piece of work done by contract is not liable for the wrongful
or negligent acts of the contractor or of his servants." See *Baxter v. Pritchard*, 1992
G.W.D. 24–1385 where the sheriff principal correctly upheld a decision not to
remit averments of vicarious liability for an independent contractor to proof.

sparks. There was also a button which sent fuel to the sparks. He pressed this button at the same time as the spark button. Marshall was burned to death.

The court accepted that there was no case of employers' personal liability made out on record, particularly no averment of a failure to implement a safe system. The court held that the electrician was not an employee of the defenders, nor of anyone else. Lord Ross called him "an independent contractor or in any event a contractor with a degree of independence", yet went on to hold the employer liable. Lord Dunpark stated that: "On the evidence in this case, even if one regards Dean as a contractor rather than a servant, he was certainly not an independent contractor." Later he concluded: "while one may say that Dean was a contractor of his own labour, he cannot reasonably be classified as an independent contractor, for whose negligence the defenders are not liable." The benefit of this formulation is that it supports the general rule that there is no liability. The effect of the case seems to be to apply the doctrine of *pro hac vice* employment, by which a servant is transferred from a *de jure* employer to a *de facto* employer. In this case, for the first time, the Inner House may have transferred a *sui juris* worker to a *de facto* employer. That is innovatory and unsupported by any authority. It is also remarkable in that the onus against transfer in *pro hac vice* vicarious liability cases is so high that there is said to be no reported case this century of the transfer having been made,[31] yet, in this case of a new application of the doctrine, the onus of transfer from the *sui juris* workman to the *de facto* defender was achieved. However, it is possible that a person employing an independent contractor can incur liability as a result of his own actings. This can only be personal, and not vicarious liability: the employer is held liable for his own fault and not the fault of the independent contractor. This may occur where a person employs an incompetent or clearly unqualified contractor, *i.e.* where someone puts "an improper person to do some act which, if done by an improper person is likely to result in mischief."[32] Other cases are where the duty which has been entrusted to the contractor is really that of the employer and is a non-delegable duty. Usually these are statutory duties.[33] The House of Lords has recently held that there was no non-delegable duty upon a main contractor undertaken to subsequent occupiers, so that the main contractor was not liable

---

[31] According to Salmond and Heuston (21st ed., 1996), p. 441. There are at least two Scottish cases. See e.g. *Sime v. Sutcliffe Catering (Scotland) Ltd*, 1990 S.L.T. 687.

[32] See *Wolfson v. Forrester*, 1910 S.C. 675.

[33] See *Stephen v. Thurso Police Commissioners* (1876) 3 R. 535; Factories Act 1961, ss. 12, 13 and 14, imposing absolute liability; Carriage of Goods by Sea Act 1971; *Riverstone Meat Co. Pty Ltd v. Lancashire Shipping Co. Ltd* [1961] A.C. 807.

for the defective workmanship of an otherwise competent sub-contractor.[34] A final category of cases is where the work to be done by the independent contractor is of a dangerous nature or an extra-hazardous nature where those who instruct the work have a duty to see that precautions are taken by the contractor. Examples include excavations or other work on public roads and streets or on private property.[35] Extra-hazardous work does not cease to be such as a result of the work being the ordinary kind of work that the wrongdoer does—it is the nature of the work as being much more likely to cause harm that makes the principal liable.[36]

Other instances of vicarious liability

By statute the chief constable is liable to pay damages in respect of 10.18 delicts committed by officers under his control,[37] but this may not make him generally liable (see lawburrows, above [2.4]). *Cropper v. Chief Constable, Dumfries, and Galloway Constabulary and Secretary of State*,[38] sounds a warning that not all police officers are under the direction of a chief constable.

The Crown's immunity from action has been severely curtailed by statute. As a general rule the Crown is now liable for the delicts of its servants or agents.[39]

At common law, trade unions had been held vicariously liable for the unofficial acts of their shop stewards.[40] In addition, the Trade Union and Labour Relations (Consolidation) Act 1992 set out a statutory scheme of vicarious liability if, but only if, the delictual act (being an economic or industrial tort) was authorised or endorsed by the union or by a responsible person. "Responsible person" is defined by the legislation as being (1) the executive committee, (2) the president or general secretary, (3) a person empowered by the rules to authorise industrial action, (4) employed officials, and (5) any committee of the union to whom an employed official reports. For persons in categories (1) and (2) the union will be liable even if the person has acted outside the rules. However, for persons in categories (4) and (5)

---

[34] See *D. & F. Estates Ltd v. Church Commissioners*, n.28 above, *per* Lord Bridge at 387–388.

[35] *Sanderson v. Paisley Burgh Commissioners* (1899) 7 S.L.T. 255. See *Alcock v. Wraith* [1991] T.L.R. 600 for a modern example between private parties. For a most interesting Scottish case where the bungle was by the sub-contractors, see *MTM Construction Ltd v. William Reid Engineering Ltd*, 1998 S.L.T. 211.

[36] *Honeywil and Stein Ltd v. Larkin Bros Ltd* [1934] 1 K.B. 191; *Alcock v. Wraith*, n.35.

[37] Police (Scotland) Act 1967, s. 39.

[38] 1998 S.L.T. 548.

[39] Crown Proceedings Act 1947; Crown Proceedings (Armed Forces) Act 1987 [9.4]. See *Casebook*, Ext. 86.

[40] *Heaton's Transport (St Helens) Ltd v. TGWU* [1972] I.C.R. 308.

the union will not be vicariously liable if those persons acted outside union rules or the union repudiated their actions.[41]

It has been held that the procurator fiscal for the time being is not in the same position as a chief constable, that is liable for his deputes or assistants.[42] A named individual must be cited.

Further reading

Lewis, R., "Insurers Agreements not to Enforce Strict Legal Rights" (1985) 48 M.L.R. 275.

MacCormack, G., "*Culpa Tenet Suos Auctores*: The Application of a Principle", 1973 J.R. 159.

---

[41] 1992 Act, s. 20.

[42] *McLaren v. Procurator Fiscal for the Lothians and Borders*, 1991 G.W.D. 24–1407.

CHAPTER 11

IMMUNITIES, DEFENCES, TRANSFER AND EXTINCTION

This chapter draws together rules which result in a pursuer being 11.1 unable to proceed with a claim which would otherwise be valid. Also included is a discussion of a person's right to sue in respect of the death of a relative on the basis that the deceased's claim in delict may have been extinguished to a considerable extent. Contribution and relief between defenders are treated here.

IMMUNITIES AND DEFENCES

It should be appreciated that it is possible to defend an action based on 11.2 delict for many reasons not set out in this chapter. Many actions are defended on issues of fact—the defender simply denying one or more of the essential requirements of the delict. In an assault case, for example, the defender denies that he struck the blow. In an unintentional harm case the defender may say that he did not know some fact which, if he had known it, would have imposed upon him a duty to take care. Sometimes a case can be defended upon the basis of some contractual exclusion of liability in delict. The effectiveness of such exemption clauses is now generally, and properly, considered in works on contract.[1] The absence of title to sue is effectively a defence and many such instances are dealt with in Chapter 9.

Immunities

Immunities apply to certain persons, as opposed to persons general- 11.3 ly, allowing any action brought against them to be stopped at an early stage. However, it has to be said that the questions of immunity, defences and the title to sue and be sued of certain parties overlap.

The Sovereign as an individual is immune from court action. 11.4

---

[1] See Woolman, Chap. 7.

11.5   The Crown has no liability for an act of state which is an act of the
         executive in its dealing with foreign persons or powers outwith the
         realm.
11.6   Foreign heads of state and their households are protected by
         legislation.[2] Ambassadors, their families and staffs are also protected
         so long as exercising their diplomatic function. The immunity may be
         waived by the sending state. Private servants of the diplomatic corps
         only have such immunity as is accorded by the host state.[3] Similar
         protections are available for persons working for international orga-
         nisations and for persons who are members of visiting forces.[4]
11.7   Judges are immune from action even if they act in excess of
         jurisdiction or maliciously. Magistrates can be liable in certain
         circumstances.[5]
             In *Russell v. Dickson*,[6]

> a sheriff seemed to entertain doubts about the conduct of an
> accused person's solicitor. As a result, when the accused pled
> guilty the sheriff remanded the accused (not his solicitor!) in
> custody in Barlinnie Prison so that inquiries could be made into
> the conduct of the case. On quashing the conviction (as opposed
> to the sentence) the High Court held that the decision to remand
> was in excess of the sheriff's powers. The proceedings were
> incompetent and the decision not to allow bail was described
> as excessive and unreasonable.

The temporary judge held that the sheriff was entitled to absolute
immunity:

> "No doubt the sheriff could lose his immunity in certain situa-
> tions, even in certain situations which might arise in the course of
> his sitting on the bench. Where, as here, he is dealing with a
> complaint and with the accused person who is before him it
> cannot be said that he is not acting as a judge."[7]

With respect, this is very hard to follow, especially coming from a
judge who himself must have wrangled with difficult authorities in
deciding what was the judicial thing to do in his time. Reading this
case and the report of the High Court proceedings, a student is likely
to say that the sheriff "lost it" and in gunning for a solicitor made a

---

[2] State Immunity Act 1978.
[3] Diplomatic Privileges Act 1964.
[4] International Organisations Acts 1968 and 1981 and Visiting Forces Act 1952, s. 12.
[5] See *McPhee*, 1933 S.C. 163 and see para. [2.7]. For a discussion of the policy, see
     Olowofoyeku, "The Crumbling Citadel: Absolute Judicial Immunity De-Ratio-
     nalised", 1990 L.S. 271.
[6] 1998 S.L.T. 96.
[7] at 101E.

client suffer—and that is not what constitutional immunity is for. The temporary judge did, however, in giving a generous benefit of a definite doubt, express concern that the legislature or the Inner House should do something about this. The case—apart from being an unfortunate blot on the record of a particularly learned sheriff, a disaster for an accused person, a nightmare for a solicitor, a good case for two counsel and a firm of solicitors, a grist to the academic mill, an opportunity for a temporary judge to display his erudition, and an example of how Scots lawyers will apparently ignore even constitutionally relevant English authority—is an embarassment to us all. Not just the confusion between privilege in defamation and immunity but the obvious lack of modern professional quality systems in the judicial function, require urgent attention. Cases like this in the reports are happily rare.

Trade unions, depending upon the political complexion of the 11.8 government of the day, sometimes have immunity or a restricted immunity or no immunity at all from delictual actions. While the statutory provisions generally apply equally to employers' associations, almost all of the cases where the statutory immunity has been claimed involve trade unions.

The Trade Disputes Acts 1906 and 1965 gave the trade unions and their members extensive immunities. These were restricted drastically by the Industrial Relations Act 1971, which in turn was repealed by the Trade Union and Labour Relations Act 1974 (amended in 1976) which gave the unions immunities at least as good as those existing after the 1906 Act. But then the tide ebbed once more and the Employment Acts 1980 to 1988 eroded the unions' immunities. The Employment Act 1990 continued the trend, itself developed and (as the name suggests) was consolidated by the Trade Union and Labour Relations (Consolidation) Act 1992 (the "1992 Act").[8] The following attempts to summarise the immunities remaining to unions at present.

Trade unions are liable for any negligence, nuisance or breach of 11.9 duty resulting in personal injury to any person or from any breach of duty imposed in connection with the ownership, occupation, possession, control or use of property and also for product liability under the Consumer Protection Act 1987, and all without statutory limit.[9] However, there is a general immunity in respect of "an act done by a person" under the Trade Union and Labour Relations (Consolidation) Act 1992 in respect of acts done "in contemplation or furtherance of a trade dispute".

---

[8] As amended in some important respects by the Trade Union Reform and Employment Rights Act 1993.
[9] s. 22, Trade Union and Labour Relations (Consolidation) Act 1992.

(1) There is protection against an action based on inducing a breach of contract or interfering (or inducing another to interfere) with its performance—covering interference in contract [3.19–3.21][10]; and where there is a threat that a contract (whether or not the threatener is a party to it) will be broken or its performance interfered with or that the threatener will induce another to break or interfere with a contract—covering intimidation [3.22–3.23].[11]

(2) Also protected is an agreement between two or more persons to do or procure the doing of any act in contemplation or furtherance of a trade dispute if the act is one which, if done without any such agreement, would not be actionable, which effectively covers conspiracy [3.16–3.18].[12]

11.10 For all of these immunities to apply the acts must be in contemplation or furtherance of a trade dispute. This is defined in section 244 of the Trade Union and Labour Relations (Consolidation) Act 1992. The dispute must be one between workers and their employers (not with other workers), which relates wholly or mainly to (not just "is connected with") one or more of the following statutory factors:

(a) terms and conditions of employment, or the physical conditions in which any workers are required to work;

(b) engagement or non-engagement, or termination or suspension of employment or the duties of employment of one or more workers;

(c) allocation of work or the duties of employment as between workers or groups of workers;

(d) matters of discipline;

(e) the membership or non-membership of a trade union on the part of a worker;

(f) facilities for officials of trade unions; and

(g) machinery for negotiation or consultation, and other procedures, relating to any of the foregoing matters, including the recognition by employers or an employers' association of the right of a trade union to represent workers in any such negotiation or consultation or in the carrying out of such procedures.

11.11 There must therefore be a genuine trade dispute and not, for example, a political protest at privatisation.[13] Whether or not the action is in contemplation or furtherance of the dispute seems to be judged on a

---

[10] s. 219 (1) (a).

[11] s. 219 (1) (b); note also s. 20.

[12] s. 219(2); note also s. 20.

[13] *Mercury Communication Ltd v. Scott-Garner and the Post Office Engineering Union* [1984] Ch. 37. See generally (not on this particular point) *Square Grip Reinforcement Co. v. Macdonald,* 1966 S.L.T. 232; 1968 S.L.T. 65.

subjective basis and so it will be sufficient if the defender has an honest belief that the action will further the dispute.[14]

Picketing, which might not in any event be illegal, is expressly 11.12 declared to be lawful if (but only if) it is peaceful picketing.[15] However, if it could be actionable, perhaps as a trespass or a nuisance,[16] the Act declares it to be lawful only if a number of conditions are observed: the person must be at or near his place of work (unless a union official) and be there for the purpose only of peacefully obtaining or communicating information, or peacefully persuading any person to work or abstain from working.

In these situations the immunity will not be allowed or will be 11.13 "clawed-back".

(a) As a result of the Employment Act 1980, and now section 224 of the Trade Union and Labour Relations (Consolidation) Act 1992, "secondary action" will not, generally, attract the immunity. Such action is that taken against someone not a party to the dispute. The mechanism is to restrict the immunity in respect of interference with contracts to contracts of employment only, making interference with, for example, a charter party, unlawful.[17] Secondary action is now permitted only in the form of lawful picketing.

(b) The Trade Union Act 1984 made it necessary to hold a secret ballot before taking certain strike action which would require the immunity as a defence against the delict of interference in contract. Subsequent legislature increased the burden of requirement. There are detailed provisions in relation to such ballots which are beyond the scope of this book.[18]

(c) Action taken to enforce trade union membership is not generally protected.[19]

In relation to proceedings mainly arising from economic delicts, the amount which may be awarded against a union is capped according to the size of the membership.[20]

---

[14] *Express Newspapers Ltd v. McShane* [1980] A.C. 672; *Duport Steels Ltd v. Sirs* [1980] 1 W.L.R. 142.

[15] s. 220, 1992 Act.

[16] *Thomas v. NUM (South Wales Area)* [1985] 2 W.L.R. 1081. Now, in English law, *not* a nuisance: *Hunter v. Canary Wharf Ltd* [1997] 2 All E.R. 426.

[17] *Merkur Island Shipping Co. v. Laughton* [1983] A.C. 570.

[18] Trade Union Reform and Employment Rights Act 1993. See, generally, on the whole issue of trade unions, Craig and Miller, *Employment Law in Scotland* (2nd ed., T. & T. Clark., 1996). For a case under the 1988 Act on ballots, see *Secretary of State for Scotland v. Scottish Prison Officers Association*, 1991 S.L.T. 658.

[19] s. 222, 1992 Act. See also ss. 223, 225.

[20] See ss. 22 and 23 for restrictions on enforcement against certain property.

Defences

11.14   *Statutory authority* is a defence, subject to the sort of situation in *Lord Advocate v. North British Railways* [2.15]. If Parliament has authorised some conduct then it will not be actionable unless it could as easily be done without causing harm. In this case, waste which was being disposed of under statutory authority was left near an army barracks. The purpose of the statute could as easily have been served by not leaving it, so the defence was not available.

11.15   *Justification* can provide a defence in certain limited circumstances (see *Crofter Co.* [3.16] and *Findlay* [3.20]). The common law also protects conduct such as the reasonable chastisement of children.

11.16   *Necessity* may protect a defender against action in certain circumstances, particularly where there has been an emergency. So it is permissible to trespass in order to save life or property.[21] So too, force feeding of a prisoner has been held not to be actionable on this basis.[22] If there are general principles of law crossing pedagogic and doctrinal boundaries then cases from the criminal law, used carefully, should assist. The High Court has recently reviewed and clearly acknowledged the defence which for a long time has been regarded with suspicion. In *Moss v. Howdle*,[23] it was decided that a defence of necessity (albeit it is a form of a wider defence of coercion) is available where the accused had no choice but to do what he did, as where he is in immediate danger of death or serious bodily harm.

11.17   *Defending oneself* or one's property is a defence. Provocation may be a complete defence to an assault in civil law. Generally it will reduce damages rather than exculpate.[24]

11.18   *Damnum fatale* has been mentioned several times. Its significance is that it is one of the few defences available to a defender who is subject to strict liability. It refers to a happening which no human foresight could provide against—such as an earthquake in Edinburgh or a volcanic eruption in Thurso, but not heavy rain in Greenock (see *Caledonian Ry* [2.19]).

11.19   *Consent* to the deed done will exonerate the defender. So, generally, medical treatment is permissible and a kiss not actionable. Where, however, the conduct exceeds the consent given (expressly or impliedly) the conduct becomes actionable—*e.g.* where, the patient having agreed to a tonsillectomy, the surgeon decides to amputate a leg. If the consent is extorted then it does not provide a bar to recovery.[25] *Volenti*

---

[21]   *Cope v. Sharpe* [1912] 1 K.B. 496.
[22]   *Leigh v. Gladstone* (1909) 26 T.L.R. 139.
[23]   1997 S.C.C.R. 215.
[24]   *Ross v. Bryce*, 1972 S.L.T. (Sh.Ct.) 76.
[25]   *Adamson v. Martin*, 1916 S.C. 319.

non fit injuria (a legal wrong is not done to one who is willing) is a similar but distinct defence. Its meaning is not really very clear and it is certainly far less often encountered than once was the case. It has been said to amount to a waiver of the duty which would otherwise be incumbent upon the defender to take care for the pursuer. So much has the defence been restricted that it now only applies if the pursuer has freely and voluntarily assumed the risk of the particular harm which he actually suffered. In employment cases there must be the clearest possible evidence that the pursuer accepted the risk of the actual harm: it is not sufficient to show that the pursuer continued working knowing of the risk.[26] A tenant had been held *volenti* prior to the Occupiers' Liability (Scotland) Act 1960 by remaining in a house which was in ill repair,[27] but that has not been followed in a thoughtful Sheriff Court decision.[27a] It is often mentioned in sports cases, especially in regard to spectators, but it is seldom that a spectator can actually be said to have assumed a risk of injury.[28]

In Scotland's first skiing decision, the sheriff correctly, it is submitted, would not have applied *volenti non fit injuria* but would rather have found the pursuer's damages to be reduced by contributory negligence. This would have been the case even although the sheriff considered participants generally accepted some degree of danger.[29]

The doctrine is most easily understood in terms of the burden of proof. Initially the burden is on the pursuer to establish a duty—once that is done the defender has to show that the pursuer was *volenti*. However, where the duty is the common-law duty to take reasonable care to prevent reasonably foreseeable harm, the willingness of the pursuer to accept the risk of the actual harm might often negate the duty. If *volenti* is established, it is a complete defence.

Criminality of the pursuer may constitute a defence. The maxim 11.20 *ex turpi causa non oritur actio*, which applies in contract, has been discussed as a defence to delict claims. The difficulty arises from the reluctance of courts to award damages to one wrongdoer caused by another wrongdoer. However, instances of such situations range from the safe-blower who blows up his confederate who is keeping watch to a case where a person injures a passenger when infringing some obscure traffic regulation. The question has been regularly debated in England and has been considered recently in some detail by the Court of Appeal.[30] Australian cases have shown

---

[26] See generally *ICI v. Shatwell* [1965] A.C. 656.
[27] *Shields v. Dalziel* (1894) 24 R. 849.
[27a] *Hughes' Tutsix v. G.D.C.*, 1982 S.L.T. (Sh.Ct.) 70.
[28] See *Murray v. Harringay Arena* [1951] 2 K.B. 529; see especially *Wooldridge v. Sumner* [1962] 2 All E.R. 978.
[29] *Garven v. White Corries*, Fort William Sheriff Court, June 21, 1989, unreported.
[30] *Pitts v. Hunt* [1991] 1 Q.B. 24. *Ashton v. Turner* [1981] Q.B. 137 takes a firm line.

something of a lead in moving away from a rigorous application of the maxim.[31]

Weir v. Wyper,[32] reconsidered much previous authority:

> a 16-year-old girl went on a trip with two men and another girl. One of the men and the other girl left the car, leaving the girl with the defender at night, in the dark, in a place she did not know. Knowing that he held only a provisional licence, she asked the defender for a lift home. The defender began showing off by driving very fast and braking violently when it was necessary to stop. The car left the road and overturned.

Lord Coulsfield, it is submitted, quite properly concluded that the maxim was not to be rigorously applied nor, if the defence was restated or explained as an aspect of public policy, was it to be a complete bar to claims. The proper course was to take each case on its merits and it is probably only in cases of significant criminal activity that the defence would have a chance of success. The defence was treated as applicable to a case of an injured passenger who was knowingly in a stolen car, which on the balance of probabilities it was accepted he had helped steal.[33]

It should be mentioned that such cases are sometimes argued on the basis of a public policy against recovery and yet others are argued on the basis that, in negligence cases, it is impossible to fix a standard of duty of care—for example, as between the safe-blower and his look-out, the court will not trouble to inquire as to the standards of the reasonable man out doing a burglary. This latter argument seems unnecessary and may well have been a way out of the otherwise draconian effect of subscribing fully to the *turpis causa* rule.

11.21   *Contributory negligence*[34] is a plea to the effect that the defender failed to take reasonable care for his own safety. Formerly this was a complete defence, so older cases should be read with caution. All that need be shown is that the pursuer's carelessness was a co-operating cause of his injuries or loss—there is no need to show a breach by the pursuer of a duty of care. The onus is on the defender to establish the defence. As a result of the Law Reform (Contributory Negligence) Act

---

[31] See *Jackson v. Harrison* (1978) 138 C.L.R. 438; *Progress and Properties v. Craft* (1976) 135 C.L.R. 651 moving away from *Smith v. Jenkins* (1970) 119 C.L.R. 397. The Australian position was analysed in *Weir*, below.

[32] 1992 S.L.T. 579, considering the earlier Scottish authority *Sloan v. Triplett*, 1985 S.L.T. 294; *Ashcroft's C.B. v. Stewart*, 1988 S.L.T. 163; *Duncan v. Ross Harper & Murphy*, 1993 S.L.T. 105; *Wilson v. Price*, 1989 S.L.T. 484 and *Winnik v. Dick*, 1984 S.L.T. 185.

[33] *Duncan v. Ross Harper & Murphy*, 1993 S.L.T. 105.

[34] The Scottish Law Commission Report No. 115 proposes a classification of the defence in cl. 9 of its draft Contribution in Damages (Scotland) Bill.

1945, contributory negligence ceased to be a complete defence and instead the court was allowed to attribute fault between the parties in proportion to their share of the responsibility.[35]

> In *Davies v. Swan Motor Co.*[36] some dustbin men (including Davies) were standing on the steps and running boards of their dustbin lorry despite having been told not to do so. Davies was killed when a bus collided with the lorry. Both the bus driver and the bin lorry driver were at fault. It was held that although Davies had not owed anyone a duty of care and had not in any sense caused the accident, his actings had contributed to his injury to the extent of one-fifth.

Conduct which consists of a response to an emergency created by 11.22 the defender does not constitute contributory negligence, in terms of the so-called "agony rule".[37] Another exemption from the defence is available under the "dilemma rule" where the pursuer picks the wrong course of two open to him in a situation created by the defender.[38]

The defence has been held available against children. In *Banner's Tutor v. Kennedy's Trustees*[39]:

> a five-year-old girl got out of the back of a minibus and ran into a lorry. She had been expressly warned by the minibus driver not to go out until he opened the door but he did not take any actual steps to prevent her getting out.

The court held that she was a girl of usual intelligence and had parental guidance about roads and had seen heavy traffic. She was held to be 20 per cent liable for the accident and her damages were reduced accordingly.

TRANSFER AND EXTINCTION

Assignation

It is quite clear that a claim may be assigned at any time to someone else. 11.23 Any defences available against the original party will be valid against the assignee.[40] A claim may be transferred by way of subrogation—that is, where the insurer has indemnified his insured for a loss for which another person is legally liable he is entitled to proceed against that party without the need of an assignation. By the Third Parties (Rights Against Insurers)

---

[35] See *Casebook*, Ext. 85.
[36] [1949] 2 K.B. 291.
[37] *Laird Line v. U.S. Shipping Board*, 1924 S.C. (H.L.) 37.
[38] *Clayards v. Dethick* (1848) 12 Q.B. 439.
[39] 1978 S.L.T. (Notes) 83.
[40] See Young, "Rights of Relief on Assignation in Settlements", 1992 S.L.T. (News) 225.

Act 1930, if an insured person becomes bankrupt or unable to pay then anyone who has incurred a loss covered by the insurance may proceed directly against the insurer. The Road Traffic Act 1972 makes insurance compulsory in respect of the risk of death or personal injury to third parties (including passengers). The insurer[41] must satisfy any judgment against any insured, notwithstanding that they may be entitled to avoid the policy.[42] There is a similar arrangement in respect of employers in terms of the Employers' Liability (Compulsory Insurance) Act 1969. It has been held that where a person recovers from his insurers, an action cannot be raised in his name for the same loss under contractual indemnities, unless perhaps (and that was not decided) the loss was caused by the negligence of the indemnifier.[42a]

Contribution and relief

11.24   The Law Reform (Miscellaneous Provisions) (Scotland) Act 1940, s. 3(1) (as amended) provides:

> "Where in any action of damages in respect of loss or damage arising from any wrongful acts or negligent acts or omissions two or more defenders are in pursuance of the verdict of a jury or the judgment of a court found jointly and severally liable in damages or expenses, they shall be liable inter se to contribute to such damages or expenses in such proportions as the jury or the court, as the case may be, may deem just."

This allows the court to apportion liability between defenders sued jointly and severally according to their responsibility for the loss. An example is *Davies* above: the four-fifths of liability remaining after deduction of the pursuer's contributory negligence was apportioned between the bus company and the bin lorry company in a two-to-one proportion, *i.e.* two-thirds to the bus company and one-third to the bin lorry company.[43] As liability is generally joint and several, the pursuer will be entitled to enforce his decree in full against any party. The party paying then has to recover the proportions for which he is not responsible from the other wrongdoers and to do that he may have to exercise his right of relief.

11.25   If all the wrongdoers are not parties to the one action the position is more complicated. While there may remain a common-law right of relief, in practice the position is now regulated by statute. Section 3(2) of the 1940 Act provides that:

---

[41] Or the Policyholders Protection Board if the insurance company is in liquidation: Policyholders Protection Act 1975, s. 6.

[42] But there is some safeguard where the policy is obtained, for example, by a misrepresentation.

[42a] *EIF Enterprise (Caledonia) Ltd v. London Bridge Engineering Ltd* (1997) T.L.R. 607.

[43] Professor Walker has usefully pointed out that in the result this divides liability 3/15ths to the plaintiff, 8/15ths to one defender and 4/15ths to the other: *Delict*, p. 374.

"Where any person has paid any damages or expenses in which he has been found liable in any such action as aforesaid [a section 3(1) action] he shall be entitled to recover from any other person who, if sued, might also have been held liable in respect of the loss or damage on which the action was founded, such contribution, if any, as the court may deem just."

At common law, there is a right of relief against a wrongdoer by a person who is vicariously liable for him. So, for example, where an employee injured another employee, the employer's liability insurers were held entitled to proceed against him.[44] In this particular area there are a number of extra-legal considerations, the most significant of which is that certain insurers have agreed not to exercise this legal right against employees unless there has been collusion or wilful misconduct.

The use of third party procedure, available in the sheriff court as 11.26 well as the Court of Session, allows a defender to call any party who might be liable to contribute or indemnify as a third party to the action. This frequently prevents the need for a separate action of contribution or relief. Actions of contribution and relief are subject to a two-year limitation period commencing on the date when the right to contribution or relief accrued.[45] It is essential for a claim of relief that there should be a Scottish decree against the claimant but it does not have to have been obtained in a contested action.[46]

Transmission on death and the relatives' claim on death

The law is regulated by the Damages (Scotland) Act 1976 as 11.27 amended by the Damages (Scotland) Act 1993.[47] This law applies where a person dies in consequence of personal injuries sustained by him as a result of an act or omission of another person, being an act or omission giving rise to liability to pay damages to the injured person or his executor.[48]

---

[44] *Lister v. Romford Ice & Cold Storage Co. Ltd* [1957] 1 All E.R. 125.

[45] See s. 8A of the Prescription and Limitation (Scotland) Act 1973.

[46] *Comex Houlder Diving Ltd v. Colne Fishing Co. Ltd*, 1987 S.L.T. 443. The Scottish Law Commission have recently reported on the questions of contribution and relief, annexing a draft Contribution in Damages (Scotland) Bill (Scot. Law Com. No. 115). See the analysis of relief in Young "Rights of Relief", 1992 S.L.T. (News) 225 and *Comex Houlder Diving Ltd v. Colne Fishing Co. Ltd (No. 2)*, 1992 S.L.T. 89.

[47] For a detailed record of the genesis of this Act, including extracts from newspapers and *Hansard* and the Law Commission papers, see Chapter 1 of *Casebook*.

[48] There is certainly now an element of transmission in the claim and it is accordingly dealt with here. The calculation of damages, meanwhile, is different—another reason for separating it from the treatment of quantification in Chapter 12. However, there are related issues and the two sections might usefully be read together.

Although an apparently simple passage, it has proved difficult in relation to ante-natal injuries [see, generally, para. 9.13]. A person must have died. In *Hamilton v. Fife Health Board*[49] a mother was injured and her child, a foetus *in utero*, was injured. The child was born alive; it died three days later. The parents sued for damages under the Act alleging negligence by the doctors. The Act applies "where a person dies in consequence of injuries sustained by him." The Inner House held that injuries caused to a foetus are personal injuries and are "properly and sensibly" described as "personal injuries" even although, when inflicted, the "victim" did not enjoy legal personality. It was said: "To suppose that only one who enjoys legal personality can sustain 'personal injuries' is to attach an artificial legal meaning to the adjective 'personal' in s. 1(1)."

The 1993 Act is one of the very few which have retrospective effect, but for compassionate reasons: as a result of one of the campaigners for reform having died of injuries while the legislative process was under way, some of the provisions apply to deaths after July 16, 1992, the date of the introduction of the Bill to Parliament. The Act substantially changes the law. It is a product of the Scottish Law Commission but its genesis lies in public concern as to the effect of the 1976 Act.[50] The general mischief was clear in the Lord Advocate's remit:

> "To consider the case for amending the law of damages in Scotland having regard to the possibility that there may be an incentive inherent in the present law for a defender to postpone making a settlement or reaching proof until after the death of the pursuer in order to minimise the amount of compensation to be paid."

The concern is even greater when the pursuer dies as a result of the injury complained of. Being a product of the Scottish Law Commission, in an appropriate case it would be appropriate to refer to the report.[51]

While, by the Damages (Scotland) Act 1976 (as originally enacted), no right to solatium for personal injuries transmitted to the representatives, the right to damages of a claimant in consequence of personal injuries will (subject to exceptions) now transfer to the executor in the same way as patrimonial loss cases.[52] The solatium is calculated up to the date of death.[53]

---

[49] 1993 S.L.T. 624.

[50] Scot. Law Com. Report No. 134, 1992. See Chap. 1 of *Casebook*.

[51] On the authority of *Pepper v. Hart* [1992] 3 W.L.R. 1032. However, note the comments of Lord McCluskey in the Extra Division in relation to the attempt to use Scot. Law Com. Nos 30 and 31 in *Hamilton v. Fife Health Board*, 1993 S.L.T. 624 at 627.

[52] 1993 Act, s. 3, inserting new s. 2 of the 1976 Act.

[53] 1993 Act, s. 3; new s. 2(1) of the 1976 Act.

In relation to verbal injury cases, a claim in respect of injury transmits to the executor, but, with the exception of patrimonial loss cases, only if the claimant brought an action while alive. The term "personal injuries" in the 1976 Act and the Administration of Justice Act 1982 was amended to include injury from defamation, verbal injury or any other verbal injury or injury to reputation.

The unamended 1976 Act gave certain relatives of a deceased **11.28** person the right to recover "loss of support" and a right to certain relatives to recover "loss of society". The 1993 Act introduced a new "relative's non-patrimonial award", discussed below, to replace loss of society and in a way which will make the award more substantial. The relatives' claims depend upon the category or categories into which they fall. Everyone who is in the immediate family is a relative, but not all relatives are in the immediate family: "immediate family" is a subset of "relatives". Loss of support is dealt with under "immediate family", below, but is also relevant to the treatment of "relative".

"Immediate family"

This is defined as parents and children of the deceased. It includes **11.29** the deceased's spouse and a cohabitee, *i.e.* any person, not being the spouse of the deceased, who was, immediately before the deceased's death, living with the deceased as husband or wife, and recently has been held to cover a woman who married a man after the delict had been committed.[54] It includes in-laws.[55]

(i)*Loss of support* These persons are entitled to claim loss of support, which is based on the actual amount of support that was usually received.[56] It is appropriate to take account of likely increases in support which would have followed[57] but not speculative matters.[58] In assessing loss of support, the court will not take into account remarriage prospects.[59] Nor will the court deduct social security benefits paid or money that will accrue from the deceased's estate such as insurance policies. Reasonable funeral expenses are recoverable.[60]

---

[54] See Administration of Justice Act 1982; *Phillips v. Grampian Health Board*, 1988 S.L.T. 628.

[55] *McAllister v. ICI plc*, 1997 S.L.T. 351; *Monteith v. Cape Insulations*, 1997 G.W.D. 28–1431.

[56] See *Hatherley v. Smith*, 1989 S.L.T. 316 (necessary averments).

[57] *Smith v. Comrie's Exrs*, 1944 S.C. 499.

[58] *Daniell v. Aviemore Station Hotel Co.*, 1951 S.L.T. (Notes) 76.

[59] Law Reform (Miscellaneous Provisions) Act 1971, s. 4.

[60] s. 1(3); *Porter v. Dickie*, 1983 S.L.T. 234; *Prentice v. Chalmers*, 1985 S.L.T. 168.

(ii) *Non-patrimonial award* Relatives are entitled to recover a new "relative's non-patrimonial award" replacing and enhancing the now deleted loss of society award.[61] The award provides for damages (without the need to specify how much is being awarded under each head) by way of compensation for all or any of: (a) distress and anxiety endured by the relative in contemplation of the suffering of the deceased before death[62]; (b) grief and sorrow of the relative caused by the deceased's death[63]; (c) the loss of such non-patrimonial benefit as the relative might have been expected to derive from the deceased's society and guidance if the deceased had not died.[64] This may be in addition to the transmitted claim of the deceased himself for solatium. This right itself transmits to the relative's executor, so that the son of a deceasing mother whose husband (his father) was negligently killed, might recover for his father's pain and suffering and his mother's grief and sorrow as well as his own. An award is also competent for any personal services rendered to the deceased and it is a legitimate head of claim to include a sum in respect of the services which the deceased would have rendered to the relative in terms of the Administration of Justice Act 1982.

Even with these reforms some have argued for more change, such as the inclusion of brothers and sisters within the "immediate family" category and the inclusion of a parent who has accepted a child into a family as his own.[65]

Relatives

11.30   Relatives, according to Schedule 1 to the 1976 Act (as amended), are immediate family as above defined, with the addition of the following: ascendants and descendants; any person who was, or was the issue of, a brother, sister, uncle or aunt of the deceased and any person who, having been a spouse of the deceased, had ceased to be so by virtue of a divorce. It does not matter that the relationship is through the mother's line rather than the father's, nor that a child or parent is a stepchild or step-parent, nor that a child is illegitimate. These persons can recover loss of support suffered or likely to be suffered. They may recover reasonable funeral expenses. The relatives, who are not also members of the immediate family, have no right to a loss of society award.

By section 9 of the 1982 Act, the same extended body of relatives are

---

[61] See *Dingwall v. Alexander*, 1981 S.L.T. 313 for discussion of the then new loss of society award.
[62] 1993 Act, s. 1; new s. 1 (4) (a) of the 1976 Act.
[63] 1993 Act, s. 1; new s. 1(4) (b) of the 1976 Act.
[64] 1993 Act, s. 1; new s. 1 (4) (c) of the 1976 Act.
[65] L.G. Moodie, "The Effect of Death on Damages" (1993) 38 J.L.S.S. 212.

entitled to claim for personal services which (i) were or might have been expected to be rendered by the deceased, (ii) were of a kind which when rendered by a person other than a relative would ordinarily be obtainable on payment, and (iii) which the deceased might have been expected to render gratuitously. This allows, *inter alia*, a working widow or widower to claim for the services of, for example, a cook or a housekeeper.

Decree

A delictual claim is discharged by decree and satisfaction of the 11.31 decree. The cause—providing, of course, that the decree was not taken in absence—is *res judicata* and cannot be raised again. Decree of *absolvitor* (of the defender) prevents the action being raised on a different basis, as where an action is raised for personal injuries instead of for damage to property, or for a negligent mis-statement instead of fraud.[66]

Decree of dismissal (in favour of the defender) only prevents an action being raised on the same point of law and so an action may be raised again on the same facts but on a different ground of law.

Discharge, compromise and settlement

A delictual action can be discharged on any terms and the discharge 11.32 can be in any form. Acceptance of social security benefits does not imply a discharge. Only the party in whose favour the discharge is granted can found upon it. If an action is raised against a number of persons jointly and severally, a discharge may be a discharge of one and not the others, but may be read as a discharge of the whole ground of action. The discharge of one joint wrongdoer does not prevent others subsequently claiming a right of relief against that party. A case can be compromised or settled with or without the court's permission on any terms. It is important that the settlement is clearly expressed. The onus of establishing a discharge by settlement is on the defender.[66a] An advocate, but not a solicitor, can compromise a case without authority from his client. In practice, discharge may be effected by a separate minute which is a formal offer of settlement and if it includes an offer of the expenses of the action it will have the effect of imperilling the offeree for expenses if he is not subsequently awarded more than the offer by the court. It is one of the skills of the experienced agent to pitch such offers at the right level. In defamation cases the offer must include a withdrawal of the alleged defamatory statement.[67]

---

[66] On this point see, generally, *Gibson & Simpson v. Pearson*, 1992 S.L.T. 894.
[66a] *Irving v. Hiddleston*, 1998 S.C.L.R. 350, a useful review of the authorities.
[67] See para. 9.12, above, with regard to minors.

Prescription and limitation

11.33   This is a very important subject in practice. Lawyers are often consulted well after an accident has taken place. It may be professional negligence on the part of a lawyer to fail to take notice of the many and various periods of prescription and limitation. Accordingly, it has to be emphasised that what follows is merely an outline account which is necessary for an understanding of the law. The position is now almost entirely statutory.[68] The difference between limitation and prescription is a simple but important one: prescription completely extinguishes the obligation and will be judicially noticed by a court without a plea being taken; limitation simply prevents an action being raised—the obligation remains and a plea has to be taken by the defender.

1. Personal injuries cases

11.34   Personal injuries cases are subject to a three-year limitation period.[69] Time begins to run from the date on which the injuries were sustained, or where there was a continuing act or omission (like pollution)—time then runs from the date on which the injuries were sustained or the date on which the act or omission ceased, whichever is the later.[70] However, the action will not be limited if one of the statutory exemptions is available, such as where the injured person is under a legal disability—for example, nonage or mental disability.[71] It has been held that nonage includes both pupillarity and minority.[72]

The period is also extended where it was not reasonably practicable for the pursuer to know that the injuries in question were sufficiently serious to justify his bringing an action of damages, on the assumption that the person against whom the action was brought did not dispute liability and was able to satisfy a decree.

The extension is also available where the pursuer was unaware that the injuries were attributable in whole or in part to an act or omission; and where he is ignorant that the defender was a person to whose act

---

[68] Prescription and Limitation (Scotland) Act 1973, as amended by the Law Reform (Miscellaneous Provisions) (Scotland) Act 1980, the Prescription and Limitation (Scotland) Act 1984, the Law Reform (Miscellaneous Provisions) (Scotland) Act 1985, and the Consumer Protection Act 1987. See *Casebook*, Ext. 93.

[69] 1973 Act, s. 17.

[70] For a contentious case, see *Hunter v. NSHB*, 1989 G.W.D. 15–645.

[71] For a detailed investigation of s. 17(3) and the meaning of "unsoundness of mind", see *Bogan's C.B. v. Graham*, 1992 G.W.D. 32–1898, 32–1907. See, in relation to those between the ages of 16 and 18, s. 8 of the Age of Legal Capacity (Scotland) Act 1991 applying a transitional provision. The period runs from the commencement of the Act (September 25, 1991), not from when the pursuer was 16 years of age.

[72] *Fyfe v. Croudace Ltd*, 1986 S.L.T. 443; *Forbes v. House of Clydesdale Ltd*, 1988 S.L.T. 594.

or omission the injuries were attributable in whole or in part, or was the employer or principal of such person (*i.e.* was vicariously liable). In the case of *Elliott v. J. & C. Finney*[73] the court refused to extend the period to take account of the entire period when an injured person was in hospital because he had had a conversation with a policeman and could have asked him, from his hospital bed, for the information necessary to pursue the action.

Even where the pursuer is not entitled to an extension, the court has   11.35
a discretion (a "section 19A discretion") to admit a claim if it seems equitable to do so. The court has to consider where the balance of the equities lies.

> In *Donald v. Rutherford*[74] a man was injured on November 3, 1975, and an action was begun on February 13, 1981. There was even a letter in this case written by representatives of the proposed defender saying that for certain purposes they accepted the writ as having been served on February 7, 1977. Negotiations continued.

A plea having been taken and upheld, the court, on appeal, refused to allow the pursuer to get back into the action since he had a claim against the insurers of the solicitors who had not raised the action on time! The court refused to offer guidance on how the discretion would be used, saying that it would always depend upon the case in question. The court did suggest, however, that it might often be appropriate to hold a preliminary proof on the facts relating to the making of the claim. Indeed, in the case of *Elliott*, above, the court, although refusing to extend on the basis of the time in hospital, did allow an extension on the equitable ground, for although an action for negligence against the solicitors might well be successful, it was not thought to be straightforward and, as the pursuer was not entitled to legal aid, would involve outlay. That is in contrast to a similar case, *Donald v. Galloway*,[75] in which the claimant had spent some time sedated in hospital, unable to find out who was responsible for his accident. While a preliminary proof was allowed on the claim for a section 17 (2) (b) (iii) extension, it was denied on the section 19A equitable grounds.

---

[73] 1989 S.L.T. 208(OH). The decision on the s. 19A question was upheld in the Inner House, 1989 S.L.T. 605. See also *Ford v. Union Insulation Co. Ltd*, 1989 G.W.D. 16–696; *Blake v. Lothian Health Board*, 1992 G.W.D. 32–1908.

[74] 1984 S.L.T. 70. For other examples of the s. 19A discretion, see *Pritchard v. Tayside Health Board*, 1989 G.W.D. 15–643; *Comber v. Greater Glasgow Health Board*, 1989 S.L.T. 639; *Ford v. Union Insulation*, 1989 G.W.D. 16–696; *Clark v. McLean*, 1993 S.L.T. 492; *Griffen v. George MacLellan Holdings Ltd*, 1992 G.W.D. 30–1787; *Bogan's C.B. v. Graham*, 1992 G.W.D. 32–1907; *Blake v. Lothian Health Board*, 1992 G.W.D. 32–1908.

[75] 1988 G.W.D. 24–1042.

The running of the limitation period is stopped by the raising of a court action.

2. *Death from personal injuries*

11.36 Where a person dies within three years of the date of an accident, there is a three-year limitation period from the date of the death, unless one of the statutory exemptions outlined above applies or the section 19A discretion is exercised.

3. *Other obligations to make reparation*

11.37 This describes cases where there is no personal injury: for example, pure economic loss cases or cases of damage to property. In such cases there is no limitation period but a five-year prescription which completely extinguishes the obligation. Time begins to run from the time when there is concurrence of loss and a legal wrong and there can be only one point of concurrence.[76] If, however, the harm is a continuing one like that resulting from nuisance, the time runs from when the continuing act ceased. If the pursuer was not aware of the damage and could not with all reasonable diligence have become so aware, then time does not run until he becomes aware of it. This is known as the discoverability formula and may assist pursuers in cases of latent damage. In the case of *Dunfermline District Council v. Blyth & Blyth*,[77] Lord MacDonald considered (*obiter*) that the pursuers had to know that the damage was caused by a legal wrong of the defenders before time would begin to run. It has been held that the prescriptive period will not begin to run until there has been actual damage.[78] In the case of a solicitor's professional negligence in failing to take a proper title, it was held in the Inner House that time did not run until the defect was noticed rather than when the error was made.[79] Not only that, in cases such as this there was no real place for reasonable diligence. The prescriptive period is interrupted by the raising of an action or the relevant acknowledgment of the claim. Nonage precludes the running of the period.[80] The onus of proof of prescription is on the defender.[81]

---

[76] Or, as is often put, the *terminus a quo* is the concurrence of *damnum* and *injuria*: see *Dunlop v. McGowans*, 1979 S.C. 22; 1980 S.C. (H.L.) 73. And see also *George Porteus (Arts) Ltd v. Dollar Rae*, 1979 S.L.T. (Sh.Ct.) 51.

[77] 1985 S.L.T. 345.

[78] *Renfrew Golf Club v. Ravenstone Securities*, 1984 S.L.T. 170.

[79] *Glasper v. Rodger*, 1996 S.L.T. 44.

[80] See also n. 71 above with regard to s. 8 of the Age of Legal Capacity (Scotland) Act 1991.

[81] *Strathclyde R.C. v. W.A. Fairhurst*, 1997 S.L.T. 658.

4. Defamation

Defamation actions are subject to a three-year limitation. The 11.38
section 19A discretion applies to such claims also.

The long negative prescription

The long negative prescription of 20 years "mops up" obligations 11.39
which might otherwise be kept outstanding forever; for example,
economic loss cases where the claimant did not reasonably know
he had a ground of action. It is worth noting that the mopping-up
period for the new statutory regime of product liability is only 10 years
from the date when the product is put into circulation. The long
negative prescription no longer applies to claims for personal injuries—effectively making such claims imprescriptible, although still
subject to the limitation period.

The positive prescription

This is of no relevance to the law of delict save that it actually confers 11.40
rights—mainly to land—and thus would entitle a person acquiring a
prescriptive right to exercise any rights of a proprietor. The "right" of a
defender to commit a nuisance cannot be acquired under the positive
prescription (of 10 years) but the right of a pursuer to complain about it
can be lost after the 20 years of the long negative prescription.

Further reading

Bennett, S., "Loss of Society Awards: Quid Juris?" 1982 S.L.T. (News) 101.
Duff, A., "Civil Actions and Sporting Injuries Sustained by Professional
    Footballers", 1994 S.L.T. (News) 175.
Hudson, A.H., "Crime, Tort and Reparation—What Solution?" 1984 S.L.T.
    (News) 321.
Hudson, A.H., "Crime, Tort and Reparation: A Common Solution", 1992
    S.L.T. (News) 203.
Ingman, T., "A History of the Defence of *Volenti Non Fit Injuria*", 1981 J.R. 1.
Jaffey, A.E., "*Volenti Non Fit Injuria*", 1985 C.L.J. 87.
Kidner, R., "The Variable Standard of Care, Contributory Negligence and
    Volenti", 1991 L.S. 1.
Kostal, R.W., "Currents in the Counter-reformation: illegality and the duty of
    care in Canada and Australia" (1995) Tort L.Rev. 100.
McEwan, V. and Paton, A., *Damages in Scotland* (2nd ed., W. Green, 1989).
McGuire, F., "The Damages (Scotland) Act 1993", 1993 S.L.T. (News) 245.
MacQueen, H.L., "Latent Defects, Collateral Warranties and Time Bar",
    1991 S.L.T. (News) 77, 91, 99.
Moodie, L.G., "The Effect of Death on Damages" (1993) 38 J.L.S.S. 212.
Olowofoyeku, A., "The Crumbling Citadel: Absolute Judicial Immunity De-
    Rationalised", 1990 L.S. 271.

Shaffer, N., "*Volenti Non Fit Injuria*", 1965 S.L.T. (News) 133.

Stewart, A., "Belated Acceptance of Judicial Tender and Defender's Expenses", 1994 S.L.T. (News) 159.

Stewart, J.B., "Football: Civil Aspects", 1981 S.L.T. (News) 157.

Stewart, W.J., "Skiing and the Law: the First Case" (1990) 35 J.L.S.S. 27.

Stewart, W.J., "Reparation—Prescription and Limitation" (1994) 39 J.L.S.S. 374.

Summers, A., "Assignation of Collateral Warranties", 1993 S.L.T. (News) 181.

Tan, C.G.S., "*Volenti Non Fit Injuria*: An Alternative Framework", 1995 Tort L. Rev. 208.

Taylor, N., "Limitation of Liability of Aircarriers to Aircrash Victims—Has the Warsaw Convention reached its retirement age?" [1994] J.P.I.L. 113.

Young, A.R.W., "Secondary Action: Recent Developments", 1991 S.L.T. (News) 367.

Young, A.R.W., "Rights of Relief", 1992 S.L.T. (News) 225.

CHAPTER 12

PRACTICAL MATTERS

This chapter deals with matters which are practical in the sense that 12.1
they usually only trouble those who practise the law. These are not,
however, contextual matters but are legal rules coming from the law of
actions, the law of procedure and the law of evidence. They are so
intimately connected with the substantive law of delict that they can
affect the law of delict itself just as the law of delict affects them.[1]

Evidence

First, the onus of proof is on the pursuer—he must aver and prove a 12.2
sufficient case or lose. The defender, as *Johnstone v. City of Glasgow
District Council*[2] demonstrates, need do nothing but lodge appropriately framed defences. In recent years the courts have been pressing for
more frank defences but it is still the case that the defender can say
"not known and not admitted" where, perhaps, someone has slipped
in a supermarket. As recently as *Robertson v. Tennent Caledonian
Brewers,*[3] it was confirmed not only that this was in order but that it
was not evasive pleading such as would support a motion for summary
decree. Being a civil action, the standard of proof is on the balance of
probabilities and not beyond a reasonable doubt as in criminal cases—
a distinction not often appreciated by motorists acquitted of a
criminal charge of careless driving who later, quite correctly, find
themselves being sued successfully in a civil action for damages.

Secondly, where something has to be shown to have caused an 12.3
accident, facts can raise an inference that the defender's actions were a
cause and shift the onus back upon him to show that they were not.
That seems to be the extent to which reliance can be placed upon
McGhee v. National Coal Board.[4] This case cannot be relied upon for

---

[1] See generally, Walker, *The Scottish Legal System* (7th rev. ed., W. Green, 1997),
Chap. 13.
[2] 1986 S.L.T. 50.
[3] 1994 G.W.D. 11–679.
[4] 1973 S.C. (H.L.) 57 and see 4.31–4.32; *Casebook*, Ext. 46 and see articles cited there
at 10.6.4.

the proposition that because there has been a breach of duty, it must have caused a loss which occurred.[5]

12.4 Thirdly, it is possible that sometimes the happening of the accident itself will substantiate the pursuer's averment that the defender did not exercise due care. In its strictest form this is known as *res ipsa loquitur*:

> "where the thing is shown to be under the management of the defendant or his servants and the accident is such as in the ordinary course of things does not happen if those who have the management use proper care, it affords reasonable evidence, in the absence of explanation by the defendants, that the accident arose from want of care."[6]

The application of the maxim can be seen in the case of *Devine v. Colvilles*[7]:

> There was an explosion in a factory. A workman was hurt when he jumped from a platform in the general panic. The disaster originated in an explosion in a hose. The most probable cause was that particles of rust had got into the hose which should have been excluded by a filter. The defenders accordingly argued they were not at fault.

However, they were held to be liable on the basis that they were, at the material time, in full control of the pipe and pipes do not usually explode. In the narrowest interpretation of the *res ipsa loquitur* doctrine, the defender's control of the thing in question is essential. It is also essential that there should be no direct evidence of the cause of the accident.[8] Where there is another explanation the doctrine cannot apply.[9]

12.5 Fourthly, the courts may, as they do in almost any kind of case, be prepared to make inferences from facts which are admitted or proved. Where there is a gap in the evidence the court may be prepared to fill in the gap. Where *res ipsa loquitur* applies, this exercise is unnecessary but it is useful where any of the elements are missing, such as was the case in *Inglis v. LMS Ry*.[10]

---

[5] See discussion of *Kay* at para 4.32. See also *Porter v. Strathclyde R.C.*, 1991 S.L.T. 446 for establishing liability, *Vize v. Scott Lithgow*, 1991 G.W.D. 9–549 for a case where the necessary foundation was missing. For comments of the Inner House on the scope of *Porter*, see *Muir v. Cumbernauld & Kilsyth D.C.*, 1993 S.L.T. 287.

[6] *Scott v. London and St Katherine's Docks* (1865) 3 H. & C. 596—Eng. Rep., Vol. 159, p. 655.

[7] 1969 S.C. (H.L.) 67.

[8] See *Binnie v. Rederij Theodoro*, 1991 G.W.D. 26–1523 for a case that failed. The maxim relates to proof and so averments should not be deleted at debate but proof before answer allowed: *Borris v. Lord Advocate*, 1993 G.W.D. 6–435.

[9] *McQueen v. Glasgow Garden Festival*, 1994 G.W.D. 9–557.

[10] 1941 S.C. 551. *Casebook*, Ext. 96.

A boy aged eight fell to his death from a railway carriage. The defenders proved that the door had been checked before the train left the station and gave evidence to the effect that even if it had been defective it should in all probability have opened of its own accord earlier in the journey. They were in effect saying that the boy had opened the door himself. However, relatives of the boy gave evidence to the effect that he had not tampered with the door—that at one moment he had been standing near the door but he was not standing there a moment later.

The *res ipsa loquitur* doctrine could not apply as the door was outside the exclusive control of the railway company. The Inner House held that the happening of the accident in these circumstances was prima facie evidence of negligence, which then only had to be brought home to the defenders. This had been achieved by excluding one of the only two persons possibly responsible for the accident—the boy or the railway company.

Inference can only take a party so far. In *Johnstone v. City of Glasgow District Council*[11] the facts were as follows:

12.6

> The pursuer fell while walking down a common stair. The defenders were the owners and as landlords were occupiers of the building. The property was in a decrepit state but there was no actual proof that the defenders knew of the missing step which caused the pursuer's fall.

It was held that no inference could be made of fault in the absence of proof that the defenders had failed to act as a reasonable occupier or landlord. All that could be done would be to speculate and speculation is not the same as inference.

Nonetheless, so long as one can infer (deduce or conclude) negligence, as opposed to speculate (conjecture) it, then certain rules apply to assist claimants. If, as was the case in *Johnstone*, the defenders do not lead evidence, then the inferences most favourable to the pursuer which the evidence can reasonably bear will be drawn.[12]

Fifthly, there is the problem of corroboration. Historically, the law of evidence required that a pursuer prove all material facts by corroborated evidence, that is evidence from two separate sources, quite often two eyewitnesses. We have seen above how this can be mitigated by certain inferences but even then sometimes a workman injured in some corner of a factory, or a pedestrian run down on a quiet street, simply could not recover. Considerable assistance was given to such pursuers by the Law Reform (Miscellaneous Provisions)

12.7

---

[11] 1986 S.L.T. 50.

[12] *Ross v. Associated Portland Cement Manufacturers* [1964] 2 All E.R. 452; and see also *Michael O'Donnell v. Murdoch McKenzie & Co.*, 1967 S.C. (H.L.) 63.

(Scotland) Act 1968, s. 9, which allowed a case of damages for personal injuries to succeed on the uncorroborated evidence of the pursuer. The Act was restrictively interpreted, partly (it seems) because the then Lord President did not approve of the Scottish Law Commission who promoted the legislation nor one of the judges who decided the first case relying on the statute to come before the court.[13] What might be called a "gloss" developed (which cannot be fully explored in this concise work) which meant among other things that the Act could only be used if there were not another witness even if that other witness were hostile.[14] It is fair to say that, taking into account the onus of proof, it is safer and better to adduce other evidence if available, but requiring the calling of adverse evidence is simply bizarre. The Civil Evidence (Scotland) Act 1988[15] allows civil actions (which includes breaches of contract) to be proved without the need for corroboration and with the admission of hearsay evidence. Unlike the 1968 Act, the 1988 Act applies to claims for economic loss as much as to personal injuries cases and so would assist the driver in the hypothetical case above. Its wording is different and a passage relied on to create the gloss is not in it.[16] Parliament discussed the gloss in detail and, while not deciding to overrule it by statute and commending the practice of calling corroboration if it were available, preferred generally the relaxation of the gloss that had been apparent. Nonetheless (and nearly incredibly) it was applied in its full rigour as recently as 1991.[17] In a series of decisions the court refused to follow the gloss in family matters.[18] In one family case Lord Coulsfield went so far as to criticise the gloss very strongly.[19] In a sheriff court delict case (a police assault) this whole issue was argued and, even although there was clearly at least one other witness present who was not called, Sheriff Principal McLeod decided that the pursuer could succeed on her own uncorroborated evidence.[20] It will probably take a decision of the Inner House to make it clear that the gloss was out of order and that reference should no longer be made to it in an era when a person can win a case on uncorroborated hearsay.

12.8   Sixthly, there are cases which involve an almost irresistible presumption of fault. These cases may look very much like strict liability

---

[13] *Morrison v. Kelly*, 1970 S.C. 65. *McGowan v. Lord Advocate*, 1972 S.C. 68 toughened the gloss to such an extent that pursuers were clearly obliged to follow it. See Stott, *Judges Diary*, (Mercat Press, 1995), especially at p. 241.

[14] For a full treatment with extracts from the relevant cases, see Sheldon, *Evidence: Cases and Materials* (W. Green, 1996), Chap. 13.

[15] See *Casebook*, Ext. 98.

[16] See *Laing v. Tayside Health Board*, 1996 Rep. L.R. 51; *Casebook*, Ext. 98.

[17] *Gordon v. Grampian Health Board*, 1991 S.C.L.R. 213.

[18] *K. v. Kennedy*, 1992 S.C.L.R. 386; *M. v. Kennedy*, 1993 S.C.L.R. 69.

[19] *Lynch v. Lynch*, 1997 G.W.D. 30–1501.

[20] *Airnes v. Chief Constable*, 1998 S.L.T. (Sh.Ct.) 15. However, see *Rae v. Chief Constable*, 1998 G.W.D. 406.

and in effect will differ very little from such liability. This kind of case was explained by Lord Fraser in *RHM Bakeries (Scotland) Ltd v. Strathclyde Regional Council*.[21] It was held in that case that nuisance did not involve liability regardless of fault but that instead where there was an intolerable continued use of land causing loss, then this would raise an almost irresistible inference of fault. This is not necessarily an easier way of proving negligence. It means that there are various ways of establishing fault, some of which in some circumstances may be easier than proving negligence.

Similarly, Professor Walker had also indicated that if the *actio de effusis vel dejectis* and the *actio de positis vel suspensis* [2.24] were not adopted into Scots law as cases of strict liability, they were instances of a heavy presumption of fault. However, this is not quite the same as saying that there is strict liability for there will have to be sufficient facts upon which the presumption can be applied—the mere happening of an event may, but will not always, be enough. This was confirmed shortly after *RHM Bakeries* where a pursuer was required to make full specification of the circumstances before fault could be inferred.[22]

Remedies

There are few serious implications of remedies in the law. The most important is that between damages and interdict. Interdict, even in the sheriff court, is governed by a specialised body of rules relevant to such actions. The reasons may be that ultimately the defender can be imprisoned for breach of interdict, and that urgent action is often required.

There is also a set of other rules which apply to the granting of interim interdict. The need for interim interdict is obvious—it might be useless to await the outcome of a contested case if the damage is already done. Many of the cases have to be dealt with immediately, when the balance of convenience is an important consideration and often operates in favour of the status quo.

12.9

Judicial review

This is a procedure to obtain remedies in matters which concern the Court of Session's supervisory jurisdiction. It is not restricted to matters of public law but applies also to cases where a jurisdiction

12.10

---

[21] 1985 S.L.T. 214 [2.15].

[22] *Argyll & Clyde Health Board v. Strathclyde R.C.*, 1988 S.L.T. 381. The pursuers had taken Lord Fraser's judgment and followed it just too literally—Lord Fraser had not been making the simple pleading point "you must aver fault"; really what is required is a full and specific averment of circumstances from which fault can be presumed. See, however, *Kennedy v. Glenbelle*, 1996 S.L.T. 1186, [1.12] in which the various different forms of fault are set out.

is given to a body to take decisions.[23] It might well be the only remedy where there is an alleged liability by omission by a local authority which is causing a continuing loss. While this may well be actionable in damages, a better remedy might be to obtain an order against the authority to prevent further loss.[24] Indeed, it is possible to obtain any remedy in an application for judicial review, including damages and including restitution, unlike the equivalent English jurisdiction.[25] Presumably the principles upon which damages might be awarded will be those of the ordinary law of delict rather than damages for breach of public law duties, but this is not necessarily so.

Actions of Harassment

The Protection from Harassment Act 1997 discussed above [2.9] is implemented *inter alia* by a separate action of harassment.

Optional procedure

12.11   A special and speedy optional procedure is provided in the Court of Session for actions of damages for personal injuries or death of a relative. If this option is chosen the right to proceed to a jury trial is lost, where one might expect in certain cases a higher award. The procedure is swifter than ordinary procedure and considerably less emphasis is placed upon written pleadings. There are useful provisions encouraging parties to exchange evidence in advance of a hearing.

Quantification of damages (personal injuries)

12.12   There are a number of special rules about the computation of damages, particularly in the area of personal injuries or in respect of the death of a relative. An outline of these follows. In respect of damage to property, readers are referred to Chapter 57 of Walker's *Civil Remedies*. Damages in verbal injuries cases are considered in Chapter 8, and damages on death are considered at paragraphs 11.27–11.30.

A distinction is made between loss to a person's estate or wealth, known as patrimonial loss and, on the other hand, pain and suffering, which is compensated by an award of solatium.

Patrimonial loss: items recoverable

12.13   (i) Wages lost to the date of the proof, together with an award for projected future loss due to the continuing effects of the injury are recoverable. In computing the amount to be paid in respect of wage loss the following calculation is made:

---

[23] See, generally, *West v. Secretary of State for Scotland*, 1992 S.L.T. 636.

[24] See *Rowling v. Takaro Properties Ltd* [1988] 2 W.L.R. 418 for an illustration.

[25] See *Woolwich v. Inland Revenue* [1992] 3 W.L.R. 366.

- calculate a figure for annual wage loss (called the multiplicand);
- multiply by a figure (called the multiplier) which reflects the years over which there will be a wage loss.

The multiplier is necessarily less than the actual number of years over which wages are prima facie lost (*e.g.* until retirement at 65) because of two main factors: (a) the fact that damages are paid in a lump sum and can therefore gain interest; and (b) the possibility that the injured person would die at some time during the period over which damages are being awarded. Thus there is usually a bigger multiplier for a young person than an old person, especially (in the latter case) if the pursuer is soon to retire. Until recently lawyers were content to look at previous cases and the facts of a case to come to a suitable multiplier. In England special tables—the Ogden tables—based on actuarial evidence have been given statutory authority—they generally provide higher multipliers. In *O'Brien's C.B. v. British Steel*[26] the traditional multiplier/multiplicand was approved. It was accepted that the Ogden tables could be taken as being within judicial knowledge. In cases, unlike ordinary future wage loss cases, where the recorded experience of practitioners and judges in fixing multipliers was not available, as in *O'Brien* itself, the use of the tables was useful as a cross-check. In determining the return to be expected from the investment of a sum awarded as damages for future pecuniary loss, the court is to take into account the rate of return laid down by the Secretary of State.[27]

Section 9 of the Damages (Scotland) Act 1976[28] provides that the court should take into consideration lost wages which a pursuer would have earned if his life expectancy had not been reduced by the accident. In personal injuries cases the multiplier is to be applied from the date of the proof, whereas in fatal accident cases the multiplier applies from the date of death. Alternatively, rather than apply a multiplier to a multiplicand, and especially if it seems that the pursuer will be able to find work or continue working, the court may award a lump sum to reflect general disadvantage in the job market.

(ii) Medical expenses generally are recoverable and will cover the cost of necessary transport between hospital and home. The cost of wheelchairs, crutches and prosthetics is recoverable.

(iii) Interest on such damages is due (subject to the court's discretion) usually from the date of the accident, by virtue of the Interest on Damages (Scotland) Act 1971. The damages are divided between prior and future loss. Thus, interest is given on the actual loss sustained to the date of the proof. Interest at half the "court rate" [12.15] is usually awarded, to reflect the fact that the loss occurred, on a week-by-week basis.

---

[26] 1991 S.L.T. 477.
[27] Damages (Scotland) Act 1996, s. 1(1) and (5).
[28] See *Casebook*, App. Ext. 11.

Deductions from patrimonial loss.

These are as follows.

12.14   (i) Any benefits received, other than from the injured person's own estate which the person would, in the court's opinion, have received or have been acquired.

(ii) Income tax from the loss of earning sum.

(iii) In terms of the Social Security (Recovery of Benefits) Act 1997 benefits are effectively taken back from damages awards.[29] The present scheme applies to all cases (including those not affected by the 1992 Scheme) where the case has not been determined or settled by October 6. The defender compensator is made liable to the Secretary of State.[30] The pursuer will appreciate that the defender has this liability and must know the extent of the clawback to enable decisions as to settlement or continued conduct of the litigation to be made. The compensator is allowed to deduct the payments he is obliged to make from the pursuer.[31] The Act provides how this is to be done, the principle being "like for like".[32] Deductions from each category of damages awarded may only extend to those paid over the relevant period—normally five years from the accident.[33] A full and final settlement brings the relevant period to a premature end.[34] Compensation has to be broken into three heads from which associated benefits are recoverable: (1) earnings lost during the relevant period[35]; (2) cost of care incurred during the relevant period[36]; loss of mobility during the relevant period.[37] Courts must now specify in their orders the amount of any compensation payment which is attributable to each of these three heads over the relevant period.[38] Settlements and tenders will have to be arranged to take account of recoupment. The 1992 Scheme allowed for a small settlements figure of £2,500. The 1997 Act permits this but it has not been reintroduced at present.

---

[29] And the associated Social Security (Recovery of Benefits) Regulations 1997 (S.I. 1997 No. 2205). See generally Maguire, F., "Compensation Recovery", 42 J.L.S.S. 352.

[30] s. 6.

[31] s. 8.

[32] Sched. 2.

[33] In the case of disease, it is five years from the first listed benefit claim.

[34] s. 3(4).

[35] Benefits recoverable are: disability working allowance; disablement pension payable under s. 103 of the 1992 Act; incapacity benefit; income support; invalidity pension and allowance; jobseekers allowance; severe disablement allowance; sickness benefit; statutory sick pay; unemployability supplement; unemployment benefit.

[36] Recoverable benefits are: attendance allowance; care component of disability living allowance; disablement pension increase payable under s. 104 or s. 105 of the 1992 Act.

[37] Recovered from mobility allowance; mobility component of disability living allowance.

[38] s. 15.

The effect of the new scheme is that if the defender or insurer is liable for a penny, they are liable for all the benefits. This should encourage defenders who are not seriously disputing liability to press for early settlement—not something which has been common heretofore. Under the previous scheme this state clawback could come out of the injured person's solatium or pain and suffering money—but no longer.

(iv) The full amount of any earnings from employment, or unemployment benefit, and any payment made by the wrongdoer (unless through a trust).

(v) Again against income, there is to be deducted any saving made by the injured person by being maintained at the public expense, *e.g.* in a hospital.

No account is to be taken of any contractual pension, or pension or retirement benefit from public funds, nor of any payment made by an employer subject to any obligation to repay in the event of the recovery of damages, nor of the proceeds of an insurance policy.[39]

There is a modern approach to compensation damages in general (this applies to solatium below) which argues for a structured settlement. "A structured settlement is an extrajudicial settlement under which the defender's insurers undertake to pay periodic payments to the insured party in lieu of the whole or part of the traditional lump sum. The defender's insurers (the general insurers) then reinsure their obligation using a life office."[40] There are tax advantages to such schemes and it may be argued by the defender that the benefit should be split.[41] The system, seldom seen in practice, has now been approved and enhanced by the legislature.[42]

Solatium

The injured person can recover for: 12.15

    (1) pain and suffering;
    (2) loss of faculties; and
    (3) shortened expectation of life.

Section 5 of the Damages (Scotland) Act 1993 added a new section 9A to the Damages (Scotland) Act 1976. The amended Act allows loss of

---

[39] Administration of Justice Act 1982, s. 10. The common-law position is the same: *Parry v. Cleaver* [1970] A.C. 1; *Forgie v. Henderson* (1818) 1 Murray 410; *Davidson v. UCS Ltd*, 1990 S.L.T. 329.

[40] Eden, "Structured Settlements" (1992) 37 J.L.S.S. 207.

[41] The English Law Commission has issued a consultation paper on this and related topics.

[42] Damages (Scotland) Act 1996, ss. 4, 5 and 6; *Casebook*, App. 18.

expectation of life to be taken into account in awarding solatium, whereas before the provision in section 9 only allowed this in relation to patrimonial loss. If the injured person's expectation of life has been reduced by the injuries and the injured person is, was, or at any time would be, likely to become aware of that reduction, the court must have regard to the consequence of that awareness he has suffered or is likely to suffer.[43]

There are complicated rules on interest on damages which are beyond the scope of this book.[44] Generally, past solatium—*i.e.* pain and suffering suffered before the proof—will attract interest at a figure representing approximately the average "court rates" for the period from the date the injuries were healed, or approximately one-half the average rate where pain continues and part of the solatium is apportioned to the past.[45]

The courts will generally take a broad brush approach to questions of quantification. Courts are assisted by awards in clearly similar cases but obviously every case has its own peculiarities.[46] It should be remembered that inflation affects the value of money and that care should be taken in comparing awards in older cases. Awards in England still tend to be higher than those in Scotland and those in the United States are many times higher.[47] Until recently jury trials were rare, yet judicial awards were based on what reasonable men would award. At the time of writing jury cases are more common and, while subject to control of excess, it is hoped that jury awards will be published and help to inform judicial awards.[48] The result is expected to be increased awards.

Pleading[49]

12.16   Two points are of particular interest. First, the technical and usually very strict rules of pleading may be relaxed in a personal injuries case to prevent a meritorious claim being lost on pleadings, if this can be done without prejudice to the defence. This has helped some people

---

[43] s. 5; new s. 9A(1). This overturns the rule in *Dalgleish v. Glasgow Corp.*, 1976 S.C. 32 in which an award was made to a comatose child.

[44] The reader is referred to the Interest on Damages (Scotland) Act 1971 and McEwan & Paton (3rd ed.).

[45] The court rates are laid down in various Acts of Sederunt. See notes to Rule of Court 66 in *Parliament House Book*, Division C, and equivalent for sheriff court in Division D.

[46] See *Baker v. Murdoch*, 1979 S.L.T. 145; *Bowers v. Strathclyde R.C.*, 1981 S.L.T. 122.

[47] This leads to what is sometimes called forum shopping—considering in detail whether jurisdiction can be established in a more generous state.

[48] *Girvan v. Inverness Farmers Dairy* (*No. 2*), 1998 S.L.T. 21.

[49] See, generally, Black, *An Introduction to Written Pleading* (Law Society of Scotland, 1982).

some of the time. It cannot be relied upon. It most certainly cannot be relied upon in the civil courts in Scotland and it may take an expensive journey to our supreme civil court in Westminster to remedy an error.[50]

Secondly, there is a part of every writ and summons which should 12.17 contain an articulate statement of the facts relied upon. However, the practice has grown up of actually averring duties, namely: the defender was under a duty not to drive blindfold; he was under a duty not to run down the pursuer. These are not really statements of fact. If a defender wants to argue that there is no duty of care on the facts averred then the proper course, and one which would increase the value of written pleadings, would be to use a specific plea to the relevancy.

There is also a need for specification. This is especially important in 12.18 negligence cases where almost every aspect depends upon the facts which bring the parties into a relationship. In novel negligence cases, the facts are crucial in giving the court material on which to decide if the parties were in a sufficiently close degree of proximity to impose a duty of care.[51]

Jurisdiction

So far as the student is concerned, this subject forms part of private 12.19 international law and so far as the practitioner is concerned there are specialist texts which must be consulted. The law is laid down in the Civil Jurisdiction and Judgments Act 1982. The principal ground of jurisdiction is domicile. But in delict cases Article 5 of Schedule 4 to the Civil Jurisdiction and Judgments Act 1982 provides that a person domiciled in a part of the United Kingdom may be sued in another part of the United Kingdom, "(3) in matters relating to tort, delict or quasi-delict, in the courts for the place where the harmful event occurred".

---

[50] *Miller v. SSEB*, 1958 S.L.T. 229.

[51] The reader who would like to have a glimpse of what sort of evidence, procedure, documents and pleadings, not to mention very difficult work, go into a run-of-the-mill defended action for damages for personal injuries, is fortunate in being able to turn to the second section of Sheriff Kearney's excellent work on Ordinary Procedure in the Sheriff Court. The sheriff reproduces the papers, letters, statements (precognitions) and even judgments of the courts (mentioning cases and materials referred to in this book) in an imaginary but quite representative case. Underneath every case cited in this book by the names of the parties, there lies just such an iceberg of human misfortune or tragedy and more or less diligent endeavour by the legal profession to serve their clients and the ends of justice—to give flesh to Justinian's precept *alterum non laedere*. The details of the book are affected by the "new" sheriff court rules but the skills and methods revealed are still valid.

Choice of law

12.20   Once it has been decided which court is the proper court to hear the dispute, it must be decided what law is to apply. This is what is meant by "choice of law" and it is one area of the subject of private international law which is well served by expert treatises.[52] Delict cases formerly were quite special and raised difficult issues based on a double actionability rule. This rule emerged from a series of cases.[53] The rule was criticised in England[54] and by Scots lawyers.[55] This resulted in the Law Commissions working to produce a joint report,[56] and legislation.[57] The general rule is that the applicable law is the law of the country in which the events constituting the tort or delict in question occur.[58] Where elements of these events occur in different countries there are three rules:

> (1) In cases of personal injury[59] or death the applicable law is that of the territory where the individual was when the injuries were sustained.[60]
> (2) For damage to property it is the law of the place where the property was when it was damaged.[61]
> (3) For all other cases it is the law of the territory where the "most significant element or elements of the events" complained of occurred; failing that, the law of the territory with which the subject-matter has the "most real and substantial connection".

The general rule may be displaced. If it appears, in all the circumstances, from a comparison of (a) the significance of the factors which connect a tort or delict with the country whose law would be the applicable law under the general rule; and (b) the significance of any factors connecting the tort or delict with another country, that it is substantially more appropriate for the applicable law for determining

---

[52] Anton and Beaumont, *Private International Law* (2nd ed., W. Green, 1990); see also Maher, *A Casebook on Private International Law* (W. Green, 1985).

[53] *Rosses v. Sir Bhagral Sinjie* (1891) 19 R. 31; *Evans v. Slein* (1904) 7 F. 65; *Naftalin v. LMS Ry*, 1933 S.C. 259; and *McElroy v. McAllister*, 1949 S.C. 110; applied as recently as *James Burrough Distilleries plc v. Speymalt Whisky Distributors Ltd*, 1989 G.W.D. 4–186.

[54] See, for example, Carter, "Choice of Law in Tort and Delict" (1991) 107 L.Q.R. 405.

[55] Black, "Delict and the conflict of laws", 1968 J.R. 40.

[56] Law Com. No. 193; Scot. Law Com. No. 129.

[57] Blaikie, "Foreign Torts and Choice of Law Flexibility", 1995 S.L.T. (News) 23.

[58] s. 11(1).

[59] This includes disease or any impairment of physical or mental condition: s. 11(3).

[60] s. 11(2) (a).

[61] s. 11(2) (b).

the issues arising in the case, or any one of those issues, to be the law of the other country, the general rule is displaced and the applicable law for determining those issues or that issue (as the case may be) is the law of that other country.

The factors which may be taken into account as connecting a tort or delict with a country for the purposes of this section include, in particular, factors relating to the parties, to any of the events which constitute the tort or delict in question, or to any of the circumstances or consequences of those events.[62]

Further reading

Ashcroft, S., "Law Commission Paper No. 224: Structured Settlements and Interim and Provisional Damages—A Practitioner's Review" [1995] J.P.I.L. 3.

Beaumont, P.R., "Jurisdiction in delict in Scotland" (1983) 28 J.L.S.S. 528.

Bennett, S.A., "Action This Day!" 1991 S.L.T. (News) 311.

Black, R., "Delict and the Conflict of Laws", 1968 J.R. 40.

Black, R., "Styles for Averring Jurisdiction under the 1982 Act", 1987 S.L.T. (News) 1.

Blaikie, J., "Personal Injury Claims: the valuation of services", 1994 S.L.T. (News) 167.

Blaikie, J., "Foreign Torts and Choice of Law Flexibility", 1995 S.L.T. (News) 23.

Blaikie, J., "Provisional damages: Please may I have some more", 1995 S.L.P.Q. 65.

Field, D., "Civil Evidence: A Quantum Leap", 1988 S.L.T. (News) 349.

Field, D., "Going it Alone", 1989 S.L.T. (News) 216.

Gow, J.J., "Delict and Private International Law" (1949) 65 L.Q.R. 313.

Leslie, R.D., "The Application of the Lex Fori Under the Double Delict Rule", 1990 S.L.T. (News) 361.

Milligan, R., "Approaching Future Wage Loss", 1995 S.L.T. (News) 173.

Morrisson, J.M., "Pleading Alternative Cases", 1987 S.L.T. (News) 193.

Ritchie, A., "*Smith* v. *Manchester* Awards: How do courts assess loss of capacity on the labour market?" [1994] J.P.I.L. 103.

Rodger, B.J., "*Bouygnes* and the Scottish Choice of Law Rules in Delict", 1995 S.L.P.Q. 58.

Rodger, B., "*The Halley*: Holed and now Sunk: Part III of the Private International Law (Miscellaneous Provisions) Act 1995", 1996 S.L.P.Q. 397.

Russell, J.A., "Further Observations—Pleading Alternative Cases", 1987 S.L.T. (News) 397.

Stewart, W.J., "Future Loss and Employability: Some preliminary thoughts", 1995 Rep. B. 5.

Sutherland, R.D., "Optional Procedure in the Court of Session", 1991 S.L.T. (News) 17.

---

[62] s. 12.

Chapter 13

PRINCIPLES OF RESTITUTION

INTRODUCTION

13.1 As has already been indicated, the law of obligations divides, not into two, but into at least three parts[1]: contract, delict and unjust enrichment. This chapter is devoted to obligations arising from unjust enrichment. Just as a breach of the obligation to refrain from delictual activity produces a response from the legal system called damages, a failure to redress unjust enrichment provokes the legal system to respond by ordering restitution.[2] Scots law knows of other cases where a party is obliged to make restitution or something like it which may not be, or may not be allowed by some doctrinal systems to be, cases of unjust enrichment; hence, for the benefit of the student who may become a lawyer and require to know of remedies, this chapter deals with many possible cases of restitution and related obligations.

UNJUST ENRICHMENT

Just as we have seen that, although delict means wrong or contrary to law, the meaning of the word "wrong" does not provide a legal formula for determining liability or a lack thereof, so too restitution is not ordered because someone has something and it is unfair that they should have it. In the same way that delictual liability is

---

[1] There are other miscellaneous obligations and it may well be wiser to accept a fourth category of others rather than trying to accomodate and distort the existing categories. The obligations imposed by family law are now considered statutory but for Stair were obediential obligations like delict, and thus in Scots law a space needs to be kept for such obligations. The duty of confidentiality explained above is another one which is difficult to place.

[2] See, generally, Stewart, *The Law of Restitution in Scotland* (W. Green, 1992) (Supplement, 1995); Walker, *Principles of Scottish Private Law* (4th ed., Oxford, 1988), Vol. II; Gloag and Henderson (10th ed., 1995, Chap. 29); Sellar, *Stair Encyclopaedia*, Vol. 15. For an exposition of current trends in the law, see the Restitution Law Review (Hart Mansfield Press).

moderated through analytical tests like proximity, remoteness and the duty of care, so too does the law guard jealously the availability of restitution for unjust enrichment. The title here is restitution because it is not yet entirely certain that all of the law that actually exists in the judgments can be assigned to unjust enrichment. For the student—particularly the student wanting to look after clients—it is necessary to know these restitutionary obligations whether or not they are triggered by unjust enrichment.

We have seen that the law of delict began with known heads and is ever more becoming a matter of generalised theory—the questions of fairness, justice and reasonableness replacing any rigid application of nominate heads. The law of restitution in Scotland until very recently has been, and, to an extent, still is, at the more primitive stage. It is moving now to a full historical examination of these nominate heads with comparative analysis focusing on the systems sharing the history, but seeking too to learn from other fundamentally different jurisdictions where they offer a useful juridical analysis of problems common to similar societies. Just as we started the examination of the law of delict with the nominate heads, so we shall start with the known heads of restitution in Scots law. However, the student, as much as the practitioner and the academic, should note carefully the words of the then Lord President (Hope) in the recent five-judge decision, when speaking of restitution, recompense and repetititon:

> "the important point is that these actions are all means to the same end, which is to redress an unjustified enrichment upon the broad equitable principle *nemo debet locupletari aliena jactura*."[3]

In an even more important development in an even more recent case, *Shilliday v. Smith*,[4] the present Lord President has taken the quest for principle even further by playing down the importance of the old names and remedies:

> "As the law has developed, it has identified various situations where persons are to be regarded as having unjustly enriched at another's expense and where the other person may accordingly seek to have the enrichment reversed. The authorities show that some of these situations fall into recognisable groups or categories. Since these situations correspond, if only somewhat loosely, to situations where remedies were granted in Roman Law, in referring to the relevant categories our law tends to use the terminology which is found in the Digest and Code. The terms include *condictio indebiti, condictio causa data causa non secuta*

---

[3] *Morgan Guaranty Trust Co. of New York v. Lothian R.C.*, 1995 S.L.T. 299 at 309.
[4] 1998 S.C.L.R. 502.

and—to a lesser extent—*condictio sine causa* . . . Once he has satisfied himself that he has a relevant case, anyone contemplating bringing an action must then determine how the court is to reverse the defender's enrichment if it decides in the pursuer's favour. This will depend on the particular circumstances. The person framing the pleadings must consider how the defender's enrichment has come about and then search among the usual range of remedies to find a remedy or combination of remedies which will achieve his purpose of having that enrichment reversed . . . So repetition, restitution, reduction and recompense are simply examples of remedies which the courts grant to reverse an unjust enrichment, depending on the way in which the particular enrichment has arisen."[5]

RESTITUTION CASES WITH NAMES

Introduction

13.2   The Scots law is built on Roman foundations but largely upon the received Roman law rather than the ancient Roman law. Accordingly, Scots cases are traditionally grouped under the known names. In the case of the Latin names, these are no more than headings, for no such actions exist in Scotland. A restitution claim is raised as an ordinary action—it is the pleadings which will indicate what is being sought and why, a view confirmed in *Shilliday* per the Lord President. See the quotation at para. 13.6 below. The following diagram charts the Scottish terminology.[6]

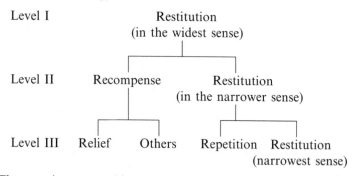

Level I	Restitution (in the widest sense)	
Level II	Recompense	Restitution (in the narrower sense)
Level III	Relief Others	Repetition Restitution (narrowest sense)

The most important thing to notice is that the term restitution is itself used in three different senses: (1) to cover the whole subject; (2) to

---

[5] *Quaere*, can the proprietary remedy of restitution given for breach of constructive trust be treated as a remedy for unjust enrichment?

[6] This chart is based upon Professor Birk's analysis of the Scots law.

describe cases of recovery of things certain; and (3) to describe the recovery of a specific thing which is not money. There now follows a brief treatment of the heads of restitutionary remedy set out alphabetically for, in the absence of a true theory, that is better than no order at all. One other ordering is immediately attractive—by the benefit or enrichment received—but to do this is to encourage thinking in this way, which is not necessarily beneficial.

CASES WITH NAMES

Actio de in rem verso

This ancient Roman remedy was adopted into many European legal   13.3
systems. It is recognised by Stair: "Hence arises the action in law de in rem verso; whereby whatsoever turneth to the behoof of any makes him thereby liable, though without any engagement of his own."[7] It is recognised in the writing of Kames and in a number of cases.[8]

It has, however, become forgotten, probably because of the expansion of the category of recompense. Actually, recompense (discussed below) is probably an instance of the *actio*. If this is the case then this broader principle of recovery is available in Scots law. In France, the *actio* became the basis for a general right of restitution of unjust enrichment.[9] In any case, where it is argued that unjust enrichment cannot be ordered for the want of a named Scots category, this may provide a traditional and conservative answer.

Caution

Some aspects of the law of caution are essentially restitutionary but   13.4
the law is well developed in Scotland and analysis in terms of first principles unlikely to be required. The unjust enrichment would be that the debtor for whom the cautioner has given caution would be discharged of liability, the cautioner would have paid and the creditor would no longer be interested in pursuing matters.[10]

Condictiones

In Roman law, a *condictio* was a debt action for the defender to make   13.5
over something which had been the pursuer's. Over time, various cases

---

[7] I, viii, 7; the authority cited for this is *Dig.*, 15.3.
[8] *White v. McIntyre* (1841) 3 D. 334; *Lockhart v. Brown* (1888) 15 R. 742; *Morgan v. Morgan's J.F.*, 1922 S.C. 247; *Mellor v. William Beardmore*, 1927 S.C. 597. It is still used in Quebec under that name—see 1993 R.L.R. 110–112.
[9] *Boudier* Cass civ. June 15, 1892; D.P. 1892 I. 596, S. 1893. I. 281, described by Goff and Jones as "the well-known fertiliser case": p. 40, n. 57.
[10] *Esso Petroleum v. Hall Russell & Co.*, 1988 S.L.T. 874.

came up so often that they acquired names and were set out under these headings. Somewhat unfortunately, Scotland has followed this practice. One benefit, however, is that Scots law shares a vocabulary with the law on continental Europe and other Civilian and mixed systems.

Condictio indebiti

13.6   This is an action for the recovery of money or a thing transferred by a person thinking that they were legally obliged to make the transfer. So if P pays E, instead of T, to whom P owes money, then this liability mistake is recognised as a prima facie unjust factor and the money in E's hands is an enrichment.

However, over the years certain barriers grew up to this particular claim. The first was that the payment should not be made by way of an error of the general law.[11] This was based upon the maxim *ignorantia juris neminem excusat* and a desire not to have the effects of transactions opened up. There was much force to this rule, but there was and is much to be said against it, and by far the best thing against it is the notion of unjust enrichment itself: why should E keep the money? Just as economics are often utilised in formulating or criticising tort policy, so too economics can be utilised in this question. The inability to recover a mistaken payment encourages efficiency in businesses and in personal dealings. The rule was relaxed in Scotland in relation to mistakes of law which were not errors of the general law, as where there was a misinterpretation of a deed between parties.[12] Another important barrier was the conduct of the parties. In *Youle v. Cochrane*[13] the fact that the mistake was induced by a demand by the recipient of the enrichment did not avail the pursuer.

At a stage where the English Law Commission recommended that the rule against recovery of payments made in error of law be set aside and the Scottish Law Commission was considering the same point, *Morgan Guaranty Trust Company of New York v. Lothian Regional Council*[14] came before a bench of five judges. They overruled the error of law bar which was certainly a major affirmation of the principle against unjust enrichment. While a welcome modernising decision, a good deal of legal archaeology was undertaken to try to find a good

---

[11]   *Lord Advocate v. Glasgow Corp.*, 1958 S.C. 12; it has often been pointed out that Scots law did not always subscribe to such a rule and that it was English influence which imported it: see Macdonald, "Mistaken Payments in Scots Law", 1989 J.R. 49.

[12]   *Baird's Trs v. Baird & Co.* (1877) 4 R. 1005. It was abrogated by the courts in Canada, Australia and South Africa, this latter being the most significant case for Scots lawyers: *Willis Faber Enthoven (Pty) Ltd v. Receiver of Revenue*, 1992 (4) S.A. 202 (A).

[13]   (1868) 6 M. 427.

[14]   1995 S.L.T. 299.

precedent (*Stirling v. Earl of Lauderdale*[15]) and explain away what had seemed like the last rational word on the subject (*Glasgow Corporation v. Inland Revenue*[16]). The previous rule had many practical benefits, while causing an injustice between parties—the result of the change is that there are many practical problems yet to be accommodated either by decision or legislation.[17]

More questionably, it is submitted, the court expressed the view that the argument about excusability was misconceived, although conduct was not entirely irrelevant:

> "It is not part of the law of Scotland that the error must be shown to be excusable. That is not to say that the nature of the error and the question whether it could be avoided may not play a part in a decision as to where the equities may lie if a point is raised in answer to the pursuer's claim. I consider, however, that once the pursuer has averred the necessary ingredients to show that prima facie he is entitled to the remedy, it is for the defender to raise the issues which may lead to a decision that the remedy should be refused on the grounds of equity."[18]

This can be defended on the basis that to do otherwise is to ask the pursuer to prove a negative—normally contrary to the law of evidence at least. It is a better formulation than any suggestion that the payer's conduct should be irrelevant. To take it further might mean that the payer can be very careless in the making of payments so long as actually not being aware that they are not due. In relation to individuals this may be acceptable but more thought ought to be given to the issue where the context is one of corporations, where the payment and the receipt are done as part of many thousands of transactions—the issue then is who is to pay for the extra systems to detect the error. In this context a rule which looks at the care taken by the payer is, it is submitted, justifiable. This is, of course, not to say that the care need be that of the reasonable man, and much less that it should require the breach of a duty.[19]

Condictio causa data causa non secuta

In Roman law this was a remedy to allow a person to withdraw from a 13.7
bilateral agreement, one part of which had not been performed by the

---

[15] (1733) Mor. 2930. The case rediscovered and re-analysed by D.R. Macdonald. Counsel in the case found printed opinions which helped the court.

[16] 1959 S.L.T. 230.

[17] See Scot. Law Com., Discussion Paper No.99, "Judicial abolition of the Error of Law Rule and its Aftermath".

[18] *Morgan*, per Lord President Hope, at 316.

[19] See *Bank of Scotland v. Crawford*, 1994 S.C.L.R. 913 for an example of a case decided before the opinions in *Morgan*.

other party. It only applied to innominate contracts with property effects. However, it developed into a general action for recovery of property which had been transferred on a basis whereupon that basis did not materialise. For a prime civilian view contradicting this statement, see Evans-Jones, R., "The claim to recover what was transferred for a lawful purpose outwith contract (*condictio causa data non secuta*)".[20]

The civilian example of the ring given in contemplation of marriage still stands—if the marriage does not take place, the ring must be returned. The *condictio causa data causa non secuta* was the inspiration for one of the great Scottish cases: *Cantiere San Rocco v. Clyde Shipbuilding and Engineering Co. Ltd.*[21]

> A contract was concluded between Clyde Shipbuilding and an Austrian company which, as a result of the First World War, became an enemy alien company with whom the Clyde company could not trade. This meant the contract was frustrated. Work had been done and a prepayment made.

The House of Lords allowed the money to be repaid, even although some work had been done under the contract and thus, in English analysis, there was no total failure of consideration. The House allowed the company the right to a counter-restitutionary claim for recompense for the work done. Professor Evans-Jones[22] suggests that *Cantiere* could and should have proceeded on the basis of risk in the contract rather than on a view of the *condictio causa data causa non secuta* which did not take account of the second phase of Roman influence, the period of the *jus commune*.

In *Zemhunt Holdings Ltd v. Control Securities plc*,[23] it was suggested in the Outer House that the *condictio* would be excluded if a party seeking restitution was in breach of contract, but Lord Morison in the Inner House stated what, it is submitted, is the better view:

> "that a breach of contract by the payer of part of the price which is sought by him to be recovered, following rescission of the contract by the payee on the ground of that breach, does not per se affect the equity of the claim for restitution. This is because the ordinary remedies for breach of contract are available to the payee and the payer is already fully accountable for the breach by the operation of these remedies."[24]

---

[20] Visser (ed.), *The Limit of the Law of Obligations* (Juta, 1997), p.139 *et seq.*, supportive of the view in the text in *Shilliday v. Smith*, 1998 S.C.L.R. 502.

[21] 1923 S.C. (H.L.) 105.

[22] "*Unjust Enrichment, Contract and the Third Reception of Roman Law in Scotland*" (1993) 109 L.Q.R. 663.

[23] 1991 S.L.T. 653.

[24] 1992 S.L.T. 151 at 155.

Some support for the view that there could have been a restitutionary claim in *Zemhunt (Holdings) Ltd*, had the "deposit" point been decided otherwise, can be found argued at length by Professor Hector MacQueen.[25] The argument that in principle restitution can be allowed even where a contract exists is also supported, in a civilian context, by an article by Professor Visser.[26] It is submitted, the correct view is that restitution can be obtained even where a valid contract is standing.[27]

Constructive trust

Norrie and Scobbie say that where a person owing a fiduciary 13.8 duty to another person makes a profit or gains an advantage from his position in that fiduciary relationship a constructive trust arises, the effect of which is to impose an obligation to account and applies the trust to any gains made with the property so held.[28] To that extent, it can be seen as a remedy preventing unjust enrichment. As thus put, the unjust factor is the wrongful conduct in acting in breach of duty and the enrichment is the gain. In other jurisdictions, because the remedy exists it is thought it can be applied to cases of unjust enrichment—the importance of constructive trust to the practitioner is that it provides a remedy with effects in property law because if property is held on trust it would not normally fall into an insolvent estate. If, however, that idea is applied to a *condictio indebiti* to allow a mistaken payer to recover in full, whereas an ordinary creditor gets only a dividend, it arguably becomes a very arbitrary remedy.

Despite references to the doctrine going back a very long time, there is feeling among many Scots lawyers that the institution is foreign or that it sits uneasily in Scots law. Indeed, Professor Gretton has recently tried to show that there is hardly any true authority for it and that what there is of it should be abolished.[29] Nonetheless the

---

[25] "Unjustified Enrichment and Breach of Contract", 1994 J.R. 165. See also his "Contract, Unjustified Enrichment and Concurrent Liability: A Scots Perspective" in Visser, ed. *op. cit.*, p. 176 *et seq.*

[26] "Rethinking Unjustified Enrichment: A Perspective of the Competition between Contractual and Enrichment Remedies", 1992 *Acta Juridica* 203.

[27] See *The Mortgage Corporation v. Mitchells Roberton*, 1997 S.L.T. 1305. See developments in the debate: Evans-Jones, "The claim to recover what was transferred for a lawful purpose outwith contract (*condictio causa data causa non secuta*) in *The Limits of the Law of Obligation* (Visser ed., Juta 1997), p. 139 and MacQueen, "Contract, Unjustified Enrichment and Concurrent Liability: A Scots Perspective" *op. cit.*, p. 176. See also *Transocean Maritime Agencies S.A. Monegasquev. Petit*, 1997 S.C.L.R. 534.

[28] Norrie and Scobbie, *Trusts*, pp. 54–55.

[29] Gretton, "Constructive trusts" (1996) 1 Edinburgh L.R. 281; (1997) 1 Edinburgh L.R. 408.

argument is still used, although there is now a tendency to tie it to, or offer by way of a lesser remedy, recompense.[30]

In the Inner House in *Sharp v. Thomson*,[31] Lord President Hope clearly accepted that there was a doctrine of constructive trust applicable in Scots law. It did not apply to mere contractual arrangements but where circumstances create fiduciary duties in favour of the party to whom the property is to be conveyed.[32] Thus neither student nor practitioner can yet ignore arguments based on this remedy.

Melville monument liability

13.9 The foundation of this liability is *Walker v. Milne*.[33] The pursuer raised an action against, *inter alios*, the defenders, as subscribers for a monument to the late Lord Melville (hence the name of the head of liability), alleging that they had entered into a contract with him, to place it upon his property of Coates, near Edinburgh; that they had taken possession of the site; had broken it up; had performed several other operations on it; and that he had been thus induced to make various alterations on his plans for feuing his ground.

The pursuer claimed implement of the agreement or damages. In defence it was stated that, although there had been an agreement, it related to heritage and as it was constituted by writing, there was *locus poenitentiae*. As there was no binding contract, it was argued that no damages could be due. The court found "that the pursuer is entitled to indemnification for any actual loss and damage he may have sustained, and for the expenses incurred in consequence of the alteration of the site of the monument."[34]

13.10 That case was developed in the later cases.[35] More recently, it has been examined in a couple of commercial litigations. In *Dawson International plc v. Coats Paton plc*,[36]

> Dawsons made an offer to take over the defenders which fell through. The pursuers claimed for losses they sustained, averred to be the costs of underwriting, printing and professional services.

---

[30] *Style Financial Services Ltd v. Bank of Scotland*, 1997 G.W.D. 7–255; *Mercedes-Benz Finance Ltd v. Clydesdale Bank plc*, 1996 S.C.C.R. 1005. Lesser in the sense that recompense is a personal and not a proprietory remedy.

[31] 1995 S.L.T. 837.

[32] at 854C. See *Stevenson v. Wilson*, 1907 S.C. 445 referred to in that case. The case result was reversed in the House of Lords, 1997 S.L.T. 636, but the constructive trust point was not taken in the House.

[33] (1823) 2 S. 379.

[34] *ibid.*

[35] *Allan v. Gilchrist* (1875) 2 R. 587; *Gilchrist v. Whyte*, 1907 S.C. 984; *Dobie v. Lauder's Trs* (1873) 11 M. 749.

[36] 1988 S.L.T. 854.

One basis of the case was that the target company, it was alleged, had agreed to certain terms and in particular that they would not encourage or co-operate with any other potential bidder. A joint press release was given out indicating that the target company were recommending the takeover. The target company, it was alleged, later went on to enter into an agreement with those who later purchased them. The pursuers could not afford a contested bid—a point they had made from an early stage.

It is the claim for "reimbursement" which is of interest in this context. Lord Cullen was of the view that this head of liability only applied if there was an agreement between the parties.[37]

It is difficult, then, to locate this undoubted head of liability within unjust enrichment. It may well be an instance of restitution for wrongs—it is not the case that simply because wrongdoing is involved only the law of delict may apply.

Negotiorum gestio (unauthorised administration of anothers business)[35]

In Roman law this was a right of action—the direct action—against the person who intermeddled in one's affairs. The interest in unjust enrichment is that a contrary action was granted for the expenses incurred in carrying out the work. Professor Birks described *negotiorum gestio* along with salvage as being doubtfully restitutionary. He suggested it ought to be allocated to a separate miscellaneous category or broken up.[39] The direct action can be subsumed within delict and the contrary action is not entirely a matter of restitution for unjust enrichment because sometimes the pursuer is paid more than the defenders gain. 13.11

While it has to be admitted that there may not be many claims made on the basis of *negotiorum gestio* this does not make it unimportant for three reasons. First, it is of theoretical importance for delict, recognising a legal interference into the affairs of others without their consent. Secondly, it may be important where communication breaks down which can happen even today.[40] Finally, it overlaps the territory of unjust enrichment and has been an inspiration for doctrinal developments in other jurisdications.

Stair's position is very close to the Roman law. The exceptional nature of the doctrine is respected: "Those who interpose themselves 13.12

---

[37] This view of the law was adopted in *The Governor and Company of the Bank of Scotland v. 3i plc*, unreported, OH (Lord Cameron of Lochbroom), Jan. 18, 1990.

[38] Lit. Management of affairs.

[39] *Six Questions*, pp. 249–250.

[40] McBryde and Scobbie, "The Iran and Kuwait Conflict: the Impact on Contracts", 1991 S.L.T. (News) 39.

in such cases, do so necessarily and profitably for the good of the absent, and so are under no delinquence."[41]

The following detailed rules can be taken from Stair:

> (1) the obligation is to recompense what others have necessarily or profitably done;
>
> (2) the deeds must be done "without command or commission, otherwise they come in the nature of the contract of Mandate or commission";
>
> (3) "a negotiator cannot begin any new business but only carry on that which is begun";
>
> (4) the deeds must be necessarily or profitably done;
>
> (5) the acts must not be "contrary to our will and command";
>
> (6) however, if *gestores* "do that which is necessary or profitable for carrying on our affairs, though by some accident that affair may perish or miscarry, and we no richer, but, it may be, poorer, yet are we obliged[42];
>
> (7) mutual actions arise, "the one direct, whereby he whose affair is managed, craveth accompt and restitution of the negotiator and reparation of what he hath done amiss; and the contrary action to the negotiator, whereby he craveth recompense and satisfaction of what he hath profitably expended, and for his labours and pains";
>
> (8) "the negotiator is holden not only to answer for fraud, but pro culpa levi, for his fault, though light", and if another had wanted to act instead then the negotiator who actually acted will be held liable for the lightest fault (*culpa levissima*);
>
> (9) there is however no liability on the negotiator for failing to act more profitably if the actings have in fact been profitable.[43]

13.13 Leslie in an essential study[44] has observed that Stair was prepared to allow the *gestor* to recover the value of his labour and pains (see proposition (7), above). Leslie correctly describes this as a deviation from the Roman law.[45] The argument for Stair's view is that the *dominus* would have to pay for labour if the *gestor* merely sub-contracted all of the various tasks and submitted these as expenses. To pay someone else to do something he could do

---

[41] I.viii.3.

[42] Compare with Grotius, *Inleiding* III, xxvii, 5: "Provided, of course, that the affair has turned out well, or, at least, has been conducted in such a way that according to the general judgement of competent persons a good outcome was to be expected."

[43] This paragraph is precisely as set out in Stewart, *Restitution*, para. 9.2. See *Bank of Scotland v. MacLeod Paxton Woolard & Co.*, 1998 S.L.T. 258 at 277.

[44] R.D. Leslie, "Negotiorum Gestio in Scots Law: The Claim of the Privileged Gestor", 1983 J.R. 12.

[45] pp. 21–22.

[46] *Stair Encyclopaedia*, Vol. 15, paras 87–143.

himself is inefficient. The argument the other way is that it might encourage a *gestor* to make a profit out of what is an act based on altruism.

There is now an exhaustive treatment of the subject to which readers must be referred.[46] The following may serve as an example, albeit not a paradigm case, of the potential application of the doctrine. In *SMT Sales & Services Co. Ltd v. Motor and General Finance Co. Ltd*,[47]

> The defenders let a motorcar to a Mr Wilson on hire-purchase. The police found the car abandoned. Mr Wilson was advised, indicated that the vehicle was stolen, but did nothing. The police acting under statutory authority instructed the pursuers to remove the vehicle to their garage. The pursuers tried to have Wilson take the vehicle or pay but he simply advised of the existence and identity of the defenders. Wilson was behind on his instalment payments.

The primary claim was for recompense *quantum lucratus*. There was an alternative claim that the pursuers were *negotiorum gestores* or agents for *negotiorum gestores*. The recompense branch of the case which was successful does not concern us here but the sheriff substitute also sustained the *negotiorum gestio* claim in the alternative. Relying on Bell[48] the sheriff substitute stated,

> "The *negotiorum gestor* is entitled to be indemnified for all reasonable expenditure incurred by him. The obligation differs from recompense in that it is unnecessary to prove that the expenditure was beneficial to the person whose affairs have been thus managed. Such a person is also directly liable to any agent employed by the *negotiorum gestor* (*Fernie* v. *Robertson* (1871) 9 M. 437; *Dunbar* v. *Wilson & Dunlop's trs.* (1887) 15 R. 210). It seems to me not unreasonable in this case to regard the police as being *negotiorum gestores* and the pursuers as their agents. . . . I do not think it makes any difference that the defenders, if they had been aware of the position, could have taken charge of the car themselves. *Negotiorum gestio* always pre-supposes some form of inability on the part of the persons whose affairs are managed and the defender's ignorance of the position is just a form of such inability."[49]

Recompense

Scots law allows recovery in respect of work done where it would be 13.14 unjust for the defender to be enriched by its receipt. Indeed, the head

---

[47] 1954 S.L.T. (Sh. Ct.) 107.

[48] para. 540.

[49] 1954 S.L.T. (Sh. Ct.) 107, *per* Sheriff-Substitute J. Lindsay Duncan.

recompense is wider, it being recognised that it is based on the brocard *nemo debet locupletari ex aliena jactura*. It is also the case that it may have brought in the concepts involved in the *actio de in rem verso*, known to the modern civil law. A most useful (and often used) modern statement can be found in *Lawrence Building Co. Ltd v. Lanark County Council*,[50] where it was stated:

> "From the opinions of their Lordships of the Second Division in that case [*Varney*[51]] it may be taken to be clear that there are three factors which are essential to the success of any case based on recompense. The first is that the pursuers must have incurred a loss. The second is that the defenders must be *lucrati* by the action of the pursuers. The third is that there must have been no intention of donation on the part of the pursuers towards the defenders."

Not everything is settled in recompense, and so the foregoing is not a definition. It would be contrary to principle if error were an essential rather than one possible vitiating factor making the transfer unjust. There is also authority to suggest that recompense is a subsidiary remedy which can only be used if there is no other basis of claim, but there is more recent authority which implies the contrary.[52] The precise meaning of the absence of an intention to donate is a problem. If property is transferred with an intention to donate then there is no recompense, just as if it were transferred under a sale, and the mention of donation does not assist. Where the matter is critical to a case, a strict reading of this as a definitional requirement would oblige the pursuer to prove a negative, which is rare. The presumption against donation and the opportunity for parties to have an opponent lead at a proof might make the definition otiose.[53]

Contractual obligations must, of course, be respected. Even valuable work done in the teeth of a contract has been held, correctly, to be irrecoverable: *Bryce Houston Ltd v. Glass's Fruit Markets Ltd.*[54] Recompense has some limited place to play in domestic relations cases.[55] It is often pressed into service in the absence of a developed law of constructive trust in cases where money is diverted into the

---

[50] 1978 S.C. 30.

[51] *Varney (Scotland) Ltd v. Burgh of Lanark*, 1976 S.L.T. 46.

[52] See *Lawrence Building*, above, and *N.V. Devos Gebroeder v. Sunderland Sportswear Ltd*, 1990 S.L.T. 473.

[53] See Stewart, "Intention to Donate and Recompense and Professor Bell's Definition", 1996 S.L.T. (News) 270; *Christie v. Armstrong*, 1996 S.L.T. 948

[54] 1992 S.C.L.R. 1019.

[55] See *Newton v. Newton*, 1925 S.C. 715; *Rankin v. Wither* (1886) 13 R. 903; *Mackle v. Mackle*, 1984 S.L.T. 276; *Scanlan v. Scanlan*, Airdrie Sheriff Court, Jan. 5, 1990, unreported. See the cohabitation case of *Gray v. Kerner*, 1996 S.C.L.R. 331.

wrong hands.[56] It should be noted at this point that, although the paradigm recompense case is of outlays made or materials supplied or even of work done, money paid can be claimed under recompense.[57]

In cases designated relief, recompense can apply even where there has not been an actual payment made.[58] Particular nominate head has expanded and is capable of further expansion.

Relief

The most recent judicial pronouncement is in *Moss v. Penman*.[59] 13.15 The pursuer was one of two persons held liable jointly and severally for the same debt. The pursuer paid the creditor and the action was against the co-obligant for a one-half share by way of relief. The sheriff allowed a proof before answer but the defender appealed on the basis that the action should have been dismissed as the pursuer was not compelled to make the payment but did so voluntarily. It was held that it was not necessary for there to have been some compulsion before the defender would be liable in relief. The Lord President (Hope) began his investigation of relief by citing Stair, at I, viii, 9. Stair treats relief as an obligation of recompense.[60] Above all, when pressed by counsel the Lord President saw the fundamental question of unjust enrichment if the defender did not have to pay:

> "In the result [of the defender's plea succeeding] neither debtor is under any further liability to the creditor, and if he has no right of relief the debtor who makes the payment will be disabled for all time from recovering any part of the debt from his co-debtor. That would seem to be a clear case of unjustified enrichment for which the equitable principle of recompense ought to provide a remedy."

The Lord President went further and stated that relief is based on recompense:

> "In my opinion it is clear from these authorities that the obligation of relief was and still is based on the principle of recompense."[61]

---

[56] *Mercedes-Benz Finance Ltd v. Clydesdale Bank plc*, 1996 S.C.L.R. 1005; *Style Financial Services v. Bank of Scotland*, 1996 S.L.T. 421.

[57] *Commercial Bank v. Biggar*; *Christie v. Armstrong*, 1996 S.L.T. 948.

[58] *Christie's Exr v. Armstrong*, 1996 S.L.T. 948.

[59] 1994 S.L.T. 19.

[60] Bankton I,9,45 supported the same view. Bell's *Princ.*, para. 62 was cited to make it clear that an assignation is not required in these circumstances.

[61] At 22.

In another relatively recent case, *Christie v. Armstrong*,[62]

> an unmarried couple bought a house together. The title was in
> joint names and there was a policy in the name of the man only
> to pay off the mortgage. He died leaving no will. The title
> transferred automatically by reason of the joint names des-
> tination. The mortgage holders were automatically paid off by
> the assigned insurance policy. But the policy itself belonged to
> the deceased and was really for his intestate estate. The effect
> of all the automatic transfers was that the unmarried partner's
> joint and several debt was paid off by a policy she had no
> interest in.

The sheriff held that one could only have relief if one paid off a debt
but that there had been no payment in this case. In the Inner House it
was held that, because relief was founded on recompense and the case
was based on unjust enrichment, there was no need to show an actual
payment.

Salvage

13.16 Bell says salvage "rests on plain principles of equity, and a right
of lien."[63] Lord Carmont considered it a form of recompense. His
source, as is Professor Walker's, is Stair, I, viii, 3, which, however,
deals with *negotiorum gestio*. Professor Birks describes it as an
obligation which is doubtfully restitutionary.[64] Salvage is not based
solely upon the amount of the defender's enrichment by the salvor's
services. The salvor gets more.[65] The court takes into account the
effort of the salvors, the degree of peril and work involved and the
value of the ship salved.[66] The existence of a contract excludes
salvage claims.[67] It is submitted that salvage is excluded by a
salvage contract express or implied,[68] notwithstanding thoughtful
criticism of that proposition by Professor Forte,[69] to which a
response has been offered.[70] New statutory provisions govern
many cases of salvage.[71]

---

[62] 1996 S.L.T. 948.
[63] *Princ.*, para. 443.
[64] "Six Questions", pp. 248–249.
[65] See *Vulcan v. Berlin* (1882) 9 R. 1057.
[66] *Duncan v. Dundee, Perth and London Shipping Co.* (1878) 5 R. 742.
[67] *Smith v. Saville*, unreported, OH (Lord Weir), May 12, 1989.
[68] *Restitution*, 10.10.
[69] Forte, "Salvage Operations, Salvage Contracts and Negotiorum Gestio", 1993
J.R. 247.
[70] *Supplement*, 10.10.
[71] Prof. Forte, *op. cit.*

Statutory rights

Many statutes make provision for money to be recovered under specific circumstances and so general principle may not apply or may be restricted or enhanced. Social security payments, for example, are often recoverable and interesting questions can arise.[72]

13.17

Subrogation

Usually only heard of in the field of insurance, this is a wider principle which has the effect of redressing unjust enrichment. The definition of subrogation by Brett L.J. in *Castellain v. Preston*[73] has recently been adopted by a Scottish Lord of Appeal in a Scottish appeal to the House of Lords:

13.18

> "In his classic definition of subrogation in *Castellain v. Preston*, Brett L.J., having stated at p. 386 that the fundamental principle of insurance was that the contract of insurance contained in a marine or fire policy was a contract of indemnity whereby the assured should be fully indemnified but never more than fully indemnified, said, at pp. 388–389: 'Now it seems to me that in order to carry out the fundamental rule of insurance law, this doctrine of subrogation must be carried to the extent which I am now about to endeavour to express, namely, that as between the underwriter and the assured the underwriter is entitled to the advantage of every right of the assured, whether such right consists in contract, fulfilled or unfulfilled, or in remedy for tort capable of being insisted on or already insisted on, or in any other right, whether by way of condition or otherwise, legal or equitable, which can be, or has been exercised or has accrued, and whether such right could or could not be enforced by the insurer in the name of the assured by the exercise of acquiring of which right or condition the loss against which the assured is insured, can be, or has been diminished. That seems to me to put this doctrine of subrogation in the largest possible form, and if in that form, large as it is, it is short of fulfilling that which is the fundamental condition, I must have omitted to state something which ought to have been stated. But it will be observed that I use the words "of every right of the assured." I think that the rule does require that limit.' "[74]

---

[72] *Riches v. Secretary of State for Social Security*, 1994 S.L.T. 730. See also *Restitution* and *Supplement*, 10.49.

[73] (1883) 11 Q.B.D. 380.

[74] *Esso Petroleum v. Hall Russell & Co. Ltd*, 1988 S.L.T. 874 at 882.

ANALYSIS AND TERMINOLOGY

13.19 It would be possible to analyse and describe the law by use of the indigenous remedies and those derived from the civilian tradition. No-one however did manage to organise the material into anything resembling a coherent whole based on this tradition.[75] Everything changed in the 1980's when Professor Birks set out a theory of the law of restitution which had descriptive and predictive elements. It had its own terminology and, while developed to solve problems with English law, arguably had much to teach any legal system. He then explored the theory against the background of Scots law and provided a critique of Scots law based on fundamental principles. That approach has now been commended as the starting point in difficult cases by the Lord President in a recent case:

> "Anyone who tries to glimpse the underlying realities must start from the work of Professor Peter Birks, the Regius Professor of Civil Law at Oxford—in particular his book *An Introduction to the Law of Restitution* (paperback edition 1989), and his two ground-breaking articles on Scots Law, "Restitution: a View of the Scots Law" (1985) 38 *Current Legal Problems* 57 and "Six Questions in Search of a Subject—Unjust Enrichment in a Crisis of Identity" 1985 *Juridical Review* 227. Professor Birks (*Introduction*, pp.9–27) and many others have pondered what is meant by unjust enrichment."[76]

On the other hand the trenchant critics of the Birksian analysis of Scots law are unlikely to change their views simply because of judicial decision and so the Birksian analysis cannot yet be said to be established.[77] What follows is a concise summary of the key concepts from the new way of thinking which should enable the reader to follow the *Shilliday* approach to restitution cases.

Subtractive restitution

13.20 Most of the cases known to the law of Scotland fall into this category—cases where the plaintiff seeks from the defender something which has been taken or has gone away from him or, as the modern commentators prefer to say, subtracted from him. There are,

---

[75] More recently Dr. Clive of the Scottish Law Commission has produced a very carefully worked out 'code', see Scot. Law. Comm No.99 (1996) Appendix.

[76] An early attempt to test the analysis by restructuring Scots cases can be found in Stewart, *The Law of Restitution in Scotland* (W. Green, 1992) and Supplement (1995).

[77] See Whitty, N.R. "Some trends and issues in Scots Enrichment Law" 1994 J.R. at 132–3 describing the Birksian analysis as "anglicising" and "assimilationsist"; See Evans-Jones, R. n.27 above and 3.26 below.

in such cases, two things to be considered: (1) is there enrichment which the law will notice in the hands of the defender? (2) is it unjust that the enrichment should not be made over to the pursuer (or disgorged as the modern commentators say)? A more unusual category, restitution for wrongs, is treated next and then left aside.

Restitution for wrongs

While, as we have seen, wrongdoing can result in an award of 13.21 damages for loss caused, sometimes no loss is caused by a wrong. The most famous example is *Reading v. Attorney-General.*[77a] In this case an army sergeant charged smugglers for his looking the other way. The army had suffered no subtractive loss for they would not have charged the smugglers. Nor had they sustained a status-quo loss—they did not have less than when the episode began. However, a wrong had been done by the sergeant and the enrichment was unjustified in his hands.

In Scots cases the phrase "restitution for wrongs" will not be found. That is because almost every case of a wrong results in a loss. However, the law of delict has in the past always taken account of this sort of damage. In the cases of spuilzie, ejection and intrusion, the award of violent profits need not have been redressing a loss actually caused—rather it was making the wrongdoer restore his enrichment made at the expense of the owner. Nonetheless, restitution for wrongs is not an articulated category in Scots law. It might be helpful if it were. An example of a more modern case and a more modern sort of sophisticated wrongdoing is *Exchange Telegraph v. Giulianoti.*[78] In this case the defenders used information they knew belonged to someone else. They appropriated the information and sold it to others. Now the thing about the case is that they were not stealing the actual customers of the pursuers. Nonetheless, they were enriched and as they were enriched by wrongdoing then it is arguably unjust. The court granted interdict but did not award damages. In England, such "restitutionary damages" can be awarded but only if a doctrine, called waiver of tort, can be applied.[79] In the United States, damages have been awarded and in one other case in a situation similar to *Exchange Telegraph—Federal Sugar Refining v. U.S. Sugar Equalisation Board.*[80]

As has been seen above, there is in Scots law an equitable duty of confidence. Breach of the duty permits the granting of interdict. It is clear from the English cases, which have the same foundations as the

---

[77a] [1951] A.C. 507.
[78] 1959 S.C. 19.
[79] See Goff and Jones, Chap. 32.
[80] 268 F. 575 (1920).

Scots cases, that damages can be awarded for breach of the duty. But it may be that the pursuer wants more than damages. If the delictual damages are awarded on the basis that the loss is the loss of profits that could be made by selling the information, then that award will compensate for the enrichment. The better course, and the one which has been adopted, is to order an account of profits. Again, this is where remedies and rights confuse matters. An accounting is essentially a restitutionary award.

Finally, if this category of claim is to emerge, free of the doctrine of waiver of tort as would be the case in Scotland, then some notion of what is meant by wrongs should be established. Birks' meaning of "wrongs" is as follows:

> "The word cannot be defined in terms of moral blame, since even some torts can be committed without fault. It is used to cover all conduct, acts or omissions, whose effect in creating legal consequences is attributable to its being characterised as a breach of duty. The term thus included not only all torts but also breaches of equitable and statutory duties and breaches of contract."[81]

Many difficulties can easily be imagined in respect of some wrongs. If breach of contract is considered to be a wrong for these purposes, there would be implications for the whole economic structure. At present, generally, the law permits breach of contract in bad faith. A party can break his contract and risk an action for implement or damages—this encourages economically efficient breach. The threat of having to make over the entrepreneurial profit from bad faith breach would discourage many transactions which might otherwise take place. Defamation[82] is a wrong and to allow restitutionary damages would give the ordinary citizen with an "ordinary" reputation, as opposed to the wealthy important pursuer, a greater protection from any journal that sought to profit from making defamatory statements.[83]

ENRICHMENT

13.22 This issue is usefully studied first, because if there is no enrichment there is no need to consider the unjust issue which usually, but not always, involves more factually difficult matters. Before an enrichment

---

[81] *Introduction to the Law of Restitution*, p. 313.

[82] See, generally, Chap. 8, above.

[83] Happily, a special study on this subject looked at from the point of view of Scots law is now available: Blackie, "Enrichment and wrongs in Scots law" 1992 *Acta Juridica* 23; see also Jackman, "Restitution for Wrongs" (1989) 47 C.L.J. 302; Stewart, Restitution Supplement (1995), 3.8.; Blackie, "Enrichment, Wrongs and Invasion of rights in Scots Law" in Visser, ed., *op. cit.*

will be considered legally justiciable in Scotland, it must be at the expense of the defender.[84]

An incidental benefit is not really at the pursuer's expense. The point is made in a classic analogy by Lord President Dunedin:

> "One man heats his house, and his neighbour gets a great deal of benefit. It is absurd to suppose that the person who has heated his house can go to his neighbour and say—'Give me so much for my coal bill, because you have been warmed by what I have done, and I did not intend to give you a present of it.' "[85]

A benefit which is intercepted and thus never subtracted from the pursuer is still an enrichment in the defender's hands.[86] An overcharge is an enrichment in the defender's hands.[87] Great debate, too detailed and extensive to reproduce or summarise here, has taken place and yet takes place over the issue of indirect enrichment. This is the situation where the pursuer has lost, the defender is enriched, but, because of some three-party situation, the defender is not enriched directly at the pursuer's expense. The idea can be seen best in an example given by Goff and Jones: "A builder contracts with a third party, whom he mistakenly but reasonably believes owns Blackacre, to build a swimming pool on Blackacre. He does so. The third party who has not paid the builder is evicted by the true owner."[88]

There is a detectable reluctance by Scottish courts to allow such claims. Perhaps the case most strongly supporting a general rule against indirect enrichment is *J.B. Mackenzie (Edinburgh) Ltd v. Lord Advocate*.[89] Further evidence against indirect enrichment can be found in the refusal of a claim by a garage company that repaired a car at the request of an insurance company against the car owner: *Kirklands Garage (Kinross) Ltd v. Clark*.[90]

Non-enrichment as a defence

It follows that if a person is not enriched then they should not be 13.23 compelled to disgorge.[91] This rule is well respected in Scotland in

---

[84] See the passage in Hume, *Lectures*, Vol. III, p. 170.

[85] *Edinburgh and District Tramways Co. Ltd v. Courtenay*, 1909 S.C. 99 at 105.

[86] *Robertson v. Landell* (1843) 6 D. 170.

[87] *British Oxygen v. SSEB*, 1959 S.C. (H.L.) 17.

[88] Goff and Jones, p. 39 and see n. 48. The example is modelled on *Gouws v. Jester Pools Pty Ltd*, 1968 (3) S.A. 563 (T.), a leading South African case in which the plaintiff failed.

[89] 1972 S.C. 231. I am indebted to an unpublished paper by N.R. Whitty, for the SPTL Restitution Group 1992, for this and the next case.

[90] 1967 S.L.T. (Sh. Ct) 60.

[91] See on this point the distinction made by Visser between non-enrichment and lost enrichment: Visser, "Responsibility to Return Lost Enrichment", 1992 *Acta Juridica* 175.

relation to moveable property. If the property has gone then it need not be made over—only the profit, if any, on the transaction. In one case a person was made to pay over money he no longer had. In *Royal Bank of Scotland v. Watt*[92] a man received money for one man and passed it on to another, keeping a very small sum for his troubles. At the time of the action he had only the very small sum left. Yet the Inner House made him give it back. This case is difficult to justify, particularly as the defender had not been found to be in any way involved in wrongdoing in the lower court. In South Africa they have developed rules which treat the time of raising the action as the focus but do permit a retrospective approach if the person sought to be made liable should have known that the receipt could be an unjust enrichment. It is submitted that this is the better rule and that *Watt* was wrongly decided.

Change of position

13.24 This phrase is often used to describe a case where the defender has no enrichment at the time of the action but the issue is whether the defender has spent or used the enrichment having relied upon the receipt being genuine. Thus, it can be seen as an aspect of the "unjust" inquiry—this particularly so where the defender may still have the actual thing or sum but where he has disbursed money from his own funds as a result of having received the enrichment. In the traditional Scottish analysis this would be a recognised ground of saying it would be inequitable to order repayment.[93] It is expressly recognised in *Credit Lyonnais v. George Stevenson & Co. Ltd.*[94] It seems to have been determinative as recently as *Glenrothes Development Corp. v. Bannerman*.[95]

Subjective devaluation

13.25 This is a concept which usefully identifies a common response to a claim. The argument is that although the defender may have received something, he does not consider it to be an enrichment. Services rendered are most likely to be met by such an argument. Put simply, it is to say, "I don't think that's worth anything."

Birks suggests three ways in which the legitimate claim of subjective devaluation can be fairly controlled. These are (i) free acceptance, where a person, by knowingly permitting the enrichment to take place, is held to value it; (ii) a miscellany of other factors not frequently encountered; and (iii) the 'no reasonable man' test—no reasonable

---

[92] 1991 S.L.T. 138.

[93] Bell, *Princ.*, para. 536.

[94] (1901) 9 S.L.T. 93 and see *Bank of Scotland v. Grimm-Foxen*, 1992 G.W.D. 37–2171; the defence has been recognised in England: *Lipkin Gorman v. Karpnale* [1991] 3 W.L.R. 10.

man would say other than that the transfer was an enrichment. Some support for the no reasonable man analysis appears in the recompense/rent cases. Occupation of premises is a benefit and it is usually the case that an owner can make money from his land. The Scots courts for a long time had no difficulty in finding that someone who lived on land had been enriched. In *Earl of Fife v. Samuel Wilson*[96] possession on the basis of a lease which was later found not to exist was sufficient to allow the court to hold the possessor liable in an amount equal to the amount under the putative lease. Another benefit recognised in the law of Scotland is mere occupation of subjects: In *Glen v. Roy*[97] the defender was in occupation, applying *Young v. Cockburn*[98] the Lord Justice Clerk (Moncrieff) stated the law to be that there was a presumption that a person in occupation was presumed to pay the real worth of the subjects occupied which was the annual value unless the occupier could show that he was entitled to pay less or nothing. Although the judgment states that the defender failed to prove he was not a tenant—this obligation is not contractual but is restitution of the use made of the land. The basis is that no reasonable man would say other than that the occupation of land was a benefit.[99] A recent case in this line is an ideal one for the seminar room. In *Secretary of State for Defence v. Mary Johnstone*:[1]

> The defender was the wife of a serving airman. They separated in 1990. For some months she occupied the former marital home on terms agreed. After that she remained without agreement. The pursuer claimed an open market rent, the defenders argued that only the amound which would be charged to service personal should be charged. It was a matter of admission that if the defender had not occupied, occupation would have been by a member of the services. While the defender accepted that the cases turned on the "real worth" it was argued that the proper measure was the pursuer's loss. Decree was granted to the pursuer.

This is a case where the enrichment is awarded albeit the loss is less than the enrichment.[2]

---

[95] 1996 G.W.D. 27–1614.

[96] (1864) 3M 323.

[97] (1882) 10 R. 329.

[98] (1674) Mor. 11, 624.

[99] The foregoing is an extract from *Restitution*, para 4.25 which was approved in *Rochester Poster Services Ltd v. A.G. Barr plc.* 1994 SLT (Sh. Ct.) 3. See also *Supplement*, 4.25.

[1] Unrep. Elgin Sheriff Court, July 18, 1996.

[2] Good students will want to read Steven, 1996 J.R. 51 on these and other cases for a fine analysis differentiating some cases and suggesting that they are evidence of an unnoticed *Eingriffskondicktion* in Scots Law.

Unjust

13.26 Even under a principled system the question, 'is an enrichment unjust? cannot be left to a case by case abstract decision. There must be identifiable principles. Under the Birksian scheme there are three main categories of cases: non-voluntary transfer (comprising vitiation and qualification), free acceptance cases and others.[3] The two subsets of non-voluntary transfer have been clearly identified as applicable in Scots law in *Shilliday*:[3a]

> She does not argue that the Defender should pay her the sum in the crave simply because she paid money to him and spent money on his house from which he has derived benefit. The Pursuer points, rather, to a particular factor which makes the Defender's enrichment unjust. Where such a relevant factor exists, the factor, rather than the mere fact of expenditure by the Pursuer and benefit to the Defender, constitutes the ground of action. So in *Newton*, the Pursuer was allowed to recover from his former wife money which he had spent on a house which actually belonged to her, but which he had mistakenly thought belonged to him. The critical factor in the Pursuer's ground of action was his mistake about the title: he recovered because his wife was benefiting from sums which he would not have spent if he had been aware of the true position. In the present case also the Pursuer does not simply rely on the fact that she spent money on the Defenders property from which he has benefited. On the contrary, the critical factor in her ground of action is that she acted as she did in contemplation of the parties' marriage, which did not take place. That is why she asks to be recompensed.

Not all commentators will agree:

> "the confusion in this context [the *condictio causa data*] is reflected and often surpassed by confusion surrounding the operation of the other *condictiones* in Scots law. This in turn provided a foundation from which Scots law began down the road of a truly bizarre legal development: constructing a system of unjust factors on the back of the *condictiones*."[4]

Vitiation cases

These are cases where a transfer of an enrichment is in some way defective and although the defender as a result technically owns the property, it should be returned. The most obvious cases are ignorance,

---

[3] Professor Burrows identifies more of a list of factors (more than 11) Burrows, A. *The Law of Restitution*, (Butterworths, 1993) p.21 and n.19, a feature which is treated by the Scottish critics as suggesting a lack of principle.

[3a] 1998 S.C.L.R. 502, at p.507.

[4] Evans-Jones, *Limits*, p.175 and see S. Law. Comm. No. 95 (1993) p. 116 (also against the Birksian analysis).

fraud, mistake or duress. Misprediction, where a person makes a calculation which turns out to be ill-advised, is not generally a vitiating factor. There are many Scots cases that fill these categories and can be happily located within this framework.[4a]

Qualification (Non-Materialisation)

These cases are those where something which was contemplated and which brought about the transfer has failed to materialise. A transfer under a condition is a common instance. If the condition is not fulfilled then retention by the recipient is unjust. The leading example from Scots law is the famous and important case of *Cantiere San Rocco v. Clyde Shipbuilding & Engineering Co. Ltd.*[5] discussed above. *Shilliday v. Smith*, [13.1] itself is a decision on this particular unjust factor. The case was argued on Birksian grounds and on a plea in law based on that approach viz, the non-materialisation of a condition.

> The parties moved in together into the Pursuer's cottage. Two month's after that the Defender bought a house and the parties discussed getting married. Later they became engaged but continued to live together as man and wife in the Pursuer's cottage. When the Defender bought the house it was in a state of disrepair. They moved into the defender's house and repaired it. Various works were carried out including the installation of central heating, renovation of the bathroom and the addition of a conservatory and a garden wall. Just when the work was almost complete the parties fell out. The Pursuer had made a sustantial contribution to the repair works. She had also paid sums to the Defender who then used it to pay for materials and work. She had brought a number of the items to the house and garden which she had to leave behind. She obtained Decree for her expenditure before the Sheriff and the Sheriff Principal refused an Appeal. The defender appealed and that appeal was refused.

Free-acceptance

The unconscientious receipt of the value, where I deliberately hide behind a bush allowing you erroneously to clean my windows. This is not entirely a matter of agreement among the commentators.[6] An example of free acceptance in Scots law might arguably be *Cooke's Circus Buildings Co. v. Welding*[7]: 13.27

[4a] See Stewart, *Restitution* (1992) and *Supplement* (1995) ch.5 and *Shilliday*, passage above citing *Newton* as a mistake vitiation case.

[5] 1923 S.C. (H.L.) 105.

[6] Birks, "In Defence of Free Acceptance" in *Essays on the Law of Restitution* (Burrows ed., Oxford, 1991), 105 at 144.

[7] (1894) 21 R. 339.

Zeigler and Welding, who had only that day been introduced, went to see the manager of the circus, Sellar. Zeigler negotiated with Sellar for a lease of the circus, to use it as a music hall. Welding had been introduced to Sellar as a partner and indeed the next day Zeigler and Welding entered into a joint venture as music hall proprietors including the circus. A second lease was entered into by Zeigler for three winter seasons. He signed as an individual and with the firm name. The partnership shortly thereafter dissolved and the circus sued Welding for payment of the remainder of the rent for the first season. He was held liable.

Welding's knowledge and approval both defined his enrichment, namely the use of the theatre and the unjust nature of his failing to disgorge an equivalent.[8]

Put simply: "the three families of unjust factor can be represented in nursery terms as: (1) I didn't mean it; (2) It was bad of you to receive it; and (3) [policy grounds not discussed in this chapter] Mother says give it back anyway."[9]

Equity and good faith

13.28   These two concepts appear in many of the Scots cases. Equity, in the sense of general fairness, is a dangerous concept to utilise in restitution, which is a distinct branch of private law with its own rules—hard cases can make bad law in restitution as much as any other field. On the other hand, equity, in its primary denotation of "balance" is indeed a guiding principle of restitution and the prevention of unjust enrichment. Simply being in good faith cannot itself be a sufficient ground for restitution, but it is at least arguable that positive bad faith can enter into the "unjust" equation. The balance is difficult, for to refuse restitution on such a ground is to leave a person unjustly enriched—thus, if it is to be utilised, the bad faith ought to be at least commensurate and related to the unjust enrichment sought to be recovered. Early in Scots law a decision was taken in one branch of restitution to deny restitution to the person who built in bad faith on another's land, despite the fact that Stair had thought the bad faith irrelevant.[10]

CONCLUSIONS

13.29 The opposition of the law to parties retaining unjust enrichments is a valuable source of remedies. It is also a quite fundamental and

---

[8] See *Elcap v. Milne's Exr.* 1998 G.W.D. 263 which may reflect this idea.

[9] *The Restitution Research Resource*, Birks and Chambers (Mansfield, 1997).

[10] See *Barbour v. Halliday* (1859) 21 D. 453; Stair I, viii, 3.

independent source of obligation depending not on loss or agreement but simply on the desire of justice to achieve equity in its primary sense of balance, rather than fairness, which is a much more value-laden concept. Scots law is a little moribund and tied to the categories with names in a way reminiscent of negligence before *Donoghue v. Stevenson*, it being recalled that the Inner House had denied recovery in that case. *Morgan Guaranty* has been received, quite rightly, not as a statement of general principle but as a licence at least to argue from unjust enrichment in difficult or marginal cases around the nominate heads. The removal of the error of law rule means that the differences between the nominate heads is not so enormous as was once the case. Recompense covers a very wide range of topics and, as the Scottish Law Commission identified, there are unusual repetition cases. It should be possible for a new synthesis of all but special cases (like the core *condictio indebiti*) which would allow a practical principle to be formulated upon which the decision in actual cases could be founded. One such formulation could be that found in the dissenting opinion in the Inner House decision in *Dollar Land v. CIN Properties Ltd*,[11] and is itself said to be based on the passage quoted at the start of this chapter from the opinion of Lord President Hope in *Morgan*:

> "I deduce that the pursuers must show that the defenders have been enriched at their expense, that there is no legal justification for the enrichment, and that it would be equitable to compel the defenders to redress the enrichment."[12]

In 1992 I concluded that Scotland was nearer to having a general enrichment action than any other system which did not have one and that progress should be by development and expansion of our existing remedies along the lines that had been taken in other civilian jurisdictions, but informed by analysis in England and not by legislation.[13] In 1996 the learned contributors to Volume 15 of the *Stair Encyclopaedia*, in a closely argued section, put the case that a general action in Scotland already exists, and so it is now in order to bring that idea before undergraduate students—it is a good one.[14]

Indeed it could be said that it is the precise nature of our general action which is now the true issue. The type mentioned in the foregoing paragraph envisages an incremental growth over and around the existing nominate heads, with an argument of subsidiarity always possible. The *Shilliday* general approach is a complete

---

[11] 1997 S.L.T. 260. The case is under appeal to the Lords at the time of writing.

[12] *per* Lord Rodger at 273L.

[13] Stewart, W.J. *Restitution*, 12.20–12.25.; for a possible scheme of reform see Dr. Clives' (1994) rules, n. 79 above, published in Rose, F.D. (ed.) *Statutes on Contract, Tort and Restitution*, (7th ed., Blackstone, 1996).

[14] Paras 73–85.

liberating restructuring with all sorts of novel arguments being possible in appropriate cases along the lines of the Birksian analysis outlined above. The usual difficulties of having a general theory while nominate heads exist will arise sharply.[15]

Further reading

As in the case of "difficult duties", this further reading section is longer than the rest. Teachers not already deep into the subject, researchers and students will want to find challenges or guidance on many of the topics discussed above. All three will find both in this selection of materials.

Beatson, J., *The Use and Abuse of Unjust Enrichment* (Oxford, 1991).

Birks, P., *An Introduction to the Law of Restitution* (Clarendon Press, 1984) (published in paperback with extra notes, 1989).

Birks, P., "Restitution: A view of the Scots Law" (1985) 38 C.L.P. 57.

Birks, P., "Six Questions in Search of a Subject—Unjust Enrichment In a Crisis of Identity", 1985 J.R. 227.

Birks, P., "The English Recognition of Unjust Enrichment" [1991] L.M.C.L.Q. 473.

Birks, P., *Restitution—The Future* (The Federation Press Centre for Commercial and Resources Law, 1992.

Birks, P. and McLeod, G., "The Implied Contract Theory of Quasi-contract: Civilian opinion current in the century before Blackstone" (1986) 6 Ox.J.L.S. 46.

Blackie, J., "Enrichment and Wrongs in Scots Law" 1992 *Acta Juridica* 23.

Blackie, J., "Enrichment, Wrongs and Invasion of Rights in Scots Law" in Visser, ed., *The Limit of the Law of Obligations* (Juta, 1997)

Blaikie, J., "Unjust Enrichment in the Conflict of Laws", 1984 J.R. 112.

Borland, G.C., "Change of Position in Scots Law", 1996 S.L.T. (News) 139.

Burrows, A.S., ed., *Essays on the Law of Restitution* (Oxford, 1991).

Burrows, A.S., *The Law of Restitution* (Butterworths, 1993).

Casad, R.C., "Unjust Enrichment in Argentina: Common law in a civil law system", 22 Am. J. Comp. L. 757.

Dawson, J.P., "Restitution without Enrichment" (1981) 61 Boston Univ. L.R. 563.

De Vos, W., "Liability Arising from Unjustified Enrichment in the Law of the Union of South Africa", 1960 J.R. 125.

De Vos, W., "Enrichment at Whose expense?—A reply" 1969 S.A.L.J. 227.

Diekman, J.A. and Evans-Jones, R., "The Dark Side of *Connelly v. Simpson*", 1995 J.R. 90.

Du Plessis and Wicke, "*Woolwich Equitable v. IRC* and the *Condictio Indebiti* in Scots Law", 1993 S.L.T. (News) 303.

Ehrenzweig, A.A., "Restitution in the Conflict of Laws" (1961) 36 N.Y.U.L.R. 1298.

Eiselen, S. and Pienaar, G., *Unjustified Enrichment: A Casebook* (Durban, 1993).

Elman, P., "Unjust enrichment in Israel Law" 1968 3 Is. L.R. 526.

---

[15] As has already happened in the law of contract, see e.g. *Shepherd (LM) Ltd. v. North West Securities Ltd.*, 1991 S.C.L.R. 271, and in delict, e.g. nuisance.

Evans-Jones, R., "Identifying the Enriched", 1992 S.L.T. (News) 25.

Evans-Jones, R., "Payments in Mistake of Law—Full Circle?" (1992) 37 J.L.S.S. 92.

Evans-Jones, R., "Unjust Enrichment, Contract and the Third Reception of Roman Law in Scotland" 1993 (109) L.Q.R. 663.

Evans-Jones, R., "Repetititon of Payments in *Sponsiones Ludicrae*", 1993 S.L.G. 11.

Evans-Jones, R., "From 'undue transfer' to 'retention without a legal basis' (the *condicitio indebiti* and *condictio turpem vel inustam causam*)" in *Civil Law Tradition in Scots Law* (Evans-Jones, ed., Stair Society), Supp., Vol. 2, pp. 213–252.

Evans-Jones, R. and Hellwege, P., "Swaps, Error of Law and Unjustified Enrichment", 1995 S.L.P.Q. 1.

Evans-Jones, R. and McKenzie, D., "Towards a Profile of the *Condictio ob Turpem vel Injustam Causam* in Scots Law", 1994 J.R. 60.

Forte, A.D.M., "Salvage Operations, Salvage Contracts and Negotiorum Gestio", 1993 J.R. 247.

Garner, M., "The Role of Subjective Benefit in the Law of Unjust Enrichment", 1990 O.J.L.S. 42.

Goff and Jones, *The Law of Restitution* (4th ed., Sweet & Maxwell).

Gretton, G.L., "Reparation and Negotiorum Gestio", 1978 S.L.T. (News) 145.

Gretton, G.L., "Unjust Enrichment in Scotland" [1992] J.B.L. 108.

Gretton, G.L., "Constructive Trusts" (1996) Edin. L.R. 281.

Hood, P., "Tracing, Constructive Trust and Unjustified Enrichment", 1994 S.L.T. (News) 265.

Hume, *Lectures* (Stair Society ed.), Vol. III, XV.

Klippert, G.B., "The juridical nature of unjust enrichment" (1980) 30 University of Toronto Law Journal 356.

Leslie, R.D., "*Negotiorum Gestio* in Scots Law: The Claim of the Privileged Gestor", 1983 J.R. 12.

Lotz, J.G., "Enrichment" in *The Law of South Africa* (Joubert, W.A., ed., Butterworths, Durban), Vol. 9.

MacCormack, G., "The Early History of the *Actio de in rem verso* (Alfenus—Labeo)" (1982) 2 Studi Biscardi 319.

MacCormack, G., "The Later History of the *Actio de in rem verso* (Proculus—Ulpian)" (1982) 48 Studiae et Documenta et Juris 318.

McCormack, G., "The *Condictio Causa data Causa Non Secuta* in Civil Law Tradition in Scots Law" (Evans-Jones, ed., Stair Society), Supp., Vol. 2, pp. 253–276.

MacDonald, D.R., "Restitution and Property Law", 1988 S.L.T. (News) 81.

MacDonald, D.R., "Mistaken Payments in Scots Law", 1989 J.R. 49.

McKendrick, E., "Incontrovertible benefit—A Postscript" [1989] L.M.C.L.Q. 401.

MacQueen, H.L., "Unjustified Enrichment and Breach of Contract", 1994 J.R. 165.

MacQueen, H.L., "Unjustified Enrichment in Scots Law" [1992] J.B.L. 333.

MacQueen, H.L. and Sellar, W.D.H., "Unjust Enrichment in Scots Law" in *A Comparative Legal History of the Law of Restitution* (E.J.H. Schrage, ed., Berlin, 1994).

Nicholas, B., "Unjustified Enrichment in Civil law and Louisiana Law. Part II" (1962) 37 Tul.L.R. 49.

O'Dair, R., "Restitutionary Damages for Breach of Contract and the Theory of Efficient Breach" (1993) 46(2) C.L.P. 113.

O'Dair, R., "Remedies for Breach of Contract: A wrong turn" [1993] R.L.R. 31

Reid, K.G.C., "Unjustified Enrichment and Property Law", 1994 J.R. 167.

Rose F.(ed) *Restitution and the Conflict of Laws* (Mansfield, 1995).

Rudden, B. and Bishop, W. "Gritz and Quellmehl: Pass it on" (1981) 6 E.L.R. 243.

Scholtens, J.E., "General enrichment action that 'was'", 1966 S.A.L.J. 391.

Scholtens, J.E., "Unjust Enrichment", 1967 Annual Survey of South African Law.

Scholtens, J.E., "Enrichment at whose expense?" 1968 S.A.L.J. 371.

Steven, A.J.M., "Recompense for Interference in Scots Law", 1996 J.R. 51.

Stewart, W.J., "First Thoughts on Interest Rate Swaps in Scotland", 1992 S.L.T. (News) 315.

Stewart, W.J., "Restitution, Unjust Enrichment and Equity", 1992 S.L.T. (News) 47.

Stewart, W.J., "Intention to Donate and Recompense and Professor Bell's Definition", 1996 S.L.T. (News) 270.

Stoljar, S.J., "Restitution—Unjust Enrichment and Negotiorum Gestio" in *International Encyclopaedia of Comparative Law* (J.C.B. Mohr/Nijhoff, 1984), Vol. X, Chap. 17.

Stoljar, S.J., "Unjust Enrichment and Unjust Sacrifice" (1987) 50 M.L.R. 603.

Tettenborn, A., *Law of Restitution* (2nd ed., Cavendish Publishing Ltd, 1996).

Van Niekerk, J.P., "Salvage and Negotiorum Gestio: Exploratory Reflections on the Jurisprudential Foundation and Classification of the South African Law of Salvage" 1992 *Acta Juridica* 148.

Visser, D.P., "Rethinking Unjustified enrichment: A perspective of the competition between Contractual and Enrichment remedies", 1992 *Acta Juridica* 203.

Visser, D.P., ed., *The Limit of the Law of Obligations* (Juta, 1997).

Walker, "Equity in Scots Law" (1954) 66 J.R. 103–147.

Whitty, N.R., "Some trends and issues in Scots Enrichment Law", 1994 J.R. 127.

Whitty, N.R., "Indirect enrichment in Scots Law", 1994 J.R. 200; 237.

Whitty, N.R., "Ultra Vires Swap Contracts and Unjustified Enrichment", 1994 S.L.T. (News) 337.

Wilson, A.R., "The Constructive Trust in Scots Law", 1993 J.R. 99.

Wolffe, W.J., "Contract and recompense: ERDC Construction Ltd v. Love", 1997, 1 Edin. L.R. 469.

Zimmerman, R., "A road through the enrichment-forest? Experiences with a general enrichment action" (1985) 18 C.I.L.J.A. 1.

Zimmerman, R., *The Law of Obligations: Roman Foundations of the Civilian Tradition* (Juta, 1990; Oxford paperback, 1996).

Zweigert and Kotz, *Introduction to Comparative Law* (Oxford, 2nd. ed., 1987) (trans. Weir).

Zweigert and Mueller-Gindullis, "Quasi-contracts", Chap. 30 in *International Encyclopaedia of Comparative Law* (J.C.B. Mohr/Nijhoff).

INDEX

a caelo usque ad centrum, 2.11
abortion, 9.14
accountants, negligence, 5.7
actio de effusis vel dejectis, 2.24, 12.8
actio de in rem verso, 13.3
actio de positivis vel suspensis, 2.24, 12.8
actio injurlarum, 1.4, 2.1, 2.2, 8.1
   damages, 8.9
actio legis Aquilae, 1.4
advocates, Immunity, 5.53
aemulatio vicini, 2.20, 3.15
agency, vicarious liability, 10.3–7
agricultural produce, product liability,
   7.17
aircraft
   invasion of air space, 2.11
   occupiers liability, 7.5
animals, 1.5, 6.2, 7.23–33
   animals (Scotland) Act 1987, 7.28–33
   before 1987 Act, 7.24–27
   categories, 7.30–31
   defences, 7.25
   definitions
     attack, 7.32
     keeper, 7.29
   diseases, 7.33
   negligence, 7.27
   strict liability, defences, 7.33
   volenti non fit injurie, 6.11
armed forces, Crown liability, 9.4
assault, 2.2
   defences, 2.3
   delict, 1.3, 2.1
assignation
   assignees, title to sue, 9.17
   claims, 11.23
assythment, 1.3
automatism, 9.15

bankrupts, title to sue, 9.16
betting and gaming, 6.3
breach of confidence, 3.3–6
   restitution, 13.21

breach of contract
   damages, 13.21
   inducing, 3.15, 3.19–21
   trade unions, 9.9
breach of duty of care, 4.20–28
   harm, magnitude, 4.25
   impracticality, 6.8
   precautions, scale and expense, 4.27
   probability, degree, 4.24
   standard of care, 4.20–23
   statutory duty (see **statutory duty**)
   usual practice, 4.26
   value of activity, 4.26
building control, 5.34, 5.39
burden of proof, 12.2–3
   volenti non fit injuria, 11.19
business premises, occupiers liability,
   exclusion, 7.9

Calcutt Report, 8.29
caravan sites, occupiers liability, 7.5
carriers
   strict liability, 2.26
   wrongful refusal to contract, 3.14
causation, 4.15, 4.29–39, *see also*
     contributory negligence
   breach of statutory duty, 6.9
   'but for' test, 4.30
   industrial accidents, 7.40
   medical negligence, 5.50
   novus actus interveniens, 4.33–39,
     4.45
   product liability, 7.14
cautions, 13.4
character references, 5.11
   qualified privilege, 8.19
chastisement, whether assault, 2.3
children
   chastisement, 2.3
   contributory negligence, 11.22
   death, *in utero*, 9.11, 11.27
   enticement, religious cults, 2.5
   legal capacity, 9.12

children, *cont.*
  title to sue, 9.12
    unborn children, 9.11, 9.13
    wrongful life, 9.14
choice of law, 12.20
claims
  assignation, 11.23
  compromises, 11.32
  contributions and relief, 11.24–26
  discharge, 11.32
    decrees, 11.31
  remedies, 12.9
  settlements, 11.32
  transmission on death, 11.27–32
    immediate family, 11.29
coal mining, 6.5
codes of practice, health and safety at
  work, 7.42
compensation, *see also* **damages**
  function of delict, 1.7
  orders, 1.3
competition
  EU law, 3.17
  UK law, developments, 3.18
compromises, delictual claims, 11.32
condictiones, 13.5
  condictio cause data cause non secute,
    13.7
  condictio Indebiti, 13.6, 13.29
confidence, breach, 3.3–6
  restitution, 13.21
consent
  defence, 11.19
  medical treatment, 2.3, 5.48, 5.49
    children, 9.12
conspiracy, 3.15, 3.16–18
  trade unions, 9.9
constructive trusts, 13.8
consumer protection, 6.2, 7.15–22
contract, 1.2, *see also* **breach of contract**
  and delict, remoteness of damage, 4.40
  implied, 5.52
  negligent misrepresentation, 5.54
  wrongful refusal, 3.14
contractors, vicarious liability, 10.17
contributory negligence, 4.39
  animals, 7.33
  breach of statutory duty, 6.11
  defence, 11.21–22
  employment, 7.40
  product liability, 7.21
contumelia, 8.1
conversion, 2.21
convicium, 8.7, 8.26–27
copyright, 3.3
corporal punishment, 2.3
corporations, title to sue, 9.6–9
corroboration, 12.7

criminal injuries compensation, 1.9
criminality, defence, 11.20
Crown
  immunity, acts of state, 11.5
  title to sue, 9.4–5
  vicarious liability, 10.18
culpa, *see* **fault**

damage to property
  choice of law, 12.20
  or economic loss, 5.10
  prescription and limitation, 11.37
  pursuers not owners, 5.14
damages, 12.9
  actions for further damages, 9.3
  breach of statutory duty, 6.10–11
  defamation, 8.9–10
  product liability, 7.20
  quantification (see **quantification of
    damages**)
  restitution, 13.21
  transmission of claims on death,
    11.27–32
damnum fatale
  animals, 7.33, 11.8
  defence, 2.25, 2.26, 2.27, 2.28
    strict liability, 11.18
dangerous animals, 7.30–31
  licence, 7.33
  list, 7.33
death
  from personal injuries, prescription
    and limitation, 11.36
  transmission of claims, 11.27–32
decrees, delictual claims, 11.31
defamation
  damages, 8.9–10, 13.20
    mallce, 8.10
  defences, 8.2, 8.11–25
    absolute privilege, 8.10, 8.14–16
    fair comment, 8.24
    in rixa, 8.12
    offers of amends, 8.25
    qualified privilege, 8.17–23
    veritas, 8.3, 8.9, 8.13
  English law, 1.10
  injunctions, 8.9
  innuendo, 8.8
  interdict, 8.9
  limitation of actions, 11.38
  rehabilitation of offenders, 8.13
  requirements
    communication, 8.2
    defamatory statements, 8.4–7
    falsity, 8.3
  settlements, 11.32
  title to sue, trade unions, 9.9
defects, definition, 7.18

defences, 11.2, 11.14–22, *see also*
  contributory negligence; damnum
  fatale; Immunities
  animals, 7.25
  consent, 11.19
  criminality, 11.20
  damnum fatale (*see* **damnum fatale**)
  harassment, national security, 2.9
  justification, 2.3, 11.15
  necessity, 11.16
  nuisance, 2.13
  product liability, 7.21–22
  provocation, 8.10, 11.17
  restitution, non-enrichment, 13.22–27
  statutory authority, 11.14
  strict liability, animals, 7.33
  volenti non fit injuria (*see* **volenti non**
    fit injuria)
delict
  and contract, remoteness of damage,
    4.40
  functions
    compensation, 1.7
    deterrence, 1.6
    redistribution of costs, 1.8
    welfare, 1.9
  history, 1.3–5
  meaning, 1.1
  Scots/English differences, 1.10
delictual liability
  basis, 4.2–7
  Donoghue v. Stevenson, 4.5
  principles, 1.11–12
  Stair, 1.11
  unintentional harm, 4.1–7
detention, 2.6
deterrence, function of delict, 1.7
diplomatic immunity, 11.6
directives, 6.13–18
  consumer protection, 7.15
  health and safety at work, 7.38
  non-implementation, crown liability, 9.5
disclaimers, 5.5
  effectiveness, 5.7, 5.13
  unfair contract terms, 5.13
diseases, liability, animals, 7.33
display screen equipment, 7.48
dogs, 7.30–31
  guard dogs, 6.2, 7.33
  strict liability, 7.26
dominant position, abuse, 3.17
duty of care, 4.8–9
  basis of liability, 4.3
  breaches, 1.11
  company accountants, to buyers of
    shares, 5.7
  concept, developments, 4.18–19
  employers, to employees, 7.34–37

duty of care, *cont.*
  foreseeability, 4.13–17
  manufacturers, to consumers, 7.13
  professional negligence, 5.46–47
    standard of care, 5.48–49
  scope, 4.10–12

economic loss, 1.11, 5.1, 5.3–22
  categories of cases
    Hedley Byrne, 5.5–13
    Henderson v. Merritt, 5.20
    Simpson v. Thomson, 5.14–19
    White v. Jones, 5.21
  duty of care, fair, just and
    reasonable, 5.12
  indirect physical loss, 5.44
  legal advice, 5.52
  or damage to property, 5.10
  prescription and limitation, 11.37
  secondary loss, 5.14–19
  services by relatives of injured
    persons, 5.22
  title to sue, 9.1
  transferred loss, 5.17
ejection, 2.10
  violent profits, 13.21
elections, statements, qualified privilege,
    8.18
employers liability, 7.34–50, *see also*
    health and safety at work
  common employment, 10.1
  common law
    and statutory duty, 7.41
    competent fellow workers, 7.35
    place of work, 7.39
    safe plant and equipment, 7.34
    safe working system, 7.36
  compulsory insurance, 11.23
  Crown, 9.4
  vicarious liability, 10.8–15
  volenti non fit injuria, 7.40
employment, see **employers liability;**
    health and safety at work
enticement, 2.5
equity
  limitation of actions, 11.35
  unjust enrichment, 13.28, 13.29
Erskine, delict, 1.4
EU law
  abuse of dominant position, 3.17
  breach, reparation, 6.12–18, 9.5
  consumer protection directive, 7.15
  employers liability, 7.38, 7.43
  statutory duties, 6.1
eurorep, 6.12–18, 7.43
eurotorts, 6.1
evidence, 12.2–8
  burden of proof, 12.2–3

evidence, *cont.*
  corroboration, 12.7
  inferences, 12.5–6
  presumptions of fault, 12.8–9
  res ipsa loquitur, 2.24, 12.4
explosives, 6.4

factories
  duty of care, 7.9
  fencing, 6.7
  reasonable practicality, 6.8
fair comment, defamation, 8.24
fault, 1.4, 1.5, 1.12
  EU law, reparation, 6.17
  meaning, 4.4
  nuisance, 1.12
fire authorities
  liability, 5.37
  trespass, 2.11
foetuses, personal injuries, 9.11
foreseeability, 4.13–17, 5.9
  nervous shock, 5.27, 5.28
  'thin-skull' rule, 4.46
fraud, 2.1, 3.2, 5.46
  employees, vicarious liability, 10.15
freedom of speech, and defamation, 8.9,
  8.23
funeral expenses, 11.29

good faith, restitution, 13.27
guard dogs, 6.2, 7.33
  strict liability, 7.26

harassment, 2.9
  actions, 12.10
health and safety at work, 1.5, 6.2
  civil liability, 7.42
  display screen equipment, 7.48
  EU law, 7.38
  management, 7.44
  manual handling operations, 7.49
  personal protective equipment, 7.47
  work equipment, 7.46
  workplace, 7.45
heritable property, *see* **land**
Hillsborough disaster, nervous shock
  cases, 5.27, 5.28
hotel proprietors, strict liability, 2.27
hypothecs, 5.16

illegality, UK legislation, judicial
  review, 6.16
immunities, 11.3–13
  Crown, acts of state, 11.5
  foreign heads of state and diplomats,
    11.6
  international organisations, 11.6
  judges and magistrates, 11.7

immunities, *cont.*
  Sovereign, 11.4
  trade unions, 11.8–13
  visiting forces, 11.6
Importers, product liability, 7.19
Imprisonment, wrongful imprisonment, 2.7
Industrial actions, *see* **trade disputes**
Industrial injuries, 1.5
Injunctions, defamation, 8.9
injuria, **meaning**, 1.4
Injuries, *see* **personal injuries**
Innkeepers
  strict liability, 2.27
  wrongful refusal to contract, 3.14
Insane persons
  personal injuries cases, prescription
    and limitation, 11.34
  title to sue, 9.15
insurance
  dangerous animals, 7.33
  relevance in delict, 1.8
  subrogation, 11.23, 13.18
interdicts, 12.9
  defamation, 6.9
  nuisance, 2.17
interest
  quantification of damages, 12.13
  solatium, 12.15
Interest to sue, meaning, 9.2
Internet, defamation, 8.2
Intimidation, 3, 3.15, 23–24
  trade unions
intrusion, 2.10
  violent profits, 13.21

Joint and several liability, 4.38
  claims, discharge, 11.32
  contributions and relief, 11.24–26,
    11.32
  vicarious liability, 10.2
Judges
  Crown liability, 9.4
  immunity, 11.7
judicial proceedings, privilege, 8.16
judicial review, 12.10
  UK statute, illegality, 6.16
Jurisdiction, 12.19
Jury trials, 12.15
jus quaesitum tertio, 5.52, 5.53
justification
  assault, 2.3
  defences, 11.15

land
  occupiers' liability, 7.5
  ownership, *a caelo usque ad centrum*,
    2.11
  wrongful interference, 2.10–20

landlord and tenant, occupiers liability, 7.11
latent defects, 5.31, 7.13
lawburrows, 2.10
  contravention, 2.4
lawyers, professional negligence, 5.52–53
  advocacy, 5.53
legal capacity, children, 9.12
lex Aquillia, 1.4, 2.2
  basis of liability, 4.2
  destroyed property, 2.22
  injuria, 4.4
  verbal injuries, 8.1, 8.9
liability, *see* **delictual liability**
liens, 5.16
limitation of actions, 11.33
  damage to property, 11.37
  defamation, 11.38
  economic loss, 11.37
  personal injuries cases, 11.34–36
  product liability, 7.22
local authorities, judicial review, 12.10
loss of society
  damages, 11.28
  replacement, 11.29
loss of support
  damages, 11.28
    immediate family, 11.29

magistrates
  immunity, 11.7
  ultra vires sentences, 2.7
malice
  defamation, 8.10, 8.13
    qualified privilege, 8.17
  malicious falsehood, 8.28
  ultra vires sentences, 2.7
  use of land, *aemulatio vicini*, 2.20
manual handling operations, 7.49
married women, title to sue, 9.10
medical expenses, quantification of damages, 12.13
medical negligence, 5.50–51
medical treatment
  consent, 2.3, 5.46, 5.49
    children, 9.12
    defence, 11.19
medicines, 6.2
mens rea, 1.1
  assault, 2.2
mentally ill persons
  detention, 2.6
  personal injuries cases, prescription and limitation, 11.34
misstatements
  negligence, 5.5–7, 5.54
    employment references, 5.11

moveable property, wrongful interference, 2.21–22

national security, defence, harassment, 2.9
nautae caupones stabularil, 2.25
  carriers, 2.26
  hotel proprietors, 2.27
  stable keepers, 2.28
necessity, defence, 11.18
negligence, *see also* **duty of care, professional negligence**
  animals, common law, 7.27
  English and Scots law, 1.10
negligent misrepresentation, 5.54
negotiorum gestio, 13.11–13
nervous shock, 3.2, 5.1, 5.23–30
  foreseeability, 5.27, 5.28
  meaning, 5.23
  primary and secondary victims, 5.28–30
  proximity, 5.26
newspapers, qualified privilege, 8.22
nonage
  prescription and limitation
    other cases, 11.37
    personal injuries cases, 11.34
novus actus interveniens, 4.33–39, 4.45
nuisance, 2.12–20
  culpa, 1.12
  defences
    long practice, 2.13
    statutory authority, 2.13
  English law, 1.10
  golf balls, 4.24(n31)
  interdicts, 2.17
  liability, basis, 2.15–17
  meaning, 2.12
  prescription, 11.40
  use of land
    aemulatio vicini, 2.20
    dangerous use, 2.18
    unnatural use, 2.18–19

occupiers liability, 1.5, 5.43, 6.2, 7.2–11
  Crown, 9.4
  exclusion, 7.9
  landlord and tenant, 7.11
  meanings
    occupier, 7.4
    occupying, 7.4
    premises, 7.5
  standard of care, 7.6
  trespass, 7.8
  volenti non fit injuria, 6.11
omissions, liability, 5.40
optional procedure, 12.11

parents
death of children, *in utero*, 9.11
title to sue, 9.11
Parliament, privilege, 8.15
partnerships, title to sue, 9.8
passing-off, 2.1, 3.7–13, 6.6
pavements, occupiers liability, 7.5
personal injuries
choice of law, 12.20
claims, prescription and limitation,
11.34–36, 11.39
deterioration, 9.3
industrial injuries, 1.5
meaning, 11.27
optional procedure, 12.11
professional negligence, 5.47
quantification of damages (*see*
quantification of damages)
unborn children, 11.27
personal protective equipment, 7.47
picketing, legality, 11.12
Piper Alpha disaster, 5.29
plagium, 2.5
pleading, 12.16
relevancy, 12.17
specification, 12.18
police
chief constables, vicarious liability,
2.4, 10.18
complaints, qualified privilege, 8.18
Crown liability, 9.4
Praetor, convicium, 8.26
pregnant workers, health and safety at
work, 7.44
prescription, 11.33
damage to property, 11.37
economic loss, 11.37
long negative prescription, 11.39
personal injuries cases, 11.34–36, 11.39
positive prescription, 11.40
product liability, 7.22, 11.39
press, invasion of privacy, 9.29
privacy, intrusion, 8.27, 8.29
privilege
defamation, 8.10
absolute privilege, 8.14–16
qualified privilege, 8.17–23
qualified privilege, employment
references, 5.11
procurators fiscal, vicarious liability,
10.18
product liability, 7.12–22
causation, 7.14
common law, 7.13–14
Consumer Protection Act 1987,
7.15–22
damages, 7.20
defences, 7.21–22

product liability, *cont.*
definitions
defect, 7.18
product, 7.17
Donoghue v Stevenson, 4.5, 7.13.
intermediate examination, 7.13,
7.14
joint and several liability, 7.19
limitation of actions, 7.22
prescription, 11.39
producers and suppliers, 7.19
professional negligence, 5.1, 5.20,
5.45–55
accountants, 5.7
developments, 5.55
duty of care, 5.46–47
medical negligence, 5.50–51
personal injuries, 5.47
prescription and limitation, 11.37
solicitors, 5.21, 5.52–53
standard of care, 5.48–49
surveyors, 5.7
profits, loss, reparation under EU law,
6.17
property, wrongful interference, 2.10–22
provocation
defences, 11.17
defamation, 8.10
proximity, 5.9
basis of liability, 7.13
manufacturers to consumers, 4.6
nervous shock, 5.26, 5.27
public bodies
further damages, actions, 9.3
liability, 5.34
public interest
defence, harassment, 2.9
respect of confidences, 3.4
public law, 5.31–39

quantification of damages, 12.12
personal injuries
patrimonial loss, 12.13
deductions, 12.14
structured settlements, 12.14
solatium, 12.15
quasi-delicts, 1.1, 2.23–28
actio de effusis vel dejectis, 2.24,
12.8
actio de positivis vel suspensis, 2.24,
12.8
nautae caupones stabularii, 2.25–28

railway lines, occupiers liability, 7.8
rape, children of rape, 9.14
recompense, 1.2(n6), 13.3, 13.14, 13.29
references, 5.11
qualified privilege, 8.19

rehabilitation of offenders, defamation, 8.13
relatives
  meaning, 11.30
  non-patrimonial awards, 11.29
  parents, 9.11
  services, loss, 5.22
  transmission of claims, 11.28, 11.30
relief
  joint and several liability, 11.24–26, 11.32
  restitution, 13.15
religious cults, enticement, 2.5
remedies, 12.9, *see also* **damages; interdicts**
  harassment, 12.10
  judicial review, 12.10
remoteness of damage, 1.10, 4.40–47
  English law, 4.42
  'thin-skull' rule, 4.46
repetition, 1.2(n6)
res ipsa loquitur, 2.24, 12.4
restitution, 1.2(n6), 13.1
  actio de in rem verso, 13.3
  cautions, 13.4
  condictiones, 13.5
    condictio causa data causa non secuta, 13.7
    condictio indebiti, 13.6, 13.29
  constructive trusts, 13.8
  defences, non-enrichment, 13.23–27
  enrichment, 13.22
  equity, 13.28
  good faith, 13.28
  Melville monument liability, 13.9–10
  negotiorum gestio, 13.11–13
  recompense, 13.3, 13.14
  relief, 13.15
  salvage, 13.16
  statutory rights, 13.17
  subrogation, 13.18
  subtractive, 13.20
  unjust enrichment, 1.2, 13.1, 13.22
  violent profits, 2.10, 2.21, 13.21
  wrongs, 13.21
risk
  injuries at work, 7.49
  voluntary assumption, animals, 7.33
roads
  condition, 5.34
  occupiers liability, 7.5
  traffic, compulsory insurance, 11.23
Roman law, 1.3
  lex Aquilia (*see iex Aquilia*)

salvage, **13.16**
seduction, **2.8**
self-defence, **2.3**

sentences, *ultra vires*, 2.7
ships
  masters, detention, 2.6
  occupiers liability, 7.5
shoplifting, detention, 2.6
social security, recovery of benefits, 12.14
solatium, 8.9, 12.15
solicitors, professional negligence, 5.21, 5.52–53
Sovereign, immunity, 11.4
spouses
  enticement, 2.5
  title to sue, 9.10
spuilzie, 2.21–22, 9.12
  violent profits, 13.21
Stair
  actio de in rem verso, 13.3
  dellctual liability, 1.11
  intimidation, 3.22
  negotiorum gestio, 13.12
  relief, 13.15
  reparation and revenge, 1.3
  restitution, bad faith, 13.28
  verbal injuries, 8.1
standard of care
  criminal acts, 11.20
  occupiers liability, 7.6
  professional negligence, 5.48–49
  statutory duty, 6.8
  statutory liability, 7.1
standard of proof, 12.2
statements
  negligence, 5.5–7
  employment references, 5.11
statutory authorities
  acts of omission, 5.35
  discretionary powers, 5.32, 5.36
  public immunity, 5.37
statutory authority, defence, 11.14
statutory duty, 5.31–35, *see also* **animals; consumer protection; employers liability; occupiers liability**
  breaches, 6.8
    and breach of common law, 7.41
  causation, 6.9
  damages, 6.10–11
  reparation, 6.3
  liability, requirements, 6.4–7
  meaning, 6.1
stress, employers liability, 7.37
strict liability, 1.7
  actio de positivis vel suspensis, 2.24
  animals, 7.31
    after 1987 Act, 7.28
    apportionment, 7.33
    before 1987 Act, 7.24–27
  employment, 7.40

strict liability, *cont.*
  factories, 7.38
  nautae caupones stabularii, 2.25
  product liability, 7.12, 7.15, 7.16
  unnatural use of land, 2.19
structured settlements, personal injuries,
  12.14
subrogation, 13.18
  claims, 11.23
suppliers, product liability, 7.19
surveyors, liability, 5.7

theft, delict, 1.3
'thin-skull' rule, 4.46
third parties
  bankrupt insured persons, 11.23
  contributions and relief, 11.26
  employment, vicarious liability,
    10.16
  intervention, 5.40–43
    animals, 7.33
title to sue, 9.1
  assignees, 9.17
  bankrupts, 9.16
  children, 9.12
    unborn children, 9.11, 9.13
    wrongful life, 9.14
  Crown, 9.4–5
  defence, 11.2
  economic loss, 9.1
  incorporated bodies, 9.6
  injured persons, services of relatives,
    5.22
  insane persons, 9.15
  married women, 9.10
  members of the public, 9.18
  parents, 9.11
  partnerships, 9.8
  spouses, 9.10
  trade unions, 9.9
  unincorporated bodies, 9.7–9

torts, 1.1
  and delict, 1.10
  conversion, 2.21
  economic torts, 3.1
trade disputes, immunity, 11.9–11
trade unions
  immunities, 11.8–13
  intimidation, 3.23

trade unions, *cont.*
  title to sue, 9.9
  vicarious liability, 10.18
transferred loss, 5.17
travel packages, directive, 6.18
trespass, 1.10, 2.11
  occupiers liability, 7.8
trustees in bankruptcy, title to sue, 9.16

unborn children, title to sue, 9.11, 9.13
unfair contract terms
  disclaimers, 5.13
  occupiers liability, exclusion, 7.9
unfair dismissal, inducing, 3.20, 3–21
unjust enrichment, 1.2, 13.1, 13.22
  indirect enrichment, 13.22

verbal Injuries, 8.1, *see also* **defamation**
  claims, transmission on death, 11.27
  convicium, 8.26–27
  malicious falsehood, 8.28
vicarious liability, 1.8, 10.1
  agents, 10.3–7
  chief constables, 2.4, 10.18
  contractors, 10.17
  Crown, 9.4, 10.18
  employees, 10.8–15
    employment status, 10.10
    fraud, 10.15
    pro hac vice, 10.16
    scope of employment, 10.11–14
  joint and several liability, 10.2
  local authorities, 3.39
  procurators fiscal, 10.18
  quasi-delicts, 2.23
  relief, 11.26
  trade unions, 10.18
violent profits, 2.10, 2.21, 13.20
volenti non fit injuria
  breach of statutory duty, 6.11
  defence, 11.19
  employers liability, 7.40
  occupiers liability, 7.10

wages, quantification of damages,
  12.13
welfare state, interaction with law of
  delict, 1.9
workshops, occupiers liability, 7.5
wrongful imprisonment, 2.7